APUS ePress

# World Literature Anthology:
## Through the Renaissance

# Volume II

*Linda Silva: Volume Editor*

Contributing Editors: Linda Silva
William Overton
Program Director: Kimberly Jacobs
Production Editor: Judith Novak
Editor-in-Chief: Fred Stielow

APUS ePress
Production

APUS™
2011

*Production Editor Judith Novak*
*Contributing Editors: Linda Silva*
*William Overton*
*Editor:Fred Stielow*
*Text Design: Judith Novak*
*Jessica Radlich*
*Artwork: Victor Montoya*

*Copyright © 2011*
*American Public University Electronic press*

*This text was compiled in Charles Town WV by APUS ePress*

*Printed by Lightning Source Inc.*
*La Vergne, TN*

*Cover Illustration: Victor Montoya,*
*American Public University System Visual Arts*

*Series contents include excepts of classical literature from around the world through the Renaissance*

*ISBN 978-1-937381-00-4, 978-1-937381-01-1, 978-1-937381-02-8*
*Collection ISBN 978-1-937381-03-5*

*ISBN 978-1-937381-00-4*

*American Public University Electronic Press*
*111 West Congress Street*
*Charles Town, WV 25414*

*www.apus.edu*

# Literature 201
## Volume II

# Volume III

# Introduction
## Volume II

In Volume II, we sample the wisdom of ancient China and other far off lands. The writing style is much different from what we encounter in our own culture, but part of the enjoyment of these literatures is to be found in realizing how different these people were from us – and yet how similar.

As we move through these stories, we follow the twisted tales of fidelity and perfidy, and delve into the mythical tales of mysterious India and the gods and goddesses of that land. It is indeed a land distant from our own in time and location, as well as culture. Yet these people display some of the same character traits of people we know in our own time and perhaps even a few traits we see in ourselves. As you read, try to picture them in your mind as living, breathing humans, dealing with forces beyond themselves and teaching their audience (and us as well) some of the basic truths of the human condition.

The tales from Africa, for instance, may seem difficult to follow; one must remember that these tales began as oral traditions and as they were related through generation upon generation, changed and grew with each telling.

When you have completed this volume, you will truly have developed a different perspective on these humans, their lives, their myths, and their wisdom.

# Doctrine of the Mean

*By Confucius*

WRITTEN 500 B.C.E

What Heaven has conferred is called The Nature; an accordance with this nature is called The Path of duty; the regulation of this path is called Instruction.

The path may not be left for an instant. If it could be left, it would not be the path. On this account, the superior man does not wait till he sees things, to be cautious, nor till he hears things, to be apprehensive.

There is nothing more visible than what is secret, and nothing more manifest than what is minute. Therefore the superior man is watchful over himself, when he is alone.

While there are no stirrings of pleasure, anger, sorrow, or joy, the mind may be said to be in the state of Equilibrium. When those feelings have been stirred, and they act in their due degree, there ensues what may be called the state of Harmony. This Equilibrium is the great root from which grow all the human actings in the world, and this Harmony is the universal path which they all should pursue.

Let the states of equilibrium and harmony exist in perfection, and a happy order will prevail throughout heaven and earth, and all things will be nourished and flourish.

Chung-ni said, "The superior man embodies the course of the Mean; the mean man acts contrary to the course of the Mean.

"The superior man's embodying the course of the Mean is because he is a superior man, and so always maintains the Mean. The mean man's acting contrary to the course of the Mean is because he is a mean man, and has no caution."

The Master said, "Perfect is the virtue which is according to the Mean! Rare have they long been among the people, who could practice it!

The Master said, "I know how it is that the path of the Mean is not walked in:-The knowing go beyond it, and the stupid do not come up to it. I know how it is that the path of the Mean is not understood:-The men of talents and virtue go beyond it, and the worthless do not come up to it.

"There is no body but eats and drinks. But they are few who can distinguish flavors."

The Master said, "Alas! How is the path of the Mean untrodden!"

The Master said, "There was Shun:-He indeed was greatly wise! Shun loved to question others, and to study their words, though they might be shallow. He concealed what was bad in them and displayed what was good. He took hold of their two extremes, determined the Mean, and employed it in his government of the people. It was by this that he was Shun!"

The Master said "Men all say, 'We are wise'; but being driven forward and taken in a net, a trap, or a pitfall, they know not how to escape. Men all say, 'We are wise'; but happening to choose the course of the Mean, they are not able to keep it for a round month."

The Master said "This was the manner of Hui:-he made choice of the Mean, and whenever he got hold of what was good, he clasped it firmly, as if wearing it on his breast, and did not lose it."

The Master said, "The kingdom, its states, and its families, may be perfectly ruled; dignities and emoluments may be declined; naked weapons may be trampled under the feet; but the course of the Mean cannot be attained to."

Tsze-lu asked about energy. The Master said, "Do you mean the energy of the South, the energy of the North, or the energy which you should cultivate yourself?

"To show forbearance and gentleness in teaching others; and not to revenge unreasonable conduct:-this is the energy of southern regions, and the good man makes it his study.

"To lie under arms; and meet death without regret:-this is the energy of northern regions, and the forceful make it their study.

"Therefore, the superior man cultivates a friendly harmony, without being weak.-How firm is he in his energy! He stands erect in the middle, without inclining to either side.-How firm is he in his energy! When good principles prevail in the government of his country, he does not change from what he was in retirement. How firm is he in his energy! When bad principles prevail in the country, he maintains his course to death without changing.-How firm is he in his energy!"

The Master said, "To live in obscurity, and yet practice wonders, in order to be mentioned with honor in future ages:-this is what I do not do.

"The good man tries to proceed according to the right path, but when he has gone halfway, he abandons it:-I am not able so to stop.

"The superior man accords with the course of the Mean. Though he may be all unknown, unregarded by the world, he feels no regret.-It is only the sage who is able for this."

The way which the superior man pursues, reaches wide and far, and yet is secret.

Common men and women, however ignorant, may intermeddle with the knowledge of it; yet in its utmost reaches, there is that which even the sage does not know. Common men and women, however much below the ordinary standard of character, can carry it into practice; yet in its utmost reaches, there is that which even the sage is not able to carry into practice. Great as heaven and earth are, men still find some things in them with which to be dissatisfied. Thus it is that, were the superior man to speak of his way in all its greatness, nothing in the world would be found able to embrace it, and were he to speak of it in its minuteness, nothing in the world would be found able to split it.

It is said in the Book of Poetry, "The hawk flies up to heaven; the fishes leap in the deep." This expresses how this way is seen above and below.

The way of the superior man may be found, in its simple elements, in the intercourse of common men and women; but in its utmost reaches, it shines brightly through Heaven and earth.

The Master said "The path is not far from man. When men try to pursue a course, which is far from the common indications of consciousness, this course cannot be considered The Path.

"In the Book of Poetry, it is said, 'In hewing an ax handle, in hewing an ax handle, the pattern is not far off. We grasp one ax handle to hew the other; and yet, if we look askance from the one to the other, we may consider them as apart. Therefore, the superior man governs men, according to their nature, with what is proper to them, and as soon as they change what is wrong, he stops.

"When one cultivates to the utmost the principles of his nature, and exercises them on the principle of reciprocity, he is not far from the path. What you do not like when done to yourself, do not do to others.

"In the way of the superior man there are four things, to not one of which have I as yet attained.-To serve my father, as I would require my son to serve me: to this I have not attained; to serve my prince as I would require my minister to serve me: to this I have not attained; to serve my elder brother as I would require my younger brother to serve me: to this I have not attained; to set the example in behaving to a friend, as I would require him to behave to me: to this I have not attained. Earnest in practicing the ordinary virtues, and careful in speaking about them, if, in his practice, he has anything defective, the superior man dares not but exert himself; and if, in his words, he has any excess, he dares not allow himself such license. Thus his words have respect to his actions, and his actions have respect to his words; is it not just an entire sincerity which marks the superior man?"

The superior man does what is proper to the station in which he is; he does not desire to go beyond this.

In a position of wealth and honor, he does what is proper to a position of wealth and honor. In a poor and low position, he does what is proper to a poor and low position. Situated among barbarous tribes, he does what is proper to a situation among barbarous tribes. In a position of sorrow and difficulty, he does what is proper to a position of sorrow and difficulty. The superior man can find himself in no situation in which he is not himself.

In a high situation, he does not treat with contempt his inferiors. In a low situation, he does not court the favor of his superiors. He rectifies himself, and seeks for nothing from others, so that he has no dissatisfactions. He does not murmur against Heaven, nor grumble against men.

Thus it is that the superior man is quiet and calm, waiting for the appointments of Heaven, while the mean man walks in dangerous paths, looking for lucky occurrences.

The Master said, "In archery we have something like the way of the superior man. When the archer misses the center of the target, he turns round and seeks for the cause of his failure in himself."

The way of the superior man may be compared to what takes place in traveling, when to go to a distance we must first traverse the space that is near, and in ascending a height, when we must begin from the lower ground.

It is said in the Book of Poetry, "Happy union with wife and children is like the music of lutes and harps. When there is concord among brethren, the harmony is delightful and enduring. Thus may you regulate your family, and enjoy the pleasure of your wife and children."

The Master said, "In such a state of things, parents have entire complacence!"

The Master said, "How abundantly do spiritual beings display the powers that belong to them!

"We look for them, but do not see them; we listen to, but do not hear them; yet they enter into all things, and there is nothing without them.

"They cause all the people in the kingdom to fast and purify themselves, and array themselves in their richest dresses, in order to attend at their sacrifices. Then, like overflowing water, they seem to be over the heads, and on the right and left of their worshippers.

"It is said in the Book of Poetry, 'The approaches of the spirits, you cannot sunrise; and can you treat them with indifference?'

"Such is the manifestness of what is minute! Such is the impossibility of repressing the outgoings of sincerity!"

The Master said, "How greatly filial was Shun! His virtue was that of a sage; his dignity was the throne; his riches were all within the four seas. He offered his sacrifices in his ancestral temple, and his descendants preserved the sacrifices to himself.

"Therefore having such great virtue, it could not but be that he should obtain the throne, that he should obtain those riches, that he should obtain his fame, that he should attain to his long life.

"Thus it is that Heaven, in the production of things, is sure to be bountiful to them, according to their qualities. Hence the tree that is flourishing, it nourishes, while that which is ready to fall, it overthrows.

"In the Book of Poetry, it is said, 'The admirable amiable prince displayed conspicuously his excelling virtue, adjusting his people, and adjusting his officers. Therefore, he received from Heaven his emoluments of dignity. It protected him, assisted him, decreed him the throne; sending from Heaven these favors, as it were repeatedly.'

"We may say therefore that he who is greatly virtuous will be sure to receive the appointment of Heaven."

The Master said, "It is only King Wan of whom it can be said that he had no cause for grief! His father was King Chi, and his son was King Wu. His father laid the foundations of his dignity, and his son transmitted it.

"King Wu continued the enterprise of King T'ai, King Chi, and King Wan. He once buckled on his armor, and got possession of the kingdom. He did not lose the distinguished personal reputation which he had throughout the kingdom. His dignity was the royal throne. His riches were the possession of all within the four seas. He offered his sacrifices in his ancestral temple, and his descendants maintained the sacrifices to himself.

"It was in his old age that King Wu received the appointment to the throne, and the duke of Chau completed the virtuous course of Wan and Wu. He carried up the title of king to T'ai and Chi, and sacrificed to all the former dukes above them with the royal ceremonies. And this rule he extended to the princes of the kingdom, the great officers, the scholars, and the common people. If the father were a great officer and the son a scholar, then the burial was that due to a great officer, and the sacrifice that due to a scholar. If the father were a scholar and the son a great officer, then the burial was that due to a scholar, and the sacrifice that due to a great officer. The one year's mourning was made to extend only to the great officers, but the three years' mourning extended to the Son of Heaven. In the mourning for a father or mother, he allowed no difference between the noble and the mean.

The Master said, "How far-extending was the filial piety of King Wu and the duke of Chau!

"Now filial piety is seen in the skillful carrying out of the wishes of our forefathers, and the skillful carrying forward of their undertakings.

"In spring and autumn, they repaired and beautified the temple halls of their fathers, set forth their ancestral vessels, displayed their various robes, and presented the offerings of the several seasons.

"By means of the ceremonies of the ancestral temple, they distinguished the royal kindred according to their order of descent. By ordering the parties present according to their rank, they distinguished the more noble and the less. By the arrangement of the services, they made a distinction of talents and worth. In the ceremony of general pledging, the inferiors presented the cup to their superiors, and thus something was given the lowest to do. At the concluding feast, places were given according to the hair, and thus was made the distinction of years.

"They occupied the places of their forefathers, practiced their ceremonies, and performed their music. They reverenced those whom they honored, and loved those whom they regarded with affection. Thus they served the dead as they would have served them alive; they served the departed as they would have served them had they been continued among them.

"By the ceremonies of the sacrifices to Heaven and Earth they served God, and by the ceremonies of the ancestral temple they sacrificed to their ancestors. He who understands the ceremonies of the sacrifices to Heaven and Earth, and the meaning of the several sacrifices to ancestors, would find the government of a kingdom as easy as to look into his palm!"

The Duke Ai asked about government. The Master said, "The government of Wan and Wu is displayed in the records,-the tablets of wood and bamboo. Let there be the men and the government will flourish; but without the men, their government decays and ceases.

"With the right men the growth of government is rapid, just as vegetation is rapid in the earth; and, moreover, their government might be called an easily-growing rush.

"Therefore the administration of government lies in getting proper men. Such men are to be got by means of the ruler's own character. That character is to be cultivated by his treading in the ways of duty. And the treading those ways of duty is to be cultivated by the cherishing of benevolence.

"Benevolence is the characteristic element of humanity, and the great exercise of it is in loving relatives. Righteousness is the accordance of actions with what is right, and the great exercise of it is in honoring the worthy. The decreasing measures of the love due to relatives, and the steps in the honor due to the worthy, are produced by the principle of propriety.

"When those in inferior situations do not possess the confidence of their superiors, they cannot retain the government of the people.

"Hence the sovereign may not neglect the cultivation of his own character. Wishing to cultivate his character, he may not neglect to serve his parents. In order to serve his parents, he may not neglect to acquire knowledge of men. In order to know men, he may not dispense with a knowledge of Heaven.

"The duties of universal obligation are five and the virtues wherewith they are practiced are three. The duties are those between sovereign and minister, between father and son, between husband and wife, between elder brother and younger, and those belonging to the intercourse of friends. Those five are the duties of universal obligation. Knowledge, magnanimity, and energy, these three, are the virtues universally binding. And the means by which they carry the duties into practice is singleness.

"Some are born with the knowledge of those duties; some know them by study; and some acquire the knowledge after a painful feeling of their ignorance. But the knowledge being possessed, it comes to the same thing. Some practice them with a natural ease; some from a desire for their advantages; and some by strenuous effort. But the achievement being made, it comes to the same thing."

The Master said, "To be fond of learning is to be near to knowledge. To practice with vigor is to be near to magnanimity. To possess the feeling of shame is to be near to energy.

"He who knows these three things knows how to cultivate his own character. Knowing how to cultivate his own character, he knows how to govern other men. Knowing how to govern other men, he knows how to govern the kingdom with all its states and families.

"All who have the government of the kingdom with its states and families have nine standard rules to follow;-viz., the cultivation of their own characters; the honoring of men of virtue and talents; affection towards their relatives; respect towards the great ministers; kind and considerate treatment of the whole body of officers; dealing with the mass of the people as children; encouraging the resort of all classes of artisans; indulgent treatment of men from a distance; and the kindly cherishing of the princes of the states.

"By the ruler's cultivation of his own character, the duties of universal obligation are set forth. By honoring men of virtue and talents, he is preserved from errors of judgment. By showing affection to his relatives, there is no grumbling nor resentment among his uncles and brethren. By respecting the great ministers, he is kept from errors in the practice of government. By kind and considerate treatment of the whole body of officers, they are led to make the most grateful return for his courtesies. By dealing with the mass of the people as his children, they are led to exhort one another to what is good. By encouraging the resort of an classes of artisans, his resources for expenditure are rendered ample. By indulgent treatment of men from a distance, they are brought to resort to him from all quarters. And by kindly cherishing the princes of the states, the whole kingdom is brought to revere him.

"Self-adjustment and purification, with careful regulation of his dress, and the not making a movement contrary to the rules of propriety this is the way for a ruler to cultivate his person. Discarding slanderers, and keeping himself from the seductions of beauty; making light of riches, and giving honor to virtue-this is the way for him to encourage men of worth and talents. Giving them places of honor and large emolument. and sharing with them in their likes and dislikes-this is the way for him to encourage his relatives to love him. Giving them numerous officers to discharge their orders and commissions:-this is the way for him to encourage the great ministers. According to them a generous confidence, and making their emoluments large:-this is the way to encourage the body of officers. Employing them only at the proper times, and making the imposts light:-this is the way to encourage the people. By daily examinations and monthly trials, and by making their rations in accordance with their labors:-this is the way to encourage the classes of artisans. To escort them on their departure and meet them on their coming; to commend the good among them, and show compassion to the incompetent:-this is the way to treat indulgently men from a distance. To restore families whose line of succession has been broken, and to revive states that have been extinguished; to reduce to order states that are in confusion, and support those which are in peril; to have fixed times for their own reception at court, and the reception of their envoys; to send them away after liberal treatment, and welcome their coming with small

contributions:-this is the way to cherish the princes of the states.

"All who have the government of the kingdom with its states and families have the above nine standard rules. And the means by which they are carried into practice is singleness.

"In all things success depends on previous preparation, and without such previous preparation there is sure to be failure. If what is to be spoken be previously determined, there will be no stumbling.

If affairs be previously determined, there will be no difficulty with them. If one's actions have been previously determined, there will be no sorrow in connection with them. If principles of conduct have been previously determined, the practice of them will be inexhaustible.

"When those in inferior situations do not obtain the confidence of the sovereign, they cannot succeed in governing the people. There is a way to obtain the confidence of the sovereign;-if one is not trusted by his friends, he will not get the confidence of his sovereign. There is a way to being trusted by one's friends;-if one is not obedient to his parents, he will not be true to friends. There is a way to being obedient to one's parents;-if one, on turning his thoughts in upon himself, finds a want of sincerity, he will not be obedient to his parents. There is a way to the attainment of sincerity in one's self; -if a man do not understand what is good, he will not attain sincerity in himself.

"Sincerity is the way of Heaven. The attainment of sincerity is the way of men. He who possesses sincerity is he who, without an effort, hits what is right, and apprehends, without the exercise of thought;-he is the sage who naturally and easily embodies the right way. He who attains to sincerity is he who chooses what is good, and firmly holds it fast.

"To this attainment there are requisite the extensive study of what is good, accurate inquiry about it, careful reflection on it, the clear discrimination of it, and the earnest practice of it.

"The superior man, while there is anything he has not studied, or while in what he has studied there is anything he cannot understand, Will not intermit his labor. While there is anything he has not inquired about, or anything in what he has inquired about which he does not know, he will not intermit his labor. While there is anything which he has not reflected on, or anything in what he has reflected on which he does not apprehend, he will not intermit his labor. While there is anything which he has not discriminated or his discrimination is not clear, he will not intermit his labor. If there be anything which he has not practiced, or his practice fails in earnestness, he will not intermit his labor. If another man succeed by one effort, he will use a hundred efforts. If another man succeed by ten efforts, he will use a thousand.

"Let a man proceed in this way, and, though dull, he will surely become intelligent; though weak, he will surely become strong."

When we have intelligence resulting from sincerity, this condition is to be ascribed to nature; when we have sincerity resulting from intelligence, this condition is to be ascribed to instruction. But given the sincerity, and there shall be the intelligence; given the intelligence, and there shall be the sincerity.

It is only he who is possessed of the most complete sincerity that can exist under heaven, who can give its fun development to his nature. Able to give its full development to his own nature, he can do the same to the nature of other men. Able to give its full development to the nature of other men, he can give their full development to the natures of animals and things. Able to give their full development to the natures of creatures and things, he can assist the transforming and nourishing powers of Heaven and Earth. Able to assist the transforming and nourishing powers of Heaven and Earth, he may with Heaven and Earth form a ternion.

Next to the above is he who cultivates to the utmost the shoots of goodness in him. From those he can attain to the possession of sincerity. This sincerity becomes apparent. From being apparent, it becomes manifest. From being manifest, it becomes brilliant. Brilliant, it affects others. Affecting others, they are changed by it. Changed by it, they are transformed. It is only he who is possessed of the most complete sincerity that can exist under heaven, who can transform.

It is characteristic of the most entire sincerity to be able to foreknow. When a nation or family is about to flourish, there are sure to be happy omens; and when it is about to perish, there are sure to be unlucky omens. Such events are seen in the milfoil and tortoise, and affect the movements of the four limbs. When calamity or happiness is about to come, the good shall certainly be foreknown by him, and the evil also. Therefore the individual possessed of the most complete sincerity is like a spirit.

Sincerity is that whereby self-completion is effected, and its way is that by which man must direct himself.

Sincerity is the end and beginning of things; without sincerity there would be nothing. On this account, the superior man regards the attainment of sincerity as the most excellent thing.

The possessor of sincerity does not merely accomplish the self-completion of himself. With this quality he completes other men and things also. The completing himself shows his perfect virtue. The completing other men and things shows his knowledge. But these are virtues belonging to the nature, and this is the way by which a union is effected of the external and internal. Therefore, whenever he-the entirely sincere man-employs them,-that is, these virtues, their action will be right.

Hence to entire sincerity there belongs ceaselessness.

Not ceasing, it continues long. Continuing long, it evidences itself.

Evidencing itself, it reaches far. Reaching far, it becomes large and substantial. Large and substantial, it becomes high and brilliant.

Large and substantial;-this is how it contains all things. High and brilliant;-this is how it overspreads all things. Reaching far and continuing long;-this is how it perfects all things.

So large and substantial, the individual possessing it is the co-equal of Earth. So high and brilliant, it makes him the co-equal of Heaven. So far-reaching and long-continuing, it makes him infinite.

Such being its nature, without any display, it becomes manifested; without any movement, it produces changes; and without any effort, it accomplishes its ends.

The way of Heaven and Earth may be completely declared in one sentence.-They are without any doubleness, and so they produce things in a manner that is unfathomable.

The way of Heaven and Earth is large and substantial, high and brilliant, far-reaching and long-enduring.

The Heaven now before us is only this bright shining spot; but when viewed in its inexhaustible extent, the sun, moon, stars, and constellations of the zodiac, are suspended in it, and all things are overspread by it. The earth before us is but a handful of soil; but when regarded in its breadth and thickness, it sustains mountains like the Hwa and the Yo, without feeling their weight, and contains the rivers and seas, without their leaking away. The mountain now before us appears only a stone; but when contemplated in all the vastness of its size, we see how the grass and trees are produced on it, and birds and beasts dwell on it, and precious things which men treasure up are found on it. The water now before us appears but a ladleful; yet extending our view to its unfathomable depths, the largest tortoises, iguanas, iguanodons, dragons, fishes, and turtles, are produced in it, articles of value and sources of wealth abound in it.

It is said in the Book of Poetry, "The ordinances of Heaven, how profound are they and unceasing!" The meaning is, that it is thus that Heaven is Heaven. And again, "How illustrious was it, the singleness of the virtue of King Wan!" indicating that it was thus that King Wan was what he was. Singleness likewise is unceasing.

How great is the path proper to the Sage! Like overflowing water, it sends forth and nourishes all things, and rises up to the height of heaven.

All-complete is its greatness! It embraces the three hundred rules of ceremony, and the three thousand rules of demeanor.

It waits for the proper man, and then it is trodden. Hence it is said, "Only by perfect virtue can the perfect path, in all its courses, be made a fact."

Therefore, the superior man honors his virtuous nature, and maintains constant inquiry and study, seeking to carry it out to its breadth and greatness, so as to omit none of the more exquisite and minute points which it embraces, and to raise it to its greatest height and brilliancy, so as to pursue the course of the Mean. He cherishes his old knowledge, and is continually acquiring new. He exerts an honest, generous earnestness, in the esteem and practice of all propriety.

Thus, when occupying a high situation he is not proud, and in a low situation he is not insubordinate. When the kingdom is well governed, he is sure by his words to rise; and when it is ill governed, he is sure by his silence to command forbearance to himself. Is not this what we find in the Book of Poetry,- "Intelligent is he and prudent, and so preserves his person?"

The Master said, Let a man who is ignorant be fond of using his own judgment; let a man without rank be fond of assuming a directing power to himself; let a man who is living in the present age go back to the ways of antiquity;-on the persons of all who act thus calamities will be sure to come.

To no one but the Son of Heaven does it belong to order ceremonies, to fix the measures, and to determine the written characters.

Now over the kingdom, carriages have all wheels, of the-same size; all writing is with the same characters; and for conduct there are the same rules.

One may occupy the throne, but if he have not the proper virtue, he may not dare to make ceremonies or music. One may have the virtue, but if he do not occupy the throne, he may not presume to make ceremonies or music.

The Master said, "I may describe the ceremonies of the Hsia dynasty, but Chi cannot sufficiently attest my words. I have learned the ceremonies of the Yin dynasty, and in Sung they still continue. I have learned the ceremonies of Chau, which are now used, and I follow Chau."

He who attains to the sovereignty of the kingdom, having those three important things, shall be able to effect that there shall be few errors under his government.

However excellent may have been the regulations of those of former times, they cannot be attested. Not being attested, they cannot command credence, and not being credited, the people would not follow them. However excellent might be the regulations made by one in an inferior situation, he is not in a position to be honored. Unhonored, he cannot command credence, and not being credited, the people would not follow his rules.

Therefore the institutions of the Ruler are rooted in his own character and conduct, and sufficient attestation of them is given by the masses of the people. He examines them by comparison with those of the three kings, and finds them without mistake. He sets them up before Heaven and Earth, and finds nothing in them contrary to their mode of operation. He presents himself with them before spiritual beings, and no doubts about them arise. He is prepared to wait for the rise of a sage a hundred ages after, and has no misgivings.

His presenting himself with his institutions before spiritual beings, without any doubts arising about them, shows that he knows Heaven. His being prepared, without any misgivings, to wait for the rise of a sage a hundred ages after, shows that he knows men.

Such being the case, the movements of such a ruler, illustrating his institutions, constitute an example to the world for ages. His acts are for ages a law to the kingdom. His words are for ages a lesson to the kingdom. Those who are far from him look longingly for him; and those who are near him are never wearied with him.

It is said in the Book of Poetry,-"Not disliked there, not tired of here, from day to day and night tonight, will they perpetuate their praise." Never has there been a ruler, who did not realize this description, that obtained an early renown throughout the kingdom.

Chung-ni handed down the doctrines of Yao and Shun, as if they had been his ancestors, and elegantly displayed the regulations of Wan and Wul taking them as his model. Above, he harmonized with the times of Heaven, and below, he was conformed to the water and land.

He may be compared to Heaven and Earth in their supporting and containing, their overshadowing and curtaining, all things. He may be compared to the four seasons in their alternating progress, and to the sun and moon in their successive shining.

All things are nourished together without their injuring one another. The courses of the seasons, and of the sun and moon, are pursued without any collision among them. The smaller energies are like river currents; the greater energies are seen in mighty transformations. It is this which makes heaven and earth so great.

It is only he, possessed of all sagely qualities that can exist under heaven, who shows himself quick in apprehension, clear in discernment, of far-reaching intelligence, and all-embracing knowledge, fitted to exercise rule; magnanimous, generous, benign, and mild, fitted to exercise forbearance; impulsive, energetic, firm, and enduring, fitted to maintain a firm hold; self-adjusted, grave, never swerving from the Mean, and correct, fitted to command reverence; accomplished, distinctive, concentrative, and searching, fitted to exercise discrimination.

All-embracing is he and vast, deep and active as a fountain, sending forth in their due season his virtues.

All-embracing and vast, he is like Heaven. Deep and active as a fountain, he is like the abyss. He is seen, and the people all reverence him; he speaks, and the people all believe him; he acts, and the people all are pleased with him.

Therefore his fame overspreads the Middle Kingdom, and extends to all barbarous tribes. Wherever ships and carriages reach; wherever the strength of man penetrates; wherever the heavens overshadow and the earth sustains; wherever the sun and moon shine; wherever frosts and dews fall:-all who have blood and breath unfeignedly honor and love him. Hence it is said,-"He is the equal of Heaven."

It is only the individual possessed of the most entire sincerity that can exist under Heaven, who can adjust the great invariable relations of mankind, establish the great fundamental virtues of humanity, and know the transforming and nurturing operations of Heaven and Earth;-shall this individual have any being or anything beyond himself on which he depends?

Call him man in his ideal, how earnest is he! Call him an abyss, how deep is he! Call him Heaven, how vast is he!

Who can know him, but he who is indeed quick in apprehension, clear in discernment, of far-reaching intelligence, and all-embracing knowledge, possessing all Heavenly virtue?

It is said in the Book of Poetry, "Over her embroidered robe she puts a plain single garment," intimating a dislike to the display of the elegance of the former. Just so, it is the way of the superior man to prefer the concealment of his virtue, while it daily becomes more illustrious, and it is the way of the mean man to seek notoriety, while he daily goes more and more to ruin. It is characteristic of the superior man, appearing insipid, yet never to produce satiety; while showing a simple negligence, yet to have his accomplishments recognized; while seemingly plain, yet to be discriminating. He knows how what is distant lies in what is near. He knows where the wind proceeds from. He knows how what is minute becomes manifested. Such a one, we may be sure, will enter into virtue.

It is said in the Book of Poetry, "Although the fish sink and lie at the bottom, it is still quite clearly seen." Therefore the superior man examines his heart, that there may be nothing wrong there, and that he may have no cause for dissatisfaction with himself. That wherein the superior man cannot be equaled is simply this,-his work which other men cannot see.

It is said in the Book of Poetry, "Looked at in your apartment, be there free from shame as being exposed to the light of Heaven." Therefore, the superior man, even when he is not moving, has a feeling of reverence, and while he speaks not, he has the feeling of truthfulness.

It is said in the Book of Poetry, "In silence is the offering presented, and the spirit approached to; there is not the slightest contention." Therefore the superior man does not use rewards, and the people are stimulated to virtue. He does not show anger, and the people are awed more than by hatchets and battle-axes.

It is said in the Book of Poetry, "What needs no display is virtue. All the princes imitate it." Therefore, the superior man being sincere and reverential, the whole world is conducted to a state of happy tranquility.

It is said in the Book of Poetry, "I regard with pleasure your brilliant virtue, making no great display of itself in sounds and appearances." The Master said,

"Among the appliances to transform the people, sound and appearances are but trivial influences. It is said in another ode, 'His Virtue is light as a hair.' Still, a hair will admit of comparison as to its size. 'The doings of the supreme Heaven have neither sound nor smell. 'That is perfect virtue."

## THE END

# The Great Learning

*By Confucius*

WRITTEN 500 B.C.E

What the great learning teaches, is to illustrate illustrious virtue; to renovate the people; and to rest in the highest excellence.

The point where to rest being known, the object of pursuit is then determined; and, that being determined, a calm unperturbedness may be attained to. To that calmness there will succeed a tranquil repose. In that repose there may be careful deliberation, and that deliberation will be followed by the attainment of the desired end.

Things have their root and their branches. Affairs have their end and their beginning. To know what is first and what is last will lead near to what is taught in the Great Learning.

The ancients who wished to illustrate illustrious virtue throughout the kingdom, first ordered well their own states. Wishing to order well their states, they first regulated their families. Wishing to regulate their families, they first cultivated their persons. Wishing to cultivate their persons, they first rectified their hearts. Wishing to rectify their hearts, they first sought to be sincere in their thoughts. Wishing to be sincere in their thoughts, they first extended to the utmost their knowledge. Such extension of knowledge lay in the investigation of things.

Things being investigated, knowledge became complete. Their knowledge being complete, their thoughts were sincere. Their thoughts being sincere, their hearts were then rectified. Their hearts being rectified, their persons were cultivated. Their persons being cultivated, their families were regulated. Their families being regulated, their states were rightly governed. Their states being rightly governed, the whole kingdom was made tranquil and happy.

From the Son of Heaven down to the mass of the people, all must consider the cultivation of the person the root of everything besides.

It cannot be, when the root is neglected, that what should spring from it will be well ordered. It never has been the case that what was of great importance has been slightly cared for, and, at the same time, that what was of slight importance has been greatly cared for.

## Commentary of the philosopher Tsang

In the Announcement to K'ang, it is said, "He was able to make his virtue illustrious."

In the Tai Chia, it is said, "He contemplated and studied the illustrious decrees of Heaven."

In the Canon of the emperor (Yao), it is said, "He was able to make illustrious his lofty virtue."

These passages all show how those sovereigns made themselves illustrious.

On the bathing tub of T'ang, the following words were engraved: "If you can one day renovate yourself, do so from day to day. Yea, let there be daily renovation."

In the Announcement to K'ang, it is said, "To stir up the new people."

In the Book of Poetry, it is said, "Although Chau was an ancient state the ordinance which lighted on it was new."

Therefore, the superior man in everything uses his utmost endeavors. In the Book of Poetry, it is said, "The royal domain of a thousand li is where the people rest."

In the Book of Poetry, it is said, "The twittering yellow bird rests on a corner of the mound." The Master said, "When it rests, it knows where to rest. Is it possible that a man should not be equal to this bird?"

In the Book of Poetry, it is said, "Profound was King Wan. With how bright and unceasing a feeling of reverence did he regard his resting places!" As a sovereign, he rested in benevolence. As a minister, he rested in reverence. As a son, he rested in filial piety. As a father, he rested in kindness. In communication with his subjects, he rested in good faith.

In the Book of Poetry, it is said, "Look at that winding course of the Ch'i, with the green bamboos so luxuriant! Here is our elegant and accomplished prince! As we cut and then file; as we chisel and then grind: so has he cultivated himself. How grave is he and dignified! How majestic and distinguished! Our elegant and accomplished prince never can be forgotten." That expression-"As we cut and then file," the work of learning. "As we chisel and then grind," indicates that of self-culture. "How grave is he and dignified!" indicates the feeling of cautious reverence. "How commanding and distinguished! indicates an awe-inspiring deportment. "Our elegant and accomplished prince never can be forgotten," indicates how, when virtue is complete and excellence extreme, the people cannot forget them.

In the Book of Poetry, it is said, "Ah! the former kings are not forgotten." Future princes deem worthy what they deemed worthy, and love what they loved. The common people delight in what delighted them, and are benefited by their beneficial arrangements. It is on this account that the former kings, after they have quitted the world, are not forgotten.

The Master said, "In hearing litigations, I am like any other body. What is necessary is to cause the people to have no litigations." So, those who are devoid of principle find it impossible to carry out their speeches, and a great awe would be struck into men's minds;-this is called knowing the root.

This is called knowing the root. This is called the perfecting of knowledge.

What is meant by "making the thoughts sincere." is the allowing no self-deception, as when we hate a bad smell, and as when we love what is beautiful. This is called self-enjoyment. Therefore, the superior man must be watchful over himself when he is alone.

There is no evil to which the mean man, dwelling retired, will not proceed, but when he sees a superior man, he instantly tries to disguise himself, concealing his evil, and displaying what is good. The other beholds him, as if he saw his heart and reins;-of what use is his disguise? This is an instance of the saying -"What truly is within will be manifested without." Therefore, the superior man must be watchful over himself when he is alone.

The disciple Tsang said, "What ten eyes behold, what ten hands point to, is to be regarded with reverence!"

Riches adorn a house, and virtue adorns the person. The mind is expanded, and the body is at ease. Therefore, the superior man must make his thoughts sincere.

What is meant by, "The cultivation of the person depends on rectifying the mind may be thus illustrated:-If a man be under the influence of passion he will be incorrect in his conduct. He will be the same, if he is under the

317

influence of terror, or under the influence of fond regard, or under that of sorrow and distress.

When the mind is not present, we look and do not see; we hear and do not understand; we eat and do not know the taste of what we eat.

This is what is meant by saying that the cultivation of the person depends on the rectifying of the mind.

What is meant by "The regulation of one's family depends on the cultivation of his person is this:-men are partial where they feel affection and love; partial where they despise and dislike; partial where they stand in awe and reverence; partial where they feel sorrow and compassion; partial where they are arrogant and rude. Thus it is that there are few men in the world who love and at the same time know the bad qualities of the object of their love, or who hate and yet know the excellences of the object of their hatred.

Hence it is said, in the common adage,"A man does not know the wickedness of his son; he does not know the richness of his growing corn."

This is what is meant by saying that if the person be not cultivated, a man cannot regulate his family.

What is meant by "In order rightly to govern the state, it is necessary first to regulate the family," is this:-It is not possible for one to teach others, while he cannot teach his own family. Therefore, the ruler, without going beyond his family, completes the lessons for the state. There is filial piety:-therewith the. sovereign should be served. There is fraternal submission:-therewith elders and superiors should be served. There is kindness:-therewith the multitude should be treated.

In the Announcement to K'ang, it is said, "Act as if you were watching over an infant." If a mother is really anxious about it, though she may not hit exactly the wants of her infant, she will not be far from doing so. There never has been a girl who learned to bring up a child, that she might afterwards marry.

From the loving example of one family a whole state becomes loving, and from its courtesies the whole state becomes courteous while, from the ambition and perverseness of the One man, the whole state may be led to rebellious disorder;-such is the nature of the influence. This verifies the saying, "Affairs may be ruined by a single sentence; a kingdom may be settled by its One man."

Yao and Shun led on the kingdom with benevolence and the people followed them. Chieh and Chau led on the kingdom with violence, and people followed them. The orders which these issued were contrary to the practices which they loved, and so the people did not follow them. On this account, the ruler must himself be possessed of the good qualities, and then he may require them in the people. He must not have the bad qualities in himself, and then he may require that they shall not be in the people. Never has there been a man, who, not having reference to his own character and wishes in dealing with others, was able effectually to instruct them.

Thus we see how the government of the state depends on the regulation of the family.

In the Book of Poetry, it is said, "That peach tree, so delicate and elegant! How luxuriant is its foliage! This girl is going to her husband's house. She will rightly order her household." Let the household be rightly ordered, and then the people of the state may be taught.

In the Book of Poetry, it is said, "They can discharge their duties to their elder brothers. They can discharge their duties to their younger brothers." Let the ruler discharge his duties to his elder and younger brothers, and then he may teach the people of the state.

In the Book of Poetry, it is said, "In his deportment there is nothing wrong; he rectifies all the people of the state." Yes; when the ruler, as a father, a son, and a brother, is a model, then the people imitate him.

This is what is meant by saying, "The government of his kingdom depends on his regulation of the family."

What is meant by "The making the whole kingdom peaceful and happy depends on the government of his state," this:-When the sovereign behaves to his aged, as the aged should be behaved to, the people become final; when the sovereign behaves to his elders, as the elders should be behaved to, the people learn brotherly submission; when the sovereign treats compassionately the young and helpless, the people do the same. Thus the ruler has a principle with which, as with a measuring square, he may regulate his conduct.

What a man dislikes in his superiors, let him not display in the treatment of his inferiors; what he dislikes in inferiors, let him not display in the service of his superiors; what he hates in those who are before him, let him not therewith precede those who are behind him; what he hates in those who are behind him, let him not bestow on the left; what he hates to receive on the left, let him not bestow on the right:-this is what is called "The principle with which, as with a measuring square, to regulate one's conduct."

In the Book of Poetry, it is said, "How much to be rejoiced in are these princes, the parents of the people!" When a prince loves what the people love, and hates what the people hate, then is he what is called the parent of the people.

In the Book of Poetry, it is said, "Lofty is that southern hill, with its rugged masses of rocks! Greatly distinguished are you, O grand-teacher Yin, the people all look up to you. "Rulers of states may not neglect to be careful. If they deviate to a mean selfishness, they will be a disgrace in the kingdom.

In the Book of Poetry, it is said, "Before the sovereigns of the Yin dynasty had lost the hearts of the people, they could appear before God. Take warning from the house of Yin. The great decree is not easily preserved." This shows that, by gaining the people, the kingdom is gained, and, by losing the people, the kingdom is lost.

On this account, the ruler will first take pains about his own virtue. Possessing virtue will give him the people. Possessing the people will give the territory. Possessing the territory will give him its wealth. Possessing the wealth, he will have resources for expenditure.

Virtue is the root; wealth is the result. If he make the root his secondary object, and the result his primary, he will only wrangle with his people, and teach them rapine.

Hence, the accumulation of wealth is the way to scatter the people; and the letting it be scattered among them is the way to collect the people.

And hence, the ruler's words going forth contrary to right, will come back to him in the same way, and wealth, gotten by improper ways, will take its departure by the same.

In the Announcement to K'ang, it is said, "The decree indeed may not always rest on us"; that is, goodness obtains the decree, and the want of goodness loses it.

In the Book of Ch'u, it is said, "The kingdom of Ch'u does not consider that to be valuable. It values, instead, its good men."

Duke Wan's uncle, Fan, said, "Our fugitive does not account that to be precious. What he considers precious is the affection due to his parent."

In the Declaration of the Duke of Ch'in, it is said, "Let me have but one minister, plain and sincere, not pretending to other abilities, but with a simple, upright, mind; and possessed of generosity, regarding the talents of others as though he himself possessed them, and, where he finds accomplished and perspicacious men, loving them in his heart more than his mouth expresses, and really showing himself able to bear them and employ them:-such a minister will be able to preserve my sons and grandsons and black-haired people, and benefits likewise to the kingdom may well be looked for from him. But if it be his character, when he finds men of ability, to be jealous and hate them; and, when he finds accomplished and perspicacious men, to oppose them and not allow their advancement, showing himself really not able to bear them: such a minister will not be able to protect my sons and grandsons and people; and may he not also be pronounced dangerous to the state?"

It is only the truly virtuous man who can send away such a man and banish him, driving him out among the barbarous tribes around, determined not to dwell along with him in the Auddle Kingdom. This is in accordance with the saying, "It is only the truly virtuous man who can love or who can hate others."

To see men of worth and not be able to raise them to office; to raise them to office, but not to do so quickly:-this is disrespectful. To see bad men and not be able to remove them; to remove them, but not to do so to a distance:-this is weakness.

To love those whom men hate, and to hate those whom men love;-this is to outrage the natural feeling of men. Calamities cannot fail to come down on him who does so.

Thus we see that the sovereign has a great course to pursue. He must show entire self-devotion and sincerity to attain it, and by pride and extravagance he will fail of it.

There is a great course also for the production of wealth. Let the producers be many and the consumers few. Let there be activity in the production, and economy in the expenditure. Then the wealth will always be sufficient.

The virtuous ruler, by means of his wealth, makes himself more distinguished. The vicious ruler accumulates wealth, at the expense of his life.

Never has there been a case of the sovereign loving benevolence, and the people not loving righteousness. Never has there been a case where the people have loved righteousness, and the affairs of the sovereign have not been carried to completion. And never has there been a case where the wealth in such a state, collected in the treasuries and arsenals, did not continue in the sovereign's possession.

The officer Mang Hsien said, "He who keeps horses and a carriage does not look after fowls and pigs. The family which keeps its stores of ice does not rear cattle or sheep. So, the house which possesses a hundred chariots should not keep a minister to look out for imposts that he may lay them on the people. Than to have such a minister, it were better for that house to have one who should rob it of its revenues." This is in accordance with the saying:-

"In a state, pecuniary gain is not to be considered to be prosperity, but its prosperity will be found in righteousness."

When he who presides over a state or a family makes his revenues his chief business, he must be under the influence of some small, mean man. He may consider this man to be good; but when such a person is employed in the administration of a state or family, calamities from Heaven, and injuries from men, will befall it together, and, though a good man may take his place, he will not be able to remedy the evil. This illustrates again the saying, "In a state, gain is not to be considered prosperity, but its prosperity will be found in righteousness."

## THE END

# The Philosophy of Confucius

1. What point was Confucius making in these two pieces? Who was he writing to and to what end? How well do you think he was received?

2. Confucius writes, "It is not possible for one to teach others, while he cannot teach his own family. Do you agree with this sentiment?

3. What can we learn about the core values of ancient Chinese culture by reading Confucius? Was he representative of the people of the time or too high above it?

# Ramayana

*By Valmiki*

TRANSLATED BY ROMESH C. DUTT (1899)

# Book I

## SITA-SWAYAWARA--The Bridal of Sita

### I. AYODRYA, THE RIGHTEOUS CIT

Rich in royal worth and valour, rich in holy Vedic lore,
Dasa-ratha ruled his empire in the happy days of yore,

Loved of men in fair Ayodhya, sprung of ancient Solar Race,
Royal rishi in his duty, saintly rishi in his grace,

Great as INDRA in his prowess, bounteous as KUVERA kind,
Dauntless deeds subdued his foemen, lofty faith subdued his mind!

Like the ancient monarch Manu, father of the human race,
Dasa-ratha ruled his people with a father's loving grace,

Truth and Justice swayed each action and each baser motive quelled
People's Love and Monarch's Duty every thought and deed impelled,

And his town like INDRA'S city,--tower and dome and turret brave--
Rose in proud and peerless beauty on Sarayu's limpid wave!

Peaceful lived the righteous people, rich in wealth in merit high,
Envy dwelt not in their bosoms and their accents shaped no lie,

Fathers with their happy households owned their cattle, corn, and gold,
Galling penury and famine in Ayodhya had no hold,

Neighbours lived in mutual kindness helpful with their ample wealth,
None who begged the wasted refuse, none who lived by fraud and stealth!

And they wore the gem and earring, wreath and fragrant sandal paste,
And their arms were decked with bracelets, and their necks with nishkas graced,

Cheat and braggart and deceiver lived not in the ancient town,
Proud despiser of the lowly wore not insults in their frown,

Poorer fed not on the richer, hireling friend upon the great,
None with low and lying accents did upon the proud man wait

Men to plighted vows were faithful, faithful was each loving wife,
Impure thought and wandering fancy stained not holy wedded life,

Robed in gold and graceful garments, fair in form and fair in face,
Winsome were Ayodhya's daughters, rich in wit and woman's grace

Twice-born men were free from passion, lust of gold and impure greed,
Faithful to their Rites and Scriptures, truthful in their word and deed,

Altar blazed in every mansion, from each home was bounty given,
'Stooped no man to fulsome falsehood, questioned none the will of Heaven.

Kshatras bowed to holy Brahmans, Vaisyas to the Kshatras bowed
Toiling Sudras lived by labour, of their honest duty proud,

To the Gods and to the Fathers, to each guest in virtue trained,
Rites were done with true devotion as by holy writ ordained,

Pure each caste in due observance, stainless was each ancient rite,
And the nation thrived and prospered by its old and matchless might,

And each man in truth abiding lived a long and peaceful life,
With his sons and with his grandsons, with his loved and honoured wife.

Thus was ruled the ancient city by her monarch true and bold,
As the earth was ruled by Mann in the misty days of old,

Troops who never turned in battle, fierce as fire and strong and brave,
Guarded well her lofty ramparts as the lions guard the cave.

Steeds like INDRA'S in their swiftness came from far Kamboja's land,
From Vanaya and Vahlika and from Sindhu's rock-bound strand,

Elephants of mighty stature from the Vindhya mountains came,
Or from deep and darksome forests round Himalay's peaks of fame,

Matchless in their mighty prowess, peerless in their wondrous speed,
Nobler than the noble tuskers sprung from high celestial breed.

Thus Ayodhya, "virgin city,"--faithful to her haughty name,--
Ruled by righteous Dasa-ratha won a world-embracing fame,

Strong-barred gates and lofty arches, tower and dome and turret high
Decked the vast and peopled city fair as mansions of the sky.

Queens of proud and peerless beauty born of houses rich in fame,
Loved of royal Dasa-ratha to his happy mansion came,

Queen Kausalya blessed with virtue true and righteous Rama bore,
Queen Kaikeyi young and beauteous bore him Bharat rich in lore,

Queen Simitra bore the bright twins, Lakshman and Satruglina bold,
Four brave princes served their father in the happy days of old!

### II. MITHILA, AND THE BREAKING OF THE BOW

Janak monarch of Videha spake his memage near and far,
He shall win my peerless Sita who shall bend my bow of war,

Suitors came from farthest regions, warlike princes known to fame,
Vainly strove to wield the weapon, left Videha in their shame.

Viswa-mitra royal rishi, Rama true and Lakshman bold,
Came to fair Mithila's city from Ayodhya famed of old,

Spake in pride the royal rishi: "Monarch of Videha's throne,
Grant, the wondrous bow of RUDRA be to princely Rama shown."

Janak spake his royal mandate to his lords and warriors bold:
"Bring ye forth the bow of RUDRA decked in garlands and in gold,"

And his peers and proud retainers waiting on the monarch's call,
Brought the great and goodly weapon from the city's inner hall.

Stalwart men of ample stature pulled the mighty iron car
In which rested all-inviolate Janak's dreaded bow of war,

And where midst assembled monarchs sat Videha's godlike king,
With a mighty toil and effort did the eight-wheeled chariot bring.

"This the weapon of Videha," proudly thus the peers begun,
"Be it shewn to royal Rama, Dasa-ratha's righteous son,"

"This the bow," then spake the monarch to the risha famed of old,
To the true and righteous Rama and to Lakshman young and bold,

"This the weapon of my fathers prized by kings from age to age,
Mighty chiefs and sturdy warriors could not bend it, noble sage

Gods before the bow of RUDRA have in righteous terror quailed,
Rakshas fierce and stout Asuras have in futile effort failed,

Mortal man will struggle vainly RUDRA'S wondrous bow to bend,
Vainly strive to string the weapon and the shining dart to send,

Holy saint and royal rishi, here is Janak's ancient bow,
Shew it to Ayodhya's princes, speak to them my kingly vow!

Viswa-mitra humbly listened to the words the monarch said,
To the brave and righteous Rama, Janak's mighty bow displayed,

Rama lifted high the cover of the pond'rous iron car,
Gazed with conscious pride and prowess on the mighty bow of war.

"Let me," humbly spake the hero, "on this bow my fingers place,
Let me lift and bend the weapon, help me with your loving grace."

"Be it so," the rishi answered, "be it so," the monarch said,
Rama lifted high the weapon on his stalwart arms displayed,

Wond'ring gazed the kings assembled as the son of Raghu's race
Proudly raised the bow of RUDRA with a warrior's stately grace,

Proudly strung the bow Of RUDRA which the kings had tried in vain
Drew the cord with force resistless till the weapon snapped in twain!

Like the thunder's pealing accent rose the loud terrific clang,
And the firm earth shook and trembled and the hills in echoes rang,

And the chiefs and gathered monarchs fell and fainted in their fear,
And the men of many nations shook the dreadful sound to hear!

Pale and white the startled monarchs slowly from their terror woke,
And with royal grace and greetings Janak to the rishi spoke:

Now my ancient eyes have witnessed wond'rous deed by Rama done,
Deed surpassing thought or fancy wrought by Dasa-ratha's son,

And the proud and peerless princess, Sita glory of my house,
Sheds on me an added lustre as she weds a godlike spouse,

True shall be my plighted promise, Sita dearer than my life,
Won by worth and wond'rous valour shall be Rama's faithful wife

Grant us leave, O royal rishi, grant us blessings kind and fair,
Envoys mounted on my chariot to Ayodhya shall repair,

They shall speak to Rama's father glorious feat by Rama done,
They shall speak to Dasa-ratha, Sita is by valour won,

They shall say the noble princes safely live within our walls,
They shall ask him by his presence to adorn our palace balls

Pleased at heart the sage assented, envoys by the monarch sent,
To Ayodhya's distant city with the royal message went.

### III. THE EMBASSY TO AYODHYA

Three nights halting in their journey with their steeds fatigued and spent,
Envoys from Mithila's monarch to Ayodhya's city went,

And by royal mandate bidden stepped within the palace hall.
Where the ancient Dasa-ratha sat with peers and courtiers all,

And with greetings and obeisance spake their message calm and bold,
Softly fell their gentle accents as their happy tale they told.

Greetings to thee, mighty monarch, greetings to each priest and peer,
Wishes for thy health and safety from Videha's king we bear,

Janak monarch of Videha for thy happy life hath prayed,
And by Viswa-mitra's bidding words of gladsome message said:

'Known on earth my plighted promise, spoke by heralds near and far,
He shall win my peerless Sita who shall bend my bow of war,--

Monarchs came and princely suitors, chiefs and warriors known to fame,
Baffled in their fruitless effort left Mithila in their shame,

Rama came with gallant Lakshman by their proud preceptor led,
Bent and broke the mighty weapon, he the beauteous bride shall wed!

Rama strained the weapon stoutly till it snapped and broke in twain,
In the concourse of the monarchs, in the throng of arméd men,

Rama wins the peerless princess by the righteous will of Heaven,
I redeem my plighted promise-be thy kind permission given!

Monarch of Kosala's country! with each lord and peer and priest,
Welcome to Mithila's city, welcome to Videha's feast,

Joy thee in thy Rama's triumph, joy thee with a father's pride,
Let each prince of proud Kosala win a fair Videha-bride!'

These by Viswa-mitra's bidding are the words our monarch said
This by Sata-nanda's counsel is the quest that he hath made."

Joyful was Kosala's monarch, spake to chieftains in the hall,
Vama-deva and Vasishtha and to priests and Brahmans all:

"Priests and peers! in far Mithila, so these friendly envoys tell,
Righteous Rama, gallant Lakshman, in the royal palace dwell,

And our brother of Videha prizes Rama's warlike pride,
To each prince of proud Kosala yields a fair Videha-bride,

If it please ye, priests and chieftains, speed we to Mithila fair,
World-renowned is Janak's virtue, Heaven-inspired his learning rare!"

Spake each peer and holy Brahman: "Dasa-ratha's will be done!"
Spake the king unto the envoys: "Part we with the rising sun!"

Honoured with a regal honour, welcomed to a rich repast,
Gifted envoys from Mithila day and night in gladness passed!

*IV. MEETING OF JANAK AND DASA-RATHA*

On Ayodhya's tower and turret now the golden morning woke,
Dasa-ratha girt by courtiers thus to wise Sumantra spoke:

Bid the keepers of my treasure with their waggons lead the way,
Ride in front with royal riches, gold and gems in bright array,

Bid my warriors skilled in duty lead the four-fold ranks of war,
Elephants and noble chargers, serried foot and battle-car,

Bid my faithful chariot-driver harness quick each car of state,
With the fleetest of my coursers, and upon my orders wait.

Vama-deva and Vasishtha versed in Veda's ancient lore,
Kasyapa and good Jabali sprung from holy saints of yore,

Markandeya in his glory, Katyayana in his pride,
Let each priest and proud preceptor with Kosala's monarch ride,

Harness to my royal chariot strong and stately steeds of war,
For the envoys speed my journey and the way is long and far."

With each priest and proud retainer Dasa-ratha led the way,
Glittering ranks of forces followed in their four-fold dread array,

Four days on the way they journeyed till they reached Videha's land,
Janak with a courteous welcome came to greet the royal band,

Joyously Videha's monarch greeted every priest and peer,
Greeted ancient Dasa-ratha in his accents soft and clear:

"Hast thou come, my royal brother, on my house to yield thy grace,
Hast thou made a peaceful journey, pride of Raghu's royal race?

Welcome! for Mithila's people seek my royal guest to greet,
Welcome! for thy sons of valour long their loving sire to meet,

Welcome to the priest Vasishtha versed in Veda's ancient lore,
Welcome every righteous rishi sprung from holy saints of yore!

And my evil fates are vanquished and my race is sanctified,
With the warlike race of Raghu thus in loving bonds allied,

Sacrifice and rites auspicious we ordain with rising sun,
Ere the evening's darkness closes, happy nuptials shall be done!"

Thus in kind and courteous accents Janak spake his purpose high,
And his royal love responding, Dasa-ratha made reply:

"Gift betokens giver's bounty, so our ancient sages sing,
And thy righteous fame and virtue grace thy gift, Videha's king!

World-renowmed is Janak's bounty, Heaven-inspired his holy grace,
And we take his boon and blessina as an honour to our race!"

Royal grace and kingly greeting, marked the ancient monarch's word,
Janak with a grateful pleasure Dasa-ratha's answer heard,

And the Brahmans and preceptors joyously the midnight spent,
And in converse pure and pleasant and in sacred sweet content.

Rigliteous Rama, gallant Lakshman piously their father greet,
Duly make their deep obeisance, humbly touch his royal feet,

And the night is filled with gladness for the king revered and old,
Honoured by the saintly Janak, greeted by his children bold,

On Mithila's tower and turret stars their silent vigils keep,
When each sacred rite completed, Janak seeks his nightly sleep.

### V. THE PREPARATION

All his four heroic princes now with Dasa-ratha stayed
In Mithila's ancient city, and their father's will obeyed,

Thither came the bold Yudhajit prince of proud Kaikeya's line,
On the day that Dasa-ratha made his gifts of gold and kine,

And he met the ancient monarch, for his health and safety prayed,
Made his bow and due obeisance and in gentle accents said:

"List, O king! my royal father, monarch of Kaikeya's race,
Sends his kindly love and greetings with his blessings and his grace,

And he asks if Dasa-ratha prospers in his wonted health,
If his friends and fond relations live in happiness and wealth.

Queen Kaikeyi is my sister, and to see her son I came,
Bharat prince of peerless virtue, worthy of his father's fame,

Aye, to see that youth of valour, by my royal father sent,
To Ayodhya's ancient city with an anxious heart I went,

In the city of Mithila,--thus did all thy subjects say,
With his sons and with his kinsmen Dasa-ratha makes his stay,

Hence in haste I journeyed hither, travelling late and early dawn,
For to do thee due obeisance and to greet my sister's son!"

Spake the young and proud Kaikeya, dear and duly-greeted guest,
Dasa-ratha on his brother choicest gifts and honours pressed.

Brightly dawned the happy morning, and Kosala's king of fame
With his sons and wise Vasishtha to the sacred yajna came,

Rama and his gallant brothers decked in gem and jewel bright,
In th' auspicious hour of morning did the blest Kautuka rite,

And beside their royal father piously the princes stood,
And to fair Videlia's monarch spake Vasishtha wise and good:

"Dasa-ratha waits expectant with each proud and princely son,
Waits upon the bounteous giver, for each holy rite is done,

'Twixt the giver and the taker sacred word is sacred deed,
Seal with gift thy plighted promise, let the nuptial rites proceed

Thus the righteous-souled Vasishtha to Videha's monarch prayed,
Janak versed in holy Vedas thus in courteous accents said:

"Wherefore waits the king expectant? Free to him this royal dome,
Since my kingdom is his empire and my palace is his home,

And the maidens, flame-resplendent, done each fond Kautuka rite,
Beaming in their bridal beauty tread the sacrificial site

I beside the lighted altar wait upon thy sacred hest,
And auspicious is the moment, sage Vasishtha knows the rest

Let the peerless Dasa-ratha, proud Kosala's king of might,
With his sons and honoured sages enter on the holy site,

Let the righteous sage Vasishtha, sprung from Vedic saints of old,
Celebrate the happy wedding; be the sacred mantras told!"

*VI. THE WEDDING*

Sage Vasishtha skilled in duty placed Videha's honoured king,
Viswa-mitra, Sata-nanda, all within the sacred ring,

And he raised the holy altar as the ancient writs ordain,
Decked and graced with scented garlands grateful unto gods and men,

And he set the golden ladles, vases pierced by artists skilled,
Holy censers fresh and fragrant, cups with sacred honey filled,

Sanka bowls and shining salvers, arghya plates for honoured guest,
Parchéd rice arranged in dishes, corn unhusked that filled the rest,

And with careful hand Vasishtha grass around the altar flung,
Offered gift to lighted AGNI and the sacred mantra sung!

Softly came the sweet-eyed Sita,--bridal blush upon her brow,
Rama in his manly beauty came to take the sacred vow,

Janak placed his beauteous daughter facing Dasa-ratha's soil,
Spake with father's fond emotion and the holy rite was done:

"This is Sita child of Janak, dearer unto him than life,
Henceforth sharer of thy virtue, be. she, prince, thy faithful wife,

Of thy weal and woe partaker, be she thine in every land,
Cherish her in joy and sorrow, clasp her hand within thy hand,

As the shadow to the substance, to her lord is faithful wife,
And my Sita best of women follows thee in death or life!"

Tears bedew his ancient bosom, gods and men his wishes share,
And he sprinkles holy water on the blest and wedded pair.

Next he turned to Sita's sister, Urmila of beauty rare,
And to Lakshman young and valiant spake in accents soft and fair:

Lakshman, dauntless in thy duty, loved of men and Gods above,
Take my dear devoted daughter, Urmila of stainless love,

Lakshman, fearless in thy virtue, take thy true and faithful wife,
Clasp her hand within thy fingers, be she thine in death or life!"

To his brother's child Mandavi, Janak turned with father's love,
Yielded her to righteous Bharat, prayed for blessings from above:

"Bharat, take the fair Mandavi, be she thine in death or life,
Clasp her hand within thy fingers as thy true and faithful wife!"

Last of all was Sruta-kriti, fair in form and fair in face,
And her gentle name was honoured for her acts of righteous grace,

"Take her by the hand, Satrughna, be she thine in death or life,
As the shadow to the suistance, to her lord is faithful wife!"

Then the princes held the maidens, hand embraced in loving hand,
And Vasishtha spake the mantra, holiest priest in all the land,

And as ancient rite ordaineth, and as sacred laws require,
Stepped each bride and princely bridegroom round the altar's lighted fire,

Round Videha's ancient monarch, round the holy rishis all,
Ughtly stepped the gentle maidens, proudly stepped the princes tall!

And a rain of flowers descended from the sky serene and fair,
And a soft celestial music filled the fresh and fragrant air,

Bright Gandkarvas skilled in music waked the sweet celestial song

Fair Apsaras in their beauty on the greensward tripped along!

As the flowery rain descended and the music rose in pride,
Thrice around the lighted altar every bridegroom led his bride,

And the nuptial rites were ended, princes took their brides away,
Janak followed with his courtiers, and the town was proud and gay!

### VII. RETURN TO AYODRYA

With his wedded sons and daughters and his guard in bright array,
To the famed and fair Ayodhya, Dasa-ratha held his way,

And they reached the ancient city decked with banners bright and brave,
And the voice of drum and trumpet hailed the home-returning brave.

Fragrant blossoms strewed the pathway, song of welcome filled the air,
Joyous men and merry women issued forth in garments fair,

And they lifted up their faces and they waved their hands on high,
And they raised the voice of welcome as their righteous king drew nigh.

Greeted by his loving subjects, welcomed by his priests of fame,
Dasa-ratha, with the princes to his happy city came,

With the brides and stately princes in the town he held his way,
Entered slow his lofty palace bright as peak of Himalay.

Queen Kausalya blessed with virtue, Queen Kaikeyi in her pride,
Queen Sumitra sweetly loving, greeted every happy bride,

Soft-eyed Sita noble-destined, Urmila of spotless fame,
Mandavi and Sruta-kirti to their loving mothers came.

Decked in silk and queenly garments they performed each pious rite,
Brought their blessings on the household, bowed to Gods of holy might,

Bowed to all the honoured elders, blest the children with their love,
And with soft and sweet endearment by their loving consorts moved.

Happy were the wedded princes peerless in their warlike might,
And they dwelt in stately mansions like KUVERA'S mansions bright.

Loving wife and troops of kinsmen, wealth and glory on them wait,
Filial love and fond affection sanctify their happy fate.

Once when on the palace chambers bright the golden morning woke,
To his son the gentle Bharat, thus the ancient monarch spoke:

"Know, my son, the prince Kaikeya, Yudajit of warlike fame,
Queen Kaikeyi's honoured brother, from his distant regions came,

He hath come to take thee, Bharat, to Kaikeya's monarch bold,
Go and stay with them a season, greet thy grandsire loved of old."

Bharat heard with filial duty and he hastened to obey,
Took with him the young Satrughna in his grandsire's home to stay,

And from Rama and from Lakshman parted they with many a tear,
From their young and gentle consorts, from their parents ever dear,

And Kaikeya with the princes, with his guards and troopers gay,
To his father's western regions gladsome held his onward way.

Rama with a pious duty,--favoured by the Gods above,--
Tended still his ancient father with a never-faltering love,

In his father's sacred mandate still his noblest Duty saw,
In the weal of subject nations recognised his foremost Law!

And he pleased his happy mother with a fond and filial care,
And his elders and his kinsmen with devotion soft and fair,

Brahmans blessed the righteous Rama for his faith in gods above,
People in the town and hamlet blessed him with their loyal love!

With a woman's whole affection fond and trusting Sita loved,
And within her faithful bosom loving Rama lived and moved,

And he loved her, for their parents chose her as his faithful wife,
Loved her for her peerless beauty, for her true and trustful life,

Loved and dwelt within her bosom though he wore a form apart,
Rama in a sweet communion lived in Sita's loving heart!

Days of joy and months of gladness o'er the gentle Sita flew,
As she like the QUEEN OF BEAUTY brighter in her graces grew,

And as VISHNU with his consort dwells in skies, alone, apart,
Rama in a sweet communion lived in Sita's loving heart!

## Book II

### VANA-GAMANA-ADESA--The Banishment

#### I. THE COUNCIL CONVENED

Thus the young and brave Satrughna, Bharat ever true and bold,
Went to warlike western regions where Kaikeyas lived of old,

Where the ancient Aswa-pati ruled his kingdom broad and fair,
Hailed the sons of Dasa-ratha with a grandsire's loving care.

Tended with a fond affection, guarded with a gentle sway,
Still the princes of their father dreamt and thought by night and day,

And their father in Ayodhya, great of heart and stout of hand,
Thought of Bharat and Satrughna living in Kaikeya's land.

For his great and gallant princes were to him his life and light,
Were a part of Dasa-ratha like his hands and arms of might,

But of all his righteous children righteous Rama won his heart,
As SWAYABIBHU of all creatures, was his dearest, holiest part,

For his Rama strong and stately was his eldest and his best,
Void of every baser passion and with every virtue blest!

Soft in speech, sedate and peaceful, seeking still the holy path,
Calm in conscious worth and valour, taunt nor cavil waked his wrath,

In the field of war excelling, boldest warrior midst the bold,
In the palace chambers musing on the tales by elders told,

Faithful to the wise and learned, truthful in his deed and word,
Rama dearly loved his people and his people loved their lord!

To the Brahmans pure and holy Rama due obeisance made,

To the poor and to the helpless deeper love and honour paid,

Spirit of his race and nation was to high-souled Rama given,
Thoughts that widen human glory, deeds that ope the gates of heaven

Not intent on idle cavil Rama spake with purpose high,
And the God of speech might envy when he spake or made reply,

In the learning of the Vedas highest meed and glory won,
In the skill of arms the father scarcely matched the gallant son!

Taught by sages and by elders in the manners of his race,
Rama, grew in social virtues and each soft endearing grace,

Taught by inborn pride and wisdom patient purpose to conceal,
Deep determined was his effort, dauntless was his silent will!

Peerless in his skill and valour steed and elephant to tame,
Dauntless leader of his forces, matchless in his warlike fame,

Higher thought and nobler duty did the righteous Rama move,
By his toil and by his virtues still he sought his people's love

Dasa-ratha marked his Rama with each kingly virtue blest,
And from lifelong royal duties now he sought repose and rest:

"Shall I see my son anointed, seated on Kosala's throne,
In the evening of my lifetime ere my days on earth be done,

Shall I place my ancient empire in the youthful Rama's care,
Seek for me a higher duty and prepare for life more fair?"

Pondering thus within his bosom counsel from his courtiers sought,
And to crown his Rama, Regent, was his purpose and his thought,

For strange signs and diverse tokens now appeared on earth and sky,
And his failing strength and vigour spoke his end approaching nigh,

And he witnessed Rama's virtues filling all the world with love,
As the full-moon's radiant lustre fills the earth from skies above!

Dear to him appeared his purpose, Rama to his people dear,
Private wish and public duty made his path serene and clear,

Dasa-ratha called his Council, summoned chiefs from town and plain.
Welcomed too from distant regions monarchs and the kings of men,

Mansions meet for prince and chieftain to his guests the monarch gave,
Gracious as the Lord of Creatures held the gathering rich and brave!

Nathless to Kosala's Council nor Videha's monarch came,
Nor the warlike chief Kaikeya, Aswa-pati king of fame,

To those kings and near relations, ancient Dasa-ratha meant,
Message of the proud anointment with his greetings would be sent.

Brightly dawned the day of gathering; in the lofty Council Hall
Stately chiefs and ancient burghers came and mustered one and all,

And each prince and peer was seated on his cushion rich and high,
And on monarch Dasa-ratha eager turned his anxious eye,

Girt by crownéd kings and chieftains, burghers from the town and plain,
Dasa-ratha shone like INDRA girt by heaven's immortal train!

*333*

## II. THE PEOPLE CONSULTED

With the voice of pealing thunder Dasa-ratha spake to all,
To the princes and the burghers gathered in Ayodhya's hall:

"Known to all, the race of Raghu rules this empire broad and fair,
And hath ever loved and cherished subjects with a father's care,

Tn my fathers' footsteps treading I have sought the ancient path,
Nursed my people as my children, free from passion, pride and wrath,

Underneath this white umbrella, seated on this royal throne,
I have toiled to win their welfare and my task is almost done!

Years have passed of fruitful labour, years of work by fortune blest,
And the evening of my lifetime needs, my friends, the evening's rest,

Years have passed in watchful effort, Law and Duty to uphold,
Effort needing strength and prowess-and my feeble limbs are old!

Peers and burghers, let your monarch, now his lifelong labour done,
For the weal of lovinor subjects on his empire seat his son,

INDRA-like in peerless valour, rishi-like in holy lore,
Rama follows Dasa-ratha, but in virtues stands before!

Throned in Pushya's constellation shines the moon with fuller light
Throned to rule his father's empire Rama wins a loftier might,

He will be your gracious monarch favoured well by FORTUNE'S QUEEN,
By his virtue and his valour lord of earth he might have been!

Speak your thoughts and from this bosom lift a load of toil and care,
On the proud throne of my fathers let me place a peerless heir,

Speak your thought, my chiefs and people, if this purpose please you well,
Or if wiser, better counsel in your wisdom ye can tell,

Speak your thoughts without compulsion, though this plan to me be dear,
If some middle course were wiser, if some other way were clear!

Gathered chieftains hailed the mandate with applauses long and loud,
As the peafowls hail the thunder of the dark and laden cloud,

And the gathered subjects echoed loud and long the welcome sound,
Till the voices of the people shook the sky and solid ground!

Brahmans versed in laws of duty, chieftains in their warlike pride,
Countless men from town and hamlet heard the mandate far and wide,

And they met in consultation, joyously with one accord,
Freely and in measured accents, gave their answer to their lord:

"Years of toil and watchful labour weigh upon thee, king of men,
Young in years is righteous Rama, Heir and Regent let him reign,

We would see the princely Rama, Heir and Regent duly made,
Riding on the royal tusker in the white umbrella's shade!"

Searching still their secret purpose, seeking still their thought to know,
Spake again the ancient monarch in his measured words and slow:

"I would know your inner feelings, loyal thoughts and whispers kind,
For a doubt within me lingers and a shadow clouds my mind,

*334*

True to Law and true to Duty while I rule this kingdom fair,
Wherefore would you see my Rama seated as the Regent Heir?"

"We would see him Heir and Regent, Dasa-ratha, ancient lord,
For his heart is blessed with valour, virtue marks his deed and word,

Lives not man in all the wide earth who excels the stainless youth,
In his loyalty to Duty, in his love of righteous Truth,

Truth impels his thought and action, Truth inspires his soul with grace,
And his virtue fills the wide earth and exalts his ancient race!

Bright Immortals know his valour; with his brother Lakshman hold
He hath never failed to conquer hostile town or castled hold,

And returning from his battles, from the duties of the war,
Riding on his royal tusker or his all-resistless car,

As a father to his children to his loving men he came,
Blessed our homes and maids and matrons till our infants lisped his name,

For our humble woes and troubles Rama hath the ready tear,
To our humble tales of suffering Rama lends his willing ear!

Happy is the royal father who hath such a righteous son,
For in town and mart and hamlet every heart hath Rama won,

Burghers and the toiling tillers tales of Rama's kindness say,
Man and infant, maid and matron, morn and eve for Rama pray,

To the Gods and bright Immortals we our inmost wishes send,
May the good and godlike Rama on his father's throne ascend,

Great in gifts and great in glory, Rama doth our homage own,
We would see the princely Rama seated on his father's throne!"

### III. THE CITY DECORATED

With his consort pious Rama, pure in deed and pure in thought,
After evening's due ablutions NARAYANA'S chamber sought,

Prayed unto the Lord of Creatures, NARAYANA Ancient Sire,
Placed his offering on his forehead, poured it on the lighted fire,

Piously partook the remnant, sought for NARAYANA'S aid,
As he kept his fast and vigils on the grass of kusa spread.

With her lord the saintly Sita silent passed the sacred night,
Contemplating World's Preserver, Lord of Heaven's ethereal height,

And within the sacred chamber on the grass of kusa lay,
Till the crimson streaks of morning, ushered in the festive day,

Till the royal bards and minstrels chanted forth the morning call,
Healing through the holy chamber, echoing through the roval hall.

Past the night of sacred vigils, in his silken robes arrayed,
Message of the proud anointment Rama to the Brahmans said,

And the Brahmans spake to burghers that the festive day was come,
Till the mart and crowded pathway rang with note of pipe and drum,

And the townsmen heard rejoicing of the vigils of the night,
Kept by Rama and by Sita, for the day's auspicious rite.

Rama shall be Heir and Regent, Rama shall be crowned to-day,
Rapid flew the gladdening message with the morning's gladsome ray,

And the people of the city, maid and matron, man and boy,
Decorated fair Ayodhya in their wild tumultuous joy!

On the temple's lofty steeple high as cloud above the air,
On the crossing of the pathways, in the garden green and fair,

On the merchant's ample warehouse, on the shop with stores displayed,
On the mansion of the noble by the cunning artist made,

On the gay and bright pavilion, on the high and shady trees.
Banners rose and glittering streamers, flags that fluttered in the breeze!

Actors gay and nimble dancers, singers skilled in lightsome song,
With their antics and their music pleased the gay and gathered throng,

And the people met in conclaves, spake of Rama, Regent Heir,
And the children by the roadside lisped of Rama brave and fair!

Women wove the scented garland, merry maids the censer lit,
Men with broom and sprinkled water swept the spacious mart and street,

Rows of trees and posts they planted hung with lamps for coming night,
That the midnight dark might rival splendour of the noonday light

Troops of men and merry children laboured with a loving care,
Woman's skill and woman's fancy made the city passing fair,

So that good and kindly Rama might his people's toil approve,
So that sweet and soft-eyed Sita might accept her people's love!

Groups of joyous townsmen gathered in the square or lofty hall,
Praised the monarch Dasa-ratha, regent Rama young and tall:

"Great and good is Dasa-ratha born of Raghu's royal race,
In the fulness of his lifetime on his son he grants his grace,

And we hail the rite auspicious for our prince of peerless might,
He will guard us by his valotir, he will save our cherished right,

Dear unto his loving brothers in his father's palace hall,
As is Rama to his brothers dear is Rama to us all,

Long live ancient Dasa-ratha king of Raghu's royal race,
We shall see his son anointed by his father's righteous grace!

Thus of Rama's consecration spake the burghers one and all,
And the men from distant hamlets poured within the city wall,

From the confines of the empire, north and south and west and east,
Came to see the consecration and to share the royal feast!

And the rolling tide of nations raised their voices loud and high,
Like the tide of sounding ocean when the full moon lights the sky,

And Ayodhya thronged by people from the hamlet , mart and lea,
Was tumultuous like the ocean thronged by creatures of the sea!

*IV. INTRIGUE*

In the inner palace chamber stood the proud and peerless queen,
With a mother's joy Kaikeyi gaily watched the festive scene,

But with deep and deadly hatred Manthara, her nurse and maid,
Marked the city bright with banners, and in scornful accents said:

"Take thy presents back, Kaikeyi, for they ill befit the day,
And when clouds of sorrow darken, ill beseems thee to be gay,

And thy folly moves my laughter though an anguish wakes my sigh,
For a gladness stirs thy bosom when thy greatest woo is nigh!

Who that hath a woman's wisdom, who that is a prudent wife.
Smiles in joy when prouder rival triumphs in the race of life,

How can hapless Queen Kaikeyi greet this deed of darkness done,
When the favoured Queen Kausalya wins the empire for her son?

Know the truth, O witless woman! Bharat is unmatched in fame,
Rama, deep and darkly jealous, dreads thy Bharat's rival claim,

Younger Lakshman with devotion doth on eldest Rama wait,
Young Satrughna with affection follows Bharat's lofty fate,

Rama dreads no rising danger from the twins, the youngest-born,
But thy Bharat's claims and virtues fill his jealous heart with scorn!

Trust me, queen, thy Bharat's merits are too well and widely known,
And he stands too near and closely by a rival brother's throne,

Rama hath a wolf-like wisdom and a fang to reach the foe,
And I tremble for thy Bharat, Heaven avert untimely woe!

Happy is the Queen Kausalya, they will soon anoint her son,
When on Pushya's constellation gaily rides to-morrow's moon,

Happy is the Queen Kausalya in her regal pomp and state,
And Kaikeyi like a bond-slave must upon her rival wait!

Wilt thou do her due obeisance as we humble women do,
Will thy proud and princely Bharat as his brother's henchman go,

Will thy Bharat's gentle consort, fairest princess in this land,
In her tears and in her anguish wait on Sita's proud command?

With a woman's scornful anger Manthara proclaimed her grief,
With a mother's love for Rama thus Kaikeyi answered brief:

"What inspires thee, wicked woman, thus to rail in bitter tone,
Shall not Rama, best and eldest, fill his father's royal throne,

What alarms thee, crooked woman, in the happy rites begun,
Shall not Rama guard his brothers as a father guards his son?

And when Rama's reign is over, shall not Gods my Bharat speed,
And by law and ancient custom shall not younger son succeed,

In the present bliss of Rama and in Bharat's future hope,
What offends thee, senseless woman, wherefore dost thou idly mope?

Dear is Rama as my Bharat, ever duteous in his ways,
Rama honours Queen Kausalya, loftier honour to me pays,

Rama's realm is Bharat's kingdom, ruling partners they shall prove,
For himself than for his brothers Rama owns no deeper love!"

Scorn and anger shook her person and her bosom heaved a sigh,

As in wilder, fiercer accents Manthara thus made reply:

What insensate rage or madness clouds thy heart and blinds thine eye,
Courting thus thy own disaster, courting danger dread and high,

What dark folly clouds thy vision to the workings of thy foe,
Heedless thus to seek destruction and to sink in gulf of woe?

Know, fair queen, by law and custom, son ascends the throne of pride,
Rama's son succeedeth Rama, luckless Bharat steps aside,

Brothers do not share a kingdom, nor can one by one succeed,
Mighty were the civil discord if such custom were decreed!

For to stop all war and tumult, thus the ancient laws ordain,
Eldest son succeeds his father, younger children may not reign,

Bharat barred from Rama's empire, vainly decked with royal grace,
Friendless, joyless, long shall wander, alien from his land and race!

Thou hast home the princely Bharat, nursed him from thy gentle breast,
To a queen and to a mother need a prince's claims be pressed,

To a thoughtless heedless mother must I Bharat's virtues plead,
Must the Queen Kaikeyi witness Queen Kausalya's son succeed?

Trust thy old and faithful woman who bath nursed thee, youthful queen,
And in great and princely houses many darksome deeds hath seen,

Trust my word, the wily Rama for his spacious empire's good,
Soon will banish friendless Bharat and secure his peace with blood!

Thou hast sent the righteous Bharat to thy ancient father's land,
And Satrughna young an valiant doth beside his brother stand,

Young in years and generous-hearted, they will grow in mutual love,
As the love of elder Rama doth in Lakshman's bosom move,

Young companions grow in friendship, and our ancient legends tell,
Weeds protect a forest monarch which the woodman's axe would fell,

Crownéd Rama unto Lakshman will a loving brother prove,
But for Bharat and Satrughna, Rama's bosom owns no love,

And a danger thus ariseth if the elder wins the throne,
Haste thee, heedless Queen Kaikeyi, save the younger and thy son!

Speak thy mandate to thy husband, let thy Bharat rule at home,
In the deep and pathless jungle let the banished Rama roam,

This will please thy ancient father and thy father's kith and kin,
This will please the righteous people, Bharat knows no guile or sin!

Speak thy mandate to thy husband, win thy son a happy fate,
Doom him not to Rama's service or his unrelenting hate,

Let not Rama in his rancour shed a younger brother's blood,
As the lion slays the tiger in the deep and echoing wood!

With the magic of thy beauty thou hast won thy monarch's heart,
Queen Kausalya's bosom rankles with a woman's secret smart,

Let her not with woman's vengeance turn upon her prouder foe,
And as crownéd Rama's mother venge her in Kaikeyi's woe,

Mark my word, my child Kaikeyi, much these ancient eyes have seen,
 Rama's rule is death to Bharat, insult to my honoured queen!"

Like a slow but deadly poison worked the ancient nurse's tears,
 And a wife's undying impulse mingled with a mother's fears,

Deep within Kaikeyi's bosom worked a woman's jealous thought,
Speechless in her scorn and anger mourner's dark retreat she sought.

### V. THE QUEEN'S DEMAND

Rama shall be crowned at sunrise, so did royal bards proclaim,
 Every rite arranged and ordered, Dasa-ratha homeward came,

To the fairest of his consorts, dearest to his ancient heart,
 Came the king with eager gladness joyful message to impart,

Radiant as the Lord of Midnight, ere the eclipse casts its gloom,
Carne the old and ardent monarch heedless of his darksome doom!

Through the shady palace garden where the peacock wandered free.
Lute and lyre poured forth their music, parrot flew from tree to tree,

Through the corridor of creepers, painted rooms by artists done,
And the halls where scented Champak and the flaming Asok shone,

Through the portico of splendour graced by silver, tusk and gold.
Radiant with his thought of gladness walked the monarch proud and bold.

Through the lines of scented blossoms which by limpid waters shone,
And the rooms with seats of silver, ivory bench and golden throne.

Through the chamber of confection, where each viand wooed the taste,
 Every object in profusion as in regions of the blest,

Through Kaikeyi's inner closet lighted with a softened sheen,
 Walked the king with eager longing,--but Kaikeyi was not seen!

Thoughts of love and gentle dalliance woke-within his ancient heart,
 And the magic of her beauty and the glamour of her art,

With a soft desire the monarch vainly searched the vanished fair,
 Found her not in royal chamber, found her not in gay parterre!

Filled with love and longing languor loitered not the radiant queen,
 In her soft voluptuous chamber, in the garden, grove or green,

And he asked the faithful warder of Kaikeyi loved and lost,
 She who served him with devotion and his wishes never crost,

Spake the warder in his terror that the queen with rage distraught.
Weeping silent tears of anguish had the mourner's chamber sought!

Thither flew the stricken monarch; on the bare and unswept ground,
 Trembling with tumultuous passion was the Queen Kaikeyi found,

On the cold uncovered pavement sorrowing lay the weeping wife,
 Young wife of an ancient husband, dearer than his heart and life!

Like a bright and blossoming creeper rudely severed from the earth,
 Like a fallen fair Apsara, beauteous nymph of heavenly birth,

Like a female forest-ranger bleeding from the hunter's dart,
Whom her mate the forest-monarch soothes with soft endearing art,

Lay the queen in tears of anguish! And with sweet and gentle word
To the lotus-eyéd lady softly spake her loving lord:

Wherefore thus, my Queen and Empress, sorrow-laden is thy heart,
Who with daring slight or insult seeks to cause thy bosom smart?

If some unknown ailment pains thee, evil spirit of the air,
Skilled physicians wait upon thee, priests with incantations fair,

If from human foe some insult, wipe thy tears and doom his fate,
Rich reward or royal vengeance shall upon thy mandate wait!

Wilt thou doom to death the guiltless, free whom direst sins debase,
Wilt thou lift the poor and lowly or the proud and great disgrace,

Speak, and I and all my courtiers Queen Kaikeyi's hest obey,
For thy might is boundless, Empress, limitless thy regal sway!

Rolls my chariot-wheel revolving from the sea to farthest sea,
And the wide earth is my empire, monarchs list my proud decree,

Nations of the eastern regions and of Sindhu's western wave,
Brave Saurashtras and the races who the ocean's dangers brave,

Vangas, Angas and Magadhas, warlike Matsyas of the west,
Kasis and the southern races, brave Kosalas first and best,

Nations of my world-wide empire, rich in corn and sheep and kine,
All shall serve my Queen Kaikeyi and their treasures all are thine,

Speak, command thy king a obedience, and thy wrath will melt away,
Like the melting snow of winter 'neath the sun's reviving ray!"

Blinded was the ancient husband as he lifted up her head,
Heedless oath and word he plighted that her wish should be obeyed,

Scheming for a fatal purpose, inly then Kaikeyi smiled,
And by sacred oath and promise bound the monarch love-beguiled:

"Thou hast given, Dasa-ratha, troth and word and royal oath,
Three and thirty Gods be witness, watchers of the righteous truth,

Sun and Moon and Stars be witness, Sky and Day and sable Night,
Rolling Worlds and this our wide Earth, and each dark and unseen wight,

Witness Rangers of the forest, Household Gods that guard us both,
Mortal beings and Immortal,--witness ye the monarch's oath,

Ever faithful to his promise, ever truthful in his word,
Dasa-ratha grants my prayer, Spirits and the Gods have heard!

Call to mind, O righteous monarch, days when in a bygone strife,
Warring with thy foes immortal thou hadst almost lost thy life,

With a woman's loving tendance poor Kaikeyi cured thy wound,
Till from death and danger rescued, thou wert by a promise bound,

Two rewards my husband offered, what my loving heart might seek,
Long delayed their wished fulfilment,-now let poor Kaikeyi speak,

And if royal deeds redeem not what thy royal lips did say,
Victim to thy broken promise Queen Kaikeyi dies to-day!

By these rites ordained for Rama,-such the news my menials bring,--

Let my Bharat, and not Rama, be anointed Regent King,

Wearing skins and matted tresses, in the cave or hermit's cell,
Fourteen years in Dandak's forests let the elder Rama dwell,

These are Queen Kaikeyi's wishes, these are boons for which I pray,
I would see my son anointed, Rama banished on this day!"

### VI. THE KING'S LAMENT

Is this torturing dream or madness, do my feeble senses fail,
O'er my darkened mind and bosom doth a fainting fit prevail?

So the stricken monarch pondered and in hushed and silent fear,
Looked on her as on a tigress looks the dazed and stricken deer,

Lying on the unswept pavement still he heaved the choking sigh,
Like a wild and hissing serpent quelled by incantations high!

Sobs convulsive shook his bosom and his speech and accent failed,
And a dark and deathlike faintness o'er his feeble soul prevailed,

Stunned awhile remained the monarch, then in furious passion woke.
And his eyeballs flamed with redfire, to the queen as thus he spoke:

"Traitress to thy king and husband, fell destroyer of thy race,
Wherefore seeks thy ruthless rancour Rama rich in righteous grace,

Traitress to thy kith and kindred, Rama loves thee as thy own,
Wherefore then with causeless vengeance as a mother hate thy son!

Have I courted thee, Kaikeyi, throned thee in my heart of truth,
Nursed thee in my home and bosom like a snake of poisoned tooth,

Have I courted thee, Kaikeyi, placed thee on Ayodhya's throne,
That my Rama, loved of people, thou shouldst banish from his own?

Banish far my Queen Kausalya, Queen Sumitra saintly wife,
Wrench from me my ancient empire, from my bosom wrench my life,

But with brave and princely Rama never can his father part,
Till his ancient life is ended, cold and still his beating heart!

Sunless roll the world in darkness, rainless may the harvests thrive,
But from ri~hteous Rama severed, never can his sire survive,

Feeble is thy aged husband, few and brief on earth his day,
Lend me, wife, a woman's kindness, as a consort be my stay!

Ask for other boon, Kaikeyi, aught my sea-girt empire yields,
Wealth or treasure, gem or jewel, castled town or smiling fields,

Ask for other gift, Kaikeyi, and thy wishes shall be given,
Stain me not with crime unholy in the eye of righteous Heaven!"

Coldly spake the Queen Kaikeyi: "If thy royal heart repent,
Break thy word and plighted promise, let thy royal faith be rent,

Ever known for truth and virtue, speak to peers and monarchs all,
When from near and distant regions they shall gather in thy hall,

Speak if so it please thee, monarch, of thy evil-destined wife,
How she loved with wife's devotion, how she served and saved thy life,

How on plighted promise trusting for a humble boon she sighed,
How a monarch broke his promise, how a cheated woman died!"

"Fair thy form," resumed the monarch, "beauty dwells upon thy face,
Woman's winsome charms bedeck thee, and a woman's peerless grace,

Wherefore then within thy bosom wakes this thought of cruel wile,
And what dark and loathsome spirit stains thy heart with blackest guile?

Ever since the day, Kaikeyi, when a gentle bride you came,
By a wife's unfailing duty you have won a woman's fame,

Wherefore now this cruel purpose hath a stainless heart defiled,
Ruthless wish to send my Rama to the dark and pathless wild?

Wherefore, darkly-scheming woman, on unrighteous purpose bent,
Doth thy cruel causeless vengeance on my Rama seek a vent,

Wherefore seek by deeds unholy for thy son the throne to win,
Throne which Bharat doth not covet,-blackened byhis mother's sin?

Shall I see my banished Rama mantled in the garb of woe,
Reft of home and kin and empire to the pathless jungle go,

Shall I see disasters sweeping o'er my empire dark and deep,
As the forces of a foeman o'er a scattered army sweep?

Shall I hear assembled monarchs in their whispered voices say,
Weak and foolish in his dotapre, Dasa-ratha holds his sway,

Shall I say to righteous elders when they blame my action done,
That by woman's mandate driven I have banished thus my son?

Queen Kansalya, dear-loved woman! she who serves me as a slave,
Soothes me like a tender sister, helps me like a consort brave,

As a fond and loving mother tends me with a watchful care,
As a daughter ever duteous doth obeisance sweet and fair,

When my fond and fair Kausalya asks me of her banished son,
How shall Dasa-ratha answer for the impious action done,

How can husband, cold and cruel, break a wife's confiding heart,
How can father, false and faithless, from his best and eldest part?"

Coldly spake the Queen Kaikeyi: "If thy royal heart repent,
Break thy word and plighted promise, let thy royal faith be rent,

Truth-abiding is our monarch, so I heard the people say,
And his word is all inviolate, stainless virtue marks his sway,

Let it now be known to nations,--righteous Dasa-ratha lied,
And a trusting, cheated woman broke her loving heart and died!"

Darker grew the shades of midnight, coldly shone each distant star,
Wilder in the monarch's bosom raged the struggle and the war:

"Starry midnight, robed in shadows! give my wearied heart relief,
Spread thy sable covering mantle o'er an impious monarch's grief,

Spread thy vast and inky darkness o'er a deed of nameless crime,
Reign perennial o'er my sorrows heedless of the lapse of time,

May a sinful monarch perish ere the dawning of the day,

O'er a dark life sin-polluted, beam not morning's righteous ray!"

### VII. THE SENTENCE

Morning came and duteous Rama to the palace bent his way,
For to make his salutation and his due obeisance pay,

And he saw his aged father shorn of kingly pomp and pride,
And he saw the Queen Kaikeyi sitting by her consort's side.

Duteously the righteous Rama touched the ancient monarch's feet,
Touched the feet of Queen Kaikeyi with a son's obeisance meet,

"Rama!" cried the feeble monarch, but the tear bedimmed his eye,
Sorrow choked his failing utterance and his bosom heaved a sigh,

Rama started in his terror at his father's grief or wrath,
Like a traveller in the jungle crossed by serpent in his path!

Reft of sense appeared the monarch, crushed beneath a load of pain,
Heaving oft a sigh of sorrow as his heart would break in twain,

Like the ocean tempest-shaken, like the sun in eclipse pale,
Like a crushed repenting rishi when his truth and virtue fail!

Breathless mused the anxious Rama,--what foul action hath he done,
What strange anger fills his father, wherefore greets he not his son?

"Speak, my mother," uttered Rama," what strange error on my part.
Unremembered sin or folly fills with grief my father's heart,

Gracious unto me is father with a father's boundless grace,
Wherefore clouds his altered visage, wherefore tears bedew his face?

Doth a piercing painful ailment rack his limbs with cruel smart,
Doth some secret silent anguish wring his tom and tortured heart,

Bharat lives with brave Satrughns, in thy father's realms afar,
Hath some cloud of dark disaster crossed their bright auspicious star?

Duteously the royal consorts on the loving monarch wait,
Hath some woe or dire misfortune dimmed the lustre of their fate.

I would yield my life and fortune ere I wound my father's heart,
Rath my unknown crime or folly caused his ancient bosom smart!

Ever dear is Queen Kaikeyi to her consort and her king,
Hath some angry accent escaped thee thus his royal heart to wring,

Speak, my ever-lovinging mother, speak the truth, for thou must know,
What distress or deep disaster pains his heart and clouds his brow?"

Mother's love nor woman's pity moved the deep-determined queen,
As in cold and cruel accents thus she spake her purpose keen:

"Grief nor woe nor sudden ailment pains thy father loved of old,
But he fears to speak his purpose to his Rama true and bold,

And his loving accents falter some unloving wish to tell,
Till you give your princely promise, you Will serve his mandate well!

Listen more, in bygone seasons,--Rama thou wert then unborn,
I had saved thy royal father, he a gracious boon had sworn,

But his feeble heart repenting is by pride and passion stirred,
He would break his royal promise as a caitiff breaks his word,

Years have passed and now the monarch would his ancient word forego,
He would build a needless causeway when the waters ceased to flow!

Truth inspires each deed attempted and each word by monarchs spoke,
Not for thee, though loved and honoured, should a royal vow be broke,

If the true and righteous Rama binds him by his father's vow,
I will tell thee of the anguish which obscures his royal brow,

If thy feeble bosom falter and thy halting purpose fail,
Unredeemed is royal promise and unspoken is my tale!

"Speak thy word," exclaimed the hero, "and my purpose shall not fail,
Rama serves his father's mandate and his bosom shall not quail,

Poisoned cup or death untimely,--what the cruel fates decree,
To his king and to his father Rama yields obedience free,

Speak my father's royal promise, hold me by his promise tied,
Rama speaks and shall not palter, for his lips have never lied."

Cold and clear Kaikeyi's accents fell as falls the hunter's knife,
"Listen then to word of promise and redeem it with thy life,

Wounded erst by foes immortal, saved by Queen Kaikeyi's care,
Two great boons your father plighted and his royal words were fair,

I have sought their due fulfilment,--brightly shines my Bharat's star.
Bharat shall be Heir and Regent, Rama shall be banished far!

If thy father's royal mandate thou wouldst list and honour still,
Fourteen years in Dandak's forest live and wander at thy will,

Seven long years and seven, my Rama, thou shalt in the jungle dwell,
Bark of trees shall be thy raiment and thy home the hermit's cell,

Over fair Kosala's empire let my princely Bharat reign,
With his cars and steeds and tuskers, wealth and gold and arméd men!

Tender-hearted is the monarch, age and sorrow dim his eye,
And the anguish of a father checks his speech and purpose high,

For the love he bears thee, Rama, cruel vow he may not speak,
I have spoke his will and mandate, and thy true obedience seek."

Calmly Rama heard the mandate, grief nor anger touched his heart,
Calmly from his father's empire and his home prepared to part.

## Book III

### DASA-RATHA-VIYOGA--The Death of the King

#### I. WOMAN'S LOVE

"Dearly loved, devoted Sita! daughter of a royal line,
Part we now, for years of wand'ring in the pathless woods is mine,

For my father, promise-fettered, to Kaikeyi yields the sway,
And she wills her son anointed,-fourteen years doth Rama stray,

But before I leave thee, Sita, in the wilderness to rove,

Yield me one more tender token of thy true and trustful love!

Serve my crownéd brother, Sita, as a faithful, duteous dame,
Tell him not of Rama's virtues, tell him not of Rama's claim,

Since my royal father willeth,--Bharat shall be regent-heir,
Serve him with a loyal duty, serve him with obeisance fair,

Since my roval father willetb,-years of banishment be mine,
Brave in sorrow and in suffering, woman's brightest fame be thine

Keep thy fasts and vigils, Sita, while thy Rama is away,
Faith in Gods and faith in virtue on thy bosom hold their sway,

In the early watch of morning to the Gods for blessings pray,
To my father Dasa-ratha honour and obeisance pay,

To my mother, Queen Kausalya, is thy dearest tendance due,
Offer her thy consolation, be a daughter fond and true!

Queen Kaikeyi and Sumitra equal love and honour claim,
With a soothing soft endearment sweetly serve each royal dame,

Cherish Bharat and Satrughna with a sister's watchful love,
And a mother's true affection and a mother's kindness prove!

Listen, Sita, unto Bharat speak no heedless angry word,
He is monarch of Kosala and of Raghu's race is lord,

Crownéd kings our willing service and our faithful duty own,
Dearest song they disinherit, cherish strangers near the throne!

Bharat's will with deep devotion and with faultless faith obey,
Truth and virtue on thy bosom ever hold their gentle sway,

And to please each dear relation, gentle Sita, be it thine,
Part we love! for years of wand'ring in the pathless woods is mine!"

Rama spake, and soft-eyed Sita, ever sweet in speech and word,
Stirred by loving woman's passion boldly answered thus her lord:

"Do I hear my husband rightly, are these words my Rama spake,
And her banished lord and husband will the wedded wife forsake?

Lightly I dismiss the counsel which my lord hath lightly said
For it ill beseems a warrior and my husband's princely grade;

For the faithful woman follows where her wedded lord may lead,
In the banishment of Rama, Sita's exile is decreed,

Sire nor son nor loving brother rules the wedded woman's state,
With her lord she falls or rises, with her consort courts her fate,

If the righteous son of Raghu wends to forests dark and drear,
Sita steps before her husband wild and thorny path to clear!

Like the tasted refuse water cast thy timid thoughts aside,
Take me to the pathless jungle, bid me by my lord abide,

Car and steed and gilded palace, vain are these to woman's life,
Dearer is her husband's shadow to the loved and loving wife!

For my mother often taught me and my father often spake,
That her home the wedded woman doth beside her husband make,

As the shadow to the substance, to her lord is faithful wife,
And she parts not from her consort till she parts with fleeting life!

Therefore bid me seek the jungle and in pathless forests roam,
Where the wild deer freely ranges and the tiger makes his home,

Happier than in father's mansions in the woods will Sita rove,
Waste no thought on home or kindred, nestling in her husband's love!

World-renowned is Rama's valour, fearless by her Rama's side,
Sita will still live and wander with a faithful woman's pride,

And the wild fruit she will gather from the fresh and fragrant wood,
And the food by Rama tasted shall be Sita's cherished food!

Bid me seek the sylvan greenwoods, wooded hills and plateaus high,
Limpid rills and crystal nullas as they softly ripple by,

And where in the lake of lotus tuneful ducks their plumage lave,
Let me with my loving Rama skim the cool translucent wave!

Years will pass in happy union,--happiest lot to woman given,--
Sita seeks not throne or empire, nor the brighter joys of heaven,

Heaven conceals not brighter mansions in its sunny fields of pride,
Where without her lord and husband faithful Sita would reside!

Therefore let me seek the jungle where the jungle-rangers rove,
Dearer than the royal palace, where I share my husband's love,

And my heart in sweet communion shall my Rama's wishes share,
And my wifely toil shall lighten Rama's load of woe and care!"

Vainly gentle Rama pleaded dangers of the jungle life,
Vainly spake of toil and trial to a true and tender wife!

### II. BROTHER'S FAITHFULNESS

Tears bedewed the face of Lakshman as he heard what Sita, said,
And he touched the feet of Rama and in gentle accents prayed:

"If my elder and his lady to the pathless forests wend,
Armed with bow and ample quiver Lakshman will on them attend,

Where the wild deer range the forest and the lordly tuskers roam,
And the bird of gorgeous plumage nestles in its jungle home,

Dearer far to me those woodlands where my elder Rama dwells,
Than the homes of bright Immortals where perennial bliss prevails!

Grant me then thy sweet permission,--faithful to thy glorious star,
Lakshman,shall not wait and tarry when his Rama wanders far,

Grant me then thyloving mandate,--Lakshman hath no wish to stay,
None shall bar the faithful younger when the elder leads the way!"

"Ever true to deeds of virtue, duteous brother, faithful friend,
Dearer than his life to Rama, thou shall not to forests wend,

Who shall stay by Queen Kausalya, Lakshman, if we both depart,
Who shall stay by Queen Sumitra, she who nursed thee on her heart?

For the king our aged father, he who ruled the earth and main,
Is a captive to Kaikeyi, fettered by her silken chain,

Little help Kaikeyi renders to our mothers in her pride,
　Little help can Bharat offer, standing by his mother's side.

Thou alone can'st serve Kausalya when for distant woods I part,
　When the memory of my exile rankles in her sorrowing heart,

Thou alone can'st serve Sumitra, soothe her sorrows with thy love,
　Stay by them, my faithful Lakshman, and thy filial virtues prove,

Be this then they sacred duty, tend our mothers in their woe,
　Little joy or consolation have they left on earth below!"

Spake the hero: "Fear no evil, well is Rama's prowess known,
　And to mighty Rama's mother Bharat will obeisance own,

Nathless if the pride of empire sways him from the righteous path,
　Blood will venge the offered insult and will quench our filial wrath!

But a thousand peopled hamlets Queen Kausalya's hests obey,
　And a thousand arméd champions own her high and queenly sway,

Aye, a thousand village-centres Queen Sumitra's state maintain,
　And a thousand swords  guard her proud and prosperous reign!

All alone with gentle Sita thou shalt track thy darksome way,
　Grant it, that thy faithful Lakshman shall protect her night and day,

Grant it, with his bow and quiver Lakshman shall the forests roam,
　And his axe shall fell the jungle, and his hands shall rear the home!

Grant it, in the deepest woodlands he shall seek the forest fruit,
　Berries dear to holy hermits and the sweet and luscious root,

And whenwith thy meek-eyed Sita thou shalt seek the mountain crest,
　Grant it, Lakshman ever duteous watch and guard thy nightly rest!"

Words of brother's deep devotion Rama heard with grateful heart,
And with Sita and with Lakshman for the woods prepared to part:

Part we then from loving kinsmen, arms and mighty weapons bring,
　Bows of war which Lord VARUNA rendered to Videha's king,

Coats of mail to sword impervious, quivers which can never fail,
　And the rapiers bright as sunshine, golden-hilted, tempered wen,

Safely rest these goodly weapons in our great preceptor's hall,
Seek and bring them, faithful brother, for me thinks we need them all!"

Rama spake; his valiant brother then the wondrous weapons brought,
Wreathed with fresh and fragrant garlands and with gold and jewels wrought,

"Welcome, brother," uttered Rama, "stronger thus to woods we go,
　Wealth and gold and useless treasure to the holy priests bestow,

To the son of saint Vasishtha, to each sage is honour due,
Then we leave our father's mansions, to our father's mandate true!"

### III. MOTHER'S BLESSINGS

Tears of sorrow and of suffering flowed from Queen Kausalya's eye,
　As she saw departing Sita for her blessings drawing nigh,

And she clasped the gentle Sits, and she kissed her moistened head,
　And her tears like summer tempest choked the loving words she said:

"Part we, dear devoted daughter, to thy husband ever true,
With a woman's whole affection render love to husband's due!

False are women loved and cherished, gentle in their speech and word,
When misfortune's shadows gather, who are faithless to their lord,

Who through years of sunny splendour smile and pass the livelong day,
When misfortune's darkness thickens, from their husband turn away,

Who with changeful fortune changing oft ignore the plighted word,
And forget a woman's duty, woman's faith to wedded lord,

Who to holy love inconstant from their wedded consort part,
Manly deed nor manly virtue wins the changeful woman's heart!

But the true and righteous woman, loving, spouse and changeless wife,
Faithful to her lord and consort holds him dearer than her life,

Ever true and righteous Sita, follow still my godlike son,
Like a God to thee is Rama in the woods or on the throne!"

"I shall do my duty, mother," said the wife with wifely pride,
"Like a God to me is Rama, Sita shall not leave his side,

From the Moon will part his lustre ere I part from wedded lord,
Ere from faithful wife's devotion falter in my deed or word,

For the stringless lute is silent, idle is the wheel-less car,
And no wife the loveless consort, inauspicious is her star!

Small the measure of affection which the sire and brother prove,
Measureless to wedded woman is her lord and husband's love,

True to Law and true to Scriptures, true to woman's plighted word,
Can I ever be, my mother, faithless, loveless to my lord?"

Tears of joy and mingled sorrow filled the Queen Kausalya's eye,
As she marked the faithful Sita true in heart, in virtue high,

And she wept the tears of sadness when with sweet obeisance due,
Spake with hands in meekness folded Rama ever good and true:

"Sorrow not, my loving mother, trust in virtue's changeless beam,
Swift will fly the years of exile like a brief and transient dream,

Girt by faithful friends and forces, blest by righteous Gods above,
Thou shalt see thy son returning to thy bosom and thy love!

Unto all the royal ladies Rama his obeisance paid,
For his failings unremembered, blessings and forgiveness prayed,

And his words were soft and gentle, and they wept to see him go,
Like the piercing cry of curlew rose the piercing voice of woe,

And in halls where drum and tabor rose in joy and regal pride,
Voice of grief and lamentation sounded far and sounded wide!

Then the true and faithful Lakshman parted from each weeping dame,
And to sorrowing Queen Sumitra with his due obeisance came,

And he bowed to Queen Sumitra and his mother kissed his head,
Stilled her anguish-laden bosom and in trembling accents said:

Dear devoted duteous Lakshman, ever to thy elder true,

When thy elder wends to forest, forest-life to thee is due,

Thou hast served him true and faithful in his glory and his fame,
This is Law for true and righteous,---serve him in his woe and shame,

This is Law for race of Raghu known on earth for holy might,
Bounteous in their sacred duty, brave and warlike in the fight!

Therefore tend him as thy father, as thy mother tend his wife,
And to thee, like fair Ayodhya be thy humble forest life,

Go, my son, the voice of Duty bids my gallant Lakshman go,
Serve thy elder with devotion and with valour meet thy foe

### IV. CITIZENS' LAMENT

Spake Sumantra chariot-driver waiting by the royal car,
"Haste thee, mighty-destined Rama, for we wander long and far,

Fourteen years in Dandak's forest shall the righteous Rama stray,
Such is Dasa-ratha's mandate, haste thee Rama and obey."

Queenly Sita bright-apparelled, with a strong and trusting heart,
Mounted on the car of splendour for the pathless woods to part,

And the king for needs providing gave her robes and precious store,
For the many years of exile in a far and unknown shore,

And a wealth of warlike weapons to the exiled princes gave,
Bow and dart and linkéd armour, sword and shield and lances brave.

Then the gallant brothers mounted on the gold-emblazoned car,
For unending was the journey and the wilderness was far,

Skilled Sumantra saw them seated, urged the swiftly-flying steed,
Faster than the speed of tempest was the noble coursers' speed.

And they parted for the forest; like a long unending night,
Gloomy shades of grief and sadness deepened on the city's might,

Mute and dumb but conscious creatures felt the woe the city bore,
Horses neighed and shook their bright bells, elephants returned a roar!

Man and boy and maid and matron followed Rama with their eye,
As the thirsty seek the water when the parchéd fields are dry,

Clinging to the rapid chariot, by its side, before, behind,
Tlironging men and wailing women wept for Rama good and kind:

"Draw the reins, benign Sumantra, slowly drive the royal car,
We would once more see our Rama, banished long and banished far,

Iron-hearted is Kausalya from her Rama thus to part,
Rends it not her mother's bosom thus to see her son depart?

True is righteous-hearted Sita cleaving to her husband still,
As the ever present sunlight cleaves to Meru's golden hill,

Faithful and heroic Lakshman! thou hast by thy brother stood,
And in duty still unchanging thou hast sought the pathless wood,

Fixed in purpose, true in valour, mighty boon to thee is given,
And the narrow path thou choosest is the righteous path to heaven!"

Thus they spake in tears and anguish as they followed him apace,
And their eyes were fixed on Rama, pride of Raghu's royal race,

Meanwhile ancient Dasa-ratha from his palace chamber came,
With each weeping queen and consort, with each woe-distracted dame!

And around the aged monarch rose the piercing voice of pain,
Like the wail of forest creatures when the forest-king is slain,

And the faint and feeble monarch was with age and anguish pale,
Like the darkened moon at eclipse when his light and radiance fail!

Rama saw his ancient father with a faltering footstep go,
Used to royal pomp and splendour, stricken now by age and woe,

Saw his mother faint and feeble to the speeding chariot hie,
As the mother-cow returneth to her young that loiters by,

Still she hastened to the chariot, "Rama! Rama!" was her cry,
And a throb was in her bosom and a tear was in her eye!

"Speed, Sumantra," uttered Rama, "from this torture let me part.
Speed, my friend, this sight of sadness breaks a much-enduring heart,

Heed not Dasa-ratha's mandate, stop not for the royal train,
Parting slow is lengthened sorrow like the sinner's lengthened pain!"

Sad Sumantra urged the coursers and the rapid chariot flew,
And the royal chiefs and courtiers round their fainting monarch drew,

And they spake to Dasa-ratha: "Follow not thy banished son,
He whom thou wouldst keep beside thee comes not till his task is done!"

Dasa-ratha, faint and feeble, listened to these words of pain,
Stood and saw his son departing,--saw him not on earth again!

### V. CROSSING THE TAMASA: THE CITIZENS' RETURN

Evening's thickening shades descended on Tamasa's distant shore,
Rama rested by the river, day of toilsome journey o'er,

And Ayodhya's loving people by the limpid river lay,
Sad and sorrowing they had followed Rama's chariot through the day,

"Soft-eyed Sita, faithful Lakshman," thus the gentle Rama said,
"Hail the first night of our exile mantling us in welcome shade,

Weeps the lone and voiceless forest, and in darksome lair and nest,
Feathered bird and forest creature seek their midnight's wonted rest,

Weeps methinks our fair Ayodhya to her Rama ever dear,
And perchance her men and women shed for us a silent tear,

Loyal men and faithful women, they have loved their ancient king,
And his anguish and our exile will their gentle bosoms wring!

Most I sorrow for my father and my mother loved and lost,
Stricken by untimely anguish, by a cruel fortune crost,

But the good and righteous Bharat gently will my parents tend,
And with fond and filial duty tender consolation lend,

Well I know his stainless bosom and his virtues rare and high,
He will soothe our parents' sorrow and their trickling tear will dry!

Faithful Lakshman, thou hast nobly stood by us when sorrows fell,
Guard my Sits, by thy valour, by thy virtues tend her well,

Wait on her while from this river Rama seeks his thirst to slake,
On this first night of his exile food nor fruit shall Rama take,

Thou Sumantra, tend the horses, darkness comes with close of day,
Weary was the endless journey, weary is our onward way!"

Store of grass and welcome fodder to the steeds the driver gave,
Gave them rest and gave them water from Tamasa's limpid wave,

And performing night's devotions, for the princes made their bed,
By the softly rippling river 'neath the tree's umbrageous shade.

On a bed of leaf and verdure Rama and his Sita slept,
Faithful Lakshman with Sumantra nightly watch and vigils kept,

And the stars their silent lustre on the weary exiles shed,
And on wood and rolling river night her darksome mantle spread.

Early woke the righteous Rama and to watchful Lakshman spake:
Mark the slumb'ring city people, still their nightly rest they take,

They have left their homes and children, followed us with loyal heart,
They would take us to Ayodhya, from their princes loth to part!

Speed, my brother, for the people wake not till the morning's star,
Speed by night the silent chariot, we may travel fast and far,

So my true and loving people see us not by dawn of day,
Follow not through wood and jungle Rama in his onward way,

For a monarch meek in suffering should his burden bravely bear,
And his true and faithful people may not ask his woe to share!"

Lakshman heard the gentle mandate, and Sumantra yoked the steed,
Fresh with rest and grateful fodder, matchless in their wondrous speed,

Rama with his gentle consort and with Lakshman true and brave,
Crossed beneath the silent starlight dark Tamasa's limpid wave.

On the farther bank a pathway, fair to view and far and wide,
Stretching onwards to the forests spanned the spacious country-side,

"Leave the broad and open pathway," so the gentle Rama said,
"Follow yet a track diverging, so the people be misled.

Then returning to the pathway we shall march ere break of day,
So our true and faithful people shall not know our southward way."

Wise Sumantra hastened northward, then returning to the road,
By his master and his consort and the valiant Lakshman stood,

Raghu's sons and gentle Sita mounted on the stately car,
And Sumantra drove the coursers travelling fast and travelling far.

Morning dawned, the waking people by Tamasa's limpid wave,
Saw not Rama and his consort, saw not Lakshman young and brave,

And the tear suffused their faces and their hearts with anguish burned,
Sorrow-laden and lamenting to their cheerless homes returned.

*VI. CROSSING THE GANGES. BHARAD-VAJA'S HERMITAGE*

Morning dawned, and far they wandered, by their people loved and lost,
Drove through grove and flowering woodland, rippling rill and river crost,

Crossed the sacred Vedasruti on their still unending way,
Crossed the deep and rapid Gumti where the herds of cattle stray,

All the toilsome day they travelled, evening fell o'er wood and lea,
And they came where sea-like Ganga rolls in regal majesty,

'Neath a fall Ingudi's shadow by the river's zephyrs blest,
Second night of Rama's exile passed in sleep and gentle rest.

Morning dawned, the royal chariot Rama would no further own,
Sent Sumantra and the coursers back to fair Ayodhya's town,

Doffing then their royal garments Rama and his brother bold
Coats of bark and matted tresses wore like anchorites of old.

Guha, chief of wild Nishadas, boat and needed succour gave,
And the princes and fair Sita ventured on the sacred wave.

And by royal Rama bidden strong Nishadas plied the oar,
And the strong boat quickly bounding left fair Ganga's northern shore.

"Goddess of the mighty Ganga!" so the pious Sits, prayed,
"Exiled by his father's mandate, Rama seeks the forest shade,

Ganga! o'er the three worlds rolling, bride and empress of the sea,
And from BRAHMA'S sphere descended! banished Sita bows to thee.

May my lord return in safety, and a thousand fattened kine,
Gold and gifts and gorgeous garments, pure libations shall be thine,

And with flesh and corn I worship unseen dwellers on thy shore,
May my lord return in safety, fourteen years of exile o'er!",

On the southern shore they journeyed through the long and weary day,
Still through grove and flowering woodland held their long and weary way,

And they slayed the deer of jungle and they spread their rich repast,
Third night of the princes' exile underneath a tree was past.

Morning dawned, the soft-eyed Sits, wandered with the princes brave,
To the spot where ruddy Gangs, mingles with dark Jumna's wave,

And they crost the shady woodland, verdant lawn and grassy mead,
Till the sun was in its zenith, Rama then to Lakshman said:

"Yonder mark the famed Prayaga, spot revered from age to age,
And the line of smoke ascending speaks some rishi's hermitage,

There the waves of ruddy Gangs with the dark blue Jumna meet,
And my ear the sea-like voices of the mingling waters greet.

Mark the monarchs of the forest severed by the hermit's might,
And the logs of wood and fuel for the sacrificial rite,

Mark the tall trees in their blossom and the peaceful shady grove,
There the sages make their dwelling, thither, Lakshman, let us rove."

Slowly came the exile-wand'rers, when the sun withdrew his rays,
Where the vast and sea-like rivers met in sisters' sweet embrace,

And the asram's peaceful dwellers, bird of song and spotted deer,

Quaked to see the princely strangers in their warlike garb appear!

Rama stepped with valiant Lakshman, gentle Sits followed close,
Till behind the screening foliage hermits' peaceful dwellings rose,

And they came to Bharad-vaja, anchorite and holy saint,
Girt by true and faithful pupils on his sacred duty bent.

Famed for rites and lofty penance was the anchorite of yore,
Blest with more than mortal vision, deep in more than mortal tore,

And he sat beside the altar for the agni-hotra rite,
Rama spake in humble accents to the man of holy might:

"We are sons of Dasa-ratha and to thee our homage bring,
With rny wife, the saintly Sita, daughter of Videha's king,

Exiled by my royal father in the wilderness I roam,
And my wife and faithful brother make the pathless woods their home,

We would through these years of exile in some holy asram dwell.
And our food shall be the wild fruit and our drink from crystal well,

We would practise pious penance still on sacred rites intent,
Till our souls be filled with wisdom and our years of exile spent!"

Pleased the ancient Bharad-vaja heard the prince's humble tale.
And with kind and courteous welcome royal strangers greeted well,

And he brought the milk and argya where the guests observant stood,
Crystal water from the fountain, berries from the darksome wood,

And a low and leafy cottage for their dwelling-place assigned,
As a host receives a stranger, welcomed them with offerings kind.

In the asram's peaceful courtyard fearless browsed the jungle deer,
All unharmed the bird of forest; pecked the grain collected near,

And by holy men surrounded 'neath the trees' umbrageous shade,
In his pure and peaceful accents rishi Bharad-vaja said:

Not unknown or unexpected, princely strangers, have ye come,
I have heard of sinless Rama's causeless banishment from home,

Welcome to a hermit's forest, be this spot your place of rest,
Where the meeting of the rivers, makes our sacred asram blest,

Live amidst these peaceful woodlands, still on sacred rites intent
Till your souls be filled with wisdom and your years of exile spent!"

"Gracious are thy accents, rishi," Rama answered thus the sage.
"But fair towns and peopled hamlets border on this hermitage,

And to see the banished Sita and to see us, much I fear,
Crowds of rustics oft will trespass on thy calm devotions here,

Far from towns and peopled hamlets, grant us, rishi, in thy grace,
Some wild spot where hid in jungle we may pass these years in peace."

"Twenty miles from this Prayagya," spake the rishi pond'ring well,
"Is a lonely hill and jungle where some ancient hermits dwell,

Chitra-kuta, Peak of Beauty, where the forest creatures stray,
And in every bush and thicket herds of lightsome monkeys play,

Men who view its towering summit are on lofty thoughts inclined.
Earthly pride nor earthly passions cloud their pure and peaceful mind,

Hoary-headed ancient hermits, hundred autumns who have done,
By their faith and lofty penance heaven's eternal bliss have won,

Holy is the fair seclusion for thy purpose suited well,
Or if still thy heart inclineth, here in peace and comfort dwell!"

Spake the rishi Bharad-vaja, and with every courteous rite,
Cheered his guests with varied converse till the silent hours of night,

Fourth night of the princes' exile in Prayaga's hermitage,
Passed the brothers and fair Sita honoured by Prayaga's Sacre.

### VII. CROSSING THE JUMNA--VALMIKI'S HERMITAGE

Morning dawned, and faithful Sita with the brothers held her way,
Where the dark and eddying, waters of the sacred Jumna stray,

Pondering by the rapid river long the thoughtful brothers stood,
Then with stalwart arms and axes felled the sturdy jungle wood,

Usira of strongest fibre, slender bamboo smooth and plain,
Jambu branches intertwining, with the bent and twisting cane,

And a mighty raft constructed, and with creepers scented sweet,
Lakshman for the gentle Sita made a soft and pleasant seat.

Then the rustic bark was floated, framed with skill of woodman's craft,
By her loving lord supported Sita stepped upon the raft,

And her raiments and apparel Rama by his consort laid,
And the axes and the deerskins, bow and dart and shining blade.

Then with stalwart arms the brothers plied the bending bamboo oar,
And the strong raft gaily bounding left for Jumna's southern shore.

"Goddess of the glorious Jumna!" so the pious Sita prayed,
"Peaceful be my husband's exile in the forest's darksome shade,

May he safely reach Ayodhya, and a thousand fattened kine,
Hundred jars of sweet libation, mighty Jumna, shall be thine,

Grant that from the woods returning he may see his home again,
Grant that honoured by his kinsmen he may rule his loving men!

On her breast her arms she folded while the princes plied the oar,
And the bright bark bravely bounding reached the wooded southern shore.

And the wanderers from Ayodhya on the river's margin stood,
Where the unknown realm extended mantled by unending wood,

Gallant Lakshman with his weapons went before the path to clear,
Soft-eyed Sita followed gently, Rama followed in the rear.

Oft from tree and darksome jungle, Lakshman ever true and brave,
Plucked the fruit or smiling blossom and to gentle Sita gave,

Oft to Rama turned his consort, pleased and curious evermore,
Asked the name of tree or creeper, fruit or flower unseen before.

Still with brotherly affection Lakshman brought each dewy spray,
Bud or blossom of wild beauty from the woodland bright and gay,

Still with eager joy and pleasure Sita turned her eye once more,
Where the tuneful swans and saras flocked on Jumna's sandy shore.

Two miles thus they walked and wandered and the belt of forest passed,
Slew the wild deer of the jungle, spread on leaves their rich repast,

Peacocks flew around them gaily, monkeys leaped on branches bent,
Fifth night of their endless wanderings in the forest thus they spent.

"Wake, my love, and list the warblings and the voices of the wood,"
Thus spake Rama when the morning on the eastern mountains stood,

Sita woke and gallant Lakshman, and they sipped the sacred wave,
To the hill of Chitra-kuta held their way serene and brave.

"Mark, my love," so Rama uttered, "every bush and tree and flower,
Tinged by radiant light of morning sparkles in a golden shower,

Mark the flaming flower of Kinsuk and the Vilwa in its pride,
Luscious fruits in wild profusion ample store of food provide,

Mark the honeycombs suspended from each tall and stately tree,
How from every virgin blossom steals her store the faithless bee!

Oft the lone and startled wild cock sounds its clarion full and clear,
And from flowering fragrant forests peacocks send the answering cheer,

Oft the elephant of jungle ranges in this darksome wood,
For yon peak is Chitra-kuta loved by saints and hermits good,

Oft the chanted songs of hermits echo through its sacred grove,
Peaceful on its shady uplands, Sita, we shall live and rove!"

Gently thus the princes wandered through the fair and woodland scene,
Fruits and blossoms lit the branches, feathered songsters filled the green,

Anchorites and ancient hermits lived in every sylvan grove,
And a sweet and sacred stillness filled the woods with peace and love!

Gently thus the princes wandered to the holy hermitage,
Where in lofty contemplation lived the mighty Saint and Sage,

Heaven inspired thy song, Valmiki! Ancient Bard of ancient day,
Deeds of virtue and of valour live in thy madying lay!

And the Bard received the princes with a father's greetings kind,
Bade them live in Chitra-kuta with a pure and peaceful mind,

To the true and faithful Lakshman, Rama then his purpose said,
And of leaf and forest timber Lakshman soon a cottage made.

"So our sacred Sastras sanction," thus the righteous Rama spake,
"Holy offering we should render when our dwelling-home we make,

Slay the black buck, gallant Lakshman, and a sacrifice prepare,
For the moment is auspicious and the day is bright and fair."

Lakshman slew a mighty black-buck, with the antlered trophy came,
Placed the carcass consecrated by the altar's blazing flame,

Radiant round the mighty offering tongues of red fire curling shone,
And the buck was duly roasted and the tender meat was done.

Pure from bath, with sacred mantra Rama did the holy rite,

And invoked the bright Immortals for to bless the dwelling site,

To the kindly VISWA-DEVAS, and to RUDRA fierce and strong,
And to VISHNU Lord of Creatures, Rama raised the sacred song.

Righteous rite was duly rendered for the forest-dwelling made,
And with true and deep devotion was the sacred mantra prayed,

And the worship of the Bright Ones purified each earthly stain,
Pure-souled Rama raised the altar and the chaitya's sacred fane.

Evening spread its holy stillness, bush and tree its magic felt,
As the Gods in BRAHMA'S mansions, exiles in their cottage dwelt,

In the woods of Chitra-kuta where the Malyavati flows,
Sixth day of their weary wand'rings ended in a sweet repose.

### VIII. TALE OF THE HERMIT'S SON

Wise Sumantra chariot-driver came from Ganga's sacred wave,
And unto Ayodhya's monarch, banished Rama's message gave,

Dasa-ratha's heart was shadowed by the deepening shade of night,
As the darkness of the eclipse glooms the sun's meridian light!

On the sixth night,-when his Rama slept in Chitra-kuta's bower,-
Memory of an ancient sorrow flung on him its fatal power,

Of an ancient crime and anguish, unforgotten, dark and dread,
Through the lapse of years and seasons casting back its death-like shade!

And the gloom of midnight deepened, Dasa-ratha sinking fast,
To Kausalya sad and sorrowing spake his memories of the past:

"Deeds we do in life, Kausalya, be they bitter, be they sweet,
Bring their fruit and retribution, rich reward or suffering meet.

Heedless child is he, Kausalya, in his fate who doth not scan
Retribution of his karma, sequence of a mighty plan!

Oft in madness and in folly we destroy the mango grove,
Plant the gorgeous gay palasa for the red flower that we love,

Fruitless as the red palasa is the karma I have sown,
And my barren lifetime withers through the deed which is my own!

Listen to my tale, Kausalya, in my days of youth renowned,
I was called a sabda-bedhi, archer prince who shot by sound,

I could hit the unseen target, by the sound my aim could tell,--
Blindly drinks a child the poison, blindly in my pride I fell!

I was then my father's Regent, thou a maid to me unknown,
Hunting by the fair Sarayu in my car I drove alone,

Buffalo or jungle tusker might frequent the river's brink,
Nimble deer or watchful tiger stealing for his nightly drink,

Stalking with a hunter's patience, loitering in the forests drear,
Sound of something in the water struck my keen and listening ear,

In the dark I stood and listened, some wild beast the water drunk,
'Tis some elephant, I pondered, lifting water with its trunk.

I was called a sabda-bedhi, archer prince who shot by sound,
On the unseen fancied tusker dealt a sure and deadly wound,

Ah! too deadly was my arrow and like hissing cobra fell,
On my startled car and bosom smote a voice of human wail,

Dying voice of lamentation rose upon the midnight high,
Till my weapons fell in tremor and a darkness dimmed my eye!

Hastening with a nameless terror soon I reached Sarayu's shore,
Saw a boy with hermit's tresses, and his pitcher lay before,

Weltering in a pool of red blood, lying on a gory bed,
Feebly raised his voice the hermit, and in dying accents said:

'What offence, O mighty monarch, all-unknowing have I done,
That with quick and kingly justice slayest thus a hermit's son?

Old and feeble are my parents, sightless by the will of fate,
Thirsty in their humble cottage for their duteous boy they wait,

And thy shaft that kills me, monarch, bids my ancient parents die.
Helpless, friendless, they will perish, in their anguish deep and high!

Sacred lore and lifelong penance change not mortal's earthly state,
Wherefore else they sit unconscious when their son is doomed by fate.

Or if conscious of my danger, could they dying breath recall,
Can the tall tree save the sapling doomed by woodman's axe to fall?

Hasten to my parents, monarch, soothe their sorrow and their ire,
For the tears of good and righteous wither like the forest fire,

Short the pathway to the asram, soon the cottage thou shalt see,
Soothe their anger by entreaty, ask their grace and pardon free!

But before thou goest, monarch, take, O take thy torturing dart,
For it rankles in my bosom with a cruel burning smart,

And it eats into my young life as the river's rolling tide
By the rains of summer swollen eats into its yielding side.'

Writhing in his pain and anguish thus the wounded hermit cried,
And I drew the fatal arrow, and the holy hermit died!

Darkly fell the thickening shadows, stars their feeble radiance lent,
As I filled the hermit's pitcher, to his sightless parents went,

Darkly fell the moonless midnight, deeper gloom my bosom rent,
As with faint and falt'ring footsteps to the hermits slow I went.

Like two birds bereft of plumage, void of strength, deprived of flight,
Were the stricken ancient hermits, friendless, helpless, void of sight,

Lisping in their feeble accents still they whispered of their child.
Of the stainless boy whose red blood Dasa-ratha's hands defiled!

And the father heard my footsteps, spake in accents soft and kind:
'Come, my son, to waiting parents, wherefore dost thou stay behind,

Sporting in the rippling water didst thou midnight's hour beguile,
But thy faint and thirsting mother anxious waits for thee the while,

Rath my heedless word or utterance caused thy boyish bosom smart,

But a feeble father's failings may not wound thy filial heart,

Help of helpless, sight of sightless, and thy parents' life and joy,
Wherefore art thou mute and voiceless, speak, my brave and beauteous boy!'

Thus the sightless father welcomed cruel slayer of his son,
And an anguish tore my bosom for the action I had done.

Scarce upon the sonless parents could I lift my aching eye,
Scarce in faint and faltering accents to the father make reply,

For a tremor shook my person and my spirit sank in dread.
Straining all my utmost prowess, thus in quavering voice I said:

'Not thy son, O holy hermit, but a Khsatra warrior born,
Dasa-ratha stands before thee by a cruel anguish torn,

For I came to slay the tusker by Sarayu's wooded brink,
Buffalo or deer of jungle stealing for his midnight drink,

And I heard a distant gurgle, some wild beast the water drunk,--
So I thought,--some jungle tusker lifting water with its trunk,

And I sent my fatal arrow on the unknown, unseen prey,
Speeding to the spot I witnessed,-there a dying hermit lay!

From his pierced and quivering bosom then the cruel dart I drew,
And he sorrowed for his parents as his spirit heavenward flew,

Thus unconscious, holy father, I have slayed thy stainless son,
Speak my penance, or in mercy pardon deed unknowing done!'

Slow and sadly by their bidding to the fatal spot I led,
Long and loud bewailed the parents by the cold unconscious dead,

And with hymns and holy water they performed the funeral rite,
Then with tears that burnt and withered, spake the hermit in his might:

'Sorrow for a son beloved is a father's direst woe,
Sorrow for a son beloved, Dasa-ratha, thou shalt know!

See the parents weep and perish, grieving for a slaughtered son,
Thou shalt weep and thou shalt perish for a loved and righteous son!

Distant is the expiation,---but in fulness of the time,
Dasa-ratha's death in anguish cleanses Dasa-ratha's crime!'

Spake the old and sightless prophet; then he made the funeral pyre,
And the father and the mother perished in the lighted fire,

Years have gone and many seasons, and in fulness of the time,
Comes the fruit of pride and folly and the harvest of my crime!

Rama eldest born and dearest, Lakshman true and faithful son,
Ah! forgive a dying father and a cruel action done,

Queen Kaikeyi, thou hast heedless brought on Raghu's race this stain,
Banished are the guiltless children and thy lord and king is slain!

Lay thy hands on mine, Kausalya, wipe thy unavailing tear,
Speak a wife's consoling accents to a dying husband's ear,

Lay thy hands on mine, Sumitra, vision falls my closing eyes,
And for bravo and banished Rama wings my spirit to the skies!

Hushed and silent passed the midnight, feebly still the monarch sighed,
Blessed Kausalya and Sumitra, blest his banished sons, and died.

# Book IV

## RAMA-BHARATA-SAMBADA--The Meeting of the Princes

### I. THE MEETING OF THE BROTHERS

Sorrowing for his sire departed Bharat to Ayodhya came,
But the exile of his brother stung his noble heart to flame,

Scorning sin-polluted empire, travelling with each widowed queen,
Sought through wood and trackless jungle Chitra-kuta's peaceful scene.

Royal guards and Saint Vasishtha loitered with the dames behind,
Onward pressed the eager Bharat, Rama's hermit-home to find,

Nestled in a jungle thicket, Rama's cottage rose in sight,
Thatched with leaves and twining branches, reared by Lakshman's faithful might.

Faggots hewn of gnarléd branches, blossoms culled from bush and tree.
Coats of bark and russet garments, kusa spread upon the lea,

Store of horns and branching antlers, fire-wood for the dewy night,--
Spake the dwelling of a hermit suited for a hermit's rite.

"May the scene," so Bharat uttered, "by the righteous rishi told,
Markalvati's rippling waters, Chitra-kuta's summit bold,

Mark the dark and trackless forest where the untamed tuskers roam,
And the deep and hollow caverns where the wild beasts make their home,

Mark the spacious wooded uplands, wreaths of smoke obscure the sky,
Hermits feed their flaming altars for their worship pure and high.

Done our weary work and wand'ring, righteous Rama here we meet,
Saint and king and honoured elder! Bharat bows unto his feet,

Born a king of many nations, he hath forest refuge sought,
Yielded throne and mighty kingdom for a hermit's humble cot,

Honour unto righteous Rama, unto Sita true and bold,
Theirs be fair Kosala's empire, crown and sceptre, wealth and gold!

Stately Sal and feathered palm-tree on the cottage lent their shade.
Strewn upon the sacred altar was the grass of kusa spread,

Gaily on the walls suspended hung two bows of ample height,
And their back with gold was pencilled, bright as INDRA's bow of might,

Cased in broad unfailing quivers arrows shone like light of day,
And like flame-tongued fiery serpents cast a dread and lurid ray,

Resting in their golden scabbards lay the sword of warriors bold,
And the targets broad and ample bossed with rings of yellow gold,

Glove and gauntlet decked the cottage safe from fear of hostile men,
As from creatures of the forest is the lion's lordly den!

Calm in silent contemplation by the altar's sacred fire,
Holy in his pious purpose though begirt by weapons dire,

Clad in deer-skin pure and peaceful, poring on the sacred flame,

In his bark and hermit's tresses like an anchorite of fame,

Lion-shouldered, mighty-arméd, but with gentle lotus eye.
Lord of wide earth ocean-girdled, but intent on penance high,

Godlike as the holy BRAHMA, on a skin of dappled deer
Rama sat with meek-eyed Sita, faithful Lakshman loitered near!

"Is this he whom joyous nations called to fair Ayodhya's throne,
Now the friend of forest-rangers wandering in the woods alone,

Is this he who robed in purple made Ayodhya's mansions bright..
Now in jungle bark and deer-skin clad as holy anchorite,

Is this be whose wreathéd ringlets fresh and holy fragrance shed,
Now a hermit's matted tresses cluster round his royal head,

Is this he whose royal yajnas filled the earth with righteous fame,
Now inured to hermit's labour by the altar's sacred flame,

Is this he whose brow and forehead royal gem and jewel graced,
Heir to proud Kosala's empire, eldest, noblest, and the best!"

Thus lamented pious Bharat, for his heart was anguish-rent,
As before the feet of Rama he in loving homage bent,

"Arya!" in his choking accents this was all that Bharat said,
"Arya!" spake the young Satrughna and he bent his holy head!

Rama to his loving bosom raised his brothers from his feet,
Ah, too deep is love for utterance when divided brothers meet,

Faithful Guha, brave Sumantra, bowed to Rama's righteous feet,
And a joy and mingled sadness filled the hermit's calm retreat!

*II. BHARAT'S ENTREATY AND RAMA'S REPLY*

"Speak, my true, my faithful Bharat," so the righteous Rama cried,
"Wherefore to this jungle dwelling hast thou from Ayodhya hied,

Speak, my fond and loving brother, if our father bade thee come,
Leaving throne and spacious empire in this wilderness to roam?

Heir and Regent of Kosala! Dost thou tend our father well,
And obey the lofty mandate from his royal lips that fell,

And the ancient Dasa-ratha, glorious still in regal might,
Doth he pass his bright life's evening in each pure and holy rite?

Doth my mother, Queen Kausalya, still for Rama wet her eye,
And the gentle Queen Sumitra for her banished Lakshman sigh,

Doth the peerless Queen Kaikeyi pass her days in duties fair,
Guard her Bharat's mighty empire, tend him with a mother's care?

Is each holy rite and homage to the Gods and Fathers done,
Is the honour due to elders rendered by each duteous son,

Do thy warriors guard thy kingdom as of yore with matchless skill,
And with counsel deep and duteous do thy min'sters serve thy will?

Rich thy fields in corn and produce fed by rivers broad and deep,
Rich thy green unending pastures with the kine and fattened sheep,

Tend the herdsman and his cattle, tend the tiller of the soil,
Watch and help with all thy bounty workmen in their peaceful toil,

For the monarch's highest duty is to serve his people's weal
And the ruler's richest glory is to labour and to heal!

Guard thy forts with sleepless caution with the engines of the war,
With the men who shoot the arrow and who drive the flying car,

Guard Kosala's royal treasure, make thy gifts of wealth and food,
Not to lords and proud retainers, but to worthy and the good!

Reader justice pure and spotless as befits thy royal line,
And to save the good and guiltless, Bharat, be it ever thine,

For the tears of suffering virtue wither like the thunder levin,
And they slay our men and cattle like the wrath of righteous heaven,

Fruitful be thy lore of Veda, fruitful be each pious rite,
Be thy queen a fruitful mother, be thy empire full of might!"

Weeping, weeping, Bharat answered Dasa-ratha's eldest son,
"Dasa-ratha walks the bright sky, for his earthly task is done!

For impelled by Queen Kaikeyi to the woods he bade thee go,
And his spotless fame was clouded and his bosom sank in woe,

And my mother, late repenting, weeps her deed of deepest shame,
Weeps her wedded lord departed, and a woman's tarnished fame!

Thou alone canst wipe this insult by a deed of kindness done,
Rule o'er Dasa-ratha's empire, Dasa-ratha's eldest son,

Weeping queens and loyal subjects supplicate thy noble grace,
Rule o'er Raghu's ancient empire, son of Raghu's royal race!

For our ancient Law ordaineth and thy Duty makes it plain,
Eldest-born succeeds his father as the king of earth and main,

By the fair Earth loved and welcomed, Rama, be her wedded lord,
As by planet-jewelled Midnight is the radiant Moon adored!

And thy father's ancient min'sters and thy courtiers faithful still,
Wait to do thy righteous mandate and to serve thy royal will,

As a pupil, as a brother, as a slave, I seek thy grace,
Come and rule thy father's empire, king of Raghu's royal race!"

Weeping, on the feet of Rama, Bharat placed his lowly head,
Weeping for his sire departed, tears of sorrow Rama shed,

Then he raised his loving brother with an elder's deathless love,
Sorrow wakes our deepest kindness and our holiest feelings prove!

"But I may not," answered Rama, "seek Ayodhya's ancient throne,
For a righteous father's mandate duteous son may not disown,

And I may not, gentle brother, break the word of promise given,
To a king and to a father who is now a saint in heaven!

Not on thee, nor on thy mother, rests the censure or the blame,
Faithful to his father's wishes Rama to the forest came,

For the son and duteous consort serve the father and the lord,

Higher than an empire's glory is a father's spoken word!

All inviolate is his mandate,--on Ayodhya's jewelled throne,
Or in pathless woods and jungle Rama shall his duty own,

All inviolate is the blessing by a loving mother given,
For she blessed my life in exile like a pitying saint of heaven!

Thou shalt rule the kingdom, Bharat, guard our loving people well,
Clad in wild bark and in deer-skin I shall in the forests dwell,

So spake saintly Dasa-ratha in Ayodhya's palace hall,
And a righteous father's mandate duteous son may not recall!"

### III. KAUSALYA'S LAMENT AND RAMA'S REPLY

Slow and sad with Saint Vasishtha, with each widowed royal dame,
Unto Rama's hermit-cottage ancient Queen Kausalya came,

And she saw him clad in wild bark like a hermit stern and high,
And an anguish smote her bosom and a tear bedewed her eye.

Rama bowed unto his mother and each elder's blessings sought,
Held their feet in salutation with a holy reverence fraught,

And the queens with loving fingers, with a mother's tender care,
Swept the dust of wood and jungle from his head and bosom fair,

Lakshman too in loving homage bent before each royal dame,
And they blessed the faithful hero spotless in his righteous fame.

Lastly came the soft-eyed Sita with obeisance soft and sweet,
And with hands in meekness folded bent her tresses to their feet,

Pain and anguish smote their bosoms, round their Sita as they prest,
As a mother clasps a daughter, clasped her in their loving breast!

Torn from royal hall and mansions, ranger of the darksome wood,
Reft of home and kith and kindred by her forest but she stood!

"Hast thou, daughter of Videha," weeping thus Kausalya said,
"Dwelt in woods and leafy cottage and in pathless jungle strayed,

Hast thou, Rama's royal consort, lived a homeless anchorite
Pale with rigid fast and penance, worn with toil of righteous rite?

But thy sweet face, gentle Sita, is like faded lotus dry,
And like lily parched by sunlight, lustreless thy beauteous eye,

Like the gold untimely tarnished is thy sorrow-shaded brow,
Like the moon by shadows darkened is thy form of beauty now!

And an anguish scathes my bosom like the withering forest fire,
Thus to see thee, duteous daughter, in misfortunes deep and dire,

Dark is wide Kosala's empire, dark is Raghu's royal house,
When in woods my Rama wanders and my Rama's royal spouse!

Sweetly, gentle Sita answered, answered Rama fair and tall,
That a righteous father's mandate duteous son may not recall!

### IV. JABALI'S REASONING AND RAMA'S REPLY

Jabali a learned Brahman and a Sophist skilled in word,

Questioned Faith and Law and Duty, spake to young Ayodhya's lord:

Wherefore, Rama, idle maxims cloud thy heart and warp thy mind,
Maxims which mislead the simple and the thoughtless human kind?

Love nor friendship doth a mortal to his kith or kindred own,
Entering on his Nvide earth friendless, and departing all alone,

Foolishly upon the father and the mother dotes the son,
Kinship is an idle fancy,-save thyself thy kith is none!

In the wayside inn he halteth who in distant lands doth roam,
Leaves it with the dawning daylight for another transient home,

Thus on earth are kin and kindred, home and country, wealth and store,
We but meet them on our journey, leave them as we pass before!

Wherefore for a father's mandate leave thy empire and thy throne,
Pass thy days in trackless jungle sacrificing all thy own,

Wherefore to Ayodhya's city, as to longing wife's embrace,
Speed'st thou not to rule thy empire, lord of Raghu's royal race?

Dasa-ratha claims no duty, and this will is empty word,
View him as a foreign monarch, of thy realm thou art the lord,

Dasa-ratha is departed, gone where all the mortals go,
For a dead man's idle mandate wherefore lead this life of woe?

Ah! I weep for erring mortals who on erring duty bent
Sacrifice their dear enjoyment till their barren life is spent,

Who to Gods and to the Fathers vainly still their offerings make,
Waste of food! for God nor Father doth our pious homage take!

And the food by one partaken, can it nourish other men,
Food bestowed upon a Brahman, can it serve our Fathers then?

Crafty priests have forged these maxims and with selfish objects say,
Make thy gifts and do thy penance, leave thy worldly wealth and pray!

There is no Hereafter, Rama, vain the hope and creed of men,
Seek the pleasures of the present, spurn illusions poor and vain,

Take the course of sense and wisdom, cast all idle faith aside,
Take the kingdom Bharat offers, rule Ayodhya in thy pride!"

"Fair thy purpose," answered Rama," false thy reason leads astray,
Tortuous wisdom brings no profit, virtue shuns the crooked way,

For the deed proclaims the hero from the man of spacious lies,
Marks the true and upright Arya from the scheming worldly-wise!

If assuming virtue's mantle I should seek the sinful path,
Gods who judge our secret motives curse me with their deepest wrath,

And thy counsel helps not, rishi, mansions of the sky to win,
And a king his subjects follow adding deeper sin to sin!

Sweep aside thy crafty reasoning, Truth is still our ancient way,
Truth sustains the earth and nations and a monarch's righteous sway,

Mighty Gods and holy sages find in Truth their haven shore,
Scorning death and dark destruction, Truth survives for evermore!

Deadlier than the serpent's venom is the venom of a lie,
From the false, than from the cobra, men with deeper terror fly,

Dearer than the food to mortals, Truth as nourishment is given,
Truth sustains the wide creation, Truth upholds the highest heaven,

Vain were gifts and sacrifices, rigid penances were vain,
Profitless the holy Vedas but for Truth which they sustain,

Gifts and rites and rigid penance have no aim or purpose high,
Save in Truth which rules the wide earth and the regions of the sky!

I have plighted truth and promise and my word may not unsay,
Fourteen years in pathless forests father's mandate I obey,

And I seek no spacious reasons my relinquished throne to win,
Gods nor Fathers nor the Vedas counsel tortuous paths of sin!

Pardon, rishi, still unchanging shall remain my promise given
To my mother Queen Kaikeyi, to my father now in heaven,

Pardon, rishi, still in jungle we shall seek the forest fare,
Worship Gods who watch our actions, and pervade the earth and air!

Unto AGNI, unto VAYU, shall my constant prayers run,
I shall live like happy INDRA, hundred sacrifices done,

And the deep and darksome jangle shall be Rama's royal hall,
For a righteous father's mandate duteous son may not recall!"

### V. THE SANDALS

Tears nor sighs nor sad entreaty Rama's changeless purpose shook,
Till. once more with hands conjoinéd Bharat to his elder spoke:

"Rama, true to royal mercy, true to duties of thy race,
Grant this favour to thy mother, to thy brother grant this grace,

Vain were my unaided efforts to protect our father's throne,
Town and hamlet, lord and tiller, turn to thee and thee alone!

Unto Rama, friends and kinsmen, chiefs and warriors, turn in pain,
And each city chief and elder, and each humble village swain,

Base thy empire strong, unshaken, on a loyal nation's will,
With thy worth and with thy valour serve thy faithful people still!"

Rama raised the prostrate Bharat to his ever-loving breast,
And in voice of tuneful hansa thus his gentle speech addrest:

"Trust me, Bharat, lofty virtue, strength and will to thee belong,
Thou could'st rule a worldwide empire in thy faith and purpose strong,

And our father's ancient min'sters, ever faithful, wise and deep,
They shall help thee with their counsel and thy ancient frontiers keep.

List! the Moon may lose his lustre, Himalaya lose his snow,
Heaving Ocean pass his confines surging from the caves below,

But the truth-abiding Rama will not move from promise given,
He hath spoke and will not palter, help him righteous Gods in heaven!"

Blazing like the Sun in splendour, beauteous like the Lord of Night,
Rama vowed his Vow of Duty, changeless in his holy might!

"Humble token," answered Bharat, "still I seek from Rama's hand,
Token of his love and kindness, token of his high command,

From thy feet cast forth those sandals, they shall decorate the throne.
They shall nerve my heart to duty and shall safely guard thy own,

They shall to a loyal nation absent monarch's will proclaim,
Watch the frontiers of the empire and the people's homage claim!"

Rama gave the loosened sandals as his younger humbly prayed,
Bharat bowed to them in homage and his parting purpose said:

"Not alone will banished Rama barks and matted tresses wear,
Fourteen years the crownéd Bharat will in hermit's dress appear,

Henceforth Bharat dwells in palace guised as hermit of the wood,
In the sumptuous hall of feasting wild fruit is his only food,

Fourteen years shall pass in waiting, weary toil and penance dire
Then, if Rama comes not living, Bharat dies upon the pyre!"

*VI. THE HERMITAGE OF ATRI*

With the sandals of his elder Bharat to Ayodhya went,
Rama sought for deeper forests on his arduous duty bent,

Wandering with his wife and Lakshman slowly sought the hermitage,
Where resided saintly Atri, Vedic Bard and ancient sage.

Auasuya, wife of Atri, votaress of Gods above,
Welcomed Sita in her cottage, tended her with mother's love,

Gave her robe and holy garland, jewelled ring and chain of gold,
Heard the tale of love and sadness which the soft-eyed Sita told:

How the monarch of Videha held the plough and tilled the earth,
From the furrow made by ploughshare infant Sita sprang to birth,

How the monarch of Videha welcomed kings of worth and pride,
Rama 'midst the gathered monarchs broke the bow and won the bride,

How by Queen Kaikeyi's mandate Rama lost his father's throne,
Sita followed him in exile in the forest dark and lone!

Softly from the lips of Sita words of joy and sorrow fell,
And the pure-souled pious priestess wept to hear the tender tale,

And she kissed her on the forehead, held her on her ancient breast,
And in mother's tender accents thus her gentle thoughts exprest:

"Sweet the tale you tell me, Sita, of thy wedding and thy love,
Of the true and tender Rama, righteous as the Gods above,

And thy wifely deep devotion fills my heart with purpose high,
Stay with us my gentle daughter for the night shades gather nigh.

Hastening from each distant region feathered songsters seek their nest,
Twitter in the leafy thickets ere they seek their nightly rest,

Hastening from their pure ablutions with their pitcher smooth and fair,
In their dripping barks the hermits to their evening rites repair,

And in sacred agni-hotra holy anchorites engage,
And a wreath of smoke ascending marks the altar of each sage.

Now a deeper shadow mantles bush and brake and trees around,
And a thick and inky darkness falls upon the distant ground,

Midnight prowlers of the jungle steal beneath the sable shade,
But the tame deer by the altar seeks his wonted nightly bed.

Mark! how by the stars encircled sails the radiant Lord of Night,
With his train of silver glory streaming o'er the azure height,

And thy consort waits thee, Sita, but before thou leavest, fair,
Let me deck thy brow and bosom with these jewels rich and rare,

Old these eyes and grey these tresses, but a thrill of joy is mine,
Thus to see thy youth and beauty in this gorgeous garment shine!"

Pleased at heart the ancient priestess clad her in apparel meet,
And the young wife glad and grateful bowed to Anasuya's feet,

Robed and jewelled, bright and beauteous, sweet-eyed Sita softly came,
Where with anxious heart awaited Rama prince of righteous fame.

With a wifely love and longing Sita met her hero bold,
Anasuya's love and kindness in her grateful accents told,

Rama and his brother listened of the grace by Sita gained,
Favours of the ancient priestess, pious blessings she had rained.

In the rishi's peaceful asram Rama passed the sacred night,
In the hushed and silent forest silvered by the moon's pale light,

Daylight dawned, to deeper forests Rama went serene and proud,
As the sun in midday splendour sinks within a bank of cloud!

## Book V

### PANCHAVATI--On the Banks of the Godavari

#### I. THE HERMITAGE OF AGASTYA

Righteous Rama, soft-eyed Sita, and the gallant Lakshman stood
In the wilderness of Dandaki--trackless, pathless, boundless wood,

But within its gloomy gorges, dark and deep and known to few,
Humble homes of hermit sages rose before the princes' view.

Coats of bark and scattered kusa spake their peaceful pure abode,
Seat of pious rite and penance which with holy splendour glowed,

Forest songsters knew the asrama and the wild deer crept its blade,
And the sweet-voiced sylvan wood-nymph haunted oft its holy shade,

Brightly blazed the sacred altar, vase and ladle stood around,
Fruit and blossom, skin and faggot, sanctified the holy ground.

From the broad and bending branches ripening-, fruits in clusters hung,
And with gifts and rich libations hermits raised the ancient song,

Lotus and the virgin lily danced upon the rippling rill,
And the golden sunlight glittered on the greenwoods calm and still,

And the consecrated woodland by the holy hermits trod,
Shone like BRAHMA'S sky in lustre, hallowed by the grace of God!

Rama loosened there his bow-string and the peaceful scene surveyed,

And the holy sages welcomed wanderers in the forest shade,

Rama bright as Lord of Midnight, Sita with her saintly face,
Lakshman young and true and valiant, decked with warrior's peerless grace!

Leafy hut the holy sages to the royal guests assigned,
Brought them fruit and forest blossoms, blessed them with their blessings kind,

"Raghu's son," thus spake the sages, "helper of each holy rite,
Portion of the royal INDRA, fount of justice and of might,

On thy throne or in the forest, king of nations, lord of men,
Grant us to thy kind protection in this hermit's lonely den!

Homely fare and jungle produce were before the princes laid,
And the toil-worn, tender Sita slumbered in the asram's shade.

Thus from grove to grove they wandered, to each haunt of holy sage,
Sarabhanga's sacred dwelling and Sutikshna's hermitage,

Till they met the Saint Agastya, mightiest Saint of olden time,
Harbinger of holy culture in the wilds of Southern clime!

"Eldest born of Dasa-ratha, long and far hath Rama strayed,"
Thus to pupil of Agastya young and gallant Lakshman said,--

"With his faithful consort Sita in these wilds he wanders still,
I am righteous Rama's younger, duteous to his royal will,

And we pass these years of exile to our father's mandate true,
Fain to mighty Saint Agastya we would render homage due!"

Listening to his words the hermit sought the shrine of Sacred Fire,
Spake the message of the princes to the Saint and ancient Sire:

"Righteous Rama, valiant Lakshman, saintly Sita seek this shade,
And to see thee, radiant rishi, have in humble accents prayed."

"Hath he come," so spake Agastya, "Rama prince of Raghu's race,
Youth for whom this heart hath thirsted, youth endued with righteous grace,

Hath he come with wife and brother to accept our greetings kind,
Wherefore came ye for permission, wherefore linger they behind?

Rama and the soft-eyed Sita, were with gallant Lakshman led,
Where the dun deer free and fearless roamed within the holy shade,

Where the shrines of great Immortals stood in order thick and close,
And by bright and blazing altars chanted songs and hymns arose.

BRAHMA and the flaming AGNI, VISHNU lord of heavenly light,
INDRA and benign VIVASAT ruler of the azure height,

SOMA and the radiant BHAGA, and KUVERA lord of gold,
And VIDHATRI great Creator worshipped by the saints of old,

VAYU breath of living creatures, YAMA monarch of the dead,
And VARUNA with his fetters which the trembling sinners dread,

Holy Spirit of GAYATRI goddess of the morning prayer,
VASUS and the hooded NAGAS, golden-winged GARUDA fair,

KARTIKEYA heavenly leader strong to conquer and to bless,
DHARMA god of human duty and of human righteousness,

Shrines of all these bright Immortals ruling in the skies above,
Filled the pure and peaceful forest with a calm and holy love!

Girt by hermits righteous-hearted then the Saint Agastya came,
Rich in wealth of pious penance, rich in learning and in fame,

Mighty-arméd Rama marked him radiant like the midday sun,
Bowed and rendered due obeisance with each act of homage done,

Valiant Lakshman tall and stately to the great Agastya bent,
With a woman's soft devotion Sita, bowed unto the saint.

Saint Agastya raised the princes, greeted them in accents sweet,
Gave them fruit and herb and water, offered them the honoured seat,

With libations unto AGNI offered welcome to each guest,
Food and drink beseeming hermits on the wearied princes pressed.

"False the hermits," spake Agastya, "who to guests their dues deny,
Hunger they in life hereafter-like the speaker of a lie.

And a royal guest and wanderer doth our foremost honour claim,
Car-borne kings protect the wide earth by their prowess and their fame,

By these fruits and forest blossoms be our humble homage shewn,
By some gift, of Rama worthy, be Agastya's blessings known!

Take this bow, heroic Rama,--need for warlike arms is thine,--
Gems of more than earthly radiance on the goodly weapon shine,

Worshipper of righteous VISHNU! VISHNU'S wondrous weapon take,
Heavenly artist VISWA-KARMAN shaped this bow of heavenly make!

Take this shining dart of BRAHMA radiant like a tongue of flame,
Sped by good and worthy archer never shall it miss its aim,

And this INDRA's ample quiver filled with arrows true and keen,
Filled with arrows still unfailing in the battle's dreadful scene!

Take this sabre golden-hilted in its case of burnished gold,
Not unworthy of a monarch and a warrior true and bold,

Impious foes of bright Immortals know these weapons dread and dire,
Mowing down the ranks of foemen, scathing like the forest fire!

Be these weapons thy companions,-Rama, thou shalt need them oft,
Meet and conquers till thy foemen like the Thunder-God aloft!"

## II. THE COUNSEL OF AGASTYA

"Pleased am I," so spake Agastya, "in these forests dark and wild,
Thou hast come to seek me, Rama, with the saintly Janak's child,

But like pale and drooping blossom severed from the parent tree,
Far from home in toil and trouble, faithful Sita follows thee,

True to wedded lord and husband she hath followed Raghu's son,
With a woman's deep devotion woman's duty she hath done!

How unlike the fickle woman, true while Fame and Fortune smile,
Faithless when misfortunes gather, loveless in her wicked wile,

How unlike the changeful woman, false as light the lightnings fling,
Keen as sabre, quick as tempest, swift as bird upon its wing!

Dead to Fortune's frown or favour, Sita still in truth abides,
As the star of Arundhati in her mansion still resides,

Rest thee with thy gentle consort, farther still she may not roam,
Holier were this hermit's forest as the saintly Sita's home!"

"Great Agastya!" answered Rama, "bléssed is my banished life,
For thy kindriess to an exile and his friendless homeless wife,

But in wilder, gloomier forests lonesome we must wander still,
Where a deeper, darker shadow settles on the rock and rill."

"Be it so," Agastya answered, "two short yojans from this place,
Wild is Panchavati's forest where unseen the wild deer race,

Godavari's limpid waters through its gloomy gorges flow,
Fruit and root and luscious berries on its silent margin grow,

Seek that spot and with thy brother build a lonesome leafy home,
Tend thy true and toil-worn Sita, farther still she may not roam!

Not unknown to me the mandate by thy royal father given,
Not unseen thy endless wanderings destined by the will of Heaven,

Therefore Panchavati's forest marked I for thy woodland stay,
Where the ripening wild fruit clusters and the wild bird trills his lay,

Tend thy dear devoted Sita and protect each pious rite,
Matchless in thy warlike wcapons peerless in thy princely might!

Mark yon gloomy Mahua forest stretching o'er the boundless lea,
Pass that wood and turning northward seek an old Nyagrodha tree,

Then ascend a sloping upland by a steep and lofty hill,
Thou shalt enter Panchavati, blossom-covered, calm and still!"

Bowing to the great Agastya, Rama left the mighty sage,
Bowing to each saint and hermit, Lakshman left the hermitage,

And the princes tall and stately marched where Panchavati lay,
Soft-eyed Sita followed meekly where her Rama led the way!

### III. THE FOREST OF PANCHAVATI

Godavari's limpid waters in her gloomy gorges strayed,
Unseen rangers of the jungle nestled in the darksome shade!

"Mark the woodlands," uttered Rama, "by the Saint Agastya told,
Panchavati's lonesome forest with its blossoms red and gold,

Skilled to scan the wood and jungle, Lakshman, cast thy eye around,
For our humble home and dwelling seek a low and level ground,

Where the river laves its margin with a soft and gentle kiss,
Where my sweet and soft-eyed Sita may repose in sylvan bliss,

Where the lawn is fresh and verdant and the kwa young and bright,
And the creeper yields her blossoms for our sacrificial rite."

"Little can I help thee, brother," did the duteous Lakshman say,
"Thou art prompt to judge and fathom, Lakshman listens to obey!

"Mark this spot," so answered Rama, leading Lakshman by the hand,
"Soft the lawn of verdant kusa, beauteous blossoms light the land,

Mark the smiling lake of lotus gleaming with a radiance fair,
Wafting fresh and gentle fragrance o'er the rich and laden air,

Mark each scented shrub and creeper bending o'er the lucid wave,
Where the bank with soft caresses Godavari's waters lave!

Tuneful ducks frequent this margin, Chakravakas breathe of love,
And the timid deer of jungle browse within the shady grove,

And the valleys are resonant with the peacock's clarion cry,
And the trees with budding blossoms glitter on the mountains high,

And the rocks in well-marked strata in their glittering lines appear,
Like the streaks of white and crimson painted on our tuskers fair!

Stately Sal and feathered palm-tree guard this darksome forest-land,
Golden date and flowering mango stretch afar on either hand,

Asok thrives and blazing Kinsuk, Chandan wafts a fragrance rare,
Aswa-karna and Khadira by the Sami dark and fair,

Beauteous spot for hermit-dwelling joyous with the voice of song,
Haunted by the timid wild deer and by black buck fleet and strong!

Foe-compelling faithful Lakshman heard the words his elder said,
And by sturdy toil and labour stately home and dwelling made,

Spacious was the leafy cottage walled with moistened earth and soft,
Pillared with the stately bamboo holding high the roof aloft,

Interlacing twigs and branches, corded from the ridge to eaves,
Held the thatch of reed and branches and of jungle grass and leaves,

And the floor was pressed and levelled and the toilsome task was done
And the structure rose in beauty for the righteous Raghu's son!

To the river for ablutions Lakshman went of warlike fame,
With a store of fragrant lotus and of luscious berries came,

Sacrificing to the Bright Gods sacred hymns and mantras said,
Proudly then unto his elder shewed the home his hand had made.

In her soft and grateful accents gentle Sita praised his skill,
Praised a brother's loving labour, praised a hero's dauntless will,

Rama clasped his faithful Lakshman in a brother's fond embrace,
Spake in sweet and kindly accents with an elder's loving grace:

How can Rama, homeless wand'rer, priceless love like thine requite,
Let him hold thee in his bosom, soul of love and arm of might,

And our father good and gracious, in a righteous son like thee,
Lives again and treads the bright earth, from the bonds of YAMA free!"

Thus spake Rama, and with Lakshman and with Sita child of love,
Dwelt in Panchavati's cottage as the Bright Gods dwell above!

*IV. WINTER IN PANCHAVATI*

Came and passed the golden autumn in the forest's gloomy shade,
And the northern blasts of winter swept along the silent glade,

When the chilly night was over, once at morn the prince of fame,
For his morning's pure ablutions to the Godavari came.

Meek-eyed Sita softly followed with the pitcher in her arms,
Gallant Lakshman spake to Rama of the Indian winter's charms:

"Comes the bright and bracing winter to the royal Rama dear,
Like a bride the beauteous season doth in richest robes appear,

Frosty air and freshening zephyrs wake to life each mart and plain,
And the corn in dewdrop sparkling makes a sea of waving green,

But the village maid and matron shun the freezing river's shore,
By the fire the village elder tells the stirring tale of yore!

With the winter's ample harvest men perform each pious rite,
To the Fathers long departed, to the Gods of holy might,

With the rite of agrayana pious men their sins dispel,
And with gay and sweet observance songs of love the women tell,

And the monarchs bent on conquest mark the winter's cloudless glow,
Lead their bannered cars and forces 'gainst the rival and the foe!

Southwards rolls the solar chariot, and the cold and widowed North
Reft of 'bridal mark' and joyance coldly sighs her sorrows forth,

Southward rolls the solar chariot, Himalaya, 'home of snow,'
True to name and appellation doth in whiter garments glow,

Southward rolls the solar chariot, cold and crisp the frosty air,
And the wood of flower dismantled doth in russet robes appear!

Star of Pushya rules December and the night with rime is hoar,
And beneath the starry welkin in the woods we sleep no more,

And the pale moon mist-enshrouded sheds a faint and feeble beam,
As the breath obscures the mirror, winter mist obscures her gleam,

Hidden by the rising vapour faint she glistens on the dale,
Like our sun-embrownéd Sita with her toil and penance pale!

Sweeping blasts from western mountains through the gorges whistle by
And the saras and the curlew raise their shrill and piercing cry,

Boundless fields of wheat and barley are with dewdrops moist and wet,
And the golden rice of winter ripens like the clustering date,

Peopled marts and rural hamlets wake to life and cheerful toil,
And the peaceful happy nations prosper on their fertile soil!

Mark the sun in morning vapours-like the moon subdued and pale
Brightening as the day advances piercing through the darksome veil,

Mark his gay and golden lustre sparkling o'er the dewy lea,
Mantling hill and field and forest, painting bush and leaf and tree,

Mark it glisten on the green grass, on each bright and bending blade,
Lighten up the long-drawn vista, shooting through the gloomy glade!

Thirst-impelled the lordly tusker still avoids the freezing drink,
Wild duck and the tuneful hansa doubtful watch the river's brink,

From the rivers wrapped in vapour unseen cries the wild curlew,
Unseen rolls the misty streamlet o'er its sandbank soaked in dew,

And the drooping water-lily bends her head beneath the frost,

Lost her fresh and fragrant beauty and her tender petals lost!

Now my errant fancy wanders to Ayodhya's distant town,
Where in hermit's barks and tresses Bharat wears the royal crown,

Scorning regal state and splendoar, spurning pleasures loved of yore,
Spends his winter day in penance, sleeps at night upon the floor,

Aye! perchance Sarayu's waters seeks he now, serene and brave,
As we seek, when dawns the daylight, Godavari's limpid wave!

Rich of hue, with eye of lotus, truthful, faithful, strong of mind,
For the love he bears thee, Rama, spurns each joy of baser kind,

'False he proves unto his father who is led by mother's wile,'
Vain this ancient impious adage-Bharat spurns his mother's guile,

Bharat's mother Queen Kaikeyi, Dasa-ratha's royal spouse,
Deep in craft, hath brought disaster on Ayodhya's royal house!"

"Speak not thus," so Rama answered, "on Kaikeyi cast no blame,
Honour still the righteous Bharat, honour still the royal dame,

Fixed in purpose and unchanging still in jungle wilds I roam,
But thy accents, gentle Lakshman, wake a longing for my home!

And my loving mem'ry lingers on each word from Bharat fell
Sweeter than the draught of nectar, purer than the crystal well,

And my righteous purpose falters, shaken by a brother's love,
May we meet again our brother, if it please the Gods above!"

Waked by love, a silent tear-drop fell on Godavari's wave,
True once more to righteous purpose Rama's heart was calm and brave

Rama plunged into the river'neath the morning's crimson beam,
Sits, softly sought the waters as the lily seeks the stream,

And they prayed to Gods and Fathers with each rite and duty doue,
And they sang the ancient mantra to the red and rising Sun,

With her lord, in loosened tresses Sita to her cottage came,
As with RUDRA wanders UMA in Kailasa's hill of fame!

# The Mysterious Ramayana

1.  Although not your first epic, how would you define epic poetry now?

2.  Why does this ancient story continue to be relevant to today's Indians? Does Western civilization have comparable texts?

3.  What are some of the shared cultural values you find when reading this story?

4.  Compare and contrast the imagery of the forest with that of the sea on The Odyssey.

# Sakuntala

*From the Sanskrit of Kálidása*

AN INDIAN DRAMA
TRANSLATED BY SIR MONIER MONIER-WILLIAMS

## PERSONS REPRESENTED

DUSHYANTA- King of India
MÁ[T.]HAVYA- the jester, friend, and companion of the King
KANWA, chief of the hermits- foster-father of [S']AKOONTALÁ
[S']ÁRNGARAVA and [S']ÁRADWATA- two Bráhmans, belonging to the hermitage of KANWA
MITRÁVASU- brother-in-law of the King, and superintendent of the city police
JÁNUKA and SÚCHAKA- two constables
VÁTÁYANA- the chamberlain or attendant on the women's apartments
SOMARÁTA- the domestic priest
KARABHAKA- a messenger of the queen-mother
RAIVATIKA- the warder or doorkeeper
MÁTALI- charioteer of Indra
SARVA-DAMANA/BHARATA-
a little boy, son of DUSHYANTA by [S']AKOONTALÁ
KA[S']YAPA- a divine sage, progenitor of men and gods, son of MARÍCHI, and grandson of BRAHMÁ
[S']AKOONTALÁ- daughter of the sage VI[S']WÁMITRA and the nymph MENAKÁ, foster-child of the hermit KANWA
PRIYAMVADÁ and ANASÚYÁ- female attendants, companions of [S'] AKOONTALÁ
GAUTAMÍ- a holy matron, Superior of the female inhabitants of the hermitage
VASUMATÍ- the Queen of DUSHYANTA
SÁNUMATÍ- a nymph, friend of [S']AKOONTALÁ
TARALIKÁ- personal attendant of the Queen
CHATURIKÁ- personal attendant of the King
VETRAVATÍ-female warder or doorkeeper
PARABHRITIKÁ and MADHUKARIKÁ- maidens in charge of the royal gardens
SUVRATÁ- a nurse
ADITI- wife of KA[S']YAPA; granddaughter of BRAHMÁ through her father DAKSHA
CHARIOTEER, FISHERMAN, OFFICERS, AND HERMITS

## Prologue

BENEDICTION
Í[S']a preserve you ! he who is revealed
In these eight forms  by man perceptible—
Water, of all creation's works the first;
The Fire that bears on high the sacrifice
Presented with solemnity to heaven;
The Priest, the holy offerer of gifts;
The Sun and Moon, those two majestic orbs,
Eternal marshallers of day and night;
The subtle Ether, vehicle of sound,
Diffused throughout the boundless universe;
The Earth, by sages called 'The place of birth
Of all material essences and things';
And Air, which giveth life to all that breathe.

STAGE-MANAGER.

*After the recitation of the benediction.*
*Looking toward the living-room.*
Lady, when you have finished attiring yourself, come this way.

ACTRESS.
*Entering.*
Here I am, Sir; what are your commands?

STAGE-MANAGER.
We are here before the eyes of an audience of educated and discerning men ;
and have to represent in their presence a new drama composed by Kálidása,
called '[S']akoontalá; or, the Lost Ring .' Let the whole company exert
themselves to do justice to their several parts.

ACTRESS.
You, Sir, have so judiciously managed the cast of the characters, that nothing
will be defective in the acting.

STAGE-MANAGER.
Lady, I will tell you the exact state of the case,
  No skill in acting can I deem complete,
  Till from the wise the actor gain applause;
  Know that the heart e'en of the truly skilful,
  Shrinks from too boastful confidence in self.

ACTRESS.
*Modestly.*
You judge correctly And now, what are your commands?

STAGE-MANAGER.
What can you do better than engage the attention of the audience by some
captivating melody?

ACTRESS.
Which among the seasons shall I select as the subject of my song?

STAGE-MANAGER.
You surely ought to give the preference to the present Summer season[ that
has but recently commenced, a season so rich in enjoyment. For now
  Unceasing are the charms of halcyon days,
  When the cool bath exhilarates the frame;
  When sylvan gales are laden with the scent
  Of fragrant Pátalas ; when soothing sleep
  Creeps softly on beneath the deepening shade;
  And when, at last, the dulcet calm of eve
  Entrancing steals o'er every yielding sense.

ACTRESS.
I will:—

Sings.
  Fond maids, the chosen of their hearts to please,
  Entwine their ears with sweet [S']irísha flowers ,
  Whose fragrant lips attract the kiss of bees
  That softly murmur through the summer hours.

STAGE-MANAGER.
*377*

Charmingly sung! The audience are motionless as statues, their souls riveted by the enchanting strain. What subject shall we select for representation, that we may ensure a continuance of their favour?

**ACTRESS.**
Why not the same, Sir, announced by you at first? Let the drama called '[S'] akoontalá; or, the Lost Ring,' be the subject of our dramatic performance.

**STAGE-MANAGER.**
Rightly reminded! For the moment I had forgotten it.
  Your song's transporting melody decoyed
  My thoughts, and rapt with ecstasy my soul;
  As now the bounding antelope allures
  The King Dushyanta  on the chase intent.

*Exeunt*

---

# *Act I*

## SCENE-A Forest.

*Enter King DUSHYANTA, armed with a bow and arrow, in a chariot, chasing an antelope, attended by his CHARIOTEER.*

**CHARIOTEER.**

*Looking at the deer, and then at the KING.*

Great Prince,
  When on the antelope I bend my gaze,
  And on your Majesty, whose mighty bow
  Has its string firmly braced; before my eyes
  The god that wields the trident  seems revealed.
  Chasing the deer that flies from him in vain.

**KING.**
Charioteer, this fleet antelope has drawn us far from my attendants. See! there he runs:
  Aye and anon his graceful neck he bends
  To cast a glance at the pursuing car;
  And dreading now the swift-descending shaft,
  Contracts into itself his slender frame;
  About his path, in scattered fragments strewn,
  The half-chewed grass falls from his panting mouth;
  See! in his airy bounds he seems to fly,
  And leaves no trace upon th' elastic turf.

*With astonishment.*

How now! swift as is our pursuit, I scarce can see him.

**CHARIOTEER.**
Sire, the ground here is full of hollows; I have therefore drawn in the reins and checked the speed of the chariot. Hence the deer has somewhat gained upon us. Now that we are passing over level ground, we shall have no difficulty in overtaking him.

**KING.**

Loosen the reins, then.

**CHARIOTEER.**

*The King is obeyed.*
*Drives the chariot at full speed.*

Great Prince, see I see!
  Responsive to the slackened rein, the steeds,
  Chafing with eager rivalry, career
  With emulative fleetness o'er the plain;
  Their necks outstretched, their waving plumes, that late
  Fluttered above their brows, are motionless ;
  Their sprightly ears, but now erect, bent low;
  Themselves unsullied by the circling dust,
  That vainly follows on their rapid course.

**KING.**
*Joyously.*

In good sooth, the horses seem as if they would outstrip the steeds of Indra
and the Sun .
  That which but now showed to my view minute
  Quickly assumes dimension; that which seemed
  A moment since disjoined in diverse parts,
  Looks suddenly like one compacted whole;
  That which is really crooked in its shape
  In the far distance left, grows regular;
  Wondrous the chariot's speed, that in a breath,
  Makes the near distant and the distant near.
Now, Charioteer, see me kill the deer.

*Takes aim.*

**A VOICE BEHIND THE SCENES.**
Hold, O King! this deer belongs to our hermitage.
Kill it not! kill it not!

**CHARIOTEER.**
*Listening and looking.*

Great King, some hermits have stationed themselves so as to screen the
antelope at the very moment of its coming within range of your arrow.

**KING.**
*Hastily.*
Then stop the horses.

**CHARIOTEER.**
I obey.

*Stops the chariot.*
*Enter a HERMIT, and two others with him.*

**HERMIT.**
*Raising his hand.*

This deer, O King, belongs to our hermitage. Kill it not! kill it not!
  Now heaven forbid this barbed shaft descend

*379*

Upon the fragile body of a fawn,
Like fire upon a heap of tender flowers!
Can thy steel bolts no meeter quarry find
Than the warm life-blood of a harmless deer?
Restore, great Prince, thy weapon to its quiver.
More it becomes thy arms to shield the weak,
Than to bring anguish on the innocent.

**KING.**
'Tis done.

*Replaces the arrow in its quiver.*

**HERMIT.**
Worthy is this action of a Prince, the light of Puru's race .
  Well does this act befit a Prince like thee,
  Right worthy is it of thine ancestry.
  Thy guerdon be a son of peerless worth,
  Whose wide dominion shall embrace the earth.

**BOTH THE OTHER HERMITS.**
*Raising their hands.*

May heaven indeed grant thee a son, a sovereign of the earth from sea to sea!

**KING.**
*Bowing.*

I accept with gratitude a Bráhman's benediction.

**HERMIT.**
We came hither, mighty Prince, to collect sacrificial wood. Here on the banks
of the Málini you may perceive the hermitage of the great sage Kanwa .
If other duties require not your presence, deign to enter and accept our
hospitality.
  When you behold our penitential rites
  Performed without impediment by saints
  Rich only in devotion, then with pride
  Will you reflect:—Such are the holy men
  Who call me Guardian; such the men for whom
  To wield the bow I bare my nervous arm,
  Scarred by the motion of the glancing string.

**KING.**
Is the Chief of your Society now at home?

**HERMIT.**
No; he has gone to Soma-tírtha  to propitiate Destiny, which threatens his
daughter [S']akoontalá with some calamity; but he has commissioned her in
his absence to entertain all guests with hospitality.

**KING.**
Good! I will pay her a visit. She will make me acquainted with the mighty
sage's acts of penance and devotion.

**HERMIT.**
And we will depart on our errand.

*Exit with his companions.*

**KING.**
Charioteer, urge on the horses. We will at least purify our souls by a sight of this hallowed retreat.

**CHARIOTEER.**
Your Majesty is obeyed.

*Drives the chariot with great velocity.*

**KING.**
*Looking all about him.*
Charioteer, even without being told, I should have known that these were the precincts of a grove consecrated to penitential rites.

**CHARIOTEER.**
How so?

**KING.**
Do not you observe?
  Beneath the trees, whose hollow trunks afford
  Secure retreat to many a nestling brood
  Of parrots, scattered grains of rice lie strewn.
  Lo! here and there are seen the polished slabs
  That serve to bruise the fruit of Ingudí .
  The gentle roe-deer, taught to trust in man,
  Unstartled hear our voices. On the paths
  Appear the traces of bark-woven vests
  Borne dripping from the limpid fount of waters.
And mark!
  Laved are the roots of trees by deep canals ,
  Whose glassy waters tremble in the breeze;
  The sprouting verdure of the leaves is dimmed
  By dusky wreaths of upward curling smoke
  From burnt oblations; and on new-mown lawns
  Around our car graze leisurely the fawns.

**CHARIOTEER.**
I observe it all.

**KING.**
*Advancing a little further.*

The inhabitants of this sacred retreat must not be disturbed.
Stay the chariot, that I may alight.

**CHARIOTEER.**
The reins are held in. Your Majesty may descend.

**KING.**

*Alighting.*
Charioteer, groves devoted to penance must be entered in humble attire.
Take these ornaments.

*Delivers his ornaments and bow to CHARIOTEER.*

Charioteer, see that the horses are watered, and attend to them until I return from visiting the inhabitants of the hermitage.

**CHARIOTEER.**
I Will.

*Exit.*

**KING.**
*Walking and looking about.*

Here is the entrance to the hermitage. I will now go in.

*Entering and feeling a throbbing sensation in his arm.*

Serenest peace is in this calm retreat,
By passion's breath unruffled; what portends
My throbbing arm ? Why should it whisper here
Of happy love? Yet everywhere around us
Stand the closed portals of events unknown.

**A VOICE BEHIND THE SCENES.**
This way, my dear companions; this way.

**KING.**
*Listening.*

Hark! I hear voices to the right of yonder grove of trees. I will walk in that direction.

*Walking and looking about.*

Ah! here are the maidens of the hermitage coming this way to water the shrubs, carrying water-pots proportioned to their strength.

*Gazing at them.*

How graceful they look!
  In palaces such charms are rarely ours;
  The woodland plants outshine the garden flowers.
I will conceal myself in this shade and watch them.

*Stands gazing at them.*

*Enter [S']AKOONTALÁ, with her two female companions, employed in the manner described.*

**[S']AKOONTALÁ**
This way, my dear companions; this way.

**ANASÚYÁ.**
Dear [S']akoontalá, one would think that father Kanwa had more affection for the shrubs of the hermitage even than for you, seeing he assigns to you, who are yourself as delicate as the fresh-blown jasmine, the task of filling with water the trenches which encircle their roots.

**[S']AKOONTALÁ.**
Dear Anasúyá, although I am charged by my good father with this duty, yet I cannot regard it as a task. I really feel a sisterly love for these plants.

*Continues watering the shrubs.*

**KING.**
Can this be the daughter of Kanwa? The saintly man, though descended from the great Kasyapa, must be very deficient in judgment to habituate such a maiden to the life of a recluse.

The sage who would this form of artless grace
Inure to penance, thoughtlessly attempts
To cleave in twain the hard acacia's stem
With the soft edge of a blue lotus-leaf.

Well! concealed behind this tree, I will watch her without raising her suspicions.

*Conceals himself.*

**[S']AKOONTALÁ.**
Good Anasúyá, Priyamvadá has drawn this bark-dress too tightly about my chest. I pray thee, loosen it a little.

**ANASÚYÁ.**
I will. [Loosens it.

**PRIYAMVADÁ.**
*Smiling.*

Why do you lay the blame on me? Blame rather your own blooming youthfulness which imparts fulness to your bosom.

**KING.**
A most just observation!

This youthful form, whose bosom's swelling charms
By the bark's knotted tissue are concealed,
Like some fair bud close folded in its sheath,
Gives not to view the blooming of its beauty.

But what am I saying? In real truth this bark-dress, though ill-suited to her figure, sets it off like an ornament.

The lotus  with the [S']aivala  entwined
Is not a whit less brilliant; dusky spots
Heighten the lustre of the cold-rayed moon;
This lovely maiden in her dress of bark
Seems all the lovelier. E'en the meanest garb
Gives to true beauty fresh attractiveness.

**[S']AKOONTALÁ.**
*Looking before her.*
Yon Ke[S']ara-tree  beckons to me with its young shoots, which, as the breeze waves them to and fro, appear like slender fingers. I will go and attend to it.

*Walks towards it.*

**PRIYAMVADÁ.**
Dear [S']akoontalá, prithee, rest in that attitude one moment.

**[S']AKOONTALÁ.**
Why so?

**PRIYAMVADÁ**
The Ke[S']ara-tree, whilst your graceful form bends about its stem, appears as if it were wedded to some lovely twining creeper.

**[S']AKOONTALÁ.**
Ah! saucy girl, you are most appropriately named Priyamvadá ('Speaker of flattering things').

**KING.**
What Priyamvadá says, though complimentary, is nevertheless true. Verily,
  Her ruddy lip vies with the opening bud;
  Her graceful arms are as the twining stalks;
  And her whole form is radiant with the glow
  Of youthful beauty, as the tree with bloom.

**ANASÚYÁ.**
See, dear [S']akoontalá, here is the young jasmine, which you named 'the Moonlight of the Grove,' the self-elected wife of the mango-tree. Have you forgotten it?

**[S']AKOONTALÁ.**
Rather will I forget myself.

*Approaching the plant and looking at it.*

How delightful is the season when the jasmine-creeper and the mango-tree seem thus to unite in mutual embraces! The fresh blossoms of the jasmine resemble the bloom of a young bride, and the newly-formed shoots of the mango appear to make it her natural protector.

*Continues gazing at it.*

**PRIYAMVADÁ.**
Do you know, my Anasúyá, why [S']akoontalá gazes so intently at the jasmine?

**ANASÚYÁ.**
No, indeed, I cannot imagine. I pray thee tell me.

**PRIYAMVADÁ.**
She is wishing that as the jasmine is united to a suitable tree, so, in like manner, she may obtain a husband worthy of her.

**[S']AKOONTALÁ.**
Speak for yourself, girl; this is the thought in your own mind.

*Continues watering the flowers.*

**KING.**
Would that my union with her were permissible ! and yet I hardly dare hope that the maiden is sprung from a caste different from that of the Head of the hermitage. But away with doubt:
  That she is free to wed a warrior-king
  My heart attests. For, in conflicting doubts,
  The secret promptings of the good man's soul
  Are an unerring index of the truth.
However, come what may, I will ascertain the fact.

**[S']AKOONTALÁ.**
*In a flurry.*
Ah! a bee, disturbed by the sprinkling of the water, has left the young jasmine, and is trying to settle on my face.

*Attempts to drive it away.*

**KING.**
*Gazing at her ardently.*

Beautiful! there is something charming even in her repulse.
  Where'er the bee his eager onset plies,
  Now here, now there, she darts her kindling eyes;
  What love hath yet to teach, fear teaches now,
  The furtive glances and the frowning brow.

*In a tone of envy.*

  Ah, happy bee! how boldly dost thou try
  To steal the lustre from her sparkling eye;
  And in thy circling movements hover near,
  To murmur tender secrets in her ear;
  Or, as she coyly waves her hand, to sip
  Voluptuous nectar from her lower lip!
  While rising doubts my heart's fond hopes destroy,
  Thou dost the fulness of her charms enjoy.

**[S']AKOONTALÁ.**
This impertinent bee will not rest quiet. I must move elsewhere.

*Moving a few steps off, and casting a glance around.*

How now! he is following me here. Help! my dear friends, help! deliver me
from the attacks of this troublesome insect.

**PRIYAMVADÁ AND ANASÚYÁ.**
How can we deliver you? Call Dushyanta to your aid. The sacred groves are
under the King's special protection.

**KING.**
An excellent opportunity for me to show myself.
Fear not—

*Checks himself when the words are half-uttered; Aside.*
But stay, if I introduce myself in this manner, they will know me to be the
King. Be it so, I will accost them, nevertheless.

**[S']AKOONTALÁ.**

*Moving a step or two further off.*

What! it still persists in following me.

**KING.**
*Advancing hastily.*

  When mighty Puru's offspring sways the earth,
  And o'er the wayward holds his threatening rod,
  Who dares molest the gentle maids that keep
  Their holy vigils here in Kanwa's grove?

*All look at the KING, and all are embarrassed.*

**ANASÚYÁ.**
Kind Sir, no outrage has been committed; only our dear friend here was

*385*

teased by the attacks of a troublesome bee.

*Points to [S']AKOONTALÁ.*

**KING.**

*Turning to [S']AKOONTALÁ.*
I trust all is well with your devotional rites ?

*[S']AKOONTALÁ stands confused and silent.*

**ANASÚYÁ.**
All is well indeed, now that we are honoured by the reception of a
distinguished guest. Dear [S']akoontalá, go, bring from the hermitage an
offering of flowers, rice, and fruit. This water that we have brought with us
will serve to bathe our guest's feet .

**KING.**
The rites of hospitality are already performed; your truly kind words are the
best offering I can receive.

**PRIYAMVADÁ.**
At least be good enough, gentle Sir, to sit down awhile, and rest yourself on
this seat shaded by the leaves of the Sapta-parna tree .

**KING.**
You, too, must all be fatigued by your employment.

**ANASÚYÁ.**
Dear [S']akoontalá, there is no impropriety in our sitting by the side of our
guest; come, let us sit down here.

*All sit down together.*

**[S']AKOONTALÁ.**

*Aside.*

How is it that the sight of this made me sensible of emotions inconsistent
with religious vows?

**KING.**
*Gazing at them all By turns.*

How charmingly your friendship is in keeping with the equality of your ages
and appearance!

**PRIYAMVADÁ.**
*Aside to ANASÚYÁ.*
Who can this person be, whose lively yet dignified manner, and polite
conversation, bespeak him a man of high rank?

**ANASÚYÁ.**
I, too, my dear, am very curious to know. I will ask him myself.

*Aloud*
Your kind words, noble Sir, fill me with confidence, and prompt me to
inquire of what regal family our noble guest is the ornament? what country
is now mourning his absence? and what induced a person so delicately
nurtured to expose himself to the fatigue of visiting this grove of penance?

**[S']AKOONTALÁ.**
*Aside.*

Be not troubled, O my heart, Anasúyá is giving utterance to thy thoughts.

**KING.**
*Aside.*

How now shall I reply? shall I make myself known, or shall I still disguise my real rank? I have it; I will answer her thus. [Aloud.] I am the person charged by his Majesty, the descendant of Puru, with the administration of justice and religion; and am come to this sacred grove to satisfy myself that the rites of the hermits are free from obstruction.

**ANASÚYÁ.**
The hermits, then, and all the members of our religious society, have now a guardian.

*[[S']AKOONTALÁ gazes bashfully at the KING.*

**PRIYAMVADÁ AND ANASÚYÁ.**
*[Perceiving the state of her feelings, and of the KING'S. Aside to [S']AKOONTALÁ.*
Dear [S']akoontalá, if father Kanwa were but at home to-day—

**[S']AKOONTALÁ.**
*Angrily.*

What if he were?

**PRIYAMVADÁ AND ANASÚYÁ.**
He would honour this our distinguished guest with an offering of the most precious of his possessions.

**[S']AKOONTALÁ.**
Go to! you have some silly idea in your minds, I will not listen to such remarks.

**KING.**
May I be allowed, in my turn, to ask you maidens a few particulars respecting your friend?

**PRIYAMVADÁ AND ANASÚYÁ.**
Your request, Sir, is an honour.

**KING.**
The sage Kanwa lives in the constant practice of austerities.
How, then, can this friend of yours be called his daughter?

**ANASÚYÁ.**
I will explain to you. Sir. You have heard of an illustrious sage of regal caste, Vi[s']wámitra, whose family name is Kau[S']ika .

**KING.**
I have.

**ANASÚYÁ.**
Know that he is the real father of our friend. The venerable Kanwa is only her reputed father. He it was who brought her up, when she was deserted by her mother.

*387*

KING.
'Deserted by her mother!' My curiosity is excited; pray let me hear the story from the beginning.

ANASÚYÁ.
You shall hear it, Sir. Some time since, this sage of regal caste, while performing a most severe penance on the banks of the river Godávarí, excited the jealousy and alarm of the gods; insomuch that they despatched a lovely nymph named Menaká to interrupt his devotions.

KING.
The inferior gods, I am aware, are jealous of the power which the practice of excessive devotion confers on mortals.

ANASÚYÁ.
Well, then, it happened that Vi[s']wámitra, gazing on the bewitching beauty of that nymph at a season when, spring being in its glory—

*Stops short, and appears confused.*

KING.
The rest may be easily divined. [S']akoontalá, then, is the offspring of the nymph.

ANASÚYÁ.
Just so.

KING.
It is quite intelligible.
  How would a mortal to such charms give birth?
  The lightning's radiance flashes not from earth.

*[S']AKOONTALÁ remains modestly seated with downcast eyes; Aside.*

And so my desire has really scope for its indulgence. Yet I am still distracted by doubts, remembering the pleasantry of her female companions respecting her wish for a husband.

PRIYAMVADÁ.
*Looking with a smile at [S']AKOONTALÁ, and then turning towards the KING.*

You seem desirous, Sir, of asking something further.

*[S']AKOONTALÁ makes a chiding gesture with her finger.*

KING.
You conjecture truly. I am so eager to hear the particulars of your friend's history, that I have still another question to ask.

PRIYAMVADÁ.
Scruple not to do so. Persons who lead the life of hermits may be questioned unreservedly.

KING.
I wish to ascertain one point respecting your friend.
  Will she be bound by solitary vows
  Opposed to love, till her espousals only?
  Or ever dwell with these her cherished fawns,

Whose eyes, in lustre vying with her own,
Return her gaze of sisterly affection?

**PRIYAMVADÁ.**
Hitherto, Sir, she has been engaged in the practice of religious duties, and
has lived in subjection to her foster-father; but it is now his fixed intention to
give her away in marriage to a husband worthy of her.

**KING.**
*Aside.*

His intention may be easily carried into effect.
  Be hopeful, O my heart, thy harrowing doubts
  Are past and gone; that which thou didst believe
  To be as unapproachable as fire,
  Is found a glittering gem that may be touched.

**[S']AKOONTALÁ.**
*Pretending anger.*

Anasúyá, I shall leave you.

**ANASÚYÁ.**
Why so?

**[S']AKOONTALÁ.**
That I may go and report this impertinent Priyamvadá to the venerable
matron, Gautamí .

**ANASÚYÁ.**
Surely, dear friend, it would not be right to leave a distinguished guest before he
has received the rites of hospitality, and quit his presence in this wilful manner.

*[S']AKOONTALÁ, without answering a word, moves away.*

**KING.**
*Making a movement to arrest her departure, but checking himself. Aside.*

Ah! a lover's feelings betray themselves by his gestures.
  When I would fain have stayed the maid, a sense
  Of due decorum checked my bold design;
  Though I have stirred not, yet my mien betrays
  My eagerness to follow on her steps.

**PRIYAMVADÁ.**
*Holding [S']AKOONTALÁ back.*

Dear [S']akoontalá, it does not become you to go away in this manner.

**[S']AKOONTALÁ.**
*Frowning.*

Why not, pray?

**PRIYAMVADÁ.**
You are under a promise to water two more shrubs for me. When you have
paid your debt, you shall go, and not before.

*Forces her to turn back.*

389

KING.

Spare her this trouble, gentle maiden. The exertion of watering the shrubs has already fatigued her.

  The water-jar has overtasked the strength
  Of her slim arms; her shoulders droop, her hands
  Are ruddy with the glow of quickened pulses;
  E'en now her agitated breath imparts
  Unwonted tremor to her heaving breast;
  The pearly drops that mar the recent bloom
  Of the [S']irísha pendent in her ear,
  Gather in clustering circles on her cheek;
  Loosed is the fillet of her hair; her hand
  Restrains the locks that struggle to be free.

Suffer me, then, thus to discharge the debt for you.

*[Offers a ring to PRIYAMVADÁ. Both the maidens, reading the name DUSHYANTA on the seal, look at each other with surprise.*

KING.

Nay, think not that I am King Dushyanta. I am only the King's officer, and this is the ring which I have received from him as my credentials.

PRIYAMVADÁ.

The greater the reason you ought not to part with the ring from your finger. I am content to release her from her obligation at your simple request.

*With a smile.*

Now, [S']akoontalá, my love, you are at liberty to retire, thanks to the intercession of this noble stranger, or rather of this mighty prince.

[S']AKOONTALÁ.

*Aside.*

My movements are no longer under my own control.

*Aloud.*

Pray, what authority have you over me, either to send me away or keep me back?

KING.

*Gazing at [S']AKOONTALÁ. Aside.*

Would I could ascertain whether she is affected towards me as I am towards her! At any rate, my hopes are free to indulge themselves. Because,

  Although she mingles not her words with mine,
  Yet doth her listening ear drink in my speech;
  Although her eye shrinks from my ardent gaze,
  No form but mine attracts its timid glances.

A VOICE BEHIND THE SCENES.

O hermits, be ready to protect the animals belonging to our hermitage. King Dushyanta, amusing himself with hunting, is near at hand.

  Lo! by the feet of prancing horses raised,
  Thick clouds of moving dust, like glittering swarms
  Of locusts, in the glow of eventide,
  Fall on the branches of our sacred trees

Where hang the dripping vests of woven bark,
Bleached by the waters of the cleansing fountain.
And see!
Scared by the royal chariot in its course,
With headlong haste an elephant invades
The hallowed precincts of our sacred grove;
Himself the terror of the startled deer,
And an embodied hindrance to our rites.
The hedge of creepers clinging to his feet,
Feeble obstruction to his mad career,
Is dragged behind him in a tangled chain;
And with terrific shock one tusk he drives
Into the riven body of a tree,
Sweeping before him all impediments.

KING.
*Aside.*

Out upon it! my retinue are looking for me, and are disturbing this holy
retreat. Well! there is no help for it; I must go and meet them.

PRIYAMVADÁ AND ANASÚYÁ.
Noble Sir, we are terrified by the accidental disturbance caused by the wild
elephant. Permit us to return to the cottage.

KING.
*Hastily.*

Go, gentle maidens. It shall be our care that no injury happen to the hermitage.

*All rise up.*

PRIYAMVADÁ AND ANASÚYÁ.
After such poor hospitality, we are ashamed to request the honour of a
second visit from you.

KING.
Say not so. The mere sight of you, sweet maidens, has been to me the
best entertainment.

[S']AKOONTALÁ.
Anasúyá, a pointed blade of Ku[s']a-grass has pricked my foot; and my bark-
mantle is caught in the branch of a Kuruvaka-bush . Be so good as to wait for
me until I have disentangled it.

*Exit with her two companions, after making pretexts for delay, that she may steal
glances at the KING.*

KING.
I have no longer any desire to return to the city. I will therefore rejoin my
attendants, and make them encamp somewhere in the vicinity of this sacred
grove. In good truth, [S']akoontalá has taken such possession of my thoughts,
that I cannot turn myself in any other direction.
My limbs drawn onward leave my heart behind,
Like silken pennon borne against the wind.

*Act II*

SCENE.——_A plain on the skirts of the forest.

*Enter the Jester _ MÁ[T.]HAVYA, in a melancholy mood.*

## MÁ[T.]HAVYA.
*Sighing.*
Heigh-ho! what an unlucky fellow I am! worn to a shadow by my royal friend's sporting propensities. 'Here's a deer!' 'There goes a boar!' 'Yonder's a tiger!' This is the only burden of our talk, while in the heat of the meridian sun we toil on from jungle to jungle, wandering about in the paths of the woods, where the trees afford us no shelter. Are we thirsty? We have nothing to drink but the dirty water of some mountain stream mixed with dry leaves, which give it a most pungent flavour. Are we hungry? We have nothing to eat but roast game , which we must swallow down at odd times, as best we can. Even at night there is no peace to be had. Sleeping is out of the question, with joints all strained by dancing attendance upon my sporting friend; or if I do happen to doze, I am awakened at the very earliest dawn by the horrible din of a lot of rascally beaters and huntsmen, who must needs surround the wood before sunrise, and deafen me with their clatter. Nor are these my only troubles. Here's a fresh grievance, like a new boil rising upon an old one! Yesterday, while we were lagging behind, my royal friend entered yonder hermitage after a deer; and there, as ill-luck would have it, caught sight of a beautiful girl, called [S']akoontalá, the hermit's daughter. From that moment, not another thought about returning to the city! and all last night not a wink of sleep did he get for thinking of the damsel. What is to be done? At any rate I will be on the watch for him as soon as he has finished his toilet.

*Walking and looking about.*

Oh! here he comes, attended by the Yavana women , with bows in their hands, wearing garlands of wild flowers. What shall I do? I have it. I will pretend to stand in the easiest attitude for resting my bruised and crippled limbs.

*Stands leaning on a staff.*

*Enter King DUSHYANTA, followed by a retinue, in the manner described.*

## KING.
True, by no easy conquest may I win her,
Yet are my hopes encouraged by her mien,
Love is not yet triumphant; but, methinks,
The hearts of both are ripe for his delights.

*Smiling.*

Ah! thus does the lover delude himself; judging of the state of his loved one's feelings by his own desires. But yet,
The stolen glance with half-averted eye,
The hesitating gait, the quick rebuke
Addressed to her companion, who would fain
Have stayed her counterfeit departure; these
Are signs not unpropitious to my suit.
So eagerly the lover feeds his hopes,
Claiming each trivial gesture for his own.

## MÁ[T.]HAVYA.
*Still in the same attitude.*

Ah, friends, my hands cannot move to greet you with the usual salutation. I

*392*

can only just command my lips to wish your Majesty victory.

KING.
Why, what has paralysed your limbs?

MÁ[T.]HAVYA.
You might as well ask me how my eye comes to water after you have poked your finger into it.

KING.
I don't understand you; speak more intelligibly.

MÁ[T.]HAVYA.
Ah, my dear friend, is yonder upright reed transformed into a crooked plant by its own act, or by the force of the current?

KING.
The current of the river causes it, I suppose.

MÁ[T.]HAVYA.
Ay; just as you are the cause of my crippled limbs.

KING.
How so?

MÁ[T.]HAVYA.
Here are you living the life of a wild man of the woods in a savage unfrequented region, while your State-affairs are left to shift for themselves; and as for poor me, I am no longer master of my own limbs, but have to follow you about day after day in your chases after wild animals, till my bones are all crippled and out of joint. Do, my dear friend, let me have one day's rest.

KING.
*Aside.*

This fellow little knows, while he talks in this manner, that my mind is wholly engrossed by recollections of the hermit's daughter, and quite as disinclined to the chase as his own.
　No longer can I bend my well-braced bow
　Against the timid deer; nor e'er again
　With well-aimed arrows can I think to harm
　These her beloved associates, who enjoy
　The privilege of her companionship;
　Teaching her tender glances in return.

MÁ[T.]HAVYA.
*Looking in the King's face.*

I may as well speak to the winds, for any attention you pay to my requests. I suppose you have something on your mind, and are talking it over to yourself.

KING.
*Smiling.*

I was only thinking that I ought not to disregard a friend's request.

MÁ[T.]HAVYA.

*393*

Then may the King live for ever!

*Moves off.*

**KING.**
Stay a moment, my dear friend. I have something else to say to you.

**MÁ[T.]HAVYA.**
Say on, then.

**KING.**
When you have rested, you must assist me in another business which will give you no fatigue.

**MÁ[T.]HAVYA.**
In eating something nice, I hope.

**KING.**
You shall know at some future time.

**MÁ[T.]HAVYA.**
No time better than the present.

**KING.**
What ho, there!

**WARDER.**
*Entering.*
What are your Majesty's commands?

**KING.**
O Raivatika, bid the General of the forces attend.

**WARDER.**
I will, Sire.

*Exit and re-enters with the GENERAL.*

Come forward, General; his Majesty is looking towards you, and has some order to give you.

**GENERAL.**
*Looking at the KING.*

Though hunting is known to produce ill effects, my royal master has derived
only benefit from it. For
  Like the majestic elephant that roams
  O'er mountain wilds, so does the King display
  A stalwart frame, instinct with vigorous life.
  His brawny arms and manly chest are scored
  By frequent passage of the sounding string;
  Unharmed he bears the midday sun; no toil
  His mighty spirit daunts; his sturdy limbs,
  Stripped of redundant flesh, relinquish nought
  Of their robust proportions, but appear
  In muscle, nerve, and sinewy fibre cased.

*Approaching the KING.*

Victory to the King! We have tracked the wild beasts to their lairs in the forest. Why delay, when everything is ready?

**KING.**

My friend Má[T.]Havya here has been disparaging the chase, till he has taken away all my relish for it.

**GENERAL.**
*Aside to MÁ[T.]HAVYA.*

Persevere in your opposition, my good fellow; I will sound the
King's real feelings, and humour him accordingly.

*Aloud.*

The blockhead talks nonsense, and your Majesty in your own person furnishes the best proof of it. Observe, Sire, the advantage and pleasure the hunter derives from the chase.

**MÁ[T.]HAVYA.**
*Angrily.*

Away! tempter, away! The King has recovered his senses, and is himself again. As for you, you may, if you choose, wander about from forest to forest, till some old bear seizes you by the nose, and makes a mouthful of you.

**KING.**

My good General, as we are just now in the neighbourhood of a consecrated grove, your panegyric upon hunting is somewhat ill-timed, and I cannot assent to all you have said. For the present,
  All undisturbed the buffaloes shall sport
  In yonder pool, and with their ponderous horns
  Scatter its tranquil waters, while the deer,
  Couched here and there in groups beneath the shade
  Of spreading branches, ruminate in peace.
  And all securely shall the herd of boars
  Feed on the marshy sedge; and thou, my bow,
  With slackened string, enjoy a long repose.

**GENERAL.**
So please your Majesty, it shall be as you desire.

**KING.**
Recall, then, the beaters who were sent in advance to surround the forest. My troops must not be allowed to disturb this sacred retreat, and irritate its pious inhabitants.
  Know that within the calm and cold recluse
  Lurks unperceived a germ of smothered flame,
  All-potent to destroy; a latent fire
  That rashly kindled bursts with fury forth;
  As in the disc of crystal  that remains
  Cool to the touch, until the solar ray
  Falls on its polished surface, and excites
  The burning heat that lies within concealed.

**GENERAL.**
Your Majesty's commands shall be obeyed.

**MÁ[T.]HAVYA.**
Off with you, you son of a slave! Your nonsense won't go down here, my fine fellow.

*Exit GENERAL.*

**KING.**
*Looking at his attendants.*

Here, women, take my hunting-dress; and you, Raivatika, keep guard
carefully outside.

**ATTENDANTS.**
We will, Sire.

*Exeunt.*

**MÁ[T.]HAVYA.**
Now that you have got rid of these plagues, who have been buzzing about us
like so many flies, sit down, do, on that stone slab, with the shade of the tree
as your canopy, and I will seat myself by you quite comfortably.

**KING.**
Go you, and sit down first.

**MÁ[T.]HAVYA.**
Come along, then.

*Both walk on a little way, and seat themselves.*

**KING.**
Má[T.]Havya, it may be said of you that you have never beheld anything
worth seeing; for your eyes have not yet looked upon the loveliest object in
creation.

**MÁ[T.]HAVYA.**
How can you say so, when I see your Majesty before me at this moment?

**KING.**
It is very natural that every one should consider his own friend perfect; but I
was alluding to [S']akoontalá, the brightest ornament of these hallowed groves.

**MÁ[T.]HAVYA.**
*Aside.*
I understand well enough, but I am not going to humour him.

*Aloud.*

If, as you intimate, she is a hermit's daughter, you cannot lawfully ask her in
marriage. You may as well then dismiss her from your mind, for any good
the mere sight of her can do.

**KING.**
Think you that a descendant of the mighty Puru could fix his affections on
an unlawful object?
  Though, as men say, the offspring of the sage,
  The maiden to a nymph celestial owes
  Her being, and by her mother left on earth,
  Was found and nurtured by the holy man
  As his own daughter, in this hermitage.

*396*

So, when dissevered from its parent stalk,
Some falling blossom of the jasmine , wafted
Upon the sturdy sun-flower, is preserved
By its support from premature decay.

MÁ[T.]HAVYA.
*Smiling.*

This passion of yours for a rustic maiden, when you have so many gems of
women at home in your palace, seems to me very like the fancy of a man who
is tired of sweet dates, and longs for sour tamarinds as a variety.

KING.
You have not seen her, or you would not talk in this fashion.

MÁ[T.]HAVYA.
I can quite understand it must require something surpassingly attractive to
excite the admiration of such a great man as you.

KING.
I will describe her, my dear friend, in a few words,
  Man's all-wise Maker, wishing to create
  A faultless form, whose matchless symmetry
  Should far transcend Creation's choicest works,
  Did call together by his mighty will,
  And garner up in his eternal mind,
  A bright assemblage of all lovely things;
  And then, as in a picture, fashion them
  Into one perfect and ideal form—
  Such the divine, the wondrous prototype,
  Whence her fair shape was moulded into being.

MÁ[T.]HAVYA.
If that's the case, she must indeed throw all other beauties into
the shade.

KING.
To my mind she really does.
  This peerless maid is like a fragrant flower,
  Whose perfumed breath has never been diffused;
  A tender bud, that no profaning hand
  Has dared to sever from its parent stalk;
  A gem of priceless water, just released
  Pure and unblemished from its glittering bed.
  Or may the maiden haply be compared
  To sweetest honey, that no mortal lip
  Has sipped; or, rather, to the mellowed fruit
  Of virtuous actions in some former birth ,
  Now brought to full perfection? Lives the man
  Whom bounteous heaven has destined to espouse her?

MÁ[T.]HAVYA.
Make haste, then, to her aid; you have no time to lose, if you don't wish this
fruit of all the virtues to drop into the mouth of some greasy-headed rustic
of devout habits.

KING.
The lady is not her own mistress, and her foster-father is not
at home.

MÁ[T.]HAVYA.
Well, but tell me, did she look at all kindly upon you?

KING.
 Maidens brought up in a hermitage are naturally
 shy and reserved; but for all that
 She did look towards me, though she quick withdrew
 Her stealthy glances when she met my gaze;
 She smiled upon me sweetly, but disguised
 With maiden grace the secret of her smiles.
 Coy love was half unveiled; then, sudden checked
 By modesty, left half to be divined.

MÁ[T.]HAVYA.
Why, of course, my dear friend, you never could seriously expect that at the
very first sight she would fall over head ears in love with you, and without
more ado come and sit in your lap.

KING.
 When we parted from each other, she betrayed
 her liking for me by clearer indications, but still with the
 utmost modesty.
 Scarce had the fair one from my presence passed,
 When, suddenly, without apparent cause,
 She stopped; and, counterfeiting pain, exclaimed,
 'My foot is wounded by this prickly grass,'
 Then, glancing at me tenderly, she feigned
 Another charming pretext for delay,
 Pretending that a bush had caught her robe
 And turned as if to disentangle it.

MÁ[T.]HAVYA
I trust you have laid in a good stock of provisions, for I see you intend
making this consecrated grove your game-preserve, and will be roaming here
in quest of sport for some time to come.

KING.
You must know, my good fellow, that I have been recognized by some of the
inmates of the hermitage. Now I want the assistance of your fertile invention,
in devising some excuse for going there again.

MÁ[T.]HAVYA.
There is but one expedient that I can suggest. You are the King, are you not?

KING.
What then?

MÁ[T.]HAVYA.
Say you have come for the sixth part of their grain , which they owe you for
tribute.

KING.

No, no, foolish man; those hermits pay me a very different kind of tribute,
which I value more than heaps of gold or jewels; observe,
  The tribute which my other subjects bring
  Must moulder into dust, but holy men
  Present me with a portion of the fruits
  Of penitential services and prayers—
  A precious and imperishable gift.

A VOICE BEHIND THE SCENES.
We are fortunate; here is the object of our search.

KING.
*Listening.*

Surely those must be the voices of hermits, to judge by their deep tones.

WARDER.
*Entering.*
Victory to the King! two young hermits are in waiting outside, and solicit an
audience of your Majesty.

KING.
Introduce them Immediately.

WARDER.
I will, my liege.

*Goes out, and re-enters with TWO YOUNG HERMITS.*

This way, Sirs, this way.

*Both the HERMITS _look at the KING.*

FIRST HERMIT.
How majestic is his mien, and yet what confidence it inspires! But this might
be expected in a king, whose character and habits have earned for him a title
only one degree removed from that of a Sage .
  In this secluded grove, whose sacred joys
  All may participate, he deigns to dwell
  Like one of us; and daily treasures up
  A store of purest merit for himself,
  By the protection of our holy rites.
  In his own person wondrously are joined
  Both majesty and saintlike holiness;
  And often chanted by inspired bards ,
  His hallowed title of 'Imperial Sage'
  Ascends in joyous accents to the skies.

SECOND HERMIT.
Bear in mind, Gautama, that this is the great Dushyanta, the friend of Indra.

FIRST HERMIT.
What of that?

SECOND HERMIT.
  Where is the wonder if his nervous arm,
  Puissant and massive as the iron bar
  That binds a castle-gateway, singly sways

*399*

The sceptre of the universal earth,
E'en to its dark-green boundary of waters?
Or if the gods, beholden to his aid
In their fierce warfare with the powers of hell ,
Should blend his name with Indra's in their songs
Of victory, and gratefully accord
No lower meed of praise to his braced bow,
Than to the thunders of the god of heaven?

BOTH THE HERMITS.
*Approaching.*

Victory to the King!

KING.
*Rising from his seat.*

Hail to you both!

BOTH THE HERMITS.
Heaven bless your Majesty!

*[They offer fruits.*

KING.
*Respectfully receiving the offering.*

Tell me, I pray you, the object of your visit.

BOTH THE HERMITS.
The inhabitants of the hermitage, having heard of your Majesty's sojourn in our neighbourhood, make this humble petition:—

KING.
What are their commands?

BOTH THE HERMITS.
In the absence of our Superior, the great sage Kanwa, evil demons are disturbing our sacrificial rites . Deign, therefore, accompanied by your charioteer, to take up your abode in our hermitage for a few days.

KING.
I am honoured by your invitation.

MÁ[T.]HAVYA.
*Aside.*

Most opportune and convenient, certainly!

KING.
*Smiling.*

Ho, there, Raivatika! Tell the charioteer from me to bring round the chariot with my bow.

WARDER.
I will, Sire.

*Exit.*

**BOTH THE HERMITS.**
*Joyfully.*

> Well it becomes the King by acts of grace
> To emulate the virtues of his race.
> Such acts thy lofty destiny attest;
> Thy mission is to succour the distressed.

**KING.**
*Bowing to the HERMITS.*

Go first, reverend Sirs, I will follow you immediately.

**BOTH THE HERMITS.**
May victory attend you!

*Exeunt.*

**KING.**
My dear Má[T.]Havya, are not you full of longing to see
[S']akoontalá?

**MÁ[T.]HAVYA.**
To tell you the truth, though I was just now brimful of desire to see her, I have not a drop left since this piece of news about the demons.

**KING.**
Never fear; you shall keep close to me for protection.

**MÁ[T.]HAVYA.**
Well, you must be my guardian-angel, and act the part of a very

*Vishnu to me.*

**WARDER.**
*Entering.*

Sire, the chariot is ready, and only waits to conduct you to victory. But here is a messenger named Karabhaka, just arrived from your capital, with a message from the Queen, your mother.

**KING.**
*Respectfully.*

How say you? a messenger from the venerable Queen?

**WARDER.**
Even so.

**KING.**
Introduce him at once.

**WARDER.**
I will, Sire.

*Goes out and re-enters with KARABHAKA.*

Behold the King. Approach.

**KARABHAKA.**

*401*

Victory to the King! The Queen-mother bids me say that in four days from the present time she intends celebrating a solemn ceremony for the advancement and preservation of her son. She expects that your Majesty will honour her with your presence on that occasion.

KING.
This places me in a dilemma. Here, on the one hand, is the commission of these holy men to be executed; and, on the other, the command of my revered parent to be obeyed. Both duties are too sacred to be neglected. What is to be done?

MÁ[T.]HAVYA.
You will have to take up an intermediate position between the two, like King Tri[s']anku , who was suspended between heaven and earth, because the sage Vi[s']wámitra commanded him to mount up to heaven, and the gods ordered him down again.

KING.
I am certainly very much perplexed. For here,
  Two different duties are required of me
  In widely distant places; how can I
  In my own person satisfy them both?
  Thus is my mind distracted, and impelled
  In opposite directions like a stream
  That, driven back by rocks, still rushes on,
  Forming two currents in its eddying course.

*Reflecting.*

Friend Má[T.]Havya, as you were my playfellow in childhood, the Queen has already received you like a second son; go you, then, back to her, and tell her of my solemn engagement to assist these holy men. You can supply my place in the ceremony, and act the part of a son to the Queen.

MÁ[T.]HAVYA.
With the greatest pleasure in the world; but don't suppose that I am really coward enough to have the slightest fear of those trumpery demons.

KING.
Oh! of course not; a great Bráhman like you could not possibly give way to such weakness.

MÁ[T.]HAVYA.
You must let me travel in a manner suitable to the King's younger brother.

KING.
Yes, I shall send my retinue with you, that there may be no farther disturbance in this sacred forest.

MÁ[T.]HAVYA,
*With a strut.*

Already I feel quite like a young prince.

KING.
*Aside.*

This is a giddy fellow, and in all probability he will let out the truth about my present pursuit to the women of the palace. What is to be done? I must say something to deceive him.

*Aloud to MÁ[T.]HAVYA, taking him by the hand.*

Dear friend, I am going to the hermitage wholly and solely out of respect for its pious inhabitants, and not because I have really any liking for [S'] akoontalá, the hermit's daughter. Observe:—
  What suitable communion could there be
  Between a monarch and a rustic girl?
  I did but feign an idle passion, friend,
  Take not in earnest what was said in jest.

**MÁ[T.]HAVYA.**
Don't distress yourself; I quite understand.

*Exeunt.*

# Prelude to Act III

## SCENE.—The Hermitage.

*Enter a YOUNG BRÁHMAN carrying bundles of ku[S']a-grass for the use of the sacrificing priest.*

**YOUNG BRÁHMAN.**
How wonderful is the power of King Dushyanta! No sooner did he enter our hermitage, than we were able to proceed with our sacrificial rites, unmolested by the evil demons.
  No need to fix the arrow to the bow;
  The mighty monarch sounds the quivering string,
  And, by the thunder of his arms dismayed,
  Our demon foes are scattered to the wind.
I must now, therefore, make haste and deliver to the sacrificing priests these bundles of Ku[s']a-grass, to be strewn round the altar.

*Walking and looking about; then addressing someone off the stage.*

Why, Priyamvadá, for whose use are you carrying that ointment of Usíra-root and those lotus-leaves with fibres attached to them?

*Listening for her answer.*

What Say you?—that [S']akoontalá is suffering from fever produced by exposure to the sun, and that this ointment is to cool her burning frame? Nurse her with care, then, Priyamvadá, for she is cherished by our reverend Superior as the very breath of his nostrils . I, for my part, will contrive that soothing waters, hallowed in the sacrifice, he administered to her by the hands of Gautamí.

*Exit.*

# Act III

## SCENE.—The Sacred Grove.

*Enter KING DUSHYANTA, with the air of one in love.*

**KING.**
*Sighing thoughtfully.*

403

The holy sage possesses magic power
In virtue of his penance; she, his ward,
Under the shadow of his tutelage,
Rests in security, I know it well;
Yet sooner shall the rushing cataract
In foaming eddies re-ascend the steep,
Than my fond heart turn back from its pursuit.

God of love! God of the flowery shafts ! we lovers are cruelly deceived by
thee, and by the Moon, however deserving of confidence you may both
appear.

For not to us do these thine arrows seem
Pointed with tender flowerets; not to us
Doth the pale Moon irradiate the earth
With beams of silver fraught with cooling dews;
But on our fevered frames the moon-beams fall
Like darts of fire, and every flower-tipt shaft
Of Káma , as it probes our throbbing hearts,
Seems to be barbed with hardest adamant.

Adorable god of love! hast thou no pity for me?

*In a tone of anguish.*

How can thy arrows be so sharp when they are pointed with flowers? Ah! I
know the reason:

E'en now in thine unbodied essence lurks
The fire of [S']iva's anger , like the flame
That ever hidden in the secret depths
Of ocean, smoulders there unseen . How else
Could'st thou, all immaterial as thou art,
Inflame our hearts thus fiercely?—thou, whose form
Was scorched to ashes by a sudden flash
From the offended god's terrific eye.

Yet, methinks,

Welcome this anguish, welcome to my heart
These rankling wounds inflicted by the god,
Who on his scutcheon bears the monster-fish
Slain by his prowess; welcome death itself,
So that, commissioned by the lord of love,
This fair one be my executioner.

Adorable divinity! Can I by no reproaches excite your commiseration?

Have I not daily offered at thy shrine
Innumerable vows, the only food
Of thine ethereal essence? Are my prayers
Thus to be slighted? Is it meet that thou
Should'st aim thy shafts at thy true votary's heart,
Drawing thy bow-string even to thy ear?

*Pacing up and down in a melancholy manner.*

Now that the holy men have completed their rites, and have no more need of
my services, how shall I dispel my melancholy?

*Sighing.*

I have but one resource. Oh for another sight of the Idol of my soul! I will
seek her.

*Glancing at the sun.*

*404*

In all probability, as the sun's heat is now at its height, [S']akoontalá is passing her time under the shade of the bowers on the banks of the Máliní, attended by her maidens. I will go and look for her there.

*Walking and looking about.*

I suspect the fair one has but just passed by this avenue of young trees.
  Here, as she tripped along, her fingers plucked
  The opening buds; these lacerated plants,
  Shorn of their fairest blossoms by her hand,
  Seem like dismembered trunks, whose recent wounds
  Are still unclosed; while from the bleeding socket
  Of many a severed stalk, the milky juice
  Still slowly trickles, and betrays her path.

*Feeling a breeze.*

What a delicious breeze meets me in this spot!
  Here may the zephyr, fragrant with the scent
  Of lotuses, and laden with the spray
  Caught from the waters of the rippling stream,
  Fold in its close embrace my fevered limbs.

*Walking and looking about.*

She must be somewhere in the neighbourhood of this arbour of overhanging creepers enclosed by plantations of cane;

*Looking down.*

  For at the entrance here I plainly see
  A line of footsteps printed in the sand.
  Here are the fresh impressions of her feet;
  Their well-known outline faintly marked in front,
  More deeply towards the heel; betokening
  The graceful undulation of her gait .
I will peep through those branches.

*Walking and looking. With transport.*

Ah! now my eyes are gratified by an entrancing sight. Yonder is the beloved of my heart reclining on a rock strewn with flowers, and attended by her two friends. How fortunate! Concealed behind the leaves, I will listen to their conversation, without raising their suspicions.

*Stands concealed, and gazes at them.*

*[S']AKOONTALÁ and her two attendants, holding fans in their hands, are discovered as described.*

## PRIYAMVADÁ AND ANASÚYÁ.
*Fanning her. In a tone of affection.*

Dearest [S']akoontalá, is the breeze raised by these broad lotus-leaves refreshing to you?

## [S']AKOONTALÁ.
Dear friends, why should you trouble yourselves to fan me?

*PRIYAMVADÁ and ANASÚYÁ look sorrowfully at one another.*

KING.
[S']akoontalá seems indeed to be seriously ill.

*Thoughtfully.*

Can it be the intensity of the heat that has affected her? or does my heart suggest the true cause of her malady?

*Gazing at her passionately.*

Why should I doubt it?
  The maiden's spotless bosom is o'erspread
  With cooling balsam; on her slender arm
  Her only bracelet, twined with lotus-stalks,
  Hangs loose and withered; her recumbent form
  Betokens languor. Ne'er could noon-day sun
  Inflict such fair disorder on a maid—
  No, love, and love alone, is here to blame.

PRIYAMVADÁ.
*Aside to ANASÚYÁ.*

I have observed, Anasúyá, that [S']akoontalá has been indisposed ever since her first interview with King Dushyanta. Depend upon it, her ailment is to be traced to that source.

ANASÚYÁ.
The same suspicion, dear, has crossed my mind. But I will at once ask her and ascertain the truth.

*Aloud.*

Dear [S']akoontalá, I am about to put a question to you. Your indisposition is really very serious.

[S']AKOONTALÁ.
*Half rising from her couch.*

What were you going to ask?

ANASÚYÁ.
We know very little about love-matters, dear [S']akoontalá; but for all that, I cannot help suspecting your present state to be something similar to that of the lovers we have heard about in romances. Tell us frankly what is the cause of your disorder. It is useless to apply a remedy, until the disease be understood.

KING.
Anasúyá bears me out in my suspicion.

[S']AKOONTALÁ.
*Aside.*

I am, indeed, deeply in love; but cannot rashly disclose my passion to these young girls.

PRIYAMVADÁ.
What Anasúyá says, dear [S']akoontalá, is very just. Why give so little heed to your ailment? Every day you are becoming thinner; though I must confess your complexion is still as beautiful as ever.

**KING.**
Priyamvadá speaks most truly.
  Sunk is her velvet cheek; her wasted bosom
  Loses its fulness; e'en her slender waist
  Grows more attenuate; her face is wan,
  Her shoulders droop;—as when the vernal blasts
  Sear the young blossoms of the Mádhaví ,
  Blighting their bloom; so mournful is the change.
  Yet in its sadness, fascinating still,
  Inflicted by the mighty lord of love
  On the fair figure of the hermit's daughter.

**[S']AKOONTALÁ.**
Dear friends, to no one would I rather reveal the nature of my malady than to
you; but I should only be troubling you.

**PRIYAMVADÁ AND ANASÚYÁ.**
Nay, this is the very point about which we are so solicitous. Sorrow shared
with affectionate friends is relieved of half its poignancy.

**KING.**
  Pressed by the partners of her joys and griefs,
  Her much beloved companions, to reveal
  The cherished secret locked within her breast,
  She needs must utter it; although her looks
  Encourage me to hope, my bosom throbs
  As anxiously I listen for her answer.

**[S']AKOONTALÁ.**
Know then, dear friends, that from the first moment the illustrious Prince
who is the guardian of our sacred grove presented himself to my sight—

*Stops short, and appears confused.*

**PRIYAMVADÁ AND ANASÚYÁ.**
Say on, dear [S']akoontalá, say on.

**[S']AKOONTALÁ.**
Ever since that happy moment, my heart's affections have been fixed upon
him, and my energies of mind and body have all deserted me, as you see.

**KING.**
*With rapture.*

Her own lips have uttered the words I most longed to hear.
  Love lit the flame, and Love himself allays
  My burning fever, as when gathering clouds
  Rise o'er the earth in summer's dazzling noon,
  And grateful showers dispel the morning heat.

**[S']AKOONTALÁ.**
You must consent, then, dear friends, to contrive some means by which I may
find favour with the King, or you will have ere long to assist at my funeral.

**KING.**
Enough! These words remove all my doubts.

PRIYAMVADÁ.
*Aside to ANASÚYÁ.*

She is far gone in love, dear Anasúyá, and no time ought to be lost. Since she has fixed her affections on a monarch who is the ornament of Puru's line, we need not hesitate for a moment to express our approval.

ANASÚYÁ.
I quite agree with you.

PRIYAMVADÁ.
*Aloud.*

We wish you joy, dear [S']akoontalá. Your affections are fixed on an object in every respect worthy of you,. The noblest river will unite itself to the ocean, and the lovely Mádhaví-creeper clings naturally to the Mango, the only tree capable of supporting it.

KING.
Why need we wonder if the beautiful constellation Vi[s']ákhá pines to be united with the Moon ?

ANASÚYÁ.
By what stratagem can we best secure to our friend the accomplishment of her heart's desire both speedily and secretly?

PRIYAMVADÁ.
The latter point is all we have to think about. As to 'speedily,'
I look upon the whole affair as already settled.

ANASÚYÁ.
How so?

PRIYAMVADÁ.
Did you not observe how the King betrayed his liking by the tender manner in which he gazed upon her, and how thin he has become the last few days, as if he had been lying awake thinking of her?

KING.
*Looking at himself.*

Quite true! I certainly am becoming thin from want of sleep:
  As night by night in anxious thought I raise
  This wasted arm to rest my sleepless head,
  My jewelled bracelet, sullied by the tears
  That trickle from my eyes in scalding streams,
  Slips towards my elbow from my shrivelled wrist.
  Oft I replace the bauble, but in vain;
  So easily it spans the fleshless limb
  That e'en the rough and corrugated skin,
  Scarred by the bow-string, will not check its fall .

PRIYAMVADÁ.
An idea strikes me, Anasúyá. Let [S']akoontalá write a love-letter;
I will conceal it in a flower, and contrive to drop it in the
King's path. He will surely mistake it for the remains of some
sacred offering, and will, in all probability, pick it up.

**ANASÚYÁ.**
A very ingenious device! It my entire approval; but what says [S']akoontalá?

**[S']AKOONTALÁ.**
I must consider before I can consent to it.

**PRIYAMVADÁ.**
Could, you not, dear [S']akoontalá, think of some pretty composition in verse, containing a delicate declaration of your love?

**[S']AKOONTALÁ.**
Well, I will do my best; but my heart trembles when I think of the chances of a refusal.

**KING.**
*With rapture.*

Too timid maid, here stands the man from whom
Thou fearest a repulse; supremely blessed
To call thee all his own. Well might he doubt
His title to thy love; but how could'st thou
Believe thy beauty powerless to subdue him?

**PRIYAMVADÁ AND ANASÚYÁ.**
You undervalue your own merits, dear [S']akoontalá. What man in his senses would intercept with the skirt of his robe the bright rays of the autumnal moon, which alone can allay the fever of his body?

**[S']AKOONTALÁ.**
*Smiling.*

Then it seems I must do as I am bid.

*Sits down and appears to be thinking.*

**KING.**
How charming she looks! My very eyes forget to wink, jealous of losing even for an instant a sight so enchanting.
  How beautiful the movement of her brow,
  As through her mind love's tender fancies flow!
  And, as she weighs her thoughts, how sweet to trace
  The ardent passion mantling in her face!

**[S']AKOONTALÁ.**
Dear girls, I have thought of a verse, but I have no writing-materials at hand.

**PRIYAMVADÁ.**
Write the letters with your nail on this lotus-leaf, which is smooth as a parrot's breast.

**[S']AKOONTALÁ.**
*After writing the verse.*

Listen, dear friends, and tell me whether the ideas are appropriately expressed.

**PRIYAMVADÁ AND ANASÚYÁ.**
We are all attention.

## [S']AKOONTALÁ.

*Reads.*

I know not the secret thy bosom conceals,
Thy form is not near me to gladden my sight;
But sad is the tale that my fever reveals,
Of the love that consumes me by day and by night.

## KING.

*Advancing hastily towards her.*

Nay, Love does but warm thee, fair maiden,—thy frame
Only droops like the bud in the glare of the noon;
But me he consumes with a pitiless flame,
As the beams of the day-star destroy the pale moon.

## PRIYAMVADÁ AND ANASÚYÁ.

*Looking at him joyfully and rising to salute him.*

Welcome, the desire of our hearts, that so speedily presents itself!

*[S']AKOONTALÁ makes an effort to rise.*

## KING.

Nay, trouble not thyself, dear maiden.
  Move not to do me homage; let thy limbs
Still softly rest upon their flowery couch;
And gather fragrance from the lotus-stalks,
Bruised by the fevered contact of thy frame.

## ANASÚYÁ.

Deign, gentle Sir, to seat yourself on the rock on which our friend
is reposing.

*The KING sits down. [S']AKOONTALÁ is confused.*

## PRIYAMVADÁ.

Any one may see at a glance that you are deeply attached to each other. But
the affection I have for my friend prompts me to say something of which you
hardly require to be informed.

## KING.

Do not hesitate to speak out, my good girl. If you omit to say what is in your
mind, you may be sorry for it afterwards.

## PRIYAMVADÁ.

Is it not your special office as a King to remove the suffering of your subjects
who are in trouble?

## KING.

Such is my duty, most assuredly.

## PRIYAMVADÁ.

Know, then, that our dear friend has been brought to her present state of
suffering entirely through love for you. Her life is in your hands; take pity on
her and restore her to health.

## KING.

Excellent maiden, our attachment is mutual. It is I who am the most honoured by it.

[S']AKOONTALÁ.
*Looking at PRIYAMVADÁ.*

What do you mean by detaining the King, who must be anxious to return to his royal consorts after so long a separation?

KING.
Sweet maiden, banish from thy mind the thought
That I could love another. Thou dost reign
Supreme, without a rival, in my heart,
And I am thine alone; disown me not,
Else must I die a second deadlier death,
Killed by thy words, as erst by Káma's shafts.

ANASÚYÁ.
Kind Sir, we have heard it said that kings have many favourite consorts. You must not, then, by your behaviour towards our dear friend, give her relations cause to sorrow for her.

KING.
Listen, gentle maiden, while in a few words I quiet your anxiety.
Though many beauteous forms my palace grace,
Henceforth two things alone will I esteem
The glory of my royal dynasty—
My sea-girt realm, and this most lovely maid.

PRIYAMVADÁ AND ANASÚYÁ.
We are satisfied by your assurances.

PRIYAMVADÁ.
*Glancing on one side.*

See, Anasúyá, there is our favourite little fawn running about in great distress, and turning its eyes in every direction as if looking for its mother; come, let us help the little thing to find her.

*Both move away.*

[S']AKOONTALÁ.
Dear friends, dear friends, leave me not alone and unprotected.
Why need you both go?

PRIYAMVADÁ AND ANASÚYÁ.
Unprotected! when the Protector of the world is at your side.

*Exeunt.*

[S']AKOONTALÁ.
What! have they both really left me?

KING.
Distress not thyself, sweet maiden. Thy adorer is at hand to wait upon thee.
Oh let me tend thee, fair one, in the place
Of thy dear friends; and with broad lotus fans
Raise cooling breezes to refresh thy frame;

*411*

Or shall I rather, with caressing touch,
Allay the fever of thy limbs, and soothe
Thy aching feet, beauteous as blushing lilies?

[S']AKOONTALÁ.
Nay, touch me not. I will not incur the censure of those whom I am bound
to respect.

*Rises and attempts to go.*

KING.
Fair one, the heat of noon has not yet subsided, and thy body is still feeble.
  How canst thou quit thy fragrant couch of flowers,
  And from thy throbbing bosom cast aside
  Its covering of lotus-leaves, to brave
  With weak and fainting limbs the noon-day heat?

*Forces her to turn back.*

[S']AKOONTALÁ.
Infringe not the rules of decorum, mighty descendant of Puru. Remember,
though I love you, I have no power to dispose of myself.

KING.
Why this fear of offending your relations, timid maid? When your venerable
foster-father hears of it, he will not find fault with you. He knows that the
law permits us to be united without consulting him.
  In Indra's heaven, so at least 'tis said,
  No nuptial rites prevail , nor is the bride
  Led to the altar by her future lord;
  But all in secret does the bridegroom plight
  His troth, and each unto the other vow
  Mutual allegiance. Such espousals, too,
  Are authorised on earth, and many daughters
  Of royal saints thus wedded to their lords
  Have still received their father's benison.

[S']AKOONTALÁ.
Leave me, leave me; I must take counsel with my female friends.

KING.
I will leave thee when—

[S']AKOONTALÁ.
When?

KING.
  When I have gently stolen from thy lips
  Their yet untasted nectar, to allay
  The raging of my thirst, e'en as the bee
  Sips the fresh honey from the opening bud.

*Attempts to raise her face. [S']AKOONTALÁ tries to prevent him.*

A VOICE BEHIND THE SCENES.
The loving birds, doomed by fate to nightly separation , must bid farewell to
each other, for evening is at hand.

**[S']AKOONTALÁ.**

*In confusion.*

Great Prince, I hear the voice of the matron Gautamí. She is coming this way to inquire after my health. Hasten and conceal yourself behind the branches.

**KING.**
I will.

*Conceals himself.*

*Enter GAUTAMÍ with a vase in her hand, preceded by two attendants.*

**ATTENDANTS.**
This way, most venerable Gautamí.

**GAUTAMÍ.**
*Approaching [S']AKOONTALÁ.*

My child, is the fever of thy limbs allayed?

**[S']AKOONTALÁ.**
Venerable mother, there is certainly a change for the better.

**GAUTAMÍ.**
Let me sprinkle you with this holy water, and all your ailments will depart.

*Sprinkling [S']AKOONTALÁ on the head.*

The day is closing, my child; come, let us go to the cottage.

*They all move away.*

**[S']AKOONTALÁ.**
*Aside.*

Oh my heart! thou didst fear to taste of happiness when it was within thy reach. Now that the object of thy desires is torn from thee, how bitter will be thy remorse, how distracting thine anguish!

*Moving on a few steps and stopping. Aloud.*

Farewell! bower of creepers, sweet soother of my sufferings, farewell! may I soon again be happy under thy shade.

*Exit reluctantly with the others.*

**KING.**

*Returning to his former seat in the arbour. Sighing.*

Alas! how many are the obstacles to the accomplishment of our wishes!
  Albeit she did coyly turn away
  Her glowing cheek, and with her fingers guard
  Her pouting lips, that murmured a denial
  In faltering accents, she did yield herself
  A sweet reluctant captive to my will.
  As eagerly I raised her lovely face;
  But ere with gentle force I stole the kiss,
  Too envious Fate did mar my daring purpose.

*413*

Whither now shall I betake myself? I will tarry for a brief space in this bower of creepers, so endeared to me by the presence of my beloved [S']akoontalá.

*Looking round.*

Here printed on the flowery couch I see
The fair impression of her slender limbs;
Here is the sweet confession of her love,
Traced with her nail upon the lotus-leaf;
And yonder are the withered lily-stalks
That graced her wrist. While all around I view
Things that recall her image, can I quit
This bower, e'en though its living be fled?

A VOICE IN THE AIR.
Great King,
Scarce is our evening sacrifice begun,
When evil demons, lurid as the clouds
That gather round the dying orb of day,
Cluster in hideous troops, obscene and dread,
About our altars, casting far and near
Terrific shadows, while the sacred fire
Sheds a pale lustre o'er their ghostly shapes.

KING.
I come to the rescue, I come.

*Exit.*

## Prelude to Act IV

### SCENE.—The Garden of the Hermitage.

*Enter PRIYAMVADÁ and ANASÚYÁ in the act of gathering flowers_.*

ANASÚYÁ.
Although, dear Priyamvadá, it rejoices my heart to think that [S']akoontalá has been happily united to a husband in every respect worthy of her, by the form of marriage prevalent among Indra's celestial musicians, nevertheless, I cannot help feeling somewhat uneasy in my mind.

PRIYAMVADÁ.
How so?

ANASÚYÁ.
You know that the pious King was gratefully dismissed by the hermits on the successful termination of their sacrificial rites. He has now returned to his capital, leaving [S']akoontalá under our care; and it may be doubted whether, in the society of his royal consorts, he will not forget all that has taken place in this hermitage of ours.

PRIYAMVADÁ.
On that score be at ease. Persons of his noble nature are not so destitute of all honourable feeling. I confess, however, that there is one point about which I am rather anxious. What, think you, will Father Kanwa say when he hears what has occurred?

ANASÚYÁ.

In my opinion, he will approve the marriage.

PRIYAMVADÁ.
What makes you think so?

ANASÚYÁ.
From the first, it was always his fixed purpose to bestow the maiden on a husband worthy of her; and since heaven has given her such a husband, his wishes have been realized without any trouble to himself.

PRIYAMVADÁ.
*Looking at the flower-basket.*

We have gathered flowers enough for the sacred offering, dear Anasúyá.

ANASÚYÁ.
Well, then, let us now gather more, that we may have wherewith to propitiate the guardian-deity of our dear [S']akoontalá.

PRIYAMVADÁ.
By all means.

*They continue gathering.*

A VOICE BEHIND THE SCENES.
Ho there! See you not that I am here!

ANASÚYÁ.
That must be the voice of a guest announcing his arrival.

PRIYAMVADÁ.
Surely, [S']akoontalá is not absent from the cottage.

*Aside.*

Her heart at least is absent, I fear.

ANASÚYÁ.
Come along, come along; we have gathered flowers enough.

*They move away.*

THE SAME VOICE BEHIND THE SCENES.
Woe to thee, maiden, for daring to slight a guest like me!
  Shall I stand here unwelcomed—even I,
  A very mine of penitential merit,
  Worthy of all respect? Shalt thou, rash maid,
  Thus set at nought the ever sacred ties
  Of hospitality? and fix thy thoughts
  Upon the cherished object of thy love,
  While I am present? Thus I curse thee, then—
  He, even he of whom thou thinkest, he
  Shall think no more of thee; nor in his heart
  Retain thine image. Vainly shalt thou strive
  To waken his remembrance of the past;
  He shall disown thee, even as the sot,
  Roused from his midnight drunkenness, denies
  The words he uttered in his revellings.
*415*

PRIYAMVADÁ.

Alas! alas! I fear a terrible misfortune has occurred. [S']akoontalá, from absence of mind, must have offended some guest whom she was bound to treat with respect.

*Looking behind the scenes.*

Ah! yes; I see; and no less a person than the great sage Durvásas , who is known to be most irascible. He it is that has just cursed her, and is now retiring with hasty strides, trembling with passion, and looking as if nothing could turn him. His wrath is like a consuming fire.

ANASÚYÁ.

Go quickly, dear Priyamvadá, throw yourself at his feet, and persuade him to come back, while I prepare a propitiatory offering  for him, with water and refreshments.

PRIYAMVADÁ.

I will.

*Exit.*

ANASÚYÁ.

*Advancing hastily a few steps and stumbling.*

Alas! alas! this comes of being in a hurry. My foot has slipped, and my basket of flowers has fallen from my hand.

*Stays to gather them up.*

PRIYAMVADÁ.

*Re-entering*

Well, dear Anasúyá, I have done my best; but what living being could succeed in pacifying such a cross-grained, ill-tempered old fellow? However, I managed to mollify him a little.

ANASÚYÁ

*Smiling.*

Even a little was much for him. Say on.

PRIYAMVADÁ.

When he refused to turn back, I implored his forgiveness in these words: 'Most venerable sage, pardon, I beseech you, this first offence of a young and inexperienced girl, who was ignorant of the respect due to your saintly character and exalted rank.'

ANASÚYÁ

And what did he reply?

PRIYAMVADÁ.

'My word must not be falsified; but, at the sight of the ring of recognition the spell shall cease.' So saying, he disappeared.

ANASÚYÁ.

Oh! then we may breathe again; for, now I think of it, the King himself, at his departure, fastened on [S']akoontalá's finger, as a token of remembrance, a ring on which his own name was engraved. She has, therefore, a remedy for her misfortune at her own command.

**PRIYAMVADÁ.**
Come, dear Anasúyá, let us proceed with our religious duties.

*They walk round.*

**PRIYAMVADÁ.**
*Looking off the stage.*

See, Anasúyá, there sits our dear friend, motionless as a statue, resting her face on her left hand, her whole mind absorbed in thinking of her absent husband. She can pay no attention to herself, much less to a stranger.

**ANASÚYÁ.**
Priyamvadá, let this affair never pass our lips. We must spare our dear friend's feelings. Her constitution is too delicate to bear much emotion.

**PRIYAMVADÁ.**
I agree with you. Who would think of watering a tender jasmine with hot water?

## Act IV.

### Scene.—_The Neighbourhood of the Hermitage.

*Enter one of_ Kanwa's Pupils just arisen from his couch at the dawn of day.*

**PUPIL.**
My master, the venerable Kanwa, who is but lately returned from his pilgrimage, has ordered me to ascertain how the time goes. I have therefore come into the open air to see if it be still dark.

*Walking and looking about.*

Oh! the dawn has already broken.
  Lo! in one quarter of the sky, the Moon,
  Lord of the herbs and night-expanding flowers,
  Sinks towards his bed behind the western hills;
  While in the east, preceded by the Dawn,
  His blushing charioteer , the glorious Sun
  Begins his course, and far into the gloom
  Casts the first radiance of his orient beams.
  Hail! co-eternal orbs, that rise to set,
  And set to rise again; symbols divine
  Of man's reverses, life's vicissitudes.
And now,
  While the round Moon withdraws his looming disc
  Beneath the western sky, the full-blown flower
  Of the night-loving lotus  sheds her leave
  In sorrow for his loss, bequeathing nought
  But the sweet memory of her loveliness
  To my bereaved sight; e'en as the bride
  Disconsolately mourns her absent lord,
  And yields her heart a prey to anxious grief.

**ANASÚYÁ.**
*Entering abruptly.*

Little as I know of the ways of the world, I cannot help thinking that King Dushyanta is treating [S']akoontalá very improperly.

*417*

PUPIL.
Well, I must let my revered preceptor know that it is time to offer the burnt oblation.

*Exit.*

ANASÚYÁ.
I am broad awake, but what shall I do? I have no energy to go about my usual occupations. My hands and feet seem to have lost their power. Well, Love has gained his object; and Love only is to blame for having induced our dear friend, in the innocence of her heart, to confide in such a perfidious man. Possibly, however, the imprecation of Durvásas may he already taking effect. Indeed, I cannot otherwise account for the King's strange conduct, in allowing so long a time to elapse without even a letter; and that, too, after so many promises and protestations. I cannot think what to do unless we send him the ring which was to be the token of recognition. But which of these austere hermits could we ask to be the bearer of it? Then, again, Father Kanwa has just returned from his pilgrimage; and how am I to inform him of [S']akoontalá's marriage to King Dushyanta, and her expectation of becoming soon a mother? I never could bring myself to tell him, even if I felt that [S'] akoontalá had been in fault, which she certainly has not. What is to be done?

PRIYAMVADÁ.
*Entering; joyfully.*

Quick! quick! Anasúyá! come and assist in the joyful preparations for [S'] akoontalá's departure to her husband's palace.

ANASÚYÁ.
My dear girl, what can you mean?

PRIYAMVADÁ.
Listen, now, and I will tell you all about it. I went just now to

*[S']akoontalá, to inquire whether she had slept comfortably—*

ANASÚYÁ.
Well, well; go on.

PRIYAMVADÁ.
She was sitting with her face bowed down to the very ground with shame, when Father Kanwa entered, and, embracing her, of his own accord offered her his congratulations. 'I give thee joy, my child,' he said, 'we have had an auspicious omen. The priest who offered the oblation dropped it into the very centre of the sacred fire , though thick smoke obstructed his vision. Henceforth thou wilt cease to be an object of compassion. This very day I purpose sending thee, under the charge of certain trusty hermits, to the King's palace; and shall deliver thee into the hands of thy husband, as I would commit knowledge to the keeping of a wise and faithful student.'

ANASÚYÁ.
Who, then, informed the holy father of what passed in his absence?

PRIYAMVADÁ.
As he was entering the sanctuary of the consecrated fire, an invisible being chanted a verse in celestial strains.

**ANASÚYÁ.**
*With astonishment.*

Indeed! pray repeat it.

**PRIYAMVADÁ.**
*Repeating the verse.*

Glows in thy daughter King Dushyanta's glory,
As in the sacred tree the mystic fire ;
Let worlds rejoice to hear the welcome story,
And may the son immortalize the sire.

**ANASÚYÁ.**
*Embracing PRIYAMVADÁ.*

Oh, my dear Priyamvadá, what delightful news! I am pleased beyond
measure; yet when I think that we are to lose our dear [S']akoontalá this very
day, a feeling of melancholy mingles with my joy.

**PRIYAMVADÁ.**
We shall find means of consoling ourselves after her departure.
Let the dear creature only be made happy at any cost.

**ANASÚYÁ.**
Yes, yes, Priyamvadá, it shall be so; and now to prepare the bridal array.
I have always looked forward to this occasion, and some time since, I
deposited a beautiful garland of Ke[S']ara flowers in a cocoa-nut box, and
suspended it on a bough of yonder mango-tree. Be good enough to stretch
out your hand and take it down, while I compound unguents and perfumes
with this consecrated paste and these blades of sacred grass.

**PRIYAMVADÁ.**
Very well.

*Exit ANASÚYÁ. PRIYAMVADÁ takes down the flowers.*

**A VOICE BEHIND THE SCENES.**

*Gautamí, bid [S']árngarava and the others hold themselves in readiness to escort
[S']akoontalá.*

**PRIYAMVADÁ.**
*Listening.*

Quick, quick, Anasúyá! They are calling the hermits who are to go with [S']
akoontalá to Hastinápur .

**ANASÚYÁ.**
*Re-entering with the perfumed unguents in her hand.*

Come along then, Priyamvadá; I am ready to go with you.

*They walk away.*

**PRIYAMVADÁ.**
*Looking.*

See! there sits [S']akoontalá, her locks arranged even at this early hour of
the morning. The holy women of the hermitage are congratulating her, and

*419*

invoking blessings on her head, while they present her with wedding-gifts and offerings of consecrated wild-rice. Let us join them.

*[They approach.*
*[S']AKOONTALÁ is seen seated, with women surrounding her, occupied in the manner described.*

**FIRST WOMAN.**
*To [S']AKOONTALÁ.*

My child, may'st thou receive the title of 'Chief-queen,' and may thy husband delight to honour thee above all others!

**SECOND WOMAN.**
My child, may'st thou be the mother of a hero!

**THIRD WOMAN.**
My child, may'st thou be highly honoured by thy lord!

*[Exeunt all the women, excepting GAUTAMÍ, after blessing_ [S']AKOONTALÁ.*

**PRIYAMVADÁ AND ANASÚYÁ.**
*Approaching.*

Dear [S']akoontalá, we are come to assist you at your toilet, and may a blessing attend it!

**[S']AKOONTALÁ.**
Welcome, dear friends, welcome. Sit down here.

**PRIYAMVADÁ AND ANASÚYÁ.**

*[Taking the baskets containing the bridal decorations, and sitting down.*

Now, then, dearest, prepare to let us dress you. We must first rub your limbs with these perfumed unguents.

**[S']AKOONTALÁ.**
I ought indeed to be grateful for your kind offices, now that I am so soon to be deprived of them. Dear, dear friends, perhaps I shall never be dressed by you again.

*Bursts into tears.*

**PRIYAMVADÁ AND ANASÚYÁ.**
Weep not, dearest; tears are out of season on such a happy occasion.

*They wipe away her tears and begin to dress her.*

**PRIYAMVADÁ.**
Alas! these simple flowers and rude ornaments, which our hermitage offers in abundance, do not set off your beauty as it deserves.

*Enter TWO YOUNG HERMITS, bearing costly presents.*

**BOTH HERMITS.**
Here are ornaments suitable for a queen.

*The women look at them in astonishment.*

**GAUTAMÍ**

Why, Nárada, my son, whence came these?

**FIRST HERMIT.**
You owe them to the devotion of Father Kanwa.

**GAUTAMÍ.**
Did he create them by the power of his own mind?

**SECOND HERMIT.**
Certainly not; but you shall hear. The venerable sage ordered us to collect flowers for [S']akoontalá from the forest-trees; and we went to the wood for that purpose, when
  Straightway depending from a neighbouring tree
  Appeared a robe of linen tissue, pure
  And spotless as a moonbeam—mystic pledge
  Of bridal happiness; another tree
  Distilled a roseate dye wherewith to stain
  The lady's feet ; and other branches near
  Glistened with rare and costly ornaments.
  While, 'mid the leaves, the hands of forest-nymphs,
  Vying in beauty with the opening buds,
  Presented us with sylvan offerings.

**PRIYAMVADÁ.**
*Looking at [S']AKOONTALÁ.*

The wood-nymphs have done you honour, indeed. This favour doubtless signifies that you are soon to be received as a happy wife into your husband's house, and are from this time forward to become the partner of his royal fortunes.

*[S']AKOONTALÁ appears abashed.*

**FIRST HERMIT.**
Come, Gautama; Father Kanwa has finished his ablutions. Let us go and inform him of the favour we have received from the deities who preside over our trees.

**SECOND HERMIT.**
By all means.

*Exeunt.*

**PRIYAMVADÁ AND ANASÚYÁ**
Alas! what are we to do? We are unused to such splendid decorations, and are at a loss how to arrange them. Our knowledge of painting must be our guide. We will dispose the ornaments as we have seen them in pictures.

**[S']AKOONTALÁ**
Whatever pleases you, dear girls, will please me. I have perfect confidence In your taste.

*They commence dressing her.*
*Enter KANWA, having just finished his ablutions.*

**KANWA.**
  This day my loved one leaves me, and my heart
  Is heavy with its grief; the streams of sorrow,

Choked at the source, repress my faltering voice,
I have no words to speak; mine eyes are dimmed
By the dark shadows of the thoughts that rise
Within my soul. If such the force of grief
In an old hermit parted from his nursling,
What anguish must the stricken parent feel—
Bereft forever of an only daughter.

*Advances towards [S']AKOONTALÁ*

**PRIYAMVADÁ AND ANASÚYÁ.**
Now, dearest [S']akoontalá, we have finished decorating you. You have only
to put on the two linen mantles.

*[S']AKOONTALÁ rises and puts them on.*

**GAUTAMÍ.**
Daughter, see, here comes thy foster-father; he is eager to fold thee in his arms;
his eyes swim with tears of joy. Hasten to do him reverence.

**[S']AKOONTALÁ**
*Reverently.*

My father, I salute you.

**KANWA.**
My daughter,
  May'st thou be highly honoured by thy lord,
  E'en as Yayáti [S']armishthá adored !
  And, as she bore him Puru, so may'st thou
  Bring forth a son to whom the world shall bow!

**GAUTAMÍ.**
Most venerable father, she accepts your benediction as if she already
possessed the boon it confers.

**KANWA.**
Now come this way, my child, and walk reverently round these sacrificial fires.

*They all walk round.*

**KANWA.**
*Repeats a prayer in the metre of the Rig-veda.*

 Holy flames, that gleam around
 Every altar's hallowed ground;
 Holy flames, whose frequent food
 Is the consecrated wood,
 And for whose encircling bed,
 Sacred Ku[s']a-grass is spread ;
 Holy flames, that waft to heaven
 Sweet oblations daily given,
 Mortal guilt to purge away,
 IIear, oh hear me, when I pray—
 Purify my child this day!
Now then, my daughter, set out on thy journey.

*Looking on one side.*

Where are thy attendants. [S']árngarava and the others?

YOUNG HERMIT.
*Entering.*

Here we are, most venerable father.

KANWA.
Lead the way for thy sister.

[S']ÁRNGARAVA.
Come, [S']akoontalá, let us proceed.

*All move away.*

KANWA.
Hear me, ye trees that surround our hermitage!
[S']akoontalá ne'er moistened in the stream
Her own parched lips, till she had fondly poured
Its purest water on your thirsty roots;
And oft, when she would fain have decked her hair
With your thick-clustering blossoms, in her love
She robbed you not e'en of a single flower.
Her highest joy was ever to behold
The early glory of your opening buds;
Oh, then, dismiss her with a kind farewell.
This very day she quits her father's home,
To seek the palace of her wedded lord.

*The note of a Koïl is heard.*

Hark! heard'st thou not the answer of the trees,
Our sylvan sisters, warbled in the note
Of the melodious Koïl? they dismiss
Their dear [S']akoontalá with loving wishes.

VOICES IN THE AIR.
Fare thee well, journey pleasantly on amid streams
Where the lotuses bloom, and the sun's glowing beams
Never pierce the deep shade of the wide-spreading trees,
While gently around thee shall sport the cool breeze;
Then light be thy footsteps and easy thy tread,
Beneath thee shall carpets of lilies be spread;
Journey on to thy lord, let thy spirit be gay,
For the smiles of all Nature shall gladden thy way.

*All listen with astonishment.*

GAUTAMÍ.
Daughter! the nymphs of the wood, who love thee with the affection of a sister, dismiss thee with kind wishes for thy happiness. Take thou leave of them reverentially.

[S']AKOONTALÁ.
*Bowing respectfully and walking on. Aside to her friend.*

Eager as I am, dear Priyamvadá, to see my husband once more, yet my feet refuse to move, now that I am quitting for ever the home of my girlhood.

PRIYAMVADÁ.

You are not the only one, dearest, to feel the bitterness of parting. As the time of separation approaches, the whole grove seems to share your anguish.
  In sorrow for thy loss, the herd of deer
  Forget to browse; the peacock on the lawn
  Ceases its dance ; the very trees around
  Shed their pale leaves, like tears, upon the ground.

[S']AKOONTALÁ.

*Recollecting herself.*

My father, let me, before I go, bid adieu to my pet jasmine, the
Moonlight of the Grove . I love the plant almost as a sister.

KANWA.

Yes, yes, my child, I remember thy sisterly affection for the creeper. Here it is
on the right.

[S']AKOONTALÁ.

*Approaching the jasmine.*

My beloved jasmine! most brilliant of climbing plants, how sweet it is to see thee
cling thus fondly to thy husband, the mango-tree; yet, prithee, turn thy twining
arms for a moment in this direction to embrace thy sister; she is going far away,
and may never see thee again.

KANWA.

  Daughter, the cherished purpose of my heart
  Has ever been to wed thee to a man
  That should be worthy of thee; such a spouse
  Hast thou thyself, by thine own merits, won.
  To him thou goest, and about his neck
  Soon shalt thou cling confidingly, as now
  Thy favourite jasmine twines its loving arms
  Around the sturdy mango. Leave thou it
  To its protector—e'en as I consign
  Thee to thy lord, and henceforth from my mind
  Banish all anxious thought on thy behalf.
Proceed on thy journey, my child.

[S']AKOONTALÁ.

*To PRIYAMVADÁ and ANASÚYÁ.*

To you, my sweet companions, I leave it as a keepsake. Take charge of it
when I am gone.

PRIYAMVADÁ AND ANASÚYÁ.

*Bursting into tears.*

And to whose charge do you leave us, dearest? Who will care for us when you
are gone?

KANWA.

For shame, Anasúyá! dry your tears. Is this the way to cheer your friend at a
time when she needs your support and consolation?

*All move on.*

**[S']AKOONTALÁ.**
My father, see you there my pet deer, grazing close to the hermitage? She expects soon to fawn, and even now the weight of the little one she carries hinders her movements. Do not forget to send me word when she becomes a mother.

**KANWA.**
I will not forget it.

**[S']AKOONTALÁ.**
*Feeling herself drawn back.*

What can this be, fastened to my dress?

*Turns round.*

**KANWA.**
My daughter,
  It is the little fawn, thy foster-child,
  Poor helpless orphan! it remembers well
  How with a mother's tenderness and love
  Thou didst protect it, and with grains of rice
  From thine own hand didst daily nourish it;
  And, ever and anon, when some sharp thorn
  Had pierced its mouth, how gently thou didst tend
  The bleeding wound, and pour in healing balm.
  The grateful nursling clings to its protectress,
  Mutely imploring leave to follow her.

**[S']AKOONTALÁ.**
My poor little fawn! dost thou ask to follow an ungrateful wretch who hesitates not to desert her companions! When thy mother died, soon after thy birth, I supplied her place, and reared thee with my own hand; and now that thy second mother is about to leave thee, who will care for thee? My father, be thou a mother to her. My child, go back, and be a daughter to my father.

*Moves on, weeping.*

**KANWA.**
  Weep not, my daughter, check the gathering tear
  That lurks beneath thine eyelid, ere it flow
  And weaken thy resolve; be firm and true—
  True to thyself and me; the path of life
  Will lead o'er hill and plain, o'er rough and smooth,
  And all must feel the steepness of the way;
  Though rugged be thy course, press boldly on.

**[S']ÁRNGARAVA.**
Venerable Sire! the sacred precept is:—'Accompany thy friend as far as the margin of the first stream.' Here, then, we are arrived at the border of a lake. It is time for you to give us your final instructions and return.

**KANWA.**
Be it so; let us tarry for a moment under the shade of this fig-tree.

*They do so.*

**KANWA**
*Aside.*

425

I must think of some appropriate message to send to his Majesty King Dushyanta.

*[Reflects. .*

**[S']AKOONTALÁ.**
*Aside to ANASÚYÁ.*

See, see, dear Anasúyá, the poor female Chakraváka-bird , whom cruel fate dooms to nightly separation from her mate, calls to him in mournful notes from the other side of the stream, though he is only hidden from her view by the spreading leaves of the water-lily. Her cry is so piteous that I could almost fancy she was lamenting her hard lot in intelligible words.

**ANASÚYÁ**
Say not so, dearest:
  Fond bird! though sorrow lengthen out her night
  Of widowhood, yet with a cry of joy
  She hails the morning light that brings her mate
  Back to her side. The agony of parting
  Would wound us like a sword, but that its edge
  Is blunted by the hope of future meeting.

**KANWA.**
[S']árngarava! when you have introduced [S']akoontalá into the presence of the King, you must give him this message from me:—

**[S']ÁRNGARAVA**
Let me hear it, venerable father.

**KANWA.**
This is it:—
  Most puissant prince! we here present before thee
  One thou art bound to cherish and receive
  As thine own wife; yea, even to enthrone
  As thine own queen—worthy of equal love
  With thine imperial consorts. So much, Sire,
  We claim of thee as justice due to us,
  In virtue of our holy character,
  In virtue of thine honourable rank,
  In virtue of the pure spontaneous love
  That secretly grew up 'twixt thee and her,
  Without consent or privity of us.
  We ask no more—the rest we freely leave
  To thy just feeling and to destiny.

**[S']ÁRNGARAVA.**
A most suitable message! I will take care to deliver it correctly.

**KANWA.**
And, now, my child, a few words of advice for thee. We hermits, though we live secluded from the world are not ignorant of worldly matters.

**[S']ÁRNGARAVA.**
No, indeed. Wise men are conversant with all subjects.

**KANWA.**

Listen, then, my daughter. When thou reachest thy husband's palace, and art admitted into his family,

Honour thy betters; ever be respectful
To those above thee; and, should others share
Thy husband's love, ne'er yield thyself a prey
to jealousy; but ever be a friend,
A loving friend, to those who rival thee
In his affections. Should thy wedded lord
Treat thee with harshness, thou most never be
Harsh in return, but patient and submissive;
Be to thy menials courteous, and to all
Placed under thee, considerate and kind;
Be never self-indulgent, but avoid
Excess in pleasure; and, when fortune smiles,
Be not puffed up. Thus to thy husband's house
Wilt thou a blessing prove, and not a curse.

What thinks Gautamí of this advice?

GAUTAMÍ.
An excellent compendium, truly, of every wife's duties! Lay it well to heart, my daughter.

KANWA.
Come, my beloved child, one parting embrace for me and for thy companions, and then we leave thee.

[S']AKOONTALÁ.
My father, must Priyamvadá and Anasúyá really return with you? They are very dear to me.

KANWA.
Yes, my child; they, too, in good time, will be given in marriage to suitable husbands. It would not be proper for them to accompany thee to such a public place. But Gautamí shall be thy companion.

[S']AKOONTALÁ.
*Embracing him.*

Removed from thy bosom, my beloved father, like a young tendril of the sandal-tree torn from its home in the western mountains , how shall I be able to support life in a foreign soil?

KANWA.
Daughter, thy fears are groundless.

Soon shall thy lord prefer thee to the rank
Of his own consort; and unnumbered cares
Befitting his imperial dignity
Shall constantly engross thee. Then the bliss
Of bearing him a son—a noble boy,
Bright as the day-star, shall transport thy soul
With new delights, and little shalt thou reck
Of the light sorrow that afflicts thee now
At parting from thy father and thy friends.

*[[S']AKOONTALÁ throws herself at her foster-father's feet.*

KANWA.
*427*

Blessings on thee, my child! May all my hopes of thee be realized!

**[S']AKOONTALÁ**
*Approaching her friends.*

Come, my two loved companions, embrace me both of you together.

**PRIYAMVADÁ AND ANASÚYÁ.**
*Embracing her.*

Dear [S']akoontalá, remember, if the King should by any chance be slow in recognizing you, you have only to show him this ring, on which his own name is engraved.

**[S']AKOONTALÁ.**
The bare thought of it puts me in a tremor.

**PRIYAMVADÁ AND ANASÚYÁ.**
There is no real cause for fear, dearest. Excessive affection is too apt to suspect evil where none exists.

**[S']AKOONTALÁ.**
Come, lady, we must hasten on. The sun is rising in the heavens.

**[S']AKOONTALÁ.**
*Looking towards the hermitage.*

Dear father, when shall I ever see this hallowed grove again?

**KANWA.**
I will tell thee; listen:—
  When thou hast passed a long and blissful life
  As King Dushyanta's queen, and jointly shared
  With all the earth his ever-watchful care;
  And hast beheld thine own heroic son,
  Matchless in arms, united to a bride
  In happy wedlock; when his aged sire,
  Thy faithful husband, hath to him resigned
  The helm of state; then, weary of the world,
  Together with Dushyanta thou shalt seek
  The calm seclusion of thy former home ;
  There amid holy scenes to be at peace,
  Till thy pure spirit gain its last release.

**GAUTAMÍ.**
Come, my child, the favourable time for our journey is fast passing. Let thy father return. Venerable Sire, be thou the first to move homewards, or these last words will never end.

**KANWA.**
Daughter, detain me no longer. My religious duties must not be interrupted.

**[S']AKOONTALÁ.**
*Again embracing her foster-father.*

Beloved father, thy frame is much enfeebled by penitential exercises. Do not, oh! do not, allow thyself to sorrow too much on my account.

**KANWA.**
*Sighing.*

How, O my child, shall my bereaved heart
Forget its bitterness, when, day by day,
Full in my sight shall grow the tender plants
Reared by thy care, or sprang from hallowed grain
Which thy loved hands have strewn around the door—
A frequent offering to our household gods ?
Go, my daughter, and may thy journey be prosperous.

*Exit [S']AKOONTALÁ with her escort.*
*PRIYAMVADÁ AND ANASÚYÁ. [Gazing after [S']AKOONTALÁ.*

Alas! alas! she is gone, and now the trees hide our darling from
our view.

**KANWA.**
*Sighing.*

Well, Anasúyá, your sister has departed. Moderate your grief, both of you,
and follow me, I go back to the hermitage.

**PRIYAMVADÁ AND ANASÚYÁ.**
Holy father, the sacred grove will be a desert without

**[S']akoontalá.**
How can we ever return to it?

**KANWA.**
It is natural enough that your affection should make you view it in this light.

*Walking pensively on.*

As for me, I am quite surprised at myself. Now that I have fairly dismissed
her to her husband's house, my mind is easy; for, indeed,
A daughter is a loan—a precious jewel
Lent to a parent till her husband claim her.
And now that to her rightful lord and master
I have delivered her, my burdened soul
Is lightened, and I seem to breathe more freely.

*Exeunt.*

# Act V

## SCENE.—A Room in the Palace.

*The King DUSHYANTA and the Jester MÁ[T.]HAVYA are discovered seated.*

**MÁ[T.]HAVYA.**
*Listening.*

Hark! my dear friend, listen a minute, and you will hear sweet sounds
proceeding from the music-room. Some one is singing a charming air. Who
can it be? Oh! I know. The queen Hansapadiká is practising her notes, that
she may greet you with a new song.

**KING.**
Hush! Let me listen.

A VOICE SINGS BEHIND THE SCENES.
 How often hither didst thou rove,
 Sweet bee, to kiss the mango's cheek;
 Oh! leave not, then, thy early love,
 The lily's honeyed lip to seek.

KING.
A most impassioned strain, truly!

MÁ[T.]HAVYA.
Do you understand the meaning of the words?

KING.
*Smiling.*

She means to reprove me, because I once paid her great attention, and have
lately deserted her for the queen Vasumatí. Go, my dear fellow, and tell
Hansapadiká from me that I take her delicate reproof as it is intended.

MÁ[T.]HAVYA.
Very well.

*Rising from his seat.*

But stay—I don't much relish being sent to bear the brunt of her jealousy.
The chances are that she will have me seized by the hair of the head and
beaten to a jelly. I would as soon expose myself, after a vow of celibacy, to the
seductions of a lovely nymph, as encounter the fury of a jealous woman.

KING.
Go, go; you can disarm her wrath by a civil speech; but give her
my message.

MÁ[T.]HAVYA.
What must be must be, I suppose.

*Exit.*

KING.
*Aside.*

Strange! that song has filled me with a most peculiar sensation. A melancholy
feeling has come over me, and I seem to yearn after some long-forgotten
object of affection. Singular, indeed! but
 Not seldom In our happy hours of ease,
 When thought is still, the sight of some fair form,
 Or mournful fall of music breathing low,
 Will stir strange fancies, thrilling all the soul
 With a mysterious sadness, and a sense
 Of vague yet earnest longing. Can it be
 That the dim memory of events long past,
 Or friendships formed in other states of being ,
 Flits like a passing shadow o'er the spirit?

*Remains pensive and sad.*
*Enter the CHAMBERLAIN , named VÁTÁYANA.*

CHAMBERLAIN.
Alas! to what an advanced period of life have I attained!

*430*

Even this wand betrays the lapse of years;
In youthful days 'twas but a useless badge
And symbol of my office; now it serves
As a support to prop my tottering steps.

Ah me! I feel very unwilling to announce to the King that a deputation of young hermits from the sage Kanwa has arrived, and craves an immediate audience. Certainly, his Majesty ought not to neglect a matter of sacred duty, yet I hardly like to trouble him when he has just risen from the judgment-seat. Well, well; a monarch's business is to sustain the world, and he must not expect much repose; because—

Onward, for ever onward, in his car
The unwearied Sun pursues his daily course,
Nor tarries to unyoke his glittering steeds.
And, ever moving, speeds the rushing Wind
Through boundless space, filling the universe
With his life-giving breezes. Day and night,
The King of Serpents on his thousand heads
Upholds the incumbent earth; and even so,
Unceasing toil is aye the lot of kings,
Who, in return, draw nurture from their subjects.

I will therefore deliver my message.

*Walking on and looking about.*

Ah! here comes the King.

His subjects are his children; through the day,
Like a fond father, to supply their wants,
Incessantly he labours; wearied now,
The monarch seeks seclusion and repose;
E'en as the prince of elephants defies
The sun's fierce heat, and leads the fainting herd
To verdant pastures, ere his wayworn limbs
He yields to rest beneath the cooling shade.

*Approaching.*

Victory to the King! So please your Majesty, some hermits who live in a forest near the Snowy Mountains have arrived here, bringing certain women with them. They have a message to deliver from the sage Kanwa and desire an audience. I await your Majesty's commands.

KING.
*Respectfully.*

A message from the sage Kanwa, did you say?

CHAMBERLAIN.
Even so, my liege.

KING.
Tell my domestic priest Somaráta to receive the hermits with due honour, according to the prescribed form. He may then himself introduce them into my presence. I will await them in a place suitable for the reception of such holy guests.

CHAMBERLAIN.
Your Majesty's commands shall be obeyed.

*Exit.*

**KING.**
*Rising and addressing his WARDER.*

Vetravatí, lead the way to the chamber of the consecrated fire .

**WARDER.**
This way, Sire.

**KING.**
*Walking on, with the air of one oppressed by the cares of Government.*

People are generally contented and happy when they have gained their desires; but kings have no sooner attained the object of their aspirations than all their troubles begin.
'Tis a fond thought that to attain the end
And object of ambition is to rest;
Success doth only mitigate the fever
Of anxious expectation; soon the fear
Of losing what we have, the constant care
Of guarding it, doth weary. Ceaseless toil
Must be the lot of him who with his hands
Supports the canopy that shields his subjects.

**TWO HERALDS .**
*Behind the scenes.*

May the King be victorious!

**FIRST HERALD.**
Honour to him who labours day by day
For the world's weal, forgetful of his own;
Like some tall tree that with its stately head
Endures the solar beam, while underneath
It yields refreshing shelter to the weary.

**SECOND HERALD.**
Let but the monarch wield his threatening rod
And e'en the guilty tremble; at his voice
The rebel spirit cowers; his grateful subjects
Acknowledge him their guardian; rich and poor
Hail him a faithful friend—a loving kinsman.

**KING.**
Weary as I was before, this complimentary address has refreshed me.

*Walks on.*

**WARDER.**
Here is the terrace of the hallowed fire-chamber, and yonder stands the cow that yields the milk for the oblations. The sacred enclosure has been recently purified, and looks clean and beautiful. Ascend, Sire.

**KING.**
*Leans on the shoulders of his attendants and ascends_.*

Vetravatí, what can possibly be the message that the venerable

Kanwa has sent me by these hermits?
  Perchance their sacred rites have been disturbed
  By demons, or some evil has befallen
  The innocent herds, their favourites, that graze
  Within the precincts of the hermitage,
  Or haply, through my sins, some withering blight
  Has nipped the creeping plants that spread their arms
  Around the hallowed grove. Such troubled thoughts
  Crowd through my mind, and fill me with misgiving.

### WARDER.

If you ask my opinion, Sire, I think the hermits merely wish to take an opportunity of testifying their loyalty, and are therefore come to offer homage to your majesty.

*Enter the HERMITS leading [S']AKOONTALÁ, attended by GAUTAMÍ; and in advance of them, the CHAMBERLAIN and the DOMESTIC PRIEST.*

### CHAMBERLAIN.

This way, reverend Sirs, this way.

### [S']ÁRNGARAVA

O [S']áradwata,
  'Tis true the monarch lacks no royal grace,
  Nor ever swerves from justice; true, his people,
  Yea such as in life's humblest walks are found,
  Refrain from evil courses; still to me,
  A lonely hermit reared in solitude,
  This throng appears bewildering, and I seem
  To look upon a burning house, whose inmates
  Are running to and fro in wild dismay.

### [S']ÁRADWATA.

It is natural that the first sight of the King's capital should affect you in this manner; my own sensations are very similar.
  As one just bathed beholds the man polluted;
  As one late purified, the yet impure;
  As one awake looks on the yet unawakened;
  Or as the freeman gazes on the thrall,
  So I regard this crowd of pleasure-seekers.

### [S']AKOONTALÁ.

*Feeling a quivering sensation in her right eyelid , and suspecting a bad omen.*

Alas! what means this throbbing of my right eyelid?

### GAUTAMÍ.

Heaven avert the evil omen, my child! May the guardian deities of thy husband's family convert it into a sign of good fortune!

*Walks on.*

### PRIEST.
*Pointing to the King.*

Most reverend Sirs, there stands the protector of the four classes of the people; the guardian of the four conditions of the priesthood . He has just left the judgment-seat, and is waiting for you. Behold him!

*433*

**[S']ÁRNGARAVA**
Great Bráhman, we are happy in thinking that the King's power is exerted
for the protection of all classes of his subjects. We have not come as
petitioners—we have the fullest confidence in the generosity of his nature.
  The loftiest trees bend humbly to the ground
  Beneath the teeming burden of their fruit;
  High in the vernal sky the pregnant clouds
  Suspend their stately course, and, hanging low,
  Scatter their sparkling treasures o'er the earth;
  And such is true benevolence; the good
  Are never rendered arrogant by riches.

**WARDER.**
So please your Majesty, I judge from the placid countenance of the hermits
that they have no alarming message to deliver.

**KING.**
*Looking at [S']AKOONTALÁ.*

But the lady there—
  Who can she be, whose form of matchless grace
  Is half concealed beneath her flowing veil?
  Among the sombre hermits she appears
  Like a fresh bud 'mid sear and yellow leaves.

**WARDER.**
So please your Majesty, my curiosity is also roused, but no conjecture occurs
to my mind. This at least is certain, that she deserves to be looked at more
closely.

**KING.**
True; but it is not right to gaze at another man's wife .

**[S']AKOONTALÁ.**
*Placing her hand on her bosom. Aside.*

O my heart, why this throbbing? Remember thy lord's affection, and take
courage.

**PRIEST.**
*Advancing.*

These holy men have been received with all due honour. One of them has
now a message to deliver from his spiritual superior. Will your Majesty deign
to hear it?

**KING.**
I am all attention.

**HERMITS.**
*Extending their hands.*

Victory to the King!

**KING.**
Accept my respectful greeting.

**HERMITS.**

May the desires of your soul be accomplished!

KING.
I trust no one is molesting you in the prosecution of your religious rites.

HERMITS.
  Who dares disturb our penitential rites
  When thou art our protector? Can the night
  Prevail to cast her shadows o'er the earth
  While the sun's beams irradiate the sky?

KING.
Such, indeed, is the very meaning of my title—'Defender of the Just.' I trust the
venerable Kanwa is in good health. The world is interested in his well-being.

HERMITS.
Holy men have health and prosperity in their own power. He bade us greet
your Majesty, and, after kind inquiries, deliver this message.

KING.
Let me hear his commands.

[S']ÁRNGARAVA.
He bade us say that he feels happy in giving his sanction to the marriage which
your Majesty contracted with this lady, his daughter, privately and by mutual
agreement. Because,
  By us thou art esteemed the most illustrious
  Of noble husbands; and [S']akoontalá,
  Virtue herself in human form revealed.
  Great Brahmá hath in equal yoke united
  A bride unto a husband worthy of her;
  Henceforth let none make blasphemous complaint
  That he is pleased with ill-assorted unions .
Since, therefore, she expects soon to be the mother of thy child, receive
her into thy palace, that she may perform, in conjunction with thee, the
ceremonies prescribed by religion on such an occasion.

GAUTAMÍ.
So please your Majesty, I would add a few words; but why should I intrude
my sentiments when an opportunity of speaking my mind has never been
allowed me?
  She took no counsel with her kindred; thou
  Didst not confer with thine, but all alone
  Didst solemnize thy nuptials with thy wife.
  Together, then, hold converse; let us leave you.

[S']AKOONTALÁ
*Aside.*

Ah! how I tremble for my lord's reply.

KING.
What strange proposal is this?

[S']AKOONTALÁ

*Aside.*

His words are like fire to me.

[S']ÁRNGARAVA
What do I hear? Dost thou, then, hesitate? Monarch, thou art well acquainted with the ways of the world, and knowest that
  A wife, however virtuous and discreet,
  If she live separate from her wedded lord,
  Though under shelter of her parent's roof,
  Is marked for vile suspicion. Let her dwell
  Beside her husband, though he hold her not
  In his affection. So her kinsmen will it.

KING.
Do you really mean to assert that I ever married this lady?

[S']AKOONTALÁ.
*Despondingly. Aside.*

O my heart, thy worst misgivings are confirmed.

[S']ÁRNGARAVA.
Is it becoming in a monarch to depart from the rules of justice, because he repents of his engagements?

KING.
I cannot answer a question which is based on a mere fabrication.

[S']ÁRNGARAVA.
Such inconstancy is fortunately not common, except in men intoxicated by power.

KING.
Is that remark aimed at me?

GAUTAMÍ.
Be not ashamed, my daughter. Let me remove thy veil for a little space. Thy husband will then recognize thee.

*Removes her veil.*

KING.
*Gazing at [S']AKOONTALÁ. Aside.*

  What charms are here revealed before mine eyes!
  Truly no blemish mars the symmetry
  Of that fair form; yet can I ne'er believe
  She is my wedded wife; and like a bee
  That circles round the flower whose nectared cup
  Teems with the dew of morning, I must pause
  Ere eagerly I taste the proffered sweetness.

*Remains wrapped in thought.*

WARDER.
How admirably does our royal master's behaviour prove his regard for justice! Who else would hesitate for a moment when good fortune offered for his acceptance a form of such rare beauty?

**[S']ÁRNGARAVA.**
Great King, why art thou silent?

**KING.**
Holy men, I have revolved the matter in my mind; but the more I think of it, the less able am I to recollect that I ever contracted an alliance with this lady. What answer, then, can I possibly give you when I do not believe myself to be her husband, and I plainly see that she is soon to become a mother?

**[S']AKOONTALÁ**
*Aside.*

Woe! woe! Is our very marriage to be called in question by my own husband? Ah me! is this to be the end of all my bright visions of wedded happiness?

**[S']ÁRNGARAVA.**
Beware!
  Beware how thou insult the holy Sage!
  Remember how he generously allowed
  Thy secret union with his foster-child;
  And how, when thou didst rob him of his treasure,
  He sought to furnish thee excuse, when rather
  He should have cursed thee for a ravisher.

**[S']ÁRADWATA.**
[S']árngarava, speak to him no more. [S']akoontalá, our part is performed; we have said all we have to say, and the King has replied in the manner thou hast heard. It is now thy turn to give him convincing evidence of thy marriage.

**[S']AKOONTALÁ.**
*Aside.*

Since his feeling towards me has undergone a complete revolution, what will it avail to revive old recollections? One thing is clear—I shall soon have to mourn my own widowhood.

*Aloud.*

My revered husband—

*Stops short.*

But no—I dare not address thee by this title, since thou hast refused to acknowledge our union. Noble descendant of Puru! It is not worthy of thee to betray an innocent-minded girl, and disown her in such terms, after having so lately and so solemnly plighted thy vows to her in the hermitage.

**KING.**
*Stopping his ears.*

I will hear no more. Be such a crime far from my thoughts!
  What evil spirit can possess thee, lady,
  That thou dost seek to sully my good name
  By base aspersions, like a swollen torrent,
  That, leaping from its narrow bed, o'erthrows
  The tree upon its bank, and strives to blend
  Its turbid waters with the crystal stream?

**[S']AKOONTALÁ.**

*437*

If, then, thou really believest me to be the wife of another, and thy present conduct proceeds from some cloud that obscures thy recollection, I will easily convince thee by this token.

KING.
An excellent idea!

[S']AKOONTALÁ.
*Feeling for the ring.*

Alas! alas! woe is me! There is no ring on my finger!

*Looks with anguish at GAUTAMÍ.*

GAUTAMÍ.
The ring must have slipped off when thou wast in the act of offering homage to the holy water of [S']achí's sacred pool, near Sakrávatára .

KING.
*Smiling.*

People may well talk of the readiness of woman's invention! Here is an instance of it.

[S']AKOONTALÁ.
Say, rather, of the omnipotence of fate. I will mention another circumstance, which may yet convince thee.

KING.
By all means let me hear it at once.

[S']AKOONTALÁ.
One day, while we were seated in a jasmine-bower, thou didst pour into the hollow of thine hand some water, sprinkled by a recent shower in the cup of a lotus-blossom—

KING.
I am listening; proceed.

[S']AKOONTALÁ.
At that instant, my adopted child, the little fawn, with soft, long eyes, came running towards us. Upon which, before tasting the water thyself, thou didst kindly offer some to the little creature, saying fondly:—'Drink first, gentle fawn.' But she could not be induced to drink from the hand of a stranger; though immediately afterwards, when I took the water in my own hand, she drank with perfect confidence. Then, with a smile, thou didst say;—'Every creature confides naturally in its own kind. You are both inhabitants of the same forest, and have learnt to trust each other.'

KING.
Voluptuaries may allow themselves to be seduced from the path of duty by falsehoods such as these, expressed in honeyed words.

GAUTAMÍ.
Speak not thus, illustrious Prince. This lady was brought up in a hermitage, and has never learnt deceit.

KING.

*438*

Holy matron,
  E'en in untutored brutes, the female sex
  Is marked by inborn subtlety—much more
  In beings gifted with intelligence.
  The wily Koïl , ere towards the sky
  She wings her sportive flight, commits her eggs
  To other nests, and artfully consigns
  The rearing of her little ones to strangers.

### [S']AKOONTALÁ.
*Angrily.*

Dishonourable man, thou judgest of others by thine own evil heart. Thou, at least, art unrivalled in perfidy, and standest alone—a base deceiver in the garb of virtue and religion—like a deep pit whose yawning mouth is concealed by smiling flowers.

### KING.
*Aside.*

Her anger, at any rate, appears genuine, and makes me almost doubt whether I am in the right. For indeed,
  When I had vainly searched my memory,
  And so with stern severity denied
  The fabled story of our secret loves,
  Her brows, that met before in graceful curves,
  Like the arched weapon of the god of love,
  Seemed by her frown dissevered; while the fire
  Of sudden anger kindled in her eyes.

*Aloud.*

My good lady, Dushyanta's character is well known to all. I comprehend not your meaning.

### [S']AKOONTALÁ.
Well do I deserve to be thought a harlot for having in the innocence of my heart, and out of the confidence I reposed in a Prince of Puru's race, entrusted my honour to a man whose mouth distils honey, while his heart is full of poison.

*Covers her face with her mantle, and bursts into tears.*

### [S']ÁRNGARAVA.
Thus it is that burning remorse must ever follow rash actions which might have been avoided, and for which one has only one's self to blame.
  Not hastily should marriage be contracted,
  And specially in secret. Many a time,
  In hearts that know not each the other's fancies,
  Fond love is changed into most bitter hate.

### KING.
How now! Do you give credence to this woman rather than to me, that you heap such accusations on me?

### [S']ÁRNGARAVA.
*Sarcastically.*

439

That would be too absurd, certainly. You have heard the proverb:—
  Hold in contempt the innocent words of those
  Who from their infancy have known no guile;
  But trust the treacherous counsels of the man
  Who makes a very science of deceit.

KING.
Most veracious Bráhman, grant that you are in the right, what end would be gained by betraying this lady?

[S']ÁRNGARAVA.
Ruin.

KING.
No one will believe that a Prince of Puru's race would seek to ruin others or himself.

[S']ÁRADWATA.
This altercation is idle, [S']árngarava. We have executed the commission of our preceptor; come, let us return.

*To the KING.*

[S']akoontalá is certainly thy bride;
  Receive her or reject her, she is thine.
  Do with her, King, according to thy pleasure—
  The husband o'er the wife is absolute.
Go on before us, Gautamí.

*They move away.*

[S']AKOONTALÁ.
What! is it not enough to have been betrayed by this perfidious man? Must you also forsake me, regardless of my tears and lamentations?

*Attempts to follow them.*

GAUTAMÍ.
*Stopping.*

My son [S']árngarava, see! [S']akoontalá is following us, and with tears implores us not to leave her. Alas! poor child, what will she do here with a cruel husband who casts her from him?

[S']ÁRNGARAVA.
*Turning angrily towards her.*

Wilful woman, dost thou seek to be independent of thy lord?

*[S']AKOONTALÁ trembles with fear.*

[S']akoontalá!
  If thou art really what the King proclaims thee,
  How can thy father e'er receive thee back
  Into his house and home? but if thy conscience
  Be witness to thy purity of soul,
  E'en should thy husband to a handmaid's lot
  Condemn thee, thou may'st cheerfully endure it.
  When ranked among the number of his household.

Thy duty therefore is to stay. As for us, we must return immediately.

KING.
Deceive not this lady, my good hermit, by any such expectations.
  The moon expands the lotus of the night,
  The rising sun awakes the lily; each
  Is with his own contented. Even so
  The virtuous man is master of his passions,
  And from another's wife averts his gaze.

[S']ÁRNGARAVA.
Since thy union with another woman has rendered thee oblivious of thy marriage with [S']akoontalá, whence this fear of losing thy character for constancy and virtue?

KING.
*To his domestic PRIEST.*

You must counsel me, revered Sir, as to my course of action.
Which of the two evils involves the greater or less sin?
  Whether by some dark veil my mind be clouded.
  Or this designing woman speak untruly,
  I know not. Tell me, must I rather be
  The base disowner of my wedded wife,
  Or the defiling and defiled adulterer?

PRIEST.
*After deliberation.*

You must take an intermediate course.

KING.
What course, revered Sir? Tell me at once.

PRIEST.
I will provide an asylum for the lady in my own house until the birth of her child; and my reason, if you ask me, is this: Soothsayers have predicted that your first-born will have universal dominion. Now, if the hermit's daughter bring forth a son with the discus or mark of empire in the lines of his hand , you must admit her immediately into your royal apartments with great rejoicings; if not, then determine to send her back as soon as possible to her father.

KING.
I bow to the decision of my spiritual advisor.

PRIEST.
Daughter, follow me.

[S']AKOONTALÁ.
O divine earth, open and receive me into thy bosom!

*Exit [S']AKOONTALÁ weeping, with the PRIEST and the HERMITS. The KING remains absorbed in thinking of her, though the curse still clouds his recollection.*

A VOICE BEHIND THE SCENES.
A miracle! a miracle!

**KING.**
*Listening.*

What has happened now?

**PRIEST.**
*Entering with an air of astonishment.*
Great Prince, a stupendous prodigy has just occurred.

**KING.**
What is it?

**PRIEST.**
May it please your Majesty, so soon as Kanwa's pupils had departed, [S']
akoontalá, her eyes all bathed in tears, with outstretched arms, bewailed her
cruel fate—

**KING.**
Well, well, what happened then?

**PRIEST.**
  When suddenly a shining apparition,
  In female shape, descended from the skies,
  Near the nymph's pool, and bore her up to heaven.

*All remain motionless with astonishment.*

**KING.**
My good priest, from the very first I declined having anything to do with this
matter. It is now all over, and we can never, by our conjectures, unravel the
mystery; let it rest; go, seek repose.

**PRIEST.**
*Looking at the KING.*

Be it so. Victory to the King!

*Exit.*

**KING.**
Vetravatí, I am tired out; lead the way to the bedchamber.

**WARDER.**
This way, Sire.

*They move away.*

**KING.**
  Do what I will, I cannot call to mind
  That I did e'er espouse the sage's daughter;
  Therefore I have disowned her; yet 'tis strange
  How painfully my agitated heart
  Bears witness to the truth of her assertion,
  And makes me credit her against my judgment.

*Exeunt.*

## Prelude to Act VI

## SCENE.—A Street.

*Enter the King's brother-in-law as SUPERINTENDENT of the city police; and with him TWO CONSTABLES, dragging a poor FISHERMAN, who has his hands tied behind his back.*

**BOTH THE CONSTABLES.**
*Striking the prisoner.*
Take that for a rascally thief that you are; and now tell us, sirrah, where you found this ring—aye, the King's own signet-ring. See, here is the royal name engraved on the setting of the jewel.

**FISHERMAN.**
*With a gesture of alarm.*

Mercy! kind sirs, mercy! I did not steal it; indeed I did not.

**FIRST CONSTABLE.**
Oh! then I suppose the King took you for some fine Bráhman, and made you a present of it?

**FISHERMAN.**
Only hear me. I am but a poor fisherman, living at Sakrávatára—

**SECOND CONSTABLE.**
Scoundrel, who ever asked you, pray, for a history of your birth and parentage?

**SUPERINTENDENT.**
*To one of the CONSTABLES.*

Súchaka, let the fellow tell his own story from the beginning. Don't interrupt him.

**BOTH CONSTABLES.**
As you please, master. Go on, then, sirrah, and say what you've got to say.

**FISHERMAN.**
You see in me a poor man, who supports his family by catching fish with nets, hooks, and the like.

**SUPERINTENDENT.**
*Laughing.*

A most refined occupation, certainly !

**FISHERMAN.**
Blame me not for it, master,
  The father's occupation, though despised
  By others, casts no shame upon the son,
  And he should not forsake it . Is the priest
  Who kills the animal for sacrifice
  Therefore deemed cruel? Sure a low-born man
  May, though a fisherman, be tender-hearted.

**SUPERINTENDENT.**
Well, well; go on with your story.

443

**FISHERMAN.**
One day I was cutting open a large carp  I had just hooked, when the sparkle of a jewel caught my eye, and what should I find in the fish's maw but that ring! Soon afterwards, when I was offering it for sale, I was seized by your honours. Now you know everything. Whether you kill me, or whether you let me go, this is the true account of how the ring came into my possession.

**SUPERINTENDENT.**
*To one of the CONSTABLES.*

Well, Jánuka, the rascal emits such a fishy odour that I have no doubt of his being a fisherman; but we must inquire a little more closely into this queer story about the finding of the ring. Come, we'll take him before the King's household.

**BOTH CONSTABLES.**
Very good, master. Get on with you, you cutpurse.

*All move on.*

**SUPERINTENDENT.**
Now attend, Súchaka; keep your guard here at the gate; and hark ye, sirrahs, take good care your prisoner does not escape, while I go in and lay the whole story of the discovery of this ring before the King in person. I will soon return and let you know his commands.

**BOTH CONSTABLES.**
Go in, master, by all means; and may you find favour in the King's sight.

*Exit SUPERINTENDENT. FIRST CONSTABLE.*
*After an interval.*

I say, Jánuka, the Superintendent is a long time away.

**SECOND CONSTABLE.**
Aye, aye; kings are not to be got at so easily. Folks must bide the proper opportunity.

**FIRST CONSTABLE.**
Jánuka, my fingers itch to strike the first blow at this royal victim here. We must kill him with all the honours, you know. I long to begin binding the flowers round his head .

*Pretends to strike a blow at the FISHERMAN.*

**FISHERMAN.**
Your Honour surely will not put an innocent man to a cruel death.

**SECOND CONSTABLE.**
There's our Superintendent at last, I declare. See! he is coming towards us with a paper in his hand. We shall soon know the King's command; so prepare, my fine fellow, either to become food for the vultures, or to make acquaintance with some hungry cur.

**SUPERINTENDENT.**
*Entering.*

Ho, there, Súchaka! set the fisherman at liberty, I tell you. His story about the

ring is all correct. SÚCHAKA.
Oh! very good, Sir; as you please.

**SECOND CONSTABLE.**
The fellow had one foot in hell, and now here he is in the land of the living.

*Releases him.*

**FISHERMAN.**
*Bowing to the SUPERINTENDENT.*

Now, master, what think you of my way of getting a livelihood?

**SUPERINTENDENT.**
Here, my good man, the King desired me to present you with this purse. It contains a sum of money equal to the full value of the ring.

*Gives him the money.*

**FISHERMAN.**
*Taking it and bowing.*

His Majesty does me too great honour.

**SÚCHAKA.**
You may well say so. He might as well have taken you from the gallows to seat you on his state elephant.

**JÁNUKA.**
Master, the King must value the ring very highly, or he would never have sent such a sum of money to this ragamuffin.

**SUPERINTENDENT.**
I don't think he prizes it as a costly jewel so much as a memorial of some person he tenderly loves. The moment it was shown to him he became much agitated, though in general he conceals his feelings.

**SÚCHAKA.**
Then you must have done a great service—

**JÁNUKA.**
Yes, to this husband of a fish-wife.

*Looks enviously at the FISHERMAN.*

**FISHERMAN.**
Here's half the money for you, my masters. It will serve to purchase the flowers you spoke of, if not to buy me your good-will.

**JÁNUKA.**
Well, now, that's just as it should be.

**SUPERINTENDENT.**
My good fisherman, you are an excellent fellow, and I begin to feel quite a regard for you. Let us seal our first friendship over a glass of good liquor. Come along to the next wine-shop, and we'll drink your health.

**ALL.**
By all means.

445

*Exeunt.*

# Act VI

## SCENE.—_The Garden of a Palace.

*The nymph_ SÁNUMATÍ *is seen descending in a celestial car.*

**SÁNUMATÍ.**
Behold me just arrived from attending in my proper turn at the nymph's pool, where I have left the other nymphs to perform their ablutions, whilst I seek to ascertain, with my own eyes, how it fares with King Dushyanta. My connexion with the nymph Menaká has made her daughter [S']akoontalá dearer to me than my own flesh and blood; and Menaká it was who charged me with this errand on her daughter's behalf.

*Looking round in all directions.*

How is it that I see no preparations in the King's household for celebrating the great vernal festival ? I could easily discover the reason by my divine faculty of meditation ; but respect must be shown to the wishes of my friend. How then shall I arrive at the truth? I know what I will do. I will become invisible, and place myself near those two maidens who are tending the plants in the garden.

*Descends and takes her station.*
*Enter a* MAIDEN, *who stops in front of a mango-tree, and gazes at the blossom.*
*Another* MAIDEN *is seen behind her.*

**FIRST MAIDEN.**
Hail to thee, lovely harbinger of spring! The varied radiance of thy opening flowers Is welcome to my sight. I bid thee hail, Sweet mango, soul of this enchanting season.

**SECOND MAIDEN.**
Parabhritiká, what are you saying there to yourself?

**FIRST MAIDEN.**
Dear Madhukariká, am I not named after the Koïl ? and does not the Koïl sing for joy at the first appearance of the mango-blossom?

**SECOND MAIDEN.**
*Approaching hastily, with transport.*

What! is spring really come?

**FIRST MAIDEN.**
Yes, indeed, Madhukariká, and with it the season of joy, love, and song.

**SECOND MAIDEN.**
Let me lean upon you, dear, while I stead on tiptoe and pluck a blossom, of the mango, that I may present it as an offering to the god of love.

**FIRST MAIDEN.**
Provided you let me have half the reward which the god will bestow in return.

**SECOND MAIDEN.**
To be sure you shall, and that without asking. Are we not one in heart and

soul, though divided in body?

*Leans on her friend and plucks a mango-blossom.*

Ah! here is a bud just bursting into flower. It diffuses a delicious perfume, though not yet quite expanded.

*Joining her hands reverentially.*

God of the bow, who with spring's choicest flowers
Dost point thy five unerring shafts ; to thee
I dedicate this blossom; let it serve
To barb thy truest arrow; be its mark
Some youthful heart that pines to be beloved.

*Throws down a mango-blossom.*

CHAMBERLAIN.
*Entering in a hurried manner, angrily.*

Hold there, thoughtless woman. What are you about, breaking off those mango-blossoms, when the King has forbidden the celebration of the spring festival?

BOTH MAIDENS.
*Alarmed.*

Pardon us, kind Sir, we have heard nothing of it.

CHAMBERLAIN.
You have heard nothing of it? Why, all the vernal plants and shrubs, and the very birds that lodge in their branches, show more respect to the King's order than you do.
  Yon mango-blossoms, though long since expanded,
  Gather no down upon their tender crests;
  The flower still lingers in the amaranth ,
  Imprisoned in its bud; the tuneful Koïl,
  Though winter's chilly dews be overpast,
  Suspends the liquid volume of his song
  Scarce uttered in his throat; e'en Love, dismayed,
  Restores the half-drawn arrow to his quiver.

BOTH MAIDENS.
The mighty power of King Dushyanta is not to be disputed.

FIRST MAIDEN.
It is but a few days since Mitrávasu, the King's brother-in-law, sent us to wait upon his Majesty; and, during the whole of our sojourn here, we have been entrusted with the charge of the royal pleasure-grounds. We are therefore strangers in this place, and heard nothing of the order till you informed us of it.

CHAMBERLAIN.
Well then, now you know it, take care you don't continue your preparations.

BOTH MAIDENS.
But tell us, kind Sir, why has the King prohibited the usual festivities? We are curious to hear, if we may.

SÁNUMATÍ.
*Aside.*

Men are naturally fond of festive entertainments. There must be some good reason for the prohibition.

CHAMBERLAIN.
The whole affair is now public; why should I not speak of it? Has not the gossip about the King's rejection of [S']akoontalá reached your ears yet?

BOTH MAIDENS.
Oh yes, we heard the story from the King's brother-in-law, as far, at least, as the discovery of the ring.

CHAMBERLAIN.
Then there is little more to tell you. As soon as the King's memory was restored by the sight of his own ring, he exclaimed: 'Yes, it is all true. I remember now my secret marriage with [S']akoontalá. When I repudiated her, I had lost my recollection!' Ever since that moment, he has yielded himself a prey to the bitterest remorse.
  He loathes his former pleasures; he rejects
  The daily homage of his ministers;
  On his lone couch he tosses to and fro,
  Courting repose in vain. Whene'er he meets
  The ladies of his palace, and would fain
  Address them with politeness, he confounds
  Their names; or, calling them '[S']akoontalá,'
  Is straightway silent and abashed with shame.

SÁNUMATÍ.
*Aside.*

To me this account is delightful.

CHAMBERLAIN.
In short, the King is so completely out of his mind that the festival has been prohibited.

BOTH MAIDENS.
Perfectly right.

A VOICE BEHIND THE SCENES.
The King! the King! This way, Sire, this way.

CHAMBERLAIN.
*Listening.*

Oh! here comes his Majesty in this direction. Pass on, maidens; attend to your duties.

BOTH MAIDENS.
We will, sir.

*Exeunt.*

*Enter King DUSHYANTA, dressed in deep mourning, attended his Jester, MÁ[T.] HAVYA, and preceded by VETRAVATÍ.*

CHAMBERLAIN.

*Gazing at the KING.*

Well, noble forms are certainly pleasing, under all varieties of outward circumstances. The King's person is as charming as ever, notwithstanding his sorrow of mind.

Though but a single golden bracelet spans
His wasted arm; though costly ornaments
Have given place to penitential weeds;
Though oft-repeated sighs have blanched his lips,
And robbed them of their bloom; though sleepless care
And carking thought have dimmed his beaming eye;
Yet does his form, by its inherent lustre,
Dazzle the gaze; and, like a priceless gem
Committed to some cunning polisher,
Grow more effulgent by the loss of substance.

### SÁNUMATÍ.
*Aside. Looking at the KING.*

Now that I have seen him, I can well understand why [S']akoontalá should pine after such a man, in spite of his disdainful rejection of her.

### KING.
*Walking slowly up and down in deep thought.*

When fatal lethargy o'erwhelmed my soul,
My loved one strove to rouse me, but in vain;
And now, when I would fain in slumber deep
Forget myself, full soon remorse doth wake me.

### SÁNUMATÍ.
*Aside.*

My poor [S']akoontalá's sufferings are very similar.

### MÁ[T.]HAVYA.
*Aside.*

He is taken with another attack of this odious [S']akoontalá-fever.
How shall we ever cure him?

### CHAMBERLAIN.
*Approaching.*

Victory to the King! Great Prince, the royal pleasure-grounds have been put in order. Your Majesty can resort to them for exercise and amusement whenever you think proper.

### KING.
Vetravatí, tell the worthy Pi[S']una, my prime minister, from me, that I am so exhausted by want of sleep that I cannot sit on the judgment-seat to-day. If any case of importance be brought before the tribunal, he must give it his best attention, and inform me of the circumstances by letter.

### VETRAVATÍ.
Your Majesty's commands shall be obeyed.

*Exit.*

**KING.**

*To the CHAMBERLAIN.*

And you, Vátáyana, may go about your own affairs.

**CHAMBERLAIN.**
I will, Sire.

**MÁ[T.]HAVYA.**
Now that you have rid yourself of these troublesome fellows, you can enjoy the delightful coolness of your pleasure-grounds
without interruption.

**KING.**
Ah! my dear friend, there is an old adage:—'When affliction has a mind to enter, she will find a crevice somewhere;' and it is verified in me.
  Scarce is my soul delivered from the cloud
  That darkened its remembrance of the past,
  When lo! the heart-born deity of love
  With yonder blossom of the mango barbs
  His keenest shaft, and aims it at my breast.

**MÁ[T.]HAVYA.**
Well, then, wait a moment; I will soon demolish Master Káma's  arrow with a cut of my cane.

*Raises his stick and strikes off the mango-blossom.*

**KING.**

*Smiling.*

That will do. I see very well the god of love is not a match for a Bráhman. And now, my dear friend, where shall I sit down, that I may enchant my sight by gazing on the twining plants, which seem to remind me of the graceful shape of my beloved?

**MÁ[T.]HAVYA.**
Don't you remember? you told your personal attendant, Chaturiká, that you would pass the heat of the day in the jasmine-bower; and commanded her to bring the likeness of your queen [S']akoontalá, sketched with your own hand.

**KING.**
True. The sight of her picture will refresh my soul. Lead the way to the arbour.

**MÁ[T.]HAVYA.**
This way, Sire.

*Both move on, followed by SÁNUMATÍ.*

**MÁ[T.]HAVYA.**
Here we are at the jasmine-bower. Look, it has a marble seat, and seems to bid us welcome with its offerings of delicious flowers. You have only to enter and sit down.

*Both enter and seat themselves.*

**SÁNUMATÍ**
*Aside.*

I will lean against these young jasmines. I can easily, from behind them, glance at my friend's picture, and will then hasten to inform her of her husband's ardent affection.

*Stands leaning against the creepers.*

### KING.
Oh! my dear friend, how vividly all the circumstances of my union with [S'] akoontalá present themselves to my recollection at this moment! But tell me now how it was that, between the time of my leaving her in the hermitage and my subsequent rejection of her, you never breathed her name to me? True, you were not by my side when I disowned her; but I had confided to you the story of my love, and you were acquainted with every particular. Did it pass out of your mind as it did out of mine?

### MÁ[T.]HAVYA.
No, no; trust me for that. But, if you remember, when you had finished telling me about it, you added that I was not to take the story in earnest, for that you were not really in love with a country girl, but were only jesting; and I was dull and thick-headed enough to believe you. But so fate decreed, and there is no help for it.

### SÁNUMATÍ.
*Aside.*

Exactly.

### KING.
*After deep thought.*

My dear friend, suggest some relief for my misery.

### MÁ[T.]HAVYA.
Come, come, cheer up; why do you give way? Such weakness is unworthy of you. Great men never surrender themselves to uncontrolled grief. Do not mountains remain unshaken even in a gale of wind?

### KING.
How can I be otherwise than inconsolable, when I call to mind the agonized demeanour of the dear one on the occasion of my disowning her? When cruelly I spurned her from my presence,
  She fain had left me; but the young recluse,
  Stern as the Sage, and with authority
  As from his saintly master, in a voice
  That brooked not contradiction, bade her stay.
  Then through her pleading eyes, bedimmed with tears,
  She cast on me one long reproachful look,
  Which like a poisoned shaft torments me still.

### SÁNUMATÍ.
*Aside.*

Alas! such is the force of self-reproach following a rash action. But his anguish only rejoices me.

### MÁ[T.]HAVYA
An idea has just struck me. I should not wonder if some celestial being had carried her off to heaven.

*451*

**KING.**
Very likely. Who else would have dared to lay a finger on a wife, the idol of her husband? It is said that Menaká, the nymph of heaven, gave her birth. The suspicion has certainly crossed my mind that some of her celestial companions may have taken her to their own abode.

**SÁNUMATÍ.**
*Aside.*

His present recollection of every circumstance of her history does not surprise me so much as his former forgetfulness.

**MÁ[T.]HAVYA.**
If that's the case, you will be certain to meet her before long.

**KING.**
Why?

**MÁ[T.]HAVYA.**
No father and mother can endure to see a daughter suffering the pain of separation from her husband.

**KING.**
Oh! my dear Má[T.]Havya,
  Was it a dream? or did some magic dire,
  Dulling my senses with a strange delusion,
  O'ercome my spirit? or did destiny,
  Jealous of my good actions, mar their fruit,
  And rob me of their guerdon? It is past,
  Whate'er the spell that bound me. Once again
  Am I awake, but only to behold
  The precipice o'er which my hopes have fallen.

**MÁ[T.]HAVYA.**
Do not despair in this manner. Is not this very ring a proof that what has been lost may be unexpectedly found?

**KING.**
*Gazing at the ring.*

Ah! this ring, too, has fallen from a station not easily regained, and I offer it my sympathy. O gem,
  The punishment we suffer is deserved,
  And equal is the merit of our works,
  When such our common doom. Thou didst enjoy
  The thrilling contact of those slender fingers,
  Bright as the dawn; and now how changed thy lot!

**SÁNUMATÍ.**
*Aside.*

Had it found its way to the hand of any other person, then indeed its fate would have been deplorable.

**MÁ[T.]HAVYA.**
Pray, how did the ring ever come upon her hand at all?

**SÁNUMATÍ.**

*Aside.*

I myself am curious to know.

KING.
You shall hear. When I was leaving my beloved [S']akoontalá that I might return to my own capital, she said to me, with tears in her eyes: 'How long will it be ere my lord send for me to his palace and make me his queen?'

MÁ[T.]HAVYA.
Well, what was your reply?

KING.
Then I placed the ring on her finger, and thus addressed her:—

Repeat each day one letter of the name Engraven on this gem; ere thou hast reckoned The tale of syllables, my minister Shall come to lead thee to thy husband's palace.

But, hard-hearted man that I was, I forgot to fulfil my promise, owing to the infatuation that took possession of me.

SÁNUMATÍ.
*Aside.*

A pleasant arrangement! Fate, however, ordained that the appointment should not be kept.

MÁ[T.]HAVYA.
But how did the ring contrive to pass into the stomach of that carp which the fisherman caught and was cutting up?

KING.
It must have slipped from my [S']akoontalá's hand, and fallen into the stream of the Ganges, while she was offering homage to the water of [S']achí's holy pool.

MÁ[T.]HAVYA.
Very likely.

SÁNUMATÍ.
*Aside.*

Hence it happened, I suppose, that the King, always fearful of committing the least injustice, came to doubt his marriage with my poor [S']akoontalá. But why should affection so strong as his stand in need of any token of recognition?

KING.
Let me now address a few words of reproof to this ring.

MÁ[T.]HAVYA.
*Aside.*

He is going stark mad, I verily believe.

KING.
  Hear me, then dull and undiscerning bauble!
  For so it argues thee, that thou could'st leave
  The slender fingers of her hand, to sink
  Beneath the waters. Yet what marvel is it
  That thou should'st lack discernment? let me rather

*453*

Heap curses on myself, who, though endowed
With reason, yet rejected her I loved.

**MÁ[T.]HAVYA.**
*Aside.*

And so, I suppose, I must stand here to be devoured by hunger, whilst he
goes on in this sentimental strain.

**KING.**
O forsaken one, unjustly banished from my presence, take pity on thy slave,
whose heart is consumed by the fire of remorse, and return to my sight.

*Enter CHATURIKÁ hurriedly, with a picture in her hand.*

**CHATURIKÁ.**
Here is the Queen's portrait.

*Shows the picture.*

**MÁ[T.]HAVYA.**
Excellent, my dear friend, excellent! The imitation of nature is perfect, and
the attitude of the figures is really charming. They stand out in such bold
relief that the eye is quite deceived.

**SÁNUMATÍ.**
*Aside.*

A most artistic performance! I admire the King's skill, and could almost
believe that [S']akoontalá herself was before me.

**KING.**
I own 'tis not amiss, though it portrays
But feebly her angelic loveliness.
Aught less than perfect is depicted falsely,
And fancy must supply the imperfection.

**SÁNUMATÍ.**
*Aside.*

A very just remark from a modest man, whose affection is exaggerated by
the keenness of his remorse.

**MÁ[T.]HAVYA.**
Tell me:—I see three female figures drawn on the canvas, and all of them
beautiful; which of the three is her Majesty [S']akoontalá?

**SÁNUMATÍ.**
*Aside.*

If he cannot distinguish her from the others, the simpleton might as well
have no eyes in his head.

**KING.**
Which should you imagine to be intended for her?

**MÁ[T.]HAVYA.**
She who is leaning, apparently a little tired, against the stem of that mango-
tree, the tender leaves of which glitter with the water she has poured upon

*454*

them. Her arms are gracefully extended; her face is somewhat flushed with the heat; and a few flowers have escaped from her hair, which has become unfastened, and hangs in loose tresses about her neck. That must be the queen [S']akoontalá, and the others, I presume, are her two attendants.

**KING.**
I congratulate you on your discernment. Behold the proof of my passion;
  My finger, burning with the glow of love ,
  Has left its impress on the painted tablet;
  While here and there, alas! a scalding tear
  Has fallen on the cheek and dimmed its brightness.
Chaturiká, the garden in the background of the picture is only half-painted.
Go, fetch the brush that I may finish it.

**CHATURIKÁ.**
Worthy Má[t.]havya, have the kindness to hold the picture until
I return.

**KING.**
Nay, I will hold it myself.

*Takes the picture.*
*Exit CHATURIKÁ.*

  My loved one came but lately to my presence
  And offered me herself, but in my folly
  I spurned the gift, and now I fondly cling
  To her mere image; even as a madman
  Would pass the waters of the gushing stream,
  And thirst for airy vapours of the desert .

**MÁ[T.]HAVYA.**
*Aside.*

He has been fool enough to forego the reality for the semblance, the substance for the shadow.

*Aloud.*

Tell us, I pray, what else remains to be painted.

**SÁNUMATÍ.**
*Aside.*

He longs, no doubt, to delineate some favourite spot where my

*[S']akoontalá delighted to ramble.*

**KING.**
You shall hear:—
  I wish to see the Málini portrayed,
  Its tranquil course by banks of sand impeded;
  Upon the brink a pair of swans; beyond,
  The hills adjacent to Himálaya ,
  Studded with deer; and, near the spreading shade
  Of some large tree, where 'mid the branches hang
  The hermits' vests of bark, a tender doe,
  Rubbing its downy forehead on the horn
  Of a black antelope, should be depicted.

**MÁ[T.]HAVYA.**
*Aside.*

Pooh! if I were he, I would fill up the vacant spaces with a lot of grizzly-bearded old hermits.

**KING.**
My dear Má[T.]Havya, there is still a part of [S']akoontalá's dress which I purposed to draw, but find I have omitted.

**MÁ[T.]HAVYA.**
What is that?

**SÁNUMATÍ.**
*Aside.*

Something suitable, I suppose, to the simple attire of a young and beautiful girl dwelling in a forest.

**KING.**
 A sweet [S']irísha blossom should be twined
 Behind her ear , its perfumed crest depending
 Towards her cheek; and, resting on her bosom,
 A lotus-fibre necklace, soft and bright
 As an autumnal moonbeam, should be traced.

**MÁ[T.]HAVYA.**
Pray, why does the Queen cover her lips with the tips of her fingers, bright as the blossom of a lily, as if she were afraid of something? [Looking more closely.] Oh! I see; a vagabond bee, intent on thieving honey from the flowers, has mistaken her mouth for a rosebud, and is trying to settle upon it.

**KING.**
A bee! drive off the impudent insect, will you?

**MÁ[T.]HAVYA.**
That's your business. Your royal prerogative gives you power over all offenders.

**KING.**
Very true. Listen to me, thou favourite guest of flowering plants; why give thyself the trouble of hovering here?
 See where thy partner sits on yonder flower,
 And waits for thee ere she will sip its dew.

**SÁNUMATÍ.**
*Aside.*

A most polite way of warning him off!

**MÁ[T.]HAVYA.**
You'll find the obstinate creature is not to be sent about his business so easily as you think.

**KING.**
Dost thou presume to disobey? Now hear me:—
 An thou but touch the lips of my beloved,
 Sweet as the opening blossom, whence I quaffed
 In happier days love's nectar, I will place thee

Within the hollow of yon lotus cup,
And there imprison thee for thy presumption.

**MÁ[T.]HAVYA.**
He must be bold indeed not to show any fear when you threaten him with
such an awful punishment. [Smiling, aside.] He is stark mad, that's clear; and
I believe, by keeping him company, I am beginning to talk almost as wildly.
[Aloud.] Look, it is only a painted bee.

**KING.**
Painted? impossible!

**SÁNUMATÍ.**
*Aside.*

Even I did not perceive it; how much less should he!

**KING.**
Oh! my dear friend, why were you so ill-natured as to tell me the truth?
  While all entranced, I gazed upon her picture,
  My loved one seemed to live before my eyes
  Till every fibre of my being thrilled
  With rapturous emotion. Oh! 'twas cruel
  To dissipate the day-dream, and transform
  The blissful vision to a lifeless image.

*Sheds tears.*

**SÁNUMATÍ.**
*Aside.*

Separated lovers are very difficult to please; but he seems more difficult than usual.

**KING.**
Alas! my dear Má[T.]Havya, why am I doomed to be the victim of perpetual
disappointment?
  Vain is the hope of meeting her in dreams,
  For slumber night by night forsakes my couch;
  And now that I would fain assuage my grief
  By gazing on her portrait here before me,
  Tears of despairing love obscure my sight.

**SÁNUMATÍ.**
*Aside.*

You have made ample amends for the wrong you did [S']akoontalá in
disowning her.

**CHATURIKÁ.**
*Entering.*

Victory to the King! I was coming along with the box of colours in my hand—

**KING.**
What now?

**CHATURIKÁ.**
When I met the queen Vasumatí, attended by Taraliká. She insisted on taking it
from me, and declared she would herself deliver it into your Majesty's hands.
  *457*

**MÁ[T.]HAVYA.**
By what luck did you contrive to escape her?

**CHATURIKÁ.**
While her maid was disengaging her mantle, which had caught in the branch, of a shrub, I ran away.

**KING.**
Here, my good friend, take the picture and conceal it. My attentions to the Queen have made her presumptuous. She will be here in a minute.

**MÁ[T.]HAVYA.**
Conceal the picture! conceal myself, you mean.

*Getting up and taking the picture.*

The Queen has a bitter draught in store for you, which you will have to swallow, as [S']iva did the poison at the Deluge . When you are well quit of her, you may send and call me from the Palace of
Clouds , where I shall take refuge.

*Exit, running.*

**SÁNUMATÍ.**
*Aside.*

Although the King's affections are transferred to another object, yet he respects his previous attachments. I fear his love must be somewhat fickle.

**VETRAVATÍ.**
*Entering with a dispatch in her hand.*

Victory to the King!

**KING.**
Vetravatí, did you observe the queen Vasumatí coming in this direction?

**VETRAVATÍ.**
I did; but when she saw that I had a despatch in my hand for your Majesty, she turned back.

**KING.**
The Queen has too much regard for propriety to interrupt me when I am engaged with State-affairs.

**VETRAVATÍ.**
So please your Majesty, your prime minister begs respectfully to inform you that he has devoted much time to the settlement of financial calculations, and only one case of importance has been submitted by the citizens for his consideration. He has made a written report of the facts, and requests your Majesty to cast your eyes over it.

**KING.**
Hand me the paper.

*VETRAVATÍ delivers it.*
*Reading.*

What have we here? 'A merchant named Dhanamitra, trading by sea, was lost in a late shipwreck. Though a wealthy trader, he was childless; and the whole of his immense property becomes by law forfeited to the king.' So writes the minister. Alas! alas! for his childlessness! But surely, if he was wealthy, he must have had many wives. Let an inquiry be made whether any one of them is expecting to give birth to a child.

VETRAVATÍ.
They say that his wife, the daughter of the foreman of a guild belonging to Ayodhyá , has just completed the ceremonies usual upon such expectations.

KING.
The unborn child has a title to its father's property. Such is my decree. Go, bid my minister proclaim it so.

VETRAVATÍ.
I will, my liege.

*Going.*

KING.
Stay a moment.

VETRAVATÍ.
I am at your Majesty's service.

KING.
Let there be no question whether he may or may not have left offspring;
Rather be it proclaimed that whosoe'er Of King Dushyanta's subjects be bereaved
  Of any loved relation, an it be not
  That his estates are forfeited for crimes,
  Dushyanta will himself to them supply
  That kinsman's place in tenderest affection.

VETRAVATÍ.
It shall be so proclaimed.

*Exit VETRAVATÍ, and re-enters after an interval.*

VETRAVATÍ.
Your Majesty's proclamation was received with acclamations of joy, like grateful rain at the right season.

KING.
*Drawing a deep sigh.*

So, then, the property of rich men, who have no lineal descendants, passes over to a stranger at their decease. And such, alas! must be the fate of the fortunes of the race of Puru at my death; even as when fertile soil is sown with seed at the wrong season.

VETRAVATÍ.
Heaven forbid!

KING.
Fool that I was to reject such happiness when it offered itself for my acceptance!

SÁNUMATÍ.

459

*Aside.*

He may well blame his own folly when he calls to mind his treatment of my beloved [S']akoontalá.

KING.
  Ah! woe is me! when I forsook my wife—
  My lawful wife—concealed within her breast
  There lay my second self, a child unborn,
  Hope of my race, e'en as the choicest fruit
  Lies hidden in the bosom of the earth.

SÁNUMATÍ. [Aside.
There is no fear of your race being cut off for want of a son.

CHATURIKÁ.
*Aside to VETRAVATÍ.*

The affair of the merchant's death has quite upset our royal master, and caused him sad distress. Would it not be better to fetch the worthy Má[t.]havya from the Palace of Clouds to comfort him?

VETRAVATÍ.
A very good idea.

*Exit.*

KING.
Alas! the shades of my forefathers are even now beginning to be alarmed, lest at my death they may be deprived of their funeral libations.
  No son remains in King Dushyanta's place
  To offer sacred homage to the dead
  Of Puru's noble line; my ancestors
  Must drink these glistening tears, the last libation
  A childless man can ever hope to make them.

*Falls down in an agony of grief.*

CHATURIKÁ.
*Looking at him in consternation.*
Great King, compose yourself.

SÁNUMATÍ.
*Aside.*

Alas! alas! though a bright light is shining near him, he is involved in the blackest darkness, by reason of the veil that obscures his sight. I will now reveal all, and put an end to his misery. But no; I heard the mother of the great Indra , when she was consoling [S']akoontalá, say that the gods will soon bring about a joyful union between husband and wife, being eager for the sacrifice which will be celebrated in their honour on the occasion. I must not anticipate the happy moment, but will return at once to my dear friend and cheer her with an account of what I have seen and heard.

*Rises aloft and disappears.*

A VOICE BEHIND THE SCENES.
Help! help! to the rescue!

**KING.**
*Recovering himself. Listening.*

Ha! I heard a cry of distress, and in Má[t.]havya's voice too. What ho there!

**VETRAVATÍ.**
*Entering.*

Your friend is in danger; save him, great King.

**KING.**
Who dares insult the worthy Má[t.]havya?

**VETRAVATÍ.**
Some evil demon, invisible to human eyes, has seized him, and carried him to one of the turrets of the Palace of Clouds.

**KING.**
*Rising.*

> Impossible! Have evil spirits power over my subjects,
> even in nay private apartments? Well, well;—
> Daily I seem, less able to avert
> Misfortune from myself, and o'er my actions
> Less competent to exercise control;
> How can I then direct my subjects' ways,
> Or shelter them from tyranny and wrong?

**A VOICE BEHIND THE SCENES.**
Halloo there! my dear friend; help! help!

**KING.**
*Advancing with rapid strides.*

Fear nothing—

**THE SAME VOICE BEHIND THE SCENES.**
Fear nothing, indeed! How can I help fearing when some monster is twisting back my neck, and is about to snap it as he would a sugar-cane?

**KING.**
*Looking round.*

What ho there! my bow!

**SLAVE.**
*Entering with a bow.*

Behold your bow, Sire, and your arm-guard.

*The KING snatches up the bow and arrows.*

**ANOTHER VOICE BEHIND THE SCENES.**
> Here, thirsting for thy life-blood, will I slay thee,
> As a fierce tiger rends his struggling prey.
> Call now thy friend Dushyanta to thy aid;
> His bow is mighty to defend the weak;
> Yet all its vaunted power shall be as nought.

**KING.**
*With fury.*

What! dares he defy me to my face? Hold there, monster! Prepare to die, for your time is come.

*Stringing his bow.*

Vetravatí, lead the way to the terrace.

**VETRAVATÍ.**
This way, Sire.

*They advance in haste.*

**KING.**
*Looking on every side.*

How's this? there is nothing to be seen.

**A VOICE BEHIND THE SCENES.**
Help! Save me! I can see you, though you cannot see me. I am like a mouse in the claws of a cat; my life is not worth a minute's purchase.

**KING.**
Avaunt, monster! You may pride yourself on the magic that renders you invisible, but my arrow shall find you out. Thus do I fix a shaft That shall discern between an impious demon, And a good Bráhman; bearing death to thee, To him deliverance—even as the swan Distinguishes the milk from worthless water .

*Takes aim.*
*Enter MÁTALI holding MÁ[T.]HAVYA, whom he releases.*

**MÁTALI.**
  Turn thou thy deadly arrows on the demons;
  Such is the will of Indra; let thy bow
  Be drawn against the enemies of the gods;
  But on thy friends cast only looks of favour.

**KING.**
*Putting back his arrow.*

What, Mátali! Welcome, most noble charioteer of the mighty Indra.

**MÁ[T.]HAVYA.**
So, here is a monster who thought as little about slaughtering me as if I had been a bullock for sacrifice, and you must e'en greet him with a welcome.

**MÁTALI.**
*Smiling.*

Great Prince, hear on what errand Indra sent me into your presence.

**KING.**
I am all attention.

**MÁTALI.**
There is a race of giants, the descendants of Kálanemi , whom the gods find it difficult to subdue.

KING.
So I have already heard from Nárada .

MÁTALI.
Heaven's mighty lord, who deigns to call thee 'friend,'
Appoints thee to the post of highest honour,
As leader of his armies; and commits
The subjugation of this giant brood
To thy resistless arms, e'en as the sun
Leaves the pale moon to dissipate the darkness.
Let your Majesty, therefore, ascend at once the celestial car of
Indra; and, grasping your arms, advance to victory.

KING.
The mighty Indra honours me too highly by such a mark of distinction. But
tell me, what made you act thus towards my poor friend Má[T.]Havya?

MÁTALI.
I will tell you. Perceiving that your Majesty's spirit was completely broken by
some distress of mind under which you were labouring, I determined to rouse
your energies by moving you to anger. Because To light a flame, we need but
stir the embers; The cobra, when incensed, extends his head And springs upon
his foe; the bravest men Display their courage only when provoked.

KING.
*Aside to MÁ[T.]HAVYA.*

My dear Má[T.]Havya, the commands of the great Indra must not be left
unfulfilled. Go you and acquaint my minister, Pi[S']una, with what has
happened, and say to him from me:—
Dushyanta to thy care confides his realm—
Protect with all the vigour of thy mind
The interests of his people; while his bow
Is braced against the enemies of heaven.

MÁ[T.]HAVYA.
I obey.

*Exit.*

MÁTALI
Ascend, illustrious Prince.

*The KING ascends the car.*
*Exeunt.*

# Act VII

## SCENE.—The Sky.

*Enter KING DUSHYANTA and MÁTALI in the car of Indra, moving in the air.*

KING.
My good Mátali, it appears to me incredible that I can merit such a mark of
distinction for having simply fulfilled the behests of the great Indra.

MÁTALI.
*Smiling.*

Great Prince, it seems to me that neither of you is satisfied with himself.
You underrate the services you have rendered,
And think too highly of the god's reward;
He deems it scarce sufficient recompense
For your heroic deeds on his behalf.

KING.
Nay, Mátali, say not so. My most ambitious expectations were more than
realised by the honour conferred on me at the moment when I took my leave.
For,
Tinged with celestial sandal, from the breast
Of the great Indra, where before it hung,
A garland of the ever-blooming tree
Of Nandana was cast about my neck
By his own hand; while, in the very presence
Of the assembled gods, I was enthroned
Beside their mighty lord, who smiled to see
His son Jayanta envious of the honour.

MÁTALI.
There is no mark of distinction which your Majesty does not deserve at the
hands of the immortals. See,
Heaven's hosts acknowledge thee their second saviour:
For now thy how's unerring shafts (as erst
The Lion-man's terrific claws ) have purged
The empyreal sphere from taint of demons foul.

KING.
The praise of my victory must be ascribed to the majesty
of Indra.
When mighty gods make men their delegates
In martial enterprise, to them belongs
The palm of victory; and not to mortals.
Could the pale Dawn dispel the shades of night,
Did not the god of day, whose diadem
Is jewelled with a thousand beams of light,
Place him in front of his effulgent car ?

MÁTALI.
A very just comparison!

*Driving on.*

Great King, behold! the glory of thy fame has reached even to the vault of
heaven.
Hark! yonder inmates of the starry sphere
Sing anthems worthy of thy martial deeds,
While with celestial colours they depict
The story of thy victories on scrolls
Formed of the leaves of heaven's immortal trees.

KING.
My good Mátali, yesterday, when I ascended the sky, I was so eager to do
battle with the demons, that the road by which we were travelling towards
Indra's heaven escaped my observation. Tell me, in which path of the seven
winds are we now moving?

MÁTALI.
 We journey in the path of Parivaha —
 The wind that bears along the triple Ganges
 And causes Ursa's seven stars to roll
 In their appointed orbits, scattering
 Their several rays with equal distribution.
 'Tis the same path that once was sanctified
 By the divine impression of the foot
 Of Vishnu, when, to conquer haughty Bali,
 He spanned the heavens in his second stride .

KING.
This is the reason, I suppose, that a sensation of calm repose pervades all
my senses.

*Looking down at the wheels.*

Ah! Mátali, we are descending towards the earth's atmosphere.

MÁTALI.
What makes you think so?

KING.
The car itself instructs me; we are moving
O'er pregnant clouds, surcharged with rain; below us
I see the moisture-loving Chátakas
In sportive flight dart through the spokes; the steeds
Of Indra glisten with the lightning's flash;
And a thick mist bedews the circling wheels.

MÁTALI
You are right; in a little while the chariot will touch the ground, and you will
be in your own dominions.

KING.
*Looking down.*

How wonderful the appearance of the earth as we rapidly descend!
 Stupendous prospect! yonder lofty hills
 Do suddenly uprear their towering heads
 Amid the plain, while from beneath their crests
 The ground receding sinks; the trees, whose stem
 Seemed lately hid within their leafy tresses,
 Rise into elevation, and display
 Their branching shoulders; yonder streams, whose waters,
 Like silver threads, were scarce, but now, discerned,
 Grow into mighty rivers; lo! the earth
 Seems upward hurled by some gigantic power.

MÁTALI.
Well described!

*Looking with awe.*

Grand, indeed, and lovely is the spectacle presented by the earth.

KING.
Tell me, Mátali, what is the range of mountains which, like a bank of clouds

*465*

illumined by the setting sun, pours down a stream of gold? On one side its base dips into the eastern ocean, and on the other side into the western.

**MÁTALI.**
Great Prince, it is called 'Golden-peak ,' and is the abode of the attendants of the god of wealth. In this spot the highest forms of penance are wrought out.
  There Ka[s']yapa , the great progenitor
  Of demons and of gods, himself the offspring
  Of the divine Maríchi, Brahmá's son,
  With Adití, his wife, in calm seclusion,
  Does holy penance for the good of mortals.

**KING.**
Then I must not neglect so good an opportunity of obtaining his blessing. I should much like to visit this venerable personage and offer him my homage.

**MÁTALI.**
By all means. An excellent idea!

*Guides the car to the earth.*

**KING.**
*In a tone of wonder.*

How's this?
  Our chariot wheels move noiselessly. Around
  No clouds of dust arise; no shock betokened
  Our contact with the earth; we seem to glide
  Above the ground, so lightly do we touch it.

**MÁTALI.**
Such is the difference between the car of Indra and that of your Majesty.

**KING.**
In which direction, Mátali, is Ka[s']yapa's sacred retreat?

**MÁTALI.**
*Pointing.*

  Where stands yon anchorite, towards the orb
  Of the meridian sun, immovable
  As a tree's stem, his body half-concealed
  By a huge ant-hill. Bound about his breast
  No sacred cord is twined , but in its stead
  A hideous serpent's skin. In place of necklace,
  The tendrils of a withered creeper chafe
  His wasted neck. His matted hair depends
  In thick entanglement about his shoulders,
  And birds construct their nests within its folds .

**KING.**
I salute thee, thou man of austere devotion.

**MÁTALI.**
*Holding in the reins of the car.*

Great Prince, we are now in the sacred grove of the holy Ka[s']yapa—the grove that boasts as its ornament one of the five trees of Indra's heaven, reared by Adití.

**KING.**
This sacred retreat is more delightful than heaven itself. I could almost fancy myself bathing in a pool of nectar.

**MÁTALI.**
*Stopping the chariot.*

Descend, mighty Prince.

**KING.**
*Descending.*

And what will you do, Mátali?

**MÁTALI.**
The chariot will remain where I have stopped it. We may both descend.

*Doing so.*

This way, great King.

*Walking on.*

You see around you the celebrated region where the holiest sages devote themselves to penitential rites.

**KING.**
I am filled with awe and wonder as I gaze.
  In such a place as this do saints of earth
  Long to complete their acts of penance; here,
  Beneath the shade of everlasting trees.
  Transplanted from the groves of Paradise,
  May they inhale the balmy air, and need
  No other nourishment ; here may they bathe
  In fountains sparkling with the golden dust
  Of lilies; here, on jewelled slabs of marble,
  In meditation rapt, may they recline;
  Here, in the presence of celestial nymphs,
  E'en passion's voice is powerless to move them.

**MÁTALI.**
So true is it that the aspirations of the good and great are ever soaring upwards.

*Turning round and speaking off the stage.*

Tell me, Vriddha-[S']ákalya, how is the divine son of Maríchi now engaged? What sayest thou? that he is conversing with Adití and some of the wives of the great sages, and that they are questioning him respecting the duties of a faithful wife?

**KING.**
*Listening.*

Then we must await the holy father's leisure.

**MÁTALI.**
*Looking at the KING.*

*467*

If your Majesty will rest under the shade, at the foot of this A[s']oka-tree, I will seek an opportunity of announcing your arrival to Indra's reputed father.

KING.
As you think proper.

*Remains under the tree.*

MÁTALI.
Great King, I go.

*Exit.*

KING.
*Feeling his arm throb.*

Wherefore this causeless throbbing, O mine arm ?
All hope has fled for ever; mock me not
With presages of good, when happiness
Is lost, and nought but misery remains.

A VOICE BEHIND THE SCENES.
Be not so naughty. Do you begin already to show a refractory spirit?

KING.
*Listening.*

This is no place for petulance. Who can it be whose behaviour calls for such a rebuke?

*Looking in the direction of the sound and smiling.*

A child, is it? closely attended by two holy women. His disposition seems anything but child-like. See!
  He braves the fury of yon lioness
  Suckling its savage offspring, and compels
  The angry whelp to leave the half-sucked dug,
  Tearing its tender mane in boisterous sport.

*Enter a CHILD, attended by TWO WOMEN of the hermitage, in the manner described.*

CHILD.
Open your mouth, my young lion, I want to count your teeth.

FIRST ATTENDANT.
You naughty child, why do you tease the animals? Know you not that we cherish them in this hermitage as if they were our own children? In good sooth, you have a high spirit of your own, and are beginning already to do justice to the name Sarva-damana ('All-taming'), given you by the hermits.

KING.
Strange! My heart inclines towards the boy with almost as much affection as if he were my own child. What can be the reason? I suppose my own childlessness makes me yearn towards the sons of others.

SECOND ATTENDANT.
This lioness will certainly attack you if you do not release her whelp.

**CHILD.**

*Laughing.*

Oh! indeed! let her come. Much I fear her, to be sure!

*Pouts his under-lip in defiance.*

**KING.**

The germ of mighty courage lies concealed
Within this noble infant, like a spark
Beneath the fuel, waiting but a breath
To fan the flame and raise a conflagration.

**FIRST ATTENDANT.**

Let the young lion go, like a dear child, and I will give you something else to play with.

**CHILD.**

Where is it? Give it me first.

*Stretches out his hand.*

**KING.**

*Looking at his hand.*

How's that? His hand exhibits one of those mystic marks[84] which are the sure prognostic of universal empire. See! His fingers stretched in eager expectation To grasp the wished-for toy, and knit together By a close-woven web, in shape resemble A lotus blossom, whose expanding petals The early dawn has only half unfolded.

**SECOND ATTENDANT.**

We shall never pacify him by mere words, dear Suvratá. Be kind enough to go to my cottage, and you will find there a plaything belonging to Márkandeya, one of the hermit's children. It is a peacock made of china-ware, painted in many colours. Bring it here for the child.

**FIRST ATTENDANT.**

Very well.

*Exit.*

**CHILD.**

No, no; I shall go on playing with the young lion.

*Looks at the FEMALE ATTENDANT and laughs.*

**KING.**

I feel an unaccountable affection for this wayward child.
How blessed the virtuous parents whose attire
Is soiled with dust, by raising from the ground
The child that asks a refuge in their arms!
And happy are they while with lisping prattle,
In accents sweetly inarticulate,
He charms their ears; and with his artless smiles
Gladdens their hearts , revealing to their gaze
His pearly teeth just budding into view.

ATTENDANT.
I see how it is. He pays me no manner of attention.

*Looking off the stage.*

I wonder whether any of the hermits are about here.

*Seeing the KING.*

Kind Sir, could you come hither a moment and help me to release the young lion from the clutch of this child who is teasing him in boyish play?

KING.
Approaching and smiling.

Listen to me, thou child of a mighty saint!
  Dost thou dare show a wayward spirit here?
  Here, in this hallowed region? Take thou heed
  Lest, as the serpent's young defiles the sandal ,
  Thou bring dishonour on the holy sage
  Thy tender-hearted parent, who delights
  To shield from harm the tenants of the wood.

ATTENDANT.
Gentle Sir, I thank you; but he is not the saint's son.

KING.
His behaviour and whole bearing would have led me to doubt it, had not the place of his abode encouraged the idea.

*Follows the CHILD, and takes him by the hand, according to        the request of the attendant. Aside.*

  I marvel that the touch of this strange child
  Should thrill me with delight; if so it be,
  How must the fond caresses of a son
  Transport the father's soul who gave him being!

ATTENDANT.
*Looking at them both.*

Wonderful! Prodigious!

KING.
What excites your surprise, my good woman?

ATTENDANT.
I am astonished at the striking resemblance between the child and yourself; and, what is still more extraordinary, he seems to have taken to you kindly and submissively, though you are a stranger to him.

KING.
*Fondling the CHILD.*

If he be not the son of the great sage, of what family does he come, may I ask?

ATTENDANT.
Of the race of Puru.

KING.

*Aside.*

What! are we, then, descended from the same ancestry? This, no doubt,
accounts for the resemblance she traces between the child and me. Certainly
it has always been an established usage among the princes of Puru's race,
  To dedicate the morning of their days
  To the world's weal, in palaces and halls,
  'Mid luxury and regal pomp abiding;
  Then, in the wane of life, to seek release
  From kingly cares, and make the hallowed shade
  Of sacred trees their last asylum, where
  As hermits they may practise self-abasement,
  And bind themselves by rigid vows of penance.

*Aloud.*

But how could mortals by their own power gain admission to this sacred region?

ATTENDANT.
Your remark is just; but your wonder will cease when I tell you that his
mother is the offspring of a celestial nymph, and gave him birth in the
hallowed grove of Ka[s']yapa.

KING.
*Aside.*

Strange that my hopes should be again excited!

*Aloud.*

But what, let me ask, was the name of the prince whom she deigned to
honour with her hand?

ATTENDANT.
How could I think of polluting my lips by the mention of a wretch who had
the cruelty to desert his lawful wife?

KING.
*Aside.*

Ha! the description suits me exactly. Would I could bring myself to inquire
the name of the child's mother!

*Reflecting.*

But it is against propriety to make too minute inquiries about the wife of
another man .

FIRST ATTENDANT.
*Entering with the china peacock in her hand.*

Sarva-damana, Sarva-damana, see, see, what a beautiful [S']akoonta (bird).

CHILD.
*Looking round.*

My mother! Where? Let me go to her.

BOTH ATTENDANTS.
He mistook the word [S']akoonta for [S']akoontalá. The boy dotes upon his
mother, and she is ever uppermost in his thoughts.

*471*

SECOND ATTENDANT.
Nay, my dear child, I said: Look at the beauty of this [S']akoonta.

KING.
*Aside.*

What! is his mother's name [S']akoontalá? But the name is not uncommon among women. Alas! I fear the mere similarity of a name, like the deceitful vapour of the desert , has once more raised my hopes only to dash them to the ground.

CHILD.
Dear nurse, what a beautiful peacock!

*Takes the toy.*

FIRST ATTENDANT.
*Looking at the CHILD. In great distress.*

Alas! alas! I do not see the amulet on his wrist.

KING.
Don't distress yourself. Here it is. It fell off while he was struggling with the young lion.

*Stoops to pick it up.*

BOTH ATTENDANTS.
Hold! hold! Touch it not, for your life. How marvellous! He has actually taken it up without the slightest hesitation.

*Both raise their hands to their breasts and look at each other in astonishment.*

KING.
Why did you try to prevent my touching it?

FIRST ATTENDANT.
Listen, great Monarch. This amulet, known as 'The Invincible,' was given to the boy by the divine son of Maríchi, soon after his birth, when the natal ceremony was performed. Its peculiar virtue is, that when it falls on the ground, no one except the father or mother of the child can touch it unhurt.

KING.
And suppose another person touches it?

FIRST ATTENDANT.
Then it instantly becomes a serpent, and bites him.

KING.
Have you ever witnessed the transformation with your own eyes?

BOTH ATTENDANTS.
Over and over again.

KING.
*With rapture. Aside.*

Joy! joy! Are then my dearest hopes to be fulfilled?

*Embraces the CHILD.*

**SECOND ATTENDANT.**
Come, my dear Suvratá, we must inform [S']akoontalá immediately of this
wonderful event, though we have to interrupt her in the performance of her
religious vows.

*Exeunt.*

**CHILD.**
*To the KING.*

Don't hold me. I want to go to my mother.

**KING.**
We will go to her together, and give her joy, my son.

**CHILD.**
Dushyanta is my father, not you.

**KING.**
*Smiling.*

His contradiction only convinces me the more.

*Enter [S']AKOONTALÁ, in widow's apparel, with her long hair twisted into a single
braid.*

**[S']AKOONTALÁ.**
*Aside.*

I have just heard that Sarva-damana's amulet has retained its form, though a
stranger raised it from the ground. I can hardly believe in my good fortune. Yet
why should not Sánumatí's prediction be verified?

**KING.**
Alas! can this indeed be my [S']akoontalá?
  Clad in the weeds of widowhood, her face
  Emaciate with fasting, her long hair
  Twined in a single braid , her whole demeanour
  Expressive of her purity of soul;
  With patient constancy she thus prolongs
  The vow to which my cruelty condemned her.

**[S']AKOONTALÁ.**
*Gazing at the KING, who is pale with remorse.*

Surely this is not like my husband; yet who can it be that dares pollute by
the pressure of his hand my child, whose amulet should protect him from a
stranger's touch?

**CHILD.**
*Going to his mother.*

Mother, who is this man that has been kissing me and calling me his son?

**KING.**
My best beloved, I have indeed treated thee most cruelly, but am now once more
thy fond and affectionate lover. Refuse not to acknowledge me as thy husband.

**[S']AKOONTALÁ.**

*Aside.*

Be of good cheer, my heart. The anger of Destiny is at last appeased. Heaven regards thee with compassion. But is he in very truth my husband?

KING.
  Behold me, best and loveliest of women,
  Delivered from the cloud of fatal darkness
  That erst oppressed my memory. Again
  Behold us brought together by the grace
  Of the great lord of Heaven. So the moon
  Shines forth from dim eclipse , to blend his rays
  With the soft lustre of his Rohiní.

[S']AKOONTALÁ.
May my husband be victorious—

*She stops short, her voice choked with tears.*

KING.
  O fair one, though the utterance of thy prayer
  Be lost amid the torrent of thy tears,
  Yet does the sight of thy fair countenance
  And of thy pallid lips, all unadorned
  And colourless in sorrow for my absence,
  Make me already more than conqueror.

CHILD.
Mother, who is this man?

[S']AKOONTALÁ.
My child, ask the deity that presides over thy destiny.

KING.
*Falling at [S']AKOONTALÁ's feet.*

  Fairest of women, banish from thy mind
  The memory of my cruelty; reproach
  The fell delusion that o'erpowered my soul,
  And blame not me, thy husband; 'tis the curse
  Of him in whom the power of darkness  reigns,
  That he mistakes the gifts of those he loves
  For deadly evils. Even though a friend
  Should wreathe a garland on a blind man's brow,
  Will he not cast it from him as a serpent?

[S']AKOONTALÁ.
Rise, my own husband, rise. Thou wast not to blame. My own evil deeds, committed in a former state of being , brought down this judgment upon me. How else could my husband, who was ever of a compassionate disposition, have acted so unfeelingly?

*The KING rises.*

But tell me, my husband, how did the remembrance of thine unfortunate wife return to thy mind?

KING.

As soon as my heart's anguish is removed, and its wounds are healed, I will tell thee all.

Oh! let me, fair one, chase away the drop
That still bedews the fringes of thine eye;
And let me thus efface the memory
Of every tear that stained thy velvet cheek,
Unnoticed and unheeded by thy lord,
When in his madness he rejected thee.

*Wipes away the tear.*

[S']AKOONTALÁ.
Seeing the signet-ring on his finger.

Ah! my dear husband, is that the Lost Ring?

KING.
Yes; the moment I recovered it my memory was restored.

[S']AKOONTALÁ.
The ring was to blame in allowing itself to be lost at the very time when I was anxious to convince my noble husband of the reality of my marriage.

KING.
Receive it back, as the beautiful twining-plant receives again its blossom in token of its reunion with the spring.

[S']AKOONTALÁ.
Nay; I can never more place confidence in it. Let my husband retain it.

*Enter MÁTALI.*

MÁTALI.
I congratulate your Majesty. Happy are you in your reunion with your wife; happy are you in beholding the face of your own son.

KING.
Yes, indeed. My heart's dearest wish has borne sweet fruit. But tell me, Mátali, is this joyful event known to the great Indra?

MÁTALI.
*Smiling.*

What is unknown to the gods? But come with me, noble Prince, the divine Ka[s']yapa graciously permits thee to be presented to him.

KING.
[S']akoontalá, take our child and lead the way. We will together go into the presence of the holy Sage.

[S']AKOONTALÁ.
I shrink from entering the august presence of the great Saint, even with my husband at my side.

KING.
Nay; on such a joyous occasion it is highly proper. Come, come; I entreat thee.

*[All advance.*
*KA[S']YAPA is discovered seated on a throne with his wife ADITI.*

**KA[S']YAPA.**
*Gazing at DUSHYANTA. To his wife.*

O Adití,
  This is the mighty hero, King Dushyanta,
  Protector of the earth; who, at the head
  Of the celestial armies of thy son,
  Does battle with the enemies of heaven.
  Thanks to his bow, the thunderbolt of Indra
  Rests from its work, no more the minister
  Of death and desolation to the world,
  But a mere symbol of divinity.

**ADITI.**
He bears in his noble form all the marks of dignity.

**MÁTALI.**
*To DUSHYANTA*

Sire, the venerable progenitors of the celestials are gazing at your Majesty with as much affection as if you were their son. You may advance towards them.

**KING.**
  Are these, O Mátali, the holy pair,
  Offspring of Daksha and divine Maríchi,
  Children of Brahmá's sons , by sages deemed
  Sole fountain of celestial light, diffused
  Through twelve effulgent orbs ? Are these the pair
  From whom the ruler of the triple world ,
  Sovereign of gods and lord of sacrifice,
  Sprang into being? That immortal pair
  Whom Vishnu, greater than the Self-existent ,
  Chose for his parents, when, to save mankind,
  He took upon himself the shape of mortals?

**MÁTALI.**
Even so.

**KING.**
*Prostrating himself.*

Most august of beings! Dushyanta, content to have fulfilled the commands of your son Indra, offers you his adoration.

**KA[S']YAPA.**
My son, long may'st thou live, and happily may'st thou reign over the earth!

**ADITI.**
My son, may'st thou ever be invincible in the field of battle!

**[S']AKOONTALÁ.**
I also prostrate myself before you, most adorable Beings, and my child with me.

**KA[S']YAPA.**
My daughter,
  Thy lord resembles Indra, and thy child
  Is noble as Jayanta, Indra's son;

I have no worthier blessing left for thee,
May'st thou be faithful as the god's own wife!

ADITI.

My daughter, may'st thou be always the object of thy husband's fondest love;
and may thy son live long to be the joy of both his parents! Be seated.

*All sit down in the presence of KA[S']YAPA.*

KA[S']YAPA.

*Regarding each of them by turns.*

Hail to the beautiful [S']akoontalá,
Hail to her noble son, and hail to thee,
Illustrious Prince—rare triple combination
Of virtue, wealth, and energy united!

KING.

Most venerable Ka[s']yapa, by your favour all my desires were accomplished
even before I was admitted to your presence. Never was mortal so honoured
that his boon should be granted ere it was solicited. Because—
Bloom before fruit, the clouds before the rain,
Cause first and then effect, in endless sequence,
Is the unchanging law of constant nature;
But, ere the blessing issued from thy lips,
The wishes of my heart were all fulfilled.

MÁTALI.

It is thus that the great progenitors of the world confer favours.

KING.

Most reverend Sage, this thy handmaid was married to me by the Gándharva
ceremony , and after a time was conducted to my palace by her relations.
Meanwhile a fatal delusion seized me; I lost my memory and rejected her,
thus committing a grievous offence against the venerable Kanwa, who is
of thy divine race. Afterwards the sight of this ring restored my faculties,
and brought back to my mind all the circumstances of my union with his
daughter. But my conduct still seems to me incomprehensible;
As foolish as the fancies of a man
Who, when he sees an elephant, denies
That 'tis an elephant; then afterwards,
When its huge bulk moves onward, hesitates;
Yet will not be convinced till it has passed
For ever from his sight, and left behind
No vestige of its presence save its footsteps.

KA[S']YAPA.

My son, cease to think thyself in fault. Even the delusion that possessed thy
mind was not brought about by any act of thine. Listen to me.

KING.

I am attentive.

KA[S']YAPA.

Know that when the nymph Menaká, the mother of [S']akoontalá, became
aware of her daughter's anguish in consequence of the loss of the ring at the
nymph's pool, and of thy subsequent rejection of her, she brought her and
*477*

confided her to the care of Adití. And I no sooner saw her than I ascertained by my divine faculty of meditation , that thy repudiation of thy poor faithful wife had been caused entirely by the curse of Durvásas—not by thine own fault—and that the spell would terminate on the discovery of the ring.

KING.
*Drawing a deep breath.*

Oh! what a weight is taken off my mind, now that my character is cleared of reproach.

[S']AKOONTALÁ.
*Aside.*

Joy! joy! My revered husband did not, then, reject me without good reason, though I have no recollection of the curse pronounced upon me. But, in all probability, I unconsciously brought it upon myself, when I was so distracted on being separated from my husband soon after our marriage. For I now remember that my two friends advised me not to fail to show the ring in case he should have forgotten me.

KA[S']YAPA.
At last, my daughter, thou art happy, and hast gained thy heart's desire.
Indulge, then, no feeling of resentment against thy consort. See, now,
  Though he repulsed thee, 'twas the sage's curse
  That clouded his remembrance; 'twas the curse
  That made thy tender husband harsh towards thee.
  Soon as the spell was broken, and his soul
  Delivered from its darkness, in a moment,
  Thou didst regain thine empire o'er his heart.
  So on the tarnished surface of a mirror
  No image is reflected, till the dust,
  That dimmed its wonted lustre, is removed.

KING.
Holy father, see here the hope of my royal race.

*Takes his child by the hand.*

KA[S']YAPA.
  Know that he, too, will become the monarch of the
  wholes earth. Observe,
  Soon, a resistless hero, shall he cross
  The trackless ocean, borne above the waves
  In an aërial car; and shall subdue
  The earth's seven sea-girt isles . Now has he gained,
  As the brave tamer of the forest-beasts,
  The title Sarva-damana; but then
  Mankind shall hail him as King Bharata ,
  And call him the supporter of the world.

KING.
We cannot but entertain the highest hopes of a child for whom your Highness performed the natal rites.

ADITI.
My revered husband, should not the intelligence be conveyed to Kanwa,

that his daughter's wishes are fulfilled, and her happiness complete? He is [S']akoontalá's foster-father. Menaká, who is one of my attendants, is her mother, and dearly does she love her daughter.

**[S']AKOONTALÁ.**
*Aside.*
The venerable matron has given utterance to the very wish that was in my mind.

**KA[S']YAPA.**
His penances have gained for him the faculty of omniscience, and the whole scene is already present to his mind's eye.

**KING.**
Then most assuredly he cannot be very angry with me.

**KA[S']YAPA.**
Nevertheless, it becomes us to send him intelligence of this happy event, and hear his reply. What ho there!

**PUPIL.**
*Entering.*

Holy father, what are your commands?

**KA[S']YAPA.**
My good Gálava, delay not an instant, but hasten through the air and convey to the venerable Kanwa, from me, the happy news that the fatal spell has ceased, that Dushyanta's memory is restored, that his daughter [S']akoontalá has a son, and that she is once more tenderly acknowledged by her husband.

**PUPIL.**
Your Highness' commands shall be obeyed.

*Exit.*

**KA[S']YAPA.**
And now, my dear son, take thy consort and thy child, re-ascend the car of Indra, and return to thy imperial capital.

**KING.**
Most holy father, I obey.

**KA[S']YAPA.**
And accept this blessing—
  For countless ages may the god of gods,
  Lord of the atmosphere, by copious showers
  Secure abundant harvests to thy subjects;
  And thou by frequent offerings preserve
  The Thunderer's friendship. Thus, by interchange
  Of kindly actions may you both confer
  Unnumbered benefits on earth and heaven.

**KING.**
Holy father, I will strive, as far as I am able, to attain this happiness.

**KA[S']YAPA.**
What other favour can I bestow on thee, my son?

KING.

What other can I desire? If, however, you permit me to form another wish, I would humbly beg that the saying of the sage Bharata  be fulfilled:
  May kings reign only for their subjects' weal;
  May the divine Saraswatí , the source
  Of speech, and goddess of dramatic art,
  Be ever honoured by the great and wise;
  And may the purple self-existent god ,
  Whose vital Energy  pervades all space,
  From future transmigrations save my soul.

*Exeunt omnes.*

## The End

# The Secrets of Sakuntala

1. Explain the timing and artifice of memory loss in this piece

2. Compare the hunting scene with those we have already read. How do the representation of hunter and prey differ in these stories?

3. Looking at the different relationships we've read about, how different are the pairings in Sakuntala as opposed to those from Western Literature?

4. What similarities did you find between Sakuntala and The Ramayana?

# Eastern Tales

*By Multiple Authors*

COMPILED AND EDITED FROM
ANCIENT AND MODERN AUTHORS

# Story of the Prince and the Lions.

In a great city of the East lived Prince Azgid, who grew up to manhood beloved by everyone, for he was virtuous, intelligent, and accomplished, though somewhat of a timorous disposition, and this was indeed his chief fault. His father had died, and he had reached now the proper age to mount the throne, a time having been already fixed for the ceremony, to which the young man was looking forward with great interest.

A few days previous to the event the old Vizier called upon the Prince, and telling him he wished to take a walk with him, led him out of the town to a mountain, on one side of which was a wide staircase of white marble, with a handsome balustrade on each side. It had three broad landings, and on these the Vizier and Prince rested as they ascended the stairs, for it was of great height, and they were both sorely tired before they reached the top. There was a small house on the summit, out of which came a black slave, who made a profound obeisance to the visitors, and, leading the way, took them a short distance to a kind of arena dug in the ground, and faced also with white marble. He then took out a key and opened a brazen door, whereupon the Prince drew near, and, looking down, saw a red lion of fierce aspect and tremendous size. He wondered what it all meant, and gazed with a look of inquiry into the face of the Vizier, who, having ordered the servant to retire, thus spoke:

"My son," said he, "the day is now very near on which you are to ascend the throne; but before you can do so you must fulfil a custom which has been established for many ages, and which your father and all your ancestors submitted to; in short, you must descend into this den with a dagger, and fight yonder lion. This will test your courage and fortitude, and show whether you are really worthy of governing a kingdom."

When the young man heard this, he turned pale, and almost fell to the ground.

"This is a severe task," said he; "is there no alternative, nor any method by which I may evade it?"

"None, whatever," answered the Vizier.

"Can I not have a few days granted me to think over the matter, and prepare for the sore trial?" asked the youth.

"Oh, yes!" returned the other, "that you can have, of course." Whereupon he beckoned to the slave to lock the door, and the visitors descended the stairs and returned to the palace.

The joy of Azgid's life seemed now to have fled, and he was suddenly immersed in deep despair. The horrid combat he was to engage in was continually before him. He could neither eat nor drink, but wandered about the palace like one distracted, or sat moping for hours, with his head buried in his hands, speaking to no one. He was glad when night came, that he might hide himself from observation, and retired to his chamber in tears. But he found no comfort there. Sleep fled from him, and he lay tossing upon his bed, anxiously awaiting the return of day. During the tedious hours of darkness he had meditated what course he had best pursue, and at length came to the resolution that he would extricate himself from the dilemma he was in by bidding farewell to his home, and seeking peace and safety in some far-distant land.

Accordingly, as soon as it was daylight, he hastily dressed himself, and going to the stables, mounted a fleet horse and rode off. Glad was he when he got outside the town, and turning round to take a last look, he thus exclaimed:

"Oh, cursed city! cursed home! what misery lies within you! May each hour carry me farther from you! and may these eyes never behold you again!"

With these words he put spurs to his horse, and was soon out of sight of the detested spot. He journeyed forward with a light heart, and on the third day came to a pleasant country overgrown with forest trees, intermingled with lawns and romantic vales.

Proceeding a little farther on, he heard the sound of delicious music, and soon overtook a handsome youth of ruddy countenance, somewhat younger than himself, playing on a flute, and leading a few sheep.

The shepherd, on seeing the stranger, stopped playing, and saluted him very courteously; but Azgid begged him to go on, telling him what an admirer of music he was, and that he had never in his life heard such enchanting strains.

The young man smiled at this compliment, and commenced playing some fresh tunes; and, when he had finished, he informed the Prince that he was slave to a rich shepherd named Oaxus, who lived near, and who would be rejoiced to see him, and show him some hospitality.

In a few moments they reached the abode of Oaxus.

It was a low stone building of considerable size, with a porch surrounding it, overgrown with vines and flowers. Around it was a large yard, encircled with a high wall, in which were some flocks of sheep, with a number of men tending them.

On entering, the old shepherd came forward and gave the stranger a hearty welcome, leading him into a neat apartment, and setting before him a handsome repast. After Azgid had finished eating, he thought it his duty to give his kind host some information as to who he was, and thus spoke:

"My friend," said he, "you no doubt wonder at seeing a stranger of my appearance thus suddenly visiting you, and will naturally wish to inquire who I am. This wish I can only in part gratify. Suffice it to say that I am a Prince whom troubles at home have driven abroad; but my name I cannot tell. That is a secret lodged in my own breast, to be imparted to no one. If no inconvenience to you, it would please me much to remain in this delightful spot. I have ample means at my disposal, and will remunerate you for whatever trouble I may put you to."

Oaxus replied to this speech in the kindest manner, begging the young man to say nothing about remuneration, for that the company of one so exalted and accomplished would more than repay him for any trouble he might be put to in entertaining him, and that nothing would give him more happiness than to have him remain there to the end of his days.

"But come, Asdril," said he, addressing the musician, "take the Prince and show him what is most worthy to be seen in this neighbourhood. Lead him to the waterfalls, the fountains, the rocks and vales, for I perceive our guest is one able to appreciate nature's beauties."

The young shepherd did as requested, and, taking up his flute, led the youth to all the pleasantest and most interesting spots.

They wandered about the sloping hills and deep valleys, and over beautiful lawns, sprinkled with trees of immense size. At one time they stood by the side of some gently murmuring stream, and now they were startled with a romantic cascade, whose flashing waters tumbled from mossy cliffs and echoed far and wide. They now entered a shady vale, and, seating themselves on a rock, the shepherd commenced playing his flute. The Prince listened with delight, for, as we said before, he was passionately fond of music, and had never in his life heard any one who pleased him so much. Indeed, he made up his mind that, if ever he left the place, he would endeavour to purchase from Oaxus the accomplished slave, and have him as his constant companion as long as he lived.

Thus did Azgid enjoy himself amid these delicious scenes, congratulating himself that he had escaped from all his troubles, and had at last reached a spot where he might live in peace and tranquillity for ever.

But his joy was not to last long; for young Asdril on a sudden rose up, and, taking his companion by the hand, told him it was time for them to be gone.

"Why so?" asked the Prince. "Why should we so soon leave these enchanting scenes?"

"Alas!" answered the shepherd, "this place is infested with lions. They come out at a certain hour every day, and we all have to retire within the walls of our abode and close the gates. See here," continued he, rolling up his sleeve, and showing a great scar on his arm, "this is what I received in an encounter with these fierce beasts. I once lagged behind, and was with great difficulty saved from destruction. So, let us lose no time, but make the best of our way home."

On hearing these words, the Prince turned pale; but he said nothing, and they silently returned to the house.

On reaching the gate, Azgid called for his horse, and, having mounted, told his host that he was about to leave, and thanked him for his kindness. "Farewell, Oaxus!" said he. "Farewell, young Asdril! I thought I should have remained here forever; but fate decrees otherwise. I must seek another abode, another home." And, so saying, he put spurs to his horse and galloped away.

He journeyed on and on, and soon left the groves and green valleys. The country became more barren, trees began to disappear, and, not long after, scarcely any verdure was visible. He was soon in the midst of the desert. Far as the eye could reach, the vast plain spread before him. Not a shrub or blade of grass could be seen, and nothing met the view but, now and then, some low sand-hills, piled up by the wind like drifts of snow, among which, with much fatigue to his horse, he pursued his way. The sun blazed on him with great power; and it was with much satisfaction, on the third day, that he perceived in the distance a number of black tents, which he knew to be an encampment of Arabs.

As he drew near, a band of warriors, mounted on fine horses and brandishing their spears, came forth to meet him. This was their usual mode of welcoming a stranger.

They seemed struck with the appearance of Azgid, and showed him much respect, forming a sort of guard around him, and leading him to the tent of their chief.

The latter was a person of dignified aspect, somewhat past the prime of life. His name was Sheik Hajaar. He sat smoking in front of his tent; and, when the youth approached, he rose up and cordially saluted him. He then took him inside the tent, and set before him a repast, of which, when the young man had eaten, he thought it his duty to inform his kind host who he was.

"My friend," said he, "you are no doubt surprised at seeing a stranger of my appearance thus suddenly visiting you, and will naturally wish to inquire who I am. This wish I can only in part gratify: suffice it, then, to say that I am a Prince whom troubles at home have driven abroad, but my name I cannot tell; that is a secret lodged within my own breast, to be imparted to no one. If no inconvenience to you, it would please me much to remain here. I have ample means at my command, and will remunerate you for whatever trouble I may put you to."

The Sheik replied that the company of one so exalted and accomplished was remuneration enough, and that he would be rejoiced to have him as his guest for ever. He then introduced him to a number of his friends, and leading him out, presented him with a beautiful horse of great value. Azgid thought he had never in his life seen so fine an animal; and when he mounted him he found him so gentle and docile as scarcely to require any management, for the intelligent creature seemed to anticipate all his wishes.

"But, come," said the Sheik, "it is time for us to be off: to-day we hunt the antelope; you, Prince, will of course accompany us."

Azgid, with a smile, replied in the affirmative, and they started off in pursuit of the game. They soon overtook a herd, and commenced chasing them—spears flew, and the air resounded with cries. The Prince was exhilarated with the sport, and enjoyed himself exceedingly. "Ah!" thought he, "this is a happy life, and these children of the desert are happy people: I am resolved never to quit them." The hunt lasted nearly the whole day, and about sunset the company returned with the spoil, which consisted of more than a dozen antelopes. These sports were kept up nearly every day, and Azgid's time passed most agreeably.

A week had now elapsed, and the youth had one night retired to rest, congratulating himself on the happy life he led, when the Sheik Hajaar quietly approached his couch, and thus spake:

"My son," said he, "I have come to tell you how much my people are pleased with you, and especially with the spirit you evince in the sports of the chase. But these sports do not comprise all our life: we have frequent wars with hostile tribes, where great valour is necessary. My men are all approved warriors, and, before they can have perfect confidence in you as a trusty comrade, desire to see some specimen of your prowess. Two leagues south of this is a range of hills infested with lions; rise, then, early on the morrow, mount your horse, take your sword and spear, and slay and bring us the skin of one of these savage beasts: then will we be assured of your courage, and have confidence in you in the day of battle."

Having thus spoke, the Sheik bid him good night, and retired. His words disturbed Azgid extremely. "Ah!" thought he, "here are the lions again! wherever I go I meet them. I thought I had found at last a quiet home, but I am mistaken; this is not the place for me." He then got out of bed, and, lifting up the covering of the tent, slipped out, and went first to see the horse the Sheik had given him. He found him tethered among the others, and, going up to him, threw his arms around him and kissed him. "Farewell, kind creature," said he, "I grieve to leave you!" The animal leaned his head on his shoulders, and seemed to return his good feelings. The youth then sought his own steed, and, having mounted him, started off.

He rode over the trackless sands, with the bright stars glittering above him, a homeless wanderer, not knowing whither he was going. At length morning

*487*

began to appear, and soon the sun rose and beat upon his head with its fierce rays; by the middle of the day he was rejoiced to perceive that he was leaving the desert; and late in the afternoon he reached a charming region of hill and dale, streams and meadows.

He soon after came to one of the most beautiful palaces he had ever seen. It was built of porphyry, and stood in the midst of an immense garden, where every plant and flower grew that could delight the sight or regale the senses. Trees loaded with all kinds of delicious fruits, some trimmed and cut into the most curious shapes, were seen on all sides. Statues of exquisite forms stood among them. From many of these fountains spouted upwards to a vast height, whose waters fell murmuring into large basins, where gold-fish, swans and other water-fowl were seen swimming about. Peacocks and other gorgeous birds strutted and flew around in every direction; and so many objects met the young man's eye, as he slowly rode up the broad avenue, that he stopped almost every moment to gaze and admire. At last lie reached the portico, which was raised twenty steps, and adorned with twelve columns of clear jasper.

The owner of the palace, who was an Emir of great wealth, was seated on the portico, in company with his daughter, the golden-haired Perizide.

On seeing a stranger of such dignified mien approaching, he rose up and went to welcome him. He led him up the steps, and introduced him to the young lady, who became at once interested with the looks and demeanour of the handsome youth. The Emir then took his guest inside the palace.

Azgid looked round with wonder. If the exterior of the building delighted him, how much more was he pleased with its interior? The hall was of vast size, with a noble staircase in the middle; the apartments were spacious, and shone with gold; the walls and ceilings were covered with the most exquisite paintings in fresco; and vases of precious stones, statues, and all kinds of rare curiosities were ranged around; the windows were of something that resembled pearl, and were stained with different colours, so that, as the sun shone through them, the tesselated floor received the rays, and glittered with all the tints of the rainbow. Azgid gazed with astonishment. The Emir now set before him a collation composed of the most delicate viands, delicious fruits, and wines.

After he had finished eating, the Prince thought it his duty to inform his kind host who he was.

"Sir," said he, "you no doubt wonder at one of my appearance thus suddenly visiting you, and will naturally wish to inquire who I am. This wish I can only in part gratify. Suffice it, then, to say that I am a Prince whom troubles at home have driven abroad, but my name I cannot tell: that is a secret lodged in my own breast, to be imparted to no one. If no inconvenience to you, it would delight me much to remain with you; and at some future day, if fortune should again smile upon me, I will be happy to return the favour, and reciprocate your hospitality."

The Emir replied to this speech in the kindest manner, telling the youth that he did him a great honour in making him a visit, and that he hoped he would remain to the end of his days. He further informed him that he expected that night a number of his friends to favour him with their company, and, wishing to look after the preparations for the banquet, he begged his guest to excuse him for a short time.

When the Emir retired, Azgid was left alone with the fair Perizide, and was struck more than ever with her ravishing beauty. In fact, he fell deeply in love with her. She, on her part, seemed not insensible to his merits, and exerted herself to amuse and entertain him. She led him into the garden, showing him all the rare sights, and bidding him observe the consummate art with which the shrubbery and trees were arranged, and the charming green alleys and vistas which opened before them as they walked along.

They explored the beauties of this fairy scene, seating themselves by the side of the glittering fountains, and sometimes beneath the dark shadows of the flowery arbours, through which the rays of a bright full moon began now to penetrate.

They then returned to the palace, and, approaching, heard the strains of festive music, and perceived the building illuminated from top to bottom. They passed through the throngs on the portico, and entered the house, which was lit up with hundreds of dazzling lustres, and crowded with guests, all habited in splendid dresses. Perizide led the youth into the grand saloon, and seated him on one of the purple divans.

The attendants now served up a splendid supper, brought in on gold and silver trays, and which consisted of every delicacy that could be procured. It was made up of many courses, and lasted a considerable time, and at its conclusion the room was partially cleared, and a number of dancing girls, of elegant form and richly clad, entered the apartment, and amused the guests with their graceful movements. Azgid, observing a lute lying near him, took it up, and, telling the lady how fond he was of music, begged her to favour him with an air. Perizide complied with his request very graciously, and commenced playing. The Prince listened with delight, and was drinking in the soft strains with rapt attention, when he suddenly heard a loud and very unusual sound.

"What noise is that?" asked the youth.

"I heard nothing," replied his companion; "nor do I think there was any. It is your imagination only that fancies it."

Whereupon she went on playing; but she had only proceeded a few minutes, when the Prince started a second time.

"There it is again!" said he. "Did you not hear it?"

"I heard nothing," answered Perizide, "but the sound of music and the merry voices of hundreds of happy guests. It must be your imagination, Prince, as I said before, and nothing else."

"Perhaps it is," returned the youth, striking his forehead. "You must pardon me, fair lady: I have lately passed through many trying scenes, and I fear my nerves are none of the strongest."

Perizide thereupon resumed her lute, but she had not proceeded very long, when her guest again cried out,

"Oh!" said he, "tell me not that this is imagination! I heard it most distinctly. Explain to me I pray, what it means."

"Oh," replied the young lady, laughing, "that is Boulak, our black porter. He is a great pet and a privileged character; he gets drowsy sometimes, and often yawns, and that was the sound you just heard."

"Good Heavens!" said Azgid, "what lungs he must have, to make such a yawn as that!"

Perizide made no reply except a smile, but went on playing the lute, when, having finished, the Prince complimented her highly for her performance. It was by this time pretty late, and the guests gradually retired; Perizide also went to her chamber, and the Prince and the Emir were left alone.

They passed nearly an hour smoking and conversing very pleasantly, till at length the host rose up, and telling his guest it was bed-time, took him by the hand to lead him to his chamber. They proceeded to the hall, and soon reached the great staircase, which was of white marble, with a handsome balustrade on each side. When they came to the foot of it, Azgid gazed for a moment admiring its beauty; but what was his horror, when, on looking up, he spied a black lion of immense size lying stretched on the topmost landing. He trembled and turned pale.

"What is that?" said he, pointing with his finger.

"Oh," returned the Emir, "that is Boulak, our black porter. He is tame, and will not hurt you if you are not afraid of him; but he can tell when any one fears him, and then he becomes ferocious."

"I fear him," whispered the Prince, "and fear him greatly."

"You must cast aside your fear, my son," replied the other, "and then there is not the slightest danger."

"That is easier said than done," answered the youth. "I try to cast it aside, but do not succeed. No, I believe I will not go to my chamber, but will sleep somewhere else, where there is no need of approaching this terrible beast."

"Just as you like," replied the Emir. "You can return to the saloon, and repose on one of those divans."

The Prince accordingly took up his lodgings in the saloon, and having bid his friend "Good night," he carefully locked the door and windows, making everything as secure as possible. He then lay down on the cushions, listening eagerly if he might perchance hear any sound. But all was silent; for every soul had retired, and the vast mansion presented a striking contrast to the noisy merriment which a little while before had reigned everywhere.

The young man now composed himself to rest, thinking that the lion was most probably fast asleep and would not disturb him—but he was mistaken; for in the course of an hour he heard most evidently a soft, heavy tread coming down the stairs. The beast, on reaching the hall, seemed for a moment to pause; then his steps were heard moving along the vast corridor, till it could be no longer distinguished.

Azgid now breathed more freely, and was in hopes that his tormentor had retired to some secluded part of the building, and had gone to sleep; but he was doomed to be disappointed, for in a short time he heard the faint steps approaching nearer and nearer, and perceived that the beast stopped every now and then, snuffing with his nose, as if in search of some one. At last he came to the door, putting his nose at the lower part, and snuffing louder than ever; then he sprang with his fore feet against it, giving it such a push as almost to burst it open, and at the same time uttering a tremendous roar, which echoed through the palace.

Azgid jumped from his couch in dismay, and retreated to the farthest corner of the room; his hair stood on end, and the cold perspiration rolled from his body. He believed for a certainty that the door would fly open, and then the lion would rush in and devour him; but nothing of the kind occurred, for in a few moments the beast again went upstairs, and nothing more was heard of him.

The Prince then lay down on his couch—but not to sleep: he revolved in his mind all that had happened to him since his departure from his own city, and thinking that Providence would not afflict him in such a manner for nought, but that there must be some design in it, he came to the determination that he would instantly return home, and fulfil the law and custom of his country by fighting the lion.

Early on the morrow, the Emir came to wake his guest, and bid him "Good morning." He found the young man in tears, and putting his arm round him, thus spoke:

"My son," said he, "your behaviour last night, when about to retire, surprised me greatly, and my amazement is increased now at seeing you in this unhappy state. What ails you, my son? Tell me all, and hide nothing from me; and first let me know frankly who you are?"

"I am one," replied the youth, "who has fled from duty. I am Azgid, son of the renowned King Almamoun. I fled from a work Providence assigned to me to perform—but my sin followed me. I searched far and wide for comfort, but in vain—trouble and disaster pursued me wherever I went. But I have repented, and am now going back to retrieve my error, and meet the trial from which I once endeavoured to escape."

"I am rejoiced to hear you thus speak," said the Emir. "I was well acquainted with your father, and think I know now from what duty it was you tried to escape. Go back, then, to your home, my son, and may Heaven grant you strength to perform your excellent resolution."

He then ordered his guest's horse to be brought, which when the youth hath mounted, he asked his host to remember him to the beautiful Perizide, and beg her to excuse him for leaving her in so strange and abrupt a manner.

"I will do as you desire," replied the other, "and when my daughter learns the cause of your departure, she will think more of you than ever."

Thus with mutual good wishes the two friends separated, and Azgid rode away. He pursued the same route he had travelled before, and on the second day reached the desert and the encampment of the Arabs. He found the Sheik Hajaar, sitting in his tent door, calmly smoking his pipe: the Sheik was surprised at seeing him, and begged him to dismount and refresh himself; but this the Prince refused to do, saying that he had only come to explain his past strange behaviour in leaving his hospitable abode so abruptly.

"I am Azgid," continued he, "son of the renowned King Almamoun. I was sorely troubled in mind when I visited you, for I had fled from duty; but I am now going back to retrieve my error and begin a new life. But tell me, I pray, how is that beautiful animal I used to ride with so much pleasure?"

"He is well," answered the other, "and it would please me much if you could remain and ride him again; but I feel that it would be wrong to interrupt you in such a pious journey as you now undertake. Go on, then, my son: may Heaven prosper you in your good resolutions, and peace be with you."

So saying, he bade the Prince farewell, and the latter, having returned his salutation, rode off.

*491*

He pursued his course rapidly, and in a day or two arrived at the abode of Oaxus, whom he found in the courtyard, busily engaged in tending his sheep and goats. The old man was delighted to see him, and begged him to dismount; but the Prince declined doing so, and went on to explain who he was in the same words he had used to the Sheik Hajaar. Oaxus was much astonished when he heard the account, and congratulated the young man on the happy change that had come over him.

"Go on, my friend," continued he: "may Heaven prosper you, and give you strength to carry out your wise designs."

"Farewell," replied Azgid, "and tell young Asdril that if fortune favours me, I hope one day to be back, and listen to his sweet music again in spite of the lions."

With these words he rode away, and travelling on, in due time reached his own city. He proceeded at once to the palace, and sought out the old Vizier, to whom he related all that had happened to him, and all that he intended to do, without concealing anything.

"And now," said he, "lead me at once to the lion, and let me fight him and fulfil the law, as all my ancestors have done before me."

The old man heard this speech with great pleasure, and almost wept for joy: he tenderly embraced his young friend, and, smiling, told him not to run into extremes nor to be in too great a hurry; for that his trial with the lion had better be put off for a week at least, and that in the meantime he needed rest and refreshment. To this suggestion Azgid acceded, and waited till the day his friend had fixed upon.

It at length arrived, and very early in the morning the Prince arose and prepared for the combat. He clad himself in a light garment, tying a sash around it, in which he stuck a sharp dagger, took a spear in his hand, and, accompanied by the Vizier, left the palace and proceeded to the mountain. They climbed up the high steps and reached the top, whereupon the slave met them, and, going before, unlocked the gate. The young man looked down and saw the lion, sitting on his haunches, at one end of the arena; he then shook hands with his companions, and committing himself to the care of Heaven, sprang in. The beast gave a loud roar when he saw him, and crouching down, drew himself slowly toward his opponent, glaring fiercely on him all the while. The Prince quailed not, but gazed steadily on the animal, and advanced on him spear in hand; the lion now gave another loud roar, and bounding forward, sprang over the youth's head. He then returned, and commenced licking his hands and rubbing himself against his body.

The Vizier now called out joyfully to his young friend, telling him he had conquered, and begging him to approach; and, with the assistance of the slave, he lifted him out of the den, the lion following like a dog.

"Yes, Azgid," continued the old man, embracing the Prince, "the beast is tame and will injure no one; but, ignorant of this, you encountered him, and the proof of your valour is complete. Come, then, and ascend your throne, for you are worthy of it."

They then began to descend the stairs, and Azgid, observing a couple of figures on the landing, asked the Vizier who they were.

"I know not," replied he; "I can see them, but the height is too great for me to distinguish who they are."

In a little while they reached the platform, when the new-comers proved to be Oaxus and Asdril.

"Azgid," said the old shepherd, "I have come to congratulate you on your good fortune and happy deliverance; and here, too, is young Asdril, whose music you so much admired, and whom I now present to you as your own."

"Oaxus," replied the Prince, "I heartily thank you; and as for you, Asdril, you are no longer a slave: from this moment you are free. You shall be the companion of my leisure hours, and entertain me with your delightful strains."

They now began to descend again; and Azgid, observing a group on the second landing, asked the Vizier who they were.

"I know not," replied he; "I can see them, but the height is too great for me to distinguish who they are."

In a little while they reached the platform, when the new-comers proved to be the Sheik Hajaar, with a group of Arabs, leading the beautiful horse with which the Prince had been so much pleased.

"Azgid," said the Sheik, "I have come to congratulate you on your good fortune and happy deliverance. I have brought you as a present the horse you used to ride when you honoured me with a visit: will your Highness deign to accept of it as a slight testimonial of my loyal regard?"

"Valiant Sheik," answered the young man, "I am rejoiced to see you again, and receive with gratitude your noble gift; you could not have given me anything more acceptable."

He then embraced the Sheik, and kissed the beautiful animal, who seemed to recognize him.

They then began to descend; and the Prince, observing at the bottom of the stairs quite a concourse of people, inquired of the Vizier who they were.

"I know not," replied he; "I can see them, but the height is too great for me to distinguish who they are."

In a little while they reached the end of the staircase, when the new-comers proved to be the Emir, with a large retinue of his guards, with music and banners.

"Azgid," said the Emir, "I am come to congratulate you on your good fortune and happy deliverance. I have brought no present; that I considered needless, since myself and all that I have are yours."

"Noble Emir," cried the youth, "I am rejoiced to see you—tell me, how is Perizide? as soon as I have been crowned I intend to visit her with the speed of lightning."

"There is no need of that," returned the other: "come with me;" and, so saying, he led the young man to a splendid white steed, on which sat a lady, covered with a long veil. The Emir lifted the veil, and Azgid beheld the beautiful face of his beloved mistress.

Their meeting, as may be imagined, was most tender and affectionate; and the Vizier, having ordered the music to strike up, the whole procession moved toward the palace.

"How strange it seems!" said the Prince: "when I fled from my duty everything went wrong with me; but now, after fulfilling it, good luck meets me at every step."

Azgid was crowned the same day, and in the evening his nuptials with the fair Perizide were celebrated; they lived long and happily; and the Prince ordered the story of his life to be written in the annals of the kingdom, and an inscription in gold letters to be placed over the door of the palace, with these words: "Never run from the lion."

## The City of the Demons

In days of yore there lived in the flourishing city of Cairo a Hebrew Rabbi, by name Jochonan, who was the most learned of his nation. His fame went over the East, and the most distant people sent their young men to imbibe wisdom from his lips. He was deeply skilled in the traditions of the fathers, and his word on a disputed point was decisive. He was pious, just, temperate, and strict; but he had one vice: a love of gold had seized upon his heart, and he opened not his hand to the poor. Yet he was wealthy above most: his wisdom being to him the source of riches. The Hebrews of the city were grieved at this blemish on the wisest of their people; but, though the elders of the tribes continued to reverence him for his fame, the women and children of Cairo called him by no other name than that of Rabbi Jochonan the Miser.

None knew so well as he the ceremonies necessary for initiation into the religion of Moses, and, consequently, the exercise of those solemn offices was to him another source of gain. One day, as he walked in the fields about Cairo, conversing with a youth on the interpretation of the law, it so happened that the Angel of Death smote the young man suddenly, and he fell dead before the feet of the Rabbi, even while he was yet speaking. When the Rabbi found that the youth was dead, he rent his garments, and glorified the Lord. But his heart was touched, and the thoughts of death troubled him in the visions of the night. He felt uneasy when he reflected on his hardness to the poor; and he said,

"Blessed be the name of the Lord! The first good thing that I am asked to do in that holy name will I perform." But he sighed, for he feared that some one might ask of him a portion of his gold.

While yet he thought upon these things, there came a loud cry at his gate.

"Awake, thou sleeper!" said the voice, "awake! A child is in danger of death, and the mother hath sent me for thee, that thou mayest do thine office."

"The night is dark and gloomy," said the Rabbi, coming to his casement, "and mine age is great: are there not younger men than I in Cairo?"

"For thee only, Rabbi Jochonan, whom some call the Wise, but whom others call Rabbi Jochonan the Miser, was I sent. Here is gold," said he, taking out a purse of sequins; "I want not thy labour for nothing. I adjure thee to come, in the name of the living God."

So the Rabbi thought upon the vow he had just made, and he groaned in spirit, for the purse sounded heavy.

"As thou hast adjured me by that name, I go with thee," said he to the man; "but I hope the distance is not far. Put up thy gold."

"The place is at hand," said the stranger, who was a gallant youth, in magnificent attire. "Be speedy, for time presses."

Jochonan arose, dressed himself, and accompanied the stranger, after having carefully locked up all the doors of his house, and deposited his keys in a secret place—at which the stranger smiled.

"I never remember," said the Rabbi, "so dark a night. Be thou to me as a guide, for I can hardly see the way."

"I know it well," replied the stranger with a sigh. "It is a way much frequented, and travelled hourly by many. Lean upon mine arm, and fear not."

They journeyed on, and, though the darkness was great, yet the Rabbi could see, when it occasionally brightened, that he was in a place strange to him.

"I thought," said he, "I knew all the country for leagues about Cairo, yet I know not where I am. I hope, young man," said he to his companion, "that thou hast not missed the way." And his heart misgave him.

"Fear not," returned the stranger; "your journey is even now done." And, as he spoke, the feet of the Rabbi slipped from under him, and he rolled down a great height. When he recovered, he found that his companion had fallen also, and stood by his side.

"Nay, young man," said the Rabbi, "if thus thou sportest with the grey hairs of age, thy days are numbered. Woe unto him who insults the hoary head!"

The stranger made an excuse, and they journeyed on some little farther in silence. The darkness grew less, and the astonished Rabbi, lifting up his eyes, found that they had come to the gates of a city which he had never before seen. Yet he knew all the cities of the land of Egypt, and he had walked but half an hour from his dwelling in Cairo. So he knew not what to think, but followed the man with trembling.

They soon entered the gates of the city, which was lighted up as if there were a festival in every house. The streets were full of revellers, and nothing but a sound of joy could be heard. But when Jochonan looked upon their faces, they were the faces of men pained within; and he saw, by the marks they bore, that they were Mazikin . He was terrified in his soul, and, by the light of the torches, he looked also upon the face of his companion, and, behold! he saw upon him too the mark that showed him to be a Demon. The Rabbi feared excessively—almost to fainting; but he thought it better to be silent, and sadly he followed his guide, who brought him to a splendid house in the most magnificent quarter of the city.

"Enter here," said the Demon to Jochonan, "for this house is mine. The lady and the child are in the upper chamber." And accordingly the sorrowful Rabbi ascended the stairs to find them.

The lady, whose dazzling beauty was shrouded by melancholy beyond hope, lay in bed; the child, in rich raiment, slumbered on the lap of the nurse, by her side.

"I have brought to thee, light of my eyes!" said the Demon, "Rebecca, beloved of my soul! I have brought unto thee Rabbi Jochonan the Wise, for whom thou didst desire. Let him, then, speedily begin his office; I shall fetch all things necessary, for he is in haste to depart." He smiled bitterly as he said these words, looking at the Rabbi, and left the room, followed by the nurse.

When Jochonan and the lady were alone, she turned in the bed towards him, and said,

"Unhappy man that thou art! knowest thou where thou hast been brought?"

"I do," said he, with a heavy groan. "I know that I am in a city of the Mazikin."

"Know then, further," said she, and the tears gushed from eyes brighter than the diamond, "know then, further, that up one is ever brought here unless he hath sinned before the Lord. What my sin hath been imports not to thee—and I seek not to know thine. But here thou remainest for ever—lost, even as I am lost." And she wept again.

The Rabbi dashed his turban on the ground, and, tearing his hair, exclaimed, "Woe is me! Who art thou, woman, that speakest to me thus?"

"I am a Hebrew woman," said she, "the daughter of a Doctor of the Laws, in the city of Bagdad; and being brought hither—it matters not how—I am married to a Prince among the Mazikin, even him who was sent for thee. And that child whom thou sawest is our first-born, and I could not bear the thought that the soul of our innocent babe should perish. I therefore besought my husband to try and bring hither a priest, that the law of Moses (blessed be his memory!) should be done; and thy fame, which has spread to Bagdad, and lands farther towards the rising of the sun, made me think of thee. Now, my husband, though great among the Mazikin, is more just than the other Demons; and he loves me, whom he hath ruined, with a love of despair. So he said that the name of Jochonan the Wise was familiar unto him, and that he knew thou wouldst not be able to refuse. What thou hast done to give him power over thee is known to thyself."

"I swear, before Heaven," said the Rabbi, "that I have ever diligently kept the law, and walked steadfastly according to the traditions of our fathers from the days of my youth upward. I have wronged no man in word or deed, and I have daily worshipped the Lord, minutely performing all the ceremonies thereto needful."

"Nay," said the lady, "all this thou mightest have done, and more, and yet be in the power of the Demons. But time passes, for I hear the foot of my husband mounting the stair. There is one chance of thine escape."

"What is that, O lady of beauty?" said the agonized Rabbi.

"Eat not, drink not, nor take fee or reward while here, and as long as thou canst do thus, the Mazikin have no power over thee, dead or alive. Have courage and persevere."

As she ceased from speaking, her husband entered the room, followed by the nurse, who bore all things requisite for the ministration of the Rabbi. With a heavy heart he performed his duty, and the child was numbered among the Faithful. But when, as usual, at the conclusion of the ceremony, the wine was handed round to be tasted by the child, the mother, and the Rabbi, he refused it when it came to him, saying,

"Spare me, my lord, for I have made a vow that I fast this day, and I will eat not, neither will I drink."

"Be it as thou pleasest," said the Demon; "I will not that thou shouldst break thy vow." And he laughed aloud.

So the poor Rabbi was taken into a chamber looking into a garden, where he passed the remainder of the night and the day, weeping and praying to the Lord that He would deliver him from the city of Demons. But when the twelfth hour came, and the sun was set, the Prince of the Mazikin came again unto him, and said,

"Eat now, I pray thee, for the day of thy vow is past." And he set meat before him.

"Pardon again thy servant, my lord," said Jochonan, "in this thing. I have another vow for this day also. I pray thee be not angry with thy servant."

"I am not angry," said the Demon; "be it as thou pleasest: I respect thy vow." And he laughed louder than before.

So the Rabbi sat another day in his chamber by the garden, weeping and praying; and when the sun had gone behind the hills, the Prince of the Mazikin again stood before him, and said,

"Eat now, for thou must be an hungered. It was a sore vow of thine." And he offered him daintier meats.

And Jochonan felt a strong desire to eat, but he prayed inwardly to the Lord, and the temptation passed, and he answered, "Excuse thy servant yet a third time, my lord, that I eat not. I have renewed my vow."

"Be it so, then," said the other: "arise, and follow me."

The Demon took a torch in his hand, and led the Rabbi, through winding passages of his palace, to the door of a lofty chamber, which he opened with a key that he took from a niche in the wall. On entering the room, Jochonan saw that it was of solid silver—floor, ceiling, walls, even to the threshold and the door-posts; and the curiously carved roof and borders of the ceiling shone in the torchlight as if they were the fanciful work of frost. In the midst were heaps of silver money, piled up in immense urns of the same metal, even over the brim.

"Thou hast done me a serviceable act, Rabbi," said the Demon: "take of these what thou pleasest; ay, were it the whole."

"I cannot, my lord," said Jochonan. "I was adjured by thee to come hither in the name of God, and in that name I came, not for fee or for reward."

"Follow me," said the Prince of the Mazikin; and Jochonan did so into an inner chamber.

It was of gold, as the other was of silver. Its golden roof was supported by pillars and pilasters of gold, resting upon a golden floor. The treasures of the kings of the earth would not purchase one of the four and twenty vessels of golden coins, which were disposed in six rows along the room. No wonder! for they were filled by the constant labours of the Demons of the Mine. The heart of Jochonan was moved by avarice when he saw them shining in yellow light, like the autumnal sun, as they reflected the beams of the torch. But God enabled him to persevere.

"These are thine," said the Demon: "one of the vessels which thou beholdest would make thee richest of the sons of men, and I give thee them all."

But Jochonan refused again, and the Prince of the Mazikin opened the door of a third chamber, which was called the Hall of Diamonds. When the Rabbi entered, he screamed aloud, and put his hands over his eyes, for the lustre of the jewels dazzled him, as if he had looked upon the noonday sun. In vases of agate were heaped diamonds beyond numeration, the smallest of which was larger than a pigeon's egg. On alabaster tables lay amethysts, topazes, rubies, beryls, and all other precious stones, wrought by the hands of skilful artists, beyond power of computation. The room was lighted by a carbuncle, which, from the end of the hall, poured its ever-living light, brighter than the rays of noontide, but cooler than the gentle radiance of the dewy moon. This was a sore trial to the Rabbi; but he was strengthened from above, and he refused again.

"Thou knowest me, then, I perceive, O Jochonan, son of Ben-David," said the Prince of the Mazikin. "I am a Demon who would tempt thee to destruction. As thou hast withstood so far, I tempt thee no more. Thou hast done a service which, though I value it not, is acceptable in the sight of her whose love is dearer to me than the light of life. Sad has been that love to thee, my Rebecca! Why should I do that which would make thy cureless grief more grievous?—You have yet another chamber to see," said he to Jochonan, who had closed his eyes, and was praying fervently to the Lord, beating his breast.

Far different from the other chambers, the one into which the Rabbi was next introduced was a mean and paltry apartment without furniture. On its filthy walls hung innumerable bunches of rusty keys of all sizes, disposed without order. Among them, to the astonishment of Jochonan, hung the keys of his own house—those which he had put to hide when he came on this miserable journey—and he gazed upon them intently.

"What dost thou see," said the Demon, "that makes thee look so eagerly? Can he who has refused silver and gold and diamonds be moved by a paltry bunch of rusty iron?"

"They are mine own, my lord," said the Rabbi. "Them will I take, if they be offered me."

"Take them, then," said the Demon, putting them into his hand: "thou mayst depart. But, Rabbi, open not thy house only when thou returnest to Cairo, but thy heart also. That thou didst not open it before was that which gave me power over thee. It was well that thou didst one act of charity in coming with me without reward, for it has been thy salvation. Be no more Rabbi Jochonan the Miser."

The Rabbi bowed to the ground, and blessed the Lord for his escape. "But how," said he, "am I to return, for I know not the way?"

"Close thine eyes," said the Demon.

He did so, and, in the space of a moment, heard the voice of the Prince of the Mazikin ordering him to open them again. And behold, when he opened them, he stood in the centre of his own chamber, in his house at Cairo, with the keys in his hand.

When he recovered from his surprise, and had offered thanksgivings to God, he opened his house, and his heart also. He gave alms to the poor, he cheered the heart of the widow, and lightened the destitution of the orphan. His hospitable board was open to the stranger, and his purse was at the service of all who needed to share it. His life was a perpetual act of benevolence, and the blessings showered upon him by all were returned bountifully upon him by the hand of God.

But people wondered, and said, "Is not this the man who was called Rabbi Jochonan the Miser? What hath made the change?"

And it became a saying in Cairo. When it came to the ears of the Rabbi, he called his friends together, and he avowed his former love of gold, and the danger to which it had exposed him, relating all which has been above told, in the hall of the new palace that he built by the side of the river, on the left hand, as thou goest down the course of the great stream. And wise men, who were scribes, wrote it down from his mouth for the benefit of mankind, that they might profit thereby. And a venerable man, with a beard of snow, who had read it in these books, and at whose feet I sat that I might learn the wisdom of the old time, told it to me. And I write it in the tongue of England, the merry and the free, on the tenth day of the month Nisan, in the year, according to the lesser computation, five hundred ninety and seven, that thou mayest learn good thereof. If not, the fault be upon thee.

## Sadik Beg.

Sadik Beg was of good family, handsome in person, and possessed of both sense and courage; but he was poor, having no property but his sword and his horse, with which he served as a gentleman retainer of a Pasha. The latter, satisfied with the purity of Sadik's descent, and entertaining a respect for his character, determined to make him the husband of his daughter Hooseinee, who, though beautiful as her name implied, was remarkable for her haughty manner and ungovernable temper.

Giving a husband of the condition of Sadik Beg to a lady of Hooseinee's rank was, according to usage in such unequal matches, like giving her a slave; and as she heard a good report of his personal qualities, she offered no objections to the marriage, which was celebrated soon after it was proposed, and apartments were assigned to the happy couple in the Pasha's palace.

Some of Sadik Beg's friends rejoiced in his good fortune, as they saw, in the connection he had formed, a sure prospect of his advancement. Others mourned the fate of so fine and promising a young man, now condemned to bear through life all the humours of a proud and capricious woman; but one of his friends, a little man called Merdek, who was completely henpecked, was particularly rejoiced, and quite chuckled at the thought of seeing another in the same condition with himself.

About a month after the nuptials, Merdek met his friend, and, with malicious pleasure, wished him joy of his marriage.

"Most sincerely do I congratulate you, Sadik," said he, "on this happy event."

"Thank you, my good fellow, I am very happy indeed, and rendered more so by the joy I perceive it gives my friends."

"Do you really mean to say you are happy?" said Merdek, with a smile.

"I really am so," replied Sadik.

"Nonsense!" said his friend; "do we not all know to what a termagant you are united? and her temper and high rank combined must no doubt make her a sweet companion." Here he burst into a loud laugh, and the little man actually strutted with a feeling of superiority over the bridegroom.

Sadik, who knew his situation and feelings, was amused instead of being angry. "My friend," said he, "I quite understand the grounds of your apprehension for my happiness. Before I was married, I had heard the same reports as you have done of my beloved bride's disposition; but I am happy to say, I have found it quite otherwise: she is a most docile and obedient wife."

"But how has this miraculous change been wrought?"

"Why," said Sadik, "I believe I have some merit in effecting it; but you shall hear. After the ceremonies of our nuptials were over, I went in my military

499

dress, and with my sword by my side, to the apartment of Hooseinee. She was sitting in a most dignified posture to receive me, and her looks were anything but inviting. As I entered the room, a beautiful cat, evidently a great favourite, came purring up to me. I deliberately drew my sword, struck its head off, and taking that in one hand and the body in the other, threw them out of the window. I then very unconcernedly turned to the lady, who appeared in some alarm; she, however, made no observations, but was in every way kind and submissive, and has continued so ever since."

"Thank you, my dear fellow," said little Merdek, with a significant shake of the head: "a word to the wise." And away he capered, obviously quite rejoiced.

It was near evening when this conversation took place; soon after, when the dark cloak of night had enveloped the bright radiance of day, Merdek entered the chamber of his spouse, with something of a martial swagger, armed with a scimitar. The unsuspecting cat came forward as usual, to welcome the husband of her mistress, but in an instant her head was divided from her body by a blow from the hand which had so often caressed her. Merdek, having proceeded so far courageously, stooped to take up the dissevered members of the cat, but before he could effect this, a blow upon the side of the head, from his incensed lady, laid him sprawling on the floor.

The tattle and scandal of the day spreads from zenaneh to zenaneh with surprising rapidity, and the wife of Merdek saw in a moment whose example it was that he had imitated.

"Take that!" said she, as she gave him another cuff, "take that, you paltry wretch! You should," she added, laughing him to scorn, "have killed the cat on the wedding day."

## The Four Talismans

Abouali Nabul , Emperor of the Moguls, reflecting upon his great age, felt convinced that he could not long enjoy the light of the sun; he therefore sent for his well-beloved and only son Nourgehan, and spoke to him thus:

"Nourgehan, I leave my throne to thee. You will soon fill my place: forget not to do justice equally to the poor as to the rich. Be satisfied with possessing a flourishing kingdom. Envy not the dominions of any other Prince: leave everyone in possession of that which they have inherited from their fathers. In one word, always remember that clemency and justice are the noblest titles of a Sovereign."

After having said these words, the Emperor descended from his throne, made his son ascend it, and retired into a delightful apartment (where he had passed his happiest days), where he remained till he died, which was shortly afterwards.

Nourgehan, after having paid all the honours that nature and gratitude required for so good a father, was wholly occupied in fulfilling the last counsels that he had received from him. His heart was naturally good, and his judgment just; but if every man stands in need of experience to form his mind, much more is it necessary for those who are destined to fill a throne. Nourgehan, persuaded of this important truth, was far from the presumption too common to Princes. One day, as he conversed with his courtiers upon the subject of government, he applauded those Kings who had shown the greatest love of justice. Solomon was quoted as having been the most just.

"This example is not a just one," replied Nourgehan. "Solomon was a prophet, and could easily prevent the evils which he foresaw; but a common mortal can only use his best endeavours to repair the faults of his weakness: therefore I command you all, not only to inform me of all my duties without flattery, but also to prevent or repair my faults by your counsels. When a King testifies a love for virtue, all his subjects become virtuous."

As soon as Nourgehan had ceased speaking, Abourazier rose up and said, "Great Prince, if you wish to have justice truly exercised in your dominions, you must make choice of a disinterested Vizier, who has only your glory and the good of the State in view. The satisfaction of having done right must be the only recompense he desires."

"You say well, Abourazier," returned Nourgehan; "but the difficulty is to find such a man."

"You have, my lord," replied the courtier, "one of your subjects whose moderation and wisdom made him renounce all public employments under the reign of your illustrious father: your Majesty, perhaps, is ignorant of what happened to him in the city of Shiras."

The King having commanded him to inform him of it, Abourazier pursued his discourse thus:

"Imadil Deule , in the last war which we sustained against Persia, led our victorious army as far as Shiras, which he took, and, by a sentiment of humanity, preserved from being plundered. His soldiers, however, demanded a recompense that might make them amends for the booty they expected to have obtained, and spoke to him so strongly, that he was obliged to promise one to them, though he knew not where he could procure it."

"One day as he was in his palace, thinking of this demand, he perceived a serpent creep out of a hole in the wall and return into it again. He called the officers of his harem, and said to them, 'Break open that hole, and take out the serpent that I saw enter it this moment.'

"The courtiers obeyed him, and found a vault full of presses ranged along the walls, with chests piled upon each other. They were opened, and found to be filled with sequins, while the presses were heaped up with the most magnificent stuffs. Imadil Deule returned thanks to God for this discovery, and distributed the treasure to his soldiers. He afterwards commanded a tailor to be sent for to make habits of these stuffs, with which he designed to recompense the merits of those officers who had served under his command. The most experienced tailor of the city was presented to him, who had always wrought for the late Governor. Imadil Deule said to him, 'Not only thou shalt be well paid if these habits are carefully made, but I will procure thee a further recompense, and some bowls of cassonnade.'"

"The tailor, who was deaf of one ear, understood that he was to have the bastinado, and fell a-weeping. Imagining that it was intended to exact an account of the late Governor's clothes which he had in his possession, he declared he had only twelve chests full, and those who accused him of having more had not said the truth.

"Imadil Deule could not forbear smiling at the effect which fear had produced in the poor tailor: he caused the habits to be brought, which were found to be magnificent and entirely new. The only use he made of them, as well as of the rich stuffs he found in the presses, was to clothe and adorn the officers of his army. I believe, therefore, that so disinterested a man deserves the confidence of your Majesty."

Abourazier having ceased speaking, Nourgehan said to him, "Imadil Deule shall not be my Vizier. I believe him an honest man, but he wants prudence, and I do not think him capable of supporting my authority. He had the seals of the empire, and yet knew not how to order everything necessary for his expedition; in a word, his treasure failed him, and his soldiers presumed to give him laws. Without the accident of the serpent, of which any other man would have made the same use, what would have become of him? The story of the tailor is of no consequence."

Nourgehan was continually occupied with the love of justice and the desire of reigning well. He left his palace at all hours to inform himself of the truth by his own knowledge. There was an old potter of earthen vessels who dwelt near his palace. Nourgehan, moved by seeing him every day pray to God with the most ardent and zealous fervour, stopped one day before the little hut in which he dwelt, and said to him, "Ask of me whatever thou desirest, and I promise to grant it thee."

"Command all your officers," said the potter, "to take each of them one of my pots, and pay for it that which I ask. I will not abuse this permission."

Nourgehan granted him his request, and gave orders to his guard to watch over the sale of the pots, and, above all, to do whatever the potter ordered him. He made a very modest use of the favour that he had obtained, and, satisfied with the sale of his work, he exacted no more than the value of it, thinking himself happy in being able to live by his industry, and wishing that he might give a proof of his gratitude to his Sovereign. The Vizier of Nourgehan was avaricious; but for fear of displeasing his master, he concealed that vice with the utmost care. He went one morning to the Emperor's audience, when the potter demanded a sequin for a pot which he presented to him. The Vizier refused it, and said it was a jest to ask such a sum for a thing that the least coin would sufficiently pay for.

The potter, seeing that he added menaces to his refusal, answered him, "that since he took it in that strain, he demanded a thousand sequins for his pot," and added, "that he should not enter into the Emperor's presence until he had hung the pot round his neck, and carried him upon his back to have an audience of the Emperor, that he might make his complaints of the refusal and menaces he had given him."

The Vizier made many difficulties and great entreaties to avoid these vexatious and mortifying conditions; but the hour approaching which the Emperor had appointed for an audience, and the guards refusing to let him enter till he had satisfied the desires of the potter, he was obliged to submit to them; to promise the thousand sequins, to hang the pot about his neck, and to carry the potter on his back, a condition from which he would not recede. The Emperor, surprised at seeing his Vizier arrive in a manner so ridiculous and so unsuitable to his dignity, commanded him to explain what it all meant. When he was told, he obliged the Vizier to pay the thousand sequins immediately; and comprehending of how great an injury it might be to a Prince to have an avaricious minister, he deposed him, and was pleased with the potter for having made known to him a fact that he never would have suspected otherwise.

Nourgehan formed a counsel of the most worthy men of the empire, ordained wise and prudent laws, and departed to visit his provinces, with a resolution of releasing his people from any possible abuse of an authority which is always dangerous, when those who exercise it are at too great a distance from the Sovereign. This Prince, endowed with every virtue, had no other wish than that of deserving after his death the noble epitaph of that Persian monarch who has graved upon his tomb, "Weep! for Shah Chuja is dead!"

Nourgehan, visiting all the provinces of his kingdom, had already gone through the greatest part of them, and remedied numberless disorders, when his curiosity engaged him in a journey into Tartary, his neighbouring kingdom. Finding himself so near their country, he had a desire also to see and know the manners of these Tartars, who were more civilized than others, for they had cities and fixed habitations: their women also are not shut up like those of the other Asiatics. The Tartars came to meet the Emperor of the Moguls. Some of them performed courses on their swiftest horses to do him honour, others, accompanied with their women, formed a kind of dance which, though a little savage, was not destitute of grace. In the number of the Tartar women who presented themselves before him, Nourgehan was struck with the beauty of a young person of eighteen, named Damake . She possessed great beauty; an inexpressible sense and modesty was visible in her countenance. Nourgehan did homage to so many charms, and caused a place in his harem to be proposed to her, but she refused it. Love but too often causes the greatest change in the worthiest characters. The Prince, so wise, and till then so moderate, led away by his passion, joined menaces to his entreaties; he even went so far as to threaten that he would bring a formidable army thither to obtain a beauty whose refusals did not permit him to hope to win her otherwise. He made this rash speech to Damake alone; for if the Tartars, who are a people most jealous of their liberty, had had the least knowledge of it, war would have been that moment declared. But Damake answered him with the utmost sweetness, without showing the least fear, and without losing that respect which she owed to a Sovereign; and it was with the gentle and yet resolved tone that courage and truth always inspire, that she related this little history to him:

"One of the great Lamas," said she, "of whose supreme authority in this country you are not ignorant, fell in love, in this very place, with a maiden of my tribe. She not only refused all that he offered to her, but she would not accept the proposal he made to marry her. The love she felt for a musician was the sole cause of her refusal, which she confessed to the Lama, with a hope of appearing unworthy of his attachment. But that Prince—for they are looked upon as such—distracted with anger and sorrow, caused his unworthy rival to be put to death, and under the pretext of her being agreeable to the Grand Lama, it was not difficult to have her carried off. For you are sensible, my lord, that in this country every one trembles at the very name of him, whom we look upon as a god. But the Lama enjoyed not much satisfaction from his cruelty and injustice; for after she had promised to marry him, in order to obtain a greater liberty, she precipitated herself from the top of a rock, which can be perceived from hence, and which is always shown in the country as a proof of the constancy and resolution of which the Tartar virgins are capable. It is not," continued Damake, "love for another that makes me refuse the offers of your Majesty. My heart to this hour is free; but, my lord, learn to know it thoroughly. It is noble, and perhaps worthy of the favour you condescend to honour me with. My weak charms have seduced you; but a woman who has no other merit than beauty, in my opinion, is of little value."

"Perhaps," returned Nourgehan, "the difference of our religions is an obstacle to my happiness?"

"No, my lord, I am a Mussulman," resumed Damake. "Can you imagine I could submit to the ideas that are given us of the Grand Lama? Can we believe that a man is immortal? The artifice that is made use of to persuade us of it is

503

too gross. In one word, my eyes are too much enlightened for me to hesitate between the ideas inculcated by these priests, and those by which the divinity of God is preached by his most sacred Prophet. No, my lord," continued she, "I am sensible of the risk I shall run by your goodness to me. Time causes the nightingale to perish and the rose to fade. The moon shines during the night; but its lustre fades when the day approaches. Can I expect, therefore, that time should spare me? Yet, notwithstanding these reflections, I confess, my lord, I should be flattered with the thought of pleasing a man whose virtues I esteem above his greatness. But I should wish to please him by other qualities: I should wish to have rendered myself worthy of him by services so considerable, that even a marriage thus unsuitable, far from exposing him to reproaches, should only serve to make his choice more applauded."

Nourgehan, charmed at finding such uncommon sense and such delicate sentiments in an object whose figure alone would have rendered her amiable, admired her virtue, gave her his royal promise never to constrain her inclinations, and resolved never to depart from her. He sent a numerous train of slaves and camels to the beauteous Damake, who followed him with all her family. She would never have consented to this step if she had been obliged to abandon her family, to whom she was fondly attached. The King saw her every day, and could not exist a moment without wishing to see her, or without admiring her when he did see her. In the meantime the discourses of the Court and of the populace reached the ears of Damake. She knew the evil opinion they had of her. To repair this wrong she conjured Nourgehan to assemble all the learned men of his kingdom, that she might answer their questions, and afterwards propose some to them. Nourgehan, who dreaded lest a person so young as Damake should expose herself too hastily, and return with confusion from such a dispute, used his utmost efforts to dissuade her from her request; for the fear and concern that is felt for those whom we love is most certainly far stronger than that which interests us for ourselves. His remonstrances were in vain.

Learned men were assembled to the number of twelve; and in the audience that was given them, the King was placed upon an elevated throne, in his habits of ceremony. Damake was seated lower, opposite to him, leaning upon a sofa, dressed with the greatest plainness, but shining with every charm of youth and every gift of nature, surrounded by the twelve sages, venerable by their extreme age and their flowing beards, leaning upon a large table, round which they and she were seated. The sages, who knew not with what design Nourgehan had assembled them, were extremely astonished when he made known to them the project of Damake. They looked upon the adversary who was presented to them, and kept silence, not doubting that the King did it with the design of showing them contempt. Nourgehan said to them,

"I perceive your thoughts, but I have given my royal promise, and it is your duty to acquit me of it. Propose boldly the hardest questions to this lady, who has engaged to resolve all the difficulties that your great learning gives you the opportunity of proposing to her."

The first sage demanded, "What is that which takes the colour of those who look upon it, which men cannot do without, and which of itself has neither form nor colour?"

"It is the water," replied Damake.

The second said to her, "Can you, O miracle of sense and beauty, tell me what is the thing which has neither door nor foundation, and which is within filled with yellow and white?"

"It is an egg," said the beauteous maiden.

The third sage, after having considered a little, in hopes of surpassing his brethren (for the learned men in the Mogul have a share of self-love), said to her, "There is in a certain garden a tree; this tree bears twelve branches, upon each branch there are thirty leaves, and upon each leaf there are five fruits, of which three are in the shade and two in the sun. What is this tree? and where is it to be found?"

"This tree," returned Damake, "represents the year: the twelve branches are the months, the thirty leaves the days, the five fruits the five prayers, of which two are made by day and three by night."

The sage was amazed, and the courtiers, whose minds vary like the air, and whose sentiments are changed by that which is less than nothing, began to be inwardly persuaded of the value of that which they had at first only pretended to admire.

The other sages, who had not yet spoken, would have excused themselves, and had their silence passed over in favour of the applauses they gave to the uncommon sense of her who had confounded those who preceded them. But Nourgehan, at the entreaty of Damake, having commanded them to continue the conference, one of them demanded, "What is heavier than a mountain?" the other, "What is more cutting than a sabre?" and the third, "What is swifter than an arrow?" Damake answered that the first "was the tongue of a man that complains of oppression;" the second, "Calumny," and the third, "A glance."

There were four sages remaining who had not yet proposed their difficulties. Nourgehan trembled, lest at length the mind of Damake should be exhausted, and she should lose the honour of so great a number of judicious answers. Yet this beautiful maiden appeared neither fatigued nor exalted with that which would have raised the vanity of the greatest part of mankind. But the very property of love being to submit to the will of that which it loves, Nourgehan, whom the preceding examples had not yet reassured, full of alarms and inquietudes, commanded them to speak by a sign of his head, which they durst not refuse. The first demanded of her, "What that animal was which avoided everybody, was composed of seven different animals, and inhabited desolate places." The second desired to know who that was whose habit was armed with darts, who wore a black vest, a yellow shirt, whose mother lived above a hundred years, and who was liked by the whole world. The third desired her to name that which had but one foot, which had a hole in its head, a leathern girdle, and which raised up its head when its hairs were torn off and its face was spit upon.

Damake answered to the first that it was a grasshopper, which is composed of seven animals; for it has the head of a horse, the neck of an ox, the wings of an eagle, the feet of a camel, the tail of a serpent, the horns of a stag, and the body of a scorpion.

The lady found it more difficult to answer the question of the second: for a moment the whole assembly thought her vanquished. This idea, which she perceived in the eyes of all who looked upon her, made her blush. She appeared only still more beautiful from her modesty; and Nourgehan was charmed when he saw the sage who had proposed the question agree that she had answered with her usual justness, when she said that it was a Chestnut. She answered the third without hesitation, that it was a Distaff.

So much knowledge, so much presence of mind, joined to such uncommon personal charms, threw all minds into so pleasing a confusion that, notwithstanding the awe that the presence of Nourgehan inspired, they all loudly expressed the joy, admiration, and pleasure they felt at being witnesses of so uncommon a scene. Damake then made a sign that she wished now to speak. Silence was commanded, and she desired the sages to inform her what was sweeter than honey.

Some of them answered that it was the satisfaction of having our wishes fulfilled, some that of gratitude, and others it was the pleasure of conferring obligations.

When Damake had let them speak, she applauded all their reasonable and just thoughts, but finished her discourse by asking them with gentleness if she was mistaken when she imagined the sweetest thing upon earth to be the love of a mother for her child.

An answer so suitable to her sex, who ought always to be attached to their maternal duty, and proposed with so much modesty, entirely finished the conquest of their hearts. But Damake, who had no other design upon this occasion than to conciliate their esteem and authorize the favours with which Nourgehan honoured her, was resolved to finish a scene which she did not design to repeat, resolving for the future to be occupied with schemes and ideas of a higher kind. Damake then caused instruments to be brought, and sang and played in all the different modes of music, finishing by singing the famous strain of Zeaghioule.

Nourgehan, in those transports of joy which are given by the repeated successes of those one loves, dismissed the assembly, but not without making some large presents to the sages; and when they had all retired, he threw himself at the knees of Damake, saying, "Thou art the life of my soul: haste thee to make me happy!"

The beauty answered that she was not yet worthy of him.

"What can you require further?" cried the passionate Prince. "You have charmed my whole Court; you have confounded the learning of the men most celebrated for their wisdom; the justness of your answers, the moderation of your questions, and the modesty with which you bore the advantage of so great a triumph, have dazzled them. Not satisfied with having proved your sense, what talents did not you show when you touched the musical instruments! What taste did you not express in your song! Whoever, like Damake, joined such merit to so much beauty? But I perceive you love me not," added this passionate Prince, with the utmost tenderness, "since you refuse to attach your destiny to mine. Doubtless you have an aversion for my person."

"I am very far from deserving this reproach, my lord," said Damake; "you yourself shall be the judge. The greatest pleasure and the highest satisfaction I have felt on this day, which your prejudice in my favour has made you think so glorious, was the being able to express before the whole Court, in a proper manner, the sentiments with which you have filled my heart."

"What can you wait for further to render me the happiest man upon earth?" cried Nourgehan with eagerness. "You love me, and I adore you. What wants there more? My wishes for you are become an ocean unbounded by any shore."

"I resolve to deserve you, my lord," replied she, "by talents of more value than those of music; by a justness of sense more valuable than that which your sages set such a price upon, and which is only a mere subtlety of mind. I wish to establish myself in your heart upon foundations more solid than beauty, or those superficial talents that you have had the goodness to applaud. In short, I wish that love may in you only be a passage to that esteem and friendship which I aspire to deserve. Submit your impatience to grant me this favour—it perhaps gives me more pain to ask it than your Majesty to grant: let me live some time under the shadow of your felicity."

"I am capable of nothing now," replied Nourgehan, "but of loving and adoring you; but at least permit me to give a full proof of the justice I do your merit. Assist in the divan, preside in all affairs, and give me your counsels: I can follow none that are more prudent or better judged."

"The diamond boasted," replied Damake, smiling, "that there was no stone which equalled it in strength and hardness. Allah, who loves not pride, changed its nature in favour of lead, the vilest of metals, to which He gave the power to cut it. Independently of the pride I must render myself guilty of if I accepted your offers,—Allah forbid that I should do that wrong to my Sovereign Lord!—to authorize by my behaviour the reproaches that would be thrown upon him. There would be a foundation to say that he was governed by a woman. I allow," added she, "that your Majesty ought to have a Vizier: you cannot see to everything with your own eyes, and I believe I am able to show you one worthy of Nourgehan."

"Name him to me," replied he, "and I will give him the charge this moment."

"Your Majesty," replied the beauteous Damake, "must know him before you accept him. I hope you will find in him whom I propose those virtues and talents necessary in a man dignified with so great an employment. He lives in the city of Balk, and is named Diafer. The post of Vizier to one of the most powerful Kings of the Indies has been in his family above a thousand years. Judge then, my lord, what a collection of admirable precepts he must have upon all parts of government, and yet a Prince, blinded by the pernicious counsels of his favourites, has deposed him, and he passes his days at Balk—days which might be happy if he had not lived in the habit of labour and a hurry of great affairs, which seldom leave the mind at liberty to be satisfied with anything less tumultuous."

Nourgehan immediately replied, "Diafer is my Vizier: Damake can never be mistaken."

Upon the spot he wrote to the Governor of Balk, and sent him a note for a hundred thousand sequins, to be delivered to Diafer, to defray the expenses of his journey; and he charged the same courier with a letter for Diafer, in which he conjured him to accept the post that he had destined him for.

Diafer began his journey. He was received with magnificence in every city, and the Emperor sent all the noblemen of his Court to meet him, and conduct him to the palace which he had destined for him in the kingdom of Visiapour, where he then resided. He was treated there with incredible magnificence during three days, after which he was conducted to an audience of the Prince. He appeared at the height of joy for possessing a man whom Damake esteemed so highly; but that joy was of no long duration, for the Prince, who was so gracious and so prejudiced in his favour, flew into the most dreadful anger the moment Diafer appeared in his presence.

"Go," said he to him, "depart this moment, and never see me again!"

Diafer obeyed, and retired in all the confusion, the sorrow, and the surprise that such a reception must needs give him. He returned to his apartment without being able to imagine the cause of the King's sudden anger, who, in the meantime, held a council, and examined the affairs of his kingdom, without taking any notice of what had passed with him whom he had destined to be his Vizier.

He afterwards repaired to the apartment of Damake, who, already informed of an event which employed the thoughts of the whole Court, doubted not that there was an alteration in the mind of him to whom she was so perfectly attached. The sorrow which this reflection had given her had plunged her into a state so languishing as scarce left her the use of speech. Yet making an effort to conquer herself, she said to him, after some moments' silence,

"How is it possible, my lord, that after all the expenses you have been at, and all the cares you took for the arrival of Diafer at your Court—after all the honours you have ordered to be paid him, and those that you have loaded him with, you should receive him so ill?"

"Ah! Damake," cried Nourgehan, "I should have had no regard to all that I have done for him, to his illustrious family, nor to the fatigues that he has suffered in coming so far, if anyone but you had recommended him to me. I would have had his head struck off the moment he presented himself before me, and it was wholly in regard to you that I satisfied myself with banishing him from my presence forever."

"But how did he incur your indignation?" pursued Damake.

"Know, then," resumed Nourgehan, "that when he came up to me he had the most subtle of poisons about him."

"May I ask you, my lord," returned Damake, "what certainty you have of such a fact, and if you may not doubt of the fidelity of him who made you the report?"

Nourgehan replied, "I knew it myself. I permit you to inquire into it, and you will find whether I was mistaken or not."

When Nourgehan had left Damake more reassured as to the heart of the Emperor, though alarmed at the impressions he was capable of taking so lightly, she sent for Diafer, who appeared sunk in the most violent chagrin. She conversed with him for some time, and perceiving how deeply the ill-treatment he had received from the King had plunged the poniard of sorrow into his heart, she said to him that he ought not to afflict himself so much, that the wrath of Nourgehan would be of no long duration, and that he would soon repair the affront that he had publicly given him. She added that Princes had their hasty moments, that ought to be passed by and excused. When she had a little calmed his chagrin, she finished her discourse by saying to him,

"If I have deserved your confidence, if you believe that I shall endeavour to repair the affront you have suffered—since I, by doing justice to your talents, was the innocent cause of that which has happened to you—if I deserve any return from you, vouchsafe to inform me why you had poison about you when you were presented to Nourgehan?"

Diafer, surprised at this question, after having reflected some moments, replied, "True, I had poison with me; but my heart, though I bore it about me, was as pure as the dew of the morning. I even have it now that I speak to you." Saying this, he drew a ring from his finger and presented it to her. "The setting of this ring," said he, "encloses a most subtle poison. It is a treasure that has been preserved in our family from father to son these thousand years. My ancestors have always worn it, to preserve themselves from the anger of those Princes they served, in case they should have had the misfortune to displease them in the exercise of their post of Vizier. You may believe," continued he, "that when the King sent for me, who was wholly unknown to him, to exercise that charge, and conscious of the many enemies a stranger generally meets with, I would not forget to bring this treasure. The sorrow that the cruel behaviour of Nourgehan has given me, and the shame that he has covered me with, render it still more precious to me: it will not be long before I make use of it."

Damake obtained from him that he should delay, at least for some days, this fatal design, and conjured him to wait in his palace till he heard from her.

She immediately repaired to give an account to Nourgehan of what she had learned. That Prince, perceiving by her relation that Diafer had no ill design, and that the cruelty of Princes in general authorized but too justly such a precaution, repented that he had received him so unworthily, and promised Damake the next day to make amends for the pain he had given him. She approved this design; but before she quitted him she conjured him to satisfy her curiosity by informing her how he could perceive the poison which Diafer had with him. Nourgehan replied,

"Never will I have anything concealed from the sovereign of my heart. I always wear a bracelet, which my father left me, and which has long been in our family, though I am ignorant of the name of the sage who composed it, or how it fell into the hands of my ancestors. It is of a substance that nearly resembles coral, and it has the property of discovering poison, even at a very great distance. It is moved and agitated whenever poison approaches; and when Diafer came near me, the bracelet was very nigh breaking, the poison which he bore had so much strength and violence. Had he not been recommended by you, his head should have been struck off that moment. I was the more certain that Diafer bore that dangerous poison, as my bracelet remained immovable immediately after his leaving the hall where I gave audience."

Nourgehan loosed it from his arm, and gave it to Damake. She examined it with great attention, and said to him, "This talisman, my lord, is doubtless very wonderful; yet this adventure ought to prove to you how much those who have the sovereign power are obliged to be upon their guard against appearances, and of what consequence it is for them not to give judgment rashly."

Damake retired, and Nourgehan commanded the greatest pomp and the most splendid train to conduct Diafer the next day to an audience. This order was executed. Nourgehan received him with the utmost affability, and testified the greatest regret for what had passed. Then there was presented to him, by the Sultan's command, a standish of gold, a pen and paper. Immediately he wrote in the most beautiful characters sublime sentences upon the manner in which a Vizier ought to fulfil the duties of his important post. Nourgehan admired his talents, made him clothe himself in the robe of a Vizier, and, to crown his goodness, confided to him the secret of his bracelet. Diafer strenuously advised that Prince never to part with it; and in his admiration, and the pleasure he felt at possessing so great a treasure, he asked his new Vizier if he believed that through the whole world there could be found anything so curious.

"Great Prince," replied Diafer to him, "I have seen in the city of Dioul another miracle of nature, less useful, indeed, but which for the strength of art and learning with which a sage has composed it, may be compared to this."

"What is it?" returned Nourgehan. "I should be glad to be informed of it."

Then Diafer spoke thus:

"When I had received your Majesty's command to repair to your presence, I departed at once, but was obliged to make some stay at Dioul, through which I passed in my way to Visiapour, where I knew I might join your Majesty. Notwithstanding my impatience, I was obliged to collect several things which were necessary for my journey, and made use of that time to view the beauties of the city. The Governor, whose riches and opulence astonished me, came to meet me on the day of my arrival, and conducted me to his palace. He loaded me with honours, and, during my residence there, showed me the utmost respect and favour; yet it was accompanied with a constraint that rendered his fidelity suspected by me. Among the amusements that he procured for me, was a party upon the river: I consented to join it, and we embarked the next day in a small frigate which he had provided. The weather was fair, and the conversation most agreeable. The Governor of Dioul was seated on the upper deck, and I was placed close to him. A young boy, beautiful as the sun, lay at his feet; the most exquisite wines were served upon a table which stood before us: their coldness, and that of the ice with which all the fruits were surrounded, contributed to the most seducing voluptuousness. The slaves sang and played upon different instruments. Our pleasure was thus accompanied with everything that could render it delicious; and as I was thinking upon something to say that might be agreeable to the Governor, I perceived upon his finger so magnificent a ruby, that I could not forbear giving it the praises it deserved. The Governor immediately drew it off, and presented it to me. I examined it with attention, and returned it to him again, but had great trouble to make him take it. Seeing that I absolutely refused to keep it, he was so concerned that he threw it into the river. I repented then that I had not accepted so perfect a work of nature, and testified my sorrow to the Governor, who answered, that it was my own fault.

"'Yet,' continued he, 'if you will promise me to accept it, it will not be difficult for me to find the ring again, which is really deserving of your acceptance.'

"I imagined that, having another not unlike it, he designed to offer me that; but, without saying any more to me, he immediately commanded they should steer the vessel to the land. When he was arrived there, he sent his slave to his treasurer to demand a small casket which he described to him, and cast anchor to wait the return of the slave, who was expeditious in executing the orders he had received. The Governor, having then taken out of his pocket a small gold key, opened the casket, out of which he took a small fish of the same metal and of admirable workmanship, and threw it into the river. Immediately it plunged to the bottom, and soon after appeared upon the surface of the water holding the ring in its mouth. The rowers who were in the boat took it in their hands and brought it to the Governor, to whom it delivered the ring with a motion of its head: no other person could have forced it from its teeth. The Governor again presenting the ring to me, I could not refuse it, especially as he redoubled his entreaties. The fish was replaced in the little casket and sent back to the treasury."

Diafer, after having related this history, drew the ring from his finger and presented it to Nourgehan, who, finding it to be extremely magnificent, said to him,

"Never part from this ring, which is still more precious from the virtue of the talisman which rendered you the possessor of it. But," continued he, "you ought to have informed yourself at what time, how, and by whom that wonderful masterpiece of art was composed."

"I used my utmost efforts to be informed," replied Diafer, "but they were in vain. Struck with so singular an event, I thought no more of the pleasures of the day. The Governor, perceiving that I fell into a deep reverie, said to me, 'Life is short: make use of every moment and enjoy every pleasure. The soul is a bird imprisoned in the cage of the body, which it must soon quit: rejoice while it is in your power, you know not who shall exist to-morrow.' I confessed to him that curiosity had penetrated my heart. He replied, 'I am in despair that I cannot satisfy you,' and pronounced these words with a tone that expressed his design of not giving a more particular answer. 'Let us think only of amusing ourselves agreeably,' continued he. I followed his counsels as much as it was in my power, and departed from Dioul without being able to obtain any information upon the subject, but fully persuaded that this talisman was the source of all the treasures which he possesses."

Nourgehan terminated the audience of Diafer by assuring him of his favour if he used his utmost care in the administration of justice. He afterwards gave an account to Damake of the conversation he had held with his Vizier, and told her the history of the fish.

"I have a love for these talismans," said that Prince, "and this little fish rouses my curiosity. I wish at least I knew the maker of it."

Damake promised him to use her utmost efforts to inform him. In effect, the next day, she told him, that of all the talismans which the great Seidel-Beckir had made, there existed only four—his bracelet, the little fish of which Diafer had spoken to him, and which she presented to him from the Governor of Dioul, adding, that he had just sent it as a present to his Majesty in order to obtain a life which he had deserved to lose, his faithful subjects having taken him in arms against the Sultan. The third, a poniard, very meanly adorned, which she begged him to accept.

"The others," continued she, "are either worn out (for you know, my lord they only last for a certain time), or have been destroyed by different accidents."

"Why did the Governor of Dioul," resumed Nourgehan, "conceal from Diafer that Seidel-Beckir was the maker of that which he possessed?"

"He was ignorant of it, my lord," interrupted Damake; "and perhaps, ashamed of not knowing it, he feigned it to be a secret. It is the habit of men to cover their ignorance by an affectation of mystery."

"But what is the virtue of this talisman that you offer me?" said Nourgehan, as he accepted the poniard.

"I will inform you of it, my lord," said Damake, "at the same time that I give you an account of what I have been able to learn concerning the fish. It may be about three thousand years since there appeared, in the part of Asia which we inhabit, a man named Houna, who was so great that he was surnamed Seidel-Beckir. He was a sage who possessed in perfection all those talents which acquire a general veneration. The science of talismans he possessed in so eminent a degree, that by their means he commanded the stars and the constellations. Unhappily, his writings are lost, and therefore no talismans like his can now be made. Antinmour, King of Hindostan, having found means to form a friendship with him, Seidel-Beckir, in return for his kindness and some small services that he had done him, made him a present of that little fish of

511

which your Vizier gave you an account. It always remained in the treasury of Antinmour as long as his family existed. One of the ancestors of the Governor of Dioul finding himself the Vizier of the last of that race, when the family was extinct by those revolutions which the history of the Indies relates at length, and which are universally known, seized upon this curiosity, and his successors have kept it with the utmost care till this time. Not only does this talisman bring back whatever is fallen into a river, or the sea, to the person to whom it belongs, but if you indicate to it anything to be brought out of that element, it goes in search of it with the greatest readiness, and brings it wherever it is commanded."

"I am fully satisfied," replied Nourgehan, "as to the two talismans, and never Prince was possessor of such treasures. I may now truly style myself the sovereign of the sea. What do I owe to thee, the ruler of my soul! But of what use is this one which the beauteous Damake has presented to me?"

"My lord," replied she, "when I tell you for what reason it was composed, you will know its virtue."

"We read in the revolutions of Hindostan, that Antinmour would have unjustly exacted a tribute from Keiramour, who was too weak to resist the forces of his enemy; and not knowing to whom to have recourse, he resolved to address himself to the sage Seidel-Beckir, and sent his Vizier to him with magnificent presents. The sage refused them; but he was so touched by the situation to which the King, his friend, had been reduced, that he declared Antinmour should not succeed in his designs. Immediately he composed this very poniard, which I have now presented to my Sovereign, and gave it to the Vizier. 'Tell your master from me,' said he, 'to choose out twenty of the bravest soldiers of his kingdom, and deliver the poniard into the hands of him who commands them; for this poniard has the virtue (when it is drawn) to render invisible not only the person who bears it, but all those whom he designs should participate in the virtue of the talisman. His will alone decides the effect of it. Keiramour shall send these twenty persons to Antinmour with a letter, in which he shall refuse to pay the tribute that is demanded of him. Antinmour, in the excess of his anger, will order the ambassadors to be seized. Then the law of nations being violated, he who bears the poniard shall render himself invisible by drawing it with one hand, and his sabre with the other; and his troop following his example, and doing the same, he shall obey, without hesitation, the dictates of his courage.'

"The Vizier returned to Keiramour, and all that Seidel-Beckir had commanded was executed. The son of the King was charged with the command and execution of this great enterprise. Antinmour was enraged on reading the letter that was presented to him.

"'Let this insolent ambassador be seized,' cried he, 'this moment.'

"Then the Prince, hastily drawing out his poniard and sabre, struck off the head of Antinmour. His train did the same to all those who composed the divan; and running directly into the city, an infinity of heads were flying off without knowing who caused this disorder. After this great execution, the ambassador and his train made themselves visible, and declared to the people in the public square that there was no other method of avoiding certain death but to submit to the government of Keiramour, which they did without reluctance. This poniard," continued Damake, "has been long kept in the treasury of the Princes of that country. By little and little, however, its value was forgotten, and the remembrance of its uncommon property totally lost; and when your Majesty desired an explanation of the talismans, I found that this was at Balsora in the possession of a poor Jew, a broker, who sells upon the bridge of that city all the old iron and useless weapons that are cast away. It was not difficult to procure the possession of it, therefore it was no merit in me to give my Sovereign Lord a talisman which would be absolutely useless to me, whilst the destiny of monarchs may unfortunately render such precautions necessary to them."

Nourgehan made a thousand exclamations upon the boundless ocean of her liberality, and said to her,

"Sovereign of my heart, reflect upon what you have said to me: consider that if these talismans, valuable in themselves, but mean in comparison with you, have excited my wish to possess them, how much greater must my desire be to wed the giver! All the sages, Seidel-Beckir himself, never composed a talisman so wonderful as you are. Yesterday you knew not a single word of the history of the talisman, to-day you are perfectly instructed in it. This poniard was not four and twenty hours since at Balsora, yet notwithstanding the great distance we are from that city, you have presented it to me this moment. Are you the daughter of Seidel-Beckir, or are you an enchantress yourself?"

Damake blushed at this discourse, and Nourgehan again pressing her to speak, she replied,

"Nothing is impossible when one desires to please him whom one loves. But I will explain at once all that puzzles my Sultan. Not long after my birth, my mother was seated at the foot of a palm-tree, enjoying with me the coolness of the morning, without any other thought than that of returning by her tender kisses my innocent caresses, when in a moment she perceived herself surrounded by a numerous Court who attended a Queen, beautiful, majestic, magnificently dressed, and who had herself also an infant in her arms. Notwithstanding the pomp of her train, and all the grandeur of royalty, she caressed me, young as I was, and after some moments' stay said to my mother,

"'This child whom you see in my arms, and who is mine, is by fate obliged to taste the milk of a mortal, it being a command laid upon us by Allah; and I cannot find one more modest, more wise, nor whose milk is purer than thine. Do me the pleasure, therefore, of nursing my infant for a few moments.'

"My mother consented with pleasure; and the Queen, in return for her complaisance, said to her,

"'Whenever you have any sorrow or any desire, come to the foot of a palm-tree, cut a leaf off it, burn it, and call for me—I am named the Peri Malikatada—and I will haste immediately to your assistance. I grant the same power to your little girl when she attains the age of reason.'

"My mother never importuned the Peri except for the care of my education; and I, my lord, before I knew you, had never addressed myself to her, for I knew no desire, nor had my heart formed any wish. From that time I fear I have fatigued her, so many troubles and inquietudes have seized upon my soul. It was she, as you will judge, who made Diafer known to me, who dictated to me the answers I gave the sages, who informed me of the talismans, and delivered this one to me. It was she, likewise, who caused the Governor of Dioul to be arrested, and who demands his life of you in return for the golden fish which I have given you from him; she also would have given me——" she paused.

"Go on, beauteous Damake," said Nourgehan, with tenderness; "if you love me, can you conceal anything from me?"

"She would have given me," resumed Damake, "a talisman of her composition that should force you always to love me, but I have refused it. Can there be any happy talisman in love but the heart?"

Nourgehan, struck with so many virtues, and such proofs of her attachment to him, would no longer defer his happiness. He immediately caused his whole Court, and all the grandees of his kingdom, to be assembled.

"I may boast with reason," said he to them, "that I am the happiest Prince upon earth: I possess a bracelet which preserves me from all fear of poison; all the treasures of the sea are mine by the means of a fish, which at my command will fetch them from the bottom of the waves; Damake has given me this poniard, which renders whoever I please invisible. The proof that I can make before your eyes of this magnificent talisman will convince you of their virtues better than the golden fish, which it would be more tedious and difficult to exhibit."

He drew his poniard as he spoke, and disappeared from their sight. The astonishment of the spectators was not yet dissipated, when he disappeared with all his military officers, and said to his magistrates, "Do you see such a general, such an officer that has served so long in my army?" To every question they answered No. He ceased then to be visible to the eyes of his warriors, and disappeared with his Viziers and all the Doctors of the Law, designing by that means to convince them fully, and leave no room for jealousy and suspicion. "Return thanks, then, with me," added he, "to Allah and His holy Prophet, for having made me the most powerful Prince upon earth."

He performed his action of thanks with a fervour worthy of the bounty which Heaven had shown him, and all his courtiers followed his example. When he had fulfilled that important duty, he said to them,

"The greatest vice of the human heart is ingratitude: it is to Damake that I owe these powerful treasures; her beauty alone, her merit and her virtue, would deserve the gratitude I shall my whole life preserve for her; but gratitude ought to be accompanied with more than words: I will this day unite her to me forever."

All the Court and the grandees applauded his choice; and Nourgehan, having commanded Damake to be brought, she appeared with all those modest graces that nature had adorned her. When the Prince had given her his hand in presence of the Great Imam, Damake, who had prostrated herself before him, said with an audible voice,

"When I gave an account of the talismans of the great Seidel-Beckir, I informed you, my lord, that there were four still subsisting in the world: you have yet but three."

"Have I not riches enough in possessing thee?" returned Nourgehan. "Thou art reckoned, perhaps, for the fourth; but they are not all of half thy value."

"No, my lord," resumed Damake, casting her eyes upon the ground, and presenting him with a ring, "this was wanting. This ring of steel gives you a power of penetrating into the secrets of every heart. Others, in my place, might look upon this talisman as a danger, but I shall look upon it as a blessing if you still condescend to interest yourself in the sentiments that you have for ever graved in mine; and if I have the misfortune not to deserve that interesting curiosity, it will at least make known to you, without any doubts, the characters and the fidelity of your subjects."

At that instant the Peri Malikatada appeared with her whole Court, and desired the King to pass into a garden, which by her power, and that of the genii, she had adorned with exquisite taste and magnificence. Here she honoured the nuptials with her presence, and Nourgehan lived happily ever afterwards, more happy in the love and counsels of Damake than in all the talismans upon earth, if he could have joined them to those which he already possessed.

## The Adventures of Urad; or, The Fair Wanderer.

On the banks of the river Tigris, far above where it washes the lofty city of the Faithful, lived Nouri, in poverty and widowhood, whose employment it was to tend the worm who clothes the richest and the fairest with its beautiful web. Her husband, who was a guard to the caravans of the merchants, lost his life in an engagement with the wild Arabs, and left the poor woman no other means of supporting herself, or her infant daughter Urad, but by her labours among the silk-worms, which were little more than sufficient to support nature, although her labours began ere the sunbeams played on the waters of the Tigris, and ended not till the stars were reflected from its surface. Such was the business of the disconsolate Nouri, when the voluptuous Almurah was proclaimed Sultan throughout his extensive dominions; nor was it long before his subjects felt the power of their Sultan; for, Almurah resolving to inclose a large tract of land for hunting and sporting, commanded the inhabitants of fourteen hundred villages to be expelled from the limits of his intended inclosure.

A piteous train of helpless and ruined families were in one day driven from their country and livelihood, and obliged to seek for shelter amidst the forests, the caves, and deserts, which surround the more uncultivated banks of the Tigris.

Many passed by the cottage of Nouri the widow, among whom she distributed what little remains of provision she had saved from the earnings of her labours the day before; and, her little stock being exhausted, she had nothing but wishes and prayers left for the rest.

It happened, among the numerous throngs that travelled by her cottage, that a young man came with wearied steps, bearing on his shoulders an old and feeble woman; setting her down on the ground before the door of Nouri, he besought her to give him a drop of water, to wash the sand and the dust from his parched mouth.

Nouri, having already distributed the contents of her pitcher, hastened to the river to fill it for the wearied young man; and, as she went, she begged a morsel of provisions from a neighbour, whose cottage stood on a rock which overlooked the flood.

With this, and her pitcher filled with water, the good Nouri returned, and found the feeble old woman on the ground, but the young man was not with her.

"Where," said Nouri, "O afflicted stranger, is the pious young man that dutifully bore the burden of age on his shoulders?"

"Alas!" answered the stranger, "my son has brought me hither from the tyranny of Almurah, and leaves me to perish in the deserts of Tigris. No sooner were you gone for the water, than a crowd of young damsels came this way, and led my cruel son from his perishing mother. But, courteous stranger," said she to Nouri, "give me of that water to drink, that my life fail not within me, for thirst, and hunger, and trouble are hastening to put an end to the unhappy Houadir."

The tender and benevolent Nouri invited Houadir into the cottage, and

515

there placed her on a straw bed, and gave her the provisions, and a cup of water to drink.

Houadir, being somewhat refreshed by the care of Nouri, acquainted her with the cruel decree of Almurah, who had turned her son out of his little patrimony, where, by the labour of his hands, he had for many years supported her, and that till that day she had ever found him a most dutiful and obedient son, and concluded with a wish that he would shortly return to his poor helpless parent.

Nouri did all she could to comfort the wretched Houadir, and, having persuaded her to rest awhile on the bed, returned to the labours of the day.

When her work was finished, Nouri, with the wages of the day, purchased some provisions, and brought them home to feed herself and the little Urad, whose portion of food, as well as her own, had been distributed to the unhappy wanderers.

As Nouri was giving a small morsel to Urad, Houadir awaked, and begged that Nouri would be so kind as to spare her a bit of her provisions.

Immediately, before Nouri could rise, the little Urad ran nimbly to the bed and offered her supper to the afflicted Houadir, who received it with great pleasure from her hands, being assured her mother would not let Urad be a loser by her benevolence.

Houadir continued several days with the widow Nouri, expecting the return of her son; till, giving over all hopes of seeing him, and observing that she was burdensome to the charitable widow, she one evening, after the labours of the day, thus addressed her hospitable friend:

"I perceive, benevolent Nouri, that my son has forsaken me, and that I do but rob you and your poor infant of the scanty provision which you, by your hourly toil, are earning: wherefore, listen to my proposal, and judge whether I offer you a suitable return. There are many parts of your business that, old as I am, I can help you in, as the winding your silk and feeding your worms. Employ me, therefore, in such business in the day as you think me capable of performing; and at night, while your necessary cares busy you about the house, give me leave (as I see your labour allows you no spare time) to instruct the innocent Urad how to behave herself, when your death shall leave her unsheltered from the storms and deceits of a troublesome world."

Nouri listened with pleasure to the words of Houadir.

"Yes," said she, "benevolent stranger, you well advise me how to portion my poor infant, Urad, whom I could neither provide for by my industry nor instruct without losing the daily bread I earn for her. I perceive a little is sufficient for your support; nay, I know not how, I seem to have greater plenty since you have been with me than before; whether it be owing to the blessing of Heaven on you I know not."

"Far be it from me," said Houadir, "to see my generous benefactress deceived; but the thinness of inhabitants, occasioned by the tyranny of Almurah, is the cause that your provisions are more plentiful; but yet I insist upon bearing my part in the burden of the day, and Urad shall share my evening's labour."

From this time Houadir became a useful member of the family of Nouri, and Urad was daily instructed by the good old stranger in the pleasures and benefits of a virtuous, and the horrors and curses of an evil, life.

Little Urad was greatly rejoiced at the lessons of Houadir, and was never better pleased than when she was listening to the mild and pleasing instructions of her affable mistress.

It was the custom of Houadir, whenever she taught Urad any new rule or caution, to give her a peppercorn; requiring of her, as often as she looked at them, to remember the lessons which she learnt at the time she received them.

In this manner Urad continued to be instructed; greatly improving, as well in virtue and religion, as in comeliness and beauty, till she was near woman's estate; so that Nouri could scarcely believe she was the mother of a daughter so amiable and graceful in person and manners. Neither was Urad unskilled in the labours of the family, or the silk-worm; for, Nouri growing old and sickly, she almost constantly, by her industry, supported the whole cottage.

One evening, as Houadir was lecturing her attentive pupil, Nouri, who lay sick on the straw bed, called Urad to her.

"My dear daughter," said Nouri, "I feel, alas! more for you than myself: while Houadir lives, you will have indeed a better instructor than your poor mother was capable of being unto you; but what will my innocent lamb, my lovely Urad do, when she is left alone, the helpless prey of craft or power? Consider, my dear child, that Allah would not send you into the world to be necessarily and unavoidably wicked; therefore always depend upon the assistance of our holy Prophet when you do right, and let no circumstance of life, nor any persuasion, ever bias you to live otherwise than according to the chaste and virtuous precepts of the religious Houadir. May Allah and the Prophet of the Faithful ever bless and preserve the innocence and chastity of my dutiful and affectionate Urad!"

The widow Nouri spoke not again; her breath for ever fled from its confinement, and her body was delivered to the waters of the Tigris.

The inconsolable Urad had now her most difficult lesson to learn from the patient Houadir; and scarcely did she think it dutiful to moderate the violence of her grief.

"Sorrows," said Houadir, "O duteous Urad, which arise from sin or evil actions, cannot be assuaged without contrition or amendment of life; there the soul is deservedly afflicted, and must feel before it can be cured: such sorrows may my amiable pupil never experience! But the afflictions of mortality are alike the portions of piety or iniquity: it is necessary that we should be taught to part with the desirable things of this life by degrees, and that by the frequency of such losses our affections should be loosened from their earthly attachments. While you continue good be not dejected, my obedient Urad; and remember, it is one part of virtue to bear with patience and resignation the unalterable decrees of Heaven; not but that I esteem your sorrow, which arises from gratitude, duty, and affection. I do not teach my pupil to part with her dearest friends without reluctance, or wish her to be unconcerned at the loss of those who, by a marvellous love, have sheltered her from all those storms which must have overwhelmed helpless innocence. Only remember that your tears be the tears of resignation, and that your sighs confess a heart humbly yielding to His will who ordereth all things according to His infinite knowledge and goodness."

"O pious Houadir," replied Urad, "just are thy precepts: it was Allah that created my best of parents, and Allah is pleased to take her from me; far be it from me, though an infinite sufferer, to dispute His will; the loss indeed wounds me sorely, yet will I endeavour to bear the blow with patience and resignation."

Houadir still continued her kind lessons and instructions, and Urad, with a decent solemnity, attended both her labours and her teacher, who was so pleased with the fruits which she saw spring forth from the seeds of virtue that she had sown in the breast of her pupil, that she now began to leave her more to herself, and exhorted her to set apart some portion of each day to pray to her Prophet, and frequent meditation and recollection of the rules she had given her, that so her mind might never be suffered to grow forgetful of the truths she had treasured up. "For," said the provident Houadir, "when it shall please the Prophet to snatch me also from you, my dear Urad will then have only the peppercorns to assist her."

"And how, my kind governess," said Urad, "will those corns assist me?"

"They will," answered Houadir, "each of them (if you remember the precepts I gave you with them, but not otherwise), be serviceable in the times of your necessities."

Urad, with great reluctance, from that time was obliged to go without her evening lectures; which loss affected her much, for she knew no greater pleasure in life than hanging over Houadir's persuasive tongue, and hearing, with fixed attention, the sweet doctrines of prudence, chastity, and virtue.

As Urad, according to her usual custom (after having spent some few early hours at her employment), advanced toward the bed to call her kind instructress, whose infirmities would not admit her to rise betimes, she perceived that Houadir was risen from her bed.

The young virgin was amazed at the novelty of her instructress's behaviour, especially as she seldom moved without assistance, and hastened into a little inclosure to look after her; but not finding Houadir there, she went to the neighbouring cottages, none of the inhabitants of which could give any account of the good old matron; nevertheless the anxious Urad continued her search, looking all around the woods and forest, and often peeping over the rocks of the Tigris, as fearful that some accident might have befallen her. In this fruitless labour the poor virgin fatigued herself, till the sun, as tired of her toils, refused any longer to assist her search; when, returning to her lonely cot, she spent the night in tears and lamentations.

The helpless Urad now gave herself up entirely to grief; and the remembrance of her affectionate mother added a double portion of sorrows to her heart: she neglected to open her lonely cottage, and went not forth to the labours of the silk-worm; but, day after day, with little or no nourishment, she continued weeping the loss of Houadir, her mild instructress, and Nouri, her affectionate mother.

The neighbouring cottagers, observing that Urad came no longer to the silk-worms, and that her dwelling was daily shut up, after some time knocked at her cottage, and demanded if Urad the daughter of Nouri was living. Urad, seeing the concourse of people, came weeping and trembling toward the door, and asked them the cause of their coming.

"O Urad," said her neighbours, "we saw you, not long ago, seeking your friend Houadir, and we feared you also were missing, as you have neither appeared among us, nor attended your daily labours among the worms, who feed and provide for us by their subtle spinning."

"O my friends," answered Urad, "suffer a wretched maid to deplore the loss of her dearest friends. Nouri, from whose breasts I sucked my natural life, is now a prey to the vulture on the banks of the Tigris; and Houadir, from whom I derive my better life, is passed away from me like a vision in the night."

Her rustic acquaintance laughed at these sorrows of the virgin Urad. "Alas!" said one, "Urad grieves that now she has to work for one, instead of three." "Nay," cried another, "I wish my old folks were as well bestowed." "And I," said a third, "were our house rid of the old-fashioned lumber that fills it at present (my superannuated father and mother), would soon bring a healthy young swain to supply their places with love and affection." "Ay, true," answered two or three more, "we must look out a clever young fellow for Urad; whom shall she have?" "Oh, if that be all," said a crooked old maid, who was famous for match-making, "I will send Darandu to comfort her, before night; and, if I mistake not, he very well knows his business." "Well, pretty Urad," cried they all, "Darandu will soon be here: he is fishing on the Tigris; and it is but just that the river which has robbed you of one comfort, should give you a better." At this speech, the rest laughed very heartily, and they all ran away, crying out, "Oh, she will do very well when Darandu approaches."

Urad, though she could despise the trifling of her country neighbours, yet felt an oppression on her heart at the name of Darandu, who was a youth of incomparable beauty, and added to the charms of his person an engaging air, which was far above the reach of the rest of the country swains, who lived on those remote banks of the Tigris. "But, O Houadir, O Nouri!" said the afflicted virgin to herself, "never shall Urad seek, in the arms of a lover, to forget the bounties and precepts of so kind a mistress and so indulgent a parent."

These reflections hurried the wretched Urad into her usual sorrowful train of thoughts, and she spent the rest of the day in tears and weeping, calling for ever on Nouri and Houadir, and wishing that the Prophet would permit her to follow them out of a world where she foresaw neither comfort nor peace.

In the midst of these melancholy meditations, she was disturbed by a knocking at the door. Urad arose with trembling, and asked who was there.

"It is one," answered a voice in the softest tone, "who seeketh comfort and cannot find it; who desires peace, and it is far from him."

"Alas!" answered Urad, "few are the comforts of this cottage, and peace is a stranger to this mournful roof: depart, O traveller, whosoever thou art, and suffer the disconsolate Urad to indulge in sorrows greater than those from which you wish to be relieved."

"Alas!" answered the voice without, "the griefs of the beautiful Urad are my griefs; and the sorrows which afflict her, rend the soul of the wretched Darandu!"

"Whatever may be the motive for this charitable visit, Darandu," answered Urad, "let me beseech you to depart; for ill does it become a forlorn virgin to admit the conversation of the youths that surround her: leave me, therefore, O swain, ere want of decency make you appear odious in the sight of the virgins who inhabit the rocky banks of the rapid Tigris."

"To convince the lovely Urad," answered Darandu, "that I came to soothe her cares and condole with her in her losses (which I heard but this evening), I now will quit this dear spot, which contains the treasure of my heart, as, however terrible the parting is to me, I rest satisfied that it pleases the fair conqueror of my heart, whose peace to Darandu is more precious than the pomegranate in the sultry noon, or the silver scales of ten thousand fishes enclosed in the nets of my skilful comrades."

Darandu then left the door of the cottage, and Urad reclined on the bed, till sleep finished her toils, and for a time released her from the severe afflictions of her unguarded situation.

Early in the morning the fair Urad arose, and directed her steps to the rocks of the Tigris, either invited thither by the melancholy reflections which her departed mother occasioned, or willing to take a nearer and more unobserved view of the gentle Darandu.

Darandu, who was just about to launch his vessel into the river, perceived the beauteous mourner on the rocks; but he was too well versed in love affairs to take any notice of her: he rather turned from Urad, and endeavoured by his behaviour to persuade her that he had not observed her, for it was enough for him to know that he was not indifferent to her.

Urad, though she hardly knew the cause of her morning walk, yet continued on the rocks till Darandu had taken in his nets, and, with his companions, was steering up the stream in quest of the fishes of the Tigris. She then returned to her cottage, more irresolute in her thoughts, but less than ever inclined to the labours of her profession.

At the return of the evening she was anxious lest Darandu should renew his visit—an anxiety which, though it arose from fear, was yet near allied to hope; nor was she less solicitous about provisions, as all her little stock was entirely exhausted, and she had no other prospect before her than to return to her labours, which her sorrows had rendered irksome and disagreeable to her.

While she was meditating on these things, she heard a knocking at the door, which fluttered her little less than the fears of hunger or the sorrows of her lonely life.

For some time she had not courage to answer, till, the knocking being repeated, she faintly asked who was at the door.

"It is Lahnar," answered a female: "Lahnar, your neighbour, seeks to give Urad comfort, and to condole with the distressed mourner of a mother and a friend."

"Lahnar," answered Urad, "is then a friend to the afflicted, and kindly seeks to alleviate the sorrows of the wretched Urad."

She then opened the door, and Lahnar entered with a basket on her head.

"Kind Lahnar," said the fair mourner, "leave your burden at the door, and enter this cottage of affliction. Alas! alas! there once sat Nouri, my ever-affectionate mother, and there Houadir, my kind counsellor and director; but now are their seats vacant, and sorrow and grief are the only companions of the miserable Urad!"

"Your losses are certainly great," answered Lahnar; "but you must endeavour to bear them with patience, especially as they are the common changes and alterations of life. Your good mother Nouri lived to a great age, and Houadir, though a kind friend, may yet be succeeded by one as amiable; but what I am most alarmed at, O Urad! is your manner of life. We no longer see you busied among the leaves of the mulberries, or gathering the bags of silk, or preparing them for the wheels. You purchase no provision among us; you seek no comfort in society; you live like the mole buried under the earth, which neither sees nor is seen."

"My sorrows indeed hitherto," replied Urad, "have prevented my labour; but to-morrow I shall again rise to my wonted employment."

"But even to-night," said Lahnar, "let my friend take some little nourishment, that she may rise refreshed; for fasting will deject you as well as grief; and suffer me to partake with you. And see, in this basket I have brought my provisions, some boiled rice, and a few fish, which my kind brother Darandu brought me this evening from the river Tigris."

"Excuse me, kind Lahnar," answered Urad, "but I must refuse your offer. Grief has driven away appetite to aught but itself far from me, and I am not solicitous to take provisions which I cannot use."

"At least," replied Lahnar, "permit me to sit beside you, and eat of what is here before us."

Upon which, without other excuses, Lahnar emptied her basket, and set a bowl of rice and fish before Urad, and began to feed heartily on that which she had brought for herself.

Urad was tempted by hunger and the example of Lahnar to begin, but she was doubtful about tasting the fish of Darandu; wherefore she first attempted the boiled rice, though her appetite was most inclined to the fish, of which she at last ate very heartily, when she recollected that as she had partaken with Lahnar, it was the same whatever part she accepted.

Lahnar having finished her meal, and advised Urad to think of some methods of social life, took her leave, and left the unsettled virgin to meditate on her strange visitor.

Urad, though confused, could not help expressing some pleasure at this visit; for such is the blessing of society, that it will always give comfort to those who have been disused to its sweet effects.

But Urad, though pleased with the friendship of Lahnar, yet was confounded when, some few minutes after, she perceived her again returning.

"What," said Urad, "brings back Lahnar to the sorrows of this cottage?"

"Urad," said Lahnar, "I will rest with my friend to-night, for the shades of night cast horrors around, and I dare not disturb my father's cottage by my late approach."

But as soon as she had admitted Lahnar, she perceived that it was Darandu disguised in Lahnar's clothes. Urad, greatly terrified, recollecting her lost friend Houadir, felt for a peppercorn, and let it fall to the ground.

A violent rapping was in a moment heard at the cottage, at which Urad uttered a loud cry, and Darandu, with shame and confusion, looked trembling toward the door.

Urad ran forward and opened it, when the son of Houadir entered, and asked Urad the reason of her cries.

"O thou blessed angel!" said Urad; "this wicked wretch is disguised in his sister's clothes."

But Darandu was fled, as guilt is ever fearful, mean, and base.

*521*

"Now, Urad," said the son of Houadir, "before you close your doors upon another man, let me resume my former features."

Upon which Urad looked, and beheld her old friend Houadir. At the sight of Houadir, Urad was equally astonished and abashed.

"Why blushes, Urad?" said Houadir.

"How, O genius," said Urad, "for such I perceive thou art—how is Urad guilty? I invited not Darandu hither: I wished not for him."

"Take care," answered Houadir, "what you say. If you wished not for him, you hardly wished him away, and, but for your imprudence, he had not entered your home. Consider how have your days been employed since I left you? Have you continued to watch the labours of the silk-worm? Have you repeated the lessons I gave you? or has the time of Urad been consumed in idleness and disobedience? Has she shaken off her dependence on Mahomet, and indulged the unavailing sorrows of her heart?"

"Alas!" answered the fair Urad, "repeat no more, my ever-honoured Houadir: I have indeed been guilty, under the mask of love and affection; and I now plainly see the force of your first rule, that idleness is the beginning of all evil and vice. Yes, my dearest Houadir, had I attended to your instructions I had given no handle to Darandu's insolence; but yet methinks some sorrows were allowable for the loss of such a mother and such a friend."

"Sorrows," answered Houadir, "proceed from the heart, and, totally indulged, soon require a change and vicissitude in our minds; wherefore, in the midst of your griefs, your feet involuntarily wandered after Darandu, and your soul, softened by idle sighs, was the more easily impressed by the deceits of his tongue.

"But this remember, O Urad—for I must, I find, repeat an old instruction to you—that of all things in the world, nothing should so much engage a woman's attention as the avenues which lead to her heart. Such are the wiles and deceits of men, that they are rarely to be trusted with the most advanced post; give them but footing, though that footing be innocent, and they will work night and day till their wishes are accomplished. Trust not, therefore, to yourself alone, nor suffer your heart to plead in their favour, lest it become as much your enemy as the tempter, man. Place your security in flight, and avoid every evil, lest it lead you into danger, for hard it is to turn the head and look backward when a beautiful or agreeable object is before you. Remember my instructions, O Urad! make a prudent use of your peppercorns, and leave this place, which holds a man sensible of your folly and resolute in his own dark and subtle intentions."

Urad was about to thank Houadir, but the genius was fled, and the eyelids of the morning were opening in the east.

Urad, in a little wallet, packed up her small stock of necessaries, and, full of terror and full of uncertainty, struck into the forest, and without reflection took the widest path that offered. And first, it was her care to repeat over deliberately the lessons of Houadir. She then travelled slowly forward, often looking, and fearing to behold the wicked Darandu at her heels.

After walking through the forest for the greater part of the day, she came to a steep descent, on each side overshadowed with lofty trees; this she walked down, and came to a small spot of ground surrounded by hills, woods, and rocks. Here she found a spring of water, and sat down on the grass to refresh herself after the travels of the day.

As Urad's meal was almost at an end she heard various voices issuing from the woods on the hills opposite to that which she came down. Her little heart beat quick at this alarm; and recollecting the advice of Houadir, she began to repeat the lessons of her instructress, and ere long she perceived through the trees several men coming down the hill, who, at sight of her, gave a loud halloo, and ran forward, each being eager who should first seize the prize.

Urad, trembling and sighing at her danger, forgot not to drop one of her peppercorns, and immediately she found herself changed into a pismire, and with great pleasure she looked for a hole in the ground, and crept into it.

The robbers, coming down to the bottom of the vale, were surprised to find their prize eloped; but they divided into separate bodies, resolved to hunt till night, and then appointed that little vale as the place of rendezvous.

Urad, perceiving that they were gone, wished herself into her original form, but alas! her wish was not granted, and the once beautiful Urad still continued an ugly pismire.

Late at night the robbers returned, and the moon shining bright, reflected a gloomy horror upon their despairing faces. Urad shuddered at the sight of them, though so well concealed, and dared hardly peep out of her hole—so difficult is it to forget our former fears. The gang resolved to spend the rest of the night in that place, and therefore unloaded their wallets, and spread their wine and provisions on the banks of the spring, grumbling and cursing each other all the time for their unfortunate search.

Urad heard them lamenting their ill fortune with the utmost horror and indignation, and praised continually the gracious Allah who had rescued her from such inhuman wretches; while they with singing and drinking spent the greatest part of the night, and wishing that their comrades in the other part of the forest had been with them; at length falling into drunkenness and sleep, they left the world to silence and peace.

Urad, finding them fast asleep, crawled out of her hole, and going to the first, she stung him in each eye, and thus she went round to them all.

The poison of the little pismire working in their eyes, in a short time occasioned them to awake in the utmost tortures; and perceiving they were blind, and feeling the pain, they each supposed his neighbour had blinded him in order to get away with the booty. This so enraged them that, feeling about, they fell upon one another, and in a short time almost the whole gang was demolished.

Urad beheld with astonishment the effect of her stings, and at a wish resumed her pristine form, saying at the same time to herself, "I now perceive that Providence is able by the most insignificant means to work the greatest purposes."

Continuing her journey through the forest, she was terribly afraid of meeting with the second band of robbers, and therefore she directed her steps with the greatest caution and circumspection.

As she walked forward, and cast her eyes all around, and stopped at every motion of the wind, she saw the son of Houadir coming to meet her in the path in which she was travelling.

At this sight Urad ran toward him, and with joy begged her old governess would unmask herself, and entertain her with instruction and persuasion.

"No, my dear child," answered the son of Houadir, "that I cannot do at present; the time is not as yet come. I will first, as you have been tried, lead you to the palace of the Genii of the Forest, and present your unspotted innocence before them; for, O my sweet Urad, my heavenly pupil!" said he, kissing and taking her in his arms, "your virtue is tried; I have found you worthy of the lessons which I gave you. I foresaw evils might befall you, and therefore I took pity on your innocence, and lived with Nouri your mother, that I might train up my beloved Urad in the paths of virtue; and now your trial is past, Urad shall enjoy the happiness of a genius."

Urad, though somewhat confounded at Houadir's embrace under the appearance of a man, yet with great humility thanked her benefactor; and the son of Houadir, turning to the left, led Urad into a little by-path, so concealed that few, if any, might ever find its beginning. After a long walk through various turnings and intricate windings, they came to a small mean cottage, where, the son of Houadir leading the way, Urad followed.

The son of Houadir striking fire with his stick, a bright flame arose from the centre of the floor, into which he cast divers herbs, and repeating some enchantments, the back part of the cottage opened and presented to the view of Urad a beautiful dome, where she saw sitting round a table a numerous assembly of gay persons of both sexes.

The son of Houadir, leading in Urad, said, "This, my dear pupil, is the assembly of the Genii of the Forest." And, presenting her to the company, "Behold," said he, "the beautiful and well-tried Urad. But here you may cast off your reserve, fair maid, and indulge in the innocent pleasures of the Genii of the Forest."

The son of Houadir then led her to the table, and seated her on the same sofa with himself. The remainder of the day was spent in mirth and pleasure.

Urad, having never beheld anything splendid or magnificent, was greatly delighted at the gay company and beautiful saloon, nor did she receive the caresses of the son of Houadir reluctantly.

At night, Urad was shown a glorious apartment to rest in, and the son of Houadir attended her.

"My dear Houadir," said Urad, "when shall I behold your proper shape? When shall I see you as my tutelary genius?"

"That," answered the son of Houadir, "I shall be in every shape; but call neither one nor the other my proper shape; for to a genius all shapes are assumed: neither is this my proper shape, nor the wrinkles of an old woman. But, to confess the truth, O beautiful Urad, from the first moment of your birth I resolved to make you my bride, and therefore did I so patiently watch your growing years, and instruct you in the fear of vice and the love of virtue."

Urad, astonished at the words of the son of Houadir, knew not what answer to make; but the natural timidity of her sex, and the strangeness of the proposal, filled her with strange apprehensions. However, she begged at least that the genius would, for a time, leave her to herself.

"No, my lovely Urad," answered the son of Houadir, "never, never, will thy faithful genius leave thee!"

"Why," said Urad, "didst thou bestow so many peppercorns upon me, as they now will become useless?"

"Not useless," said the son of Houadir: "they are indeed little preservatives against danger; but I have the seeds of some melons which will not only rescue you, but always preserve you from harm. Here, faithful Urad," continued he, "take these seeds, and, whenever you are fearful, swallow one of these, and no dangers shall surround you."

Urad thankfully received the seeds.

"And what," said she, "must I do with the peppercorns?"

"Give them," said the son of Houadir, "to me, and I will endue them with stronger virtues, and thou shalt by them have power also over others, as well as to defend thyself."

Urad pulled the peppercorns out of her bag, and presented them to the son of Houadir, whose eyes flashed with joy at the sight, and he immediately thrust them into the folds of his garments.

"O son of Houadir, what hast thou done?" said Urad.

"I have," answered the false son of Houadir, "gained the full possession of my lovely Urad, and now may address her in my proper shape." So saying, he resumed his natural figure, and became like a satyr of the wood.

"I am," said he, "O beautiful Urad, the enchanter Repah, who range in the solitude of the forest of the Tigris. You I saw surrounded by the influence of the genius Houadir, and therefore was obliged to use artifice to gain you as my wife."

The poor deluded victim, with tears in her eyes, implored his mercy and forbearance; but he laughed at her tears, and told her her eyes glittered the brighter for them.

Urad, in her despair, again put her hands into the bag whence she had fatally resigned the peppercorns, and felt about in agony for her lost treasure. And now finding none, and perceiving that the genius Houadir attended not to her cries, she was drawing out her hand when, in a corner of the bag, she felt one peppercorn, which had before escaped her search.

She instantly drew it out, and, throwing it on the ground, the enchanter stood motionless before her; the apartments vanished, and she found herself with him in a dark hut, with various kinds of necromantic instruments about her.

Urad, though fearful, yet was so much overcome with fatigue and fright that she sank on the ground; and, happily for her, the enchanter was in no condition to persecute her.

"Curse on my folly," said he, as he stood fixed to the ground, "that I neglected to ask for the bag itself which held the gifts of the genius Houadir! her pretty pupil had then been my slave, in spite of the many fine lessons she had been taught by that pitiful and enthusiastic genius; but now by chance, and not by the merit of thy virtues, or thy education, art thou delivered from my seraglio. But this grieves me not so much to lose a sickly girl as that I find a superior power condemns me to declare to you the causes of your error.

"Know, then, Urad—I speak not from myself, but He speaks who, from casual evil, can work out certain good—He forces me to declare that no specious appearance, no false colours, should incline the virtuous heart to listen to the wiles of deceit; for evil then comes most terrible when it is cloaked under friendship. Why, then, had Urad so great an opinion of her own judgment as to confide in the false appearance of the son of Houadir when she might have consulted her faithful monitors? The falling of a peppercorn would have taught her to trust to no appearances, nor would she have parted with her peppercorns, which were to refresh in her memory the sentiments of virtue, chastity, and honour—no, not to Houadir herself. No adviser can be good who would destroy what he himself has first inculcated; and no appearance ought to bias us to receive as truths those things which are contrary to virtue and religion. How, then, did Urad keep to the instructions of Houadir?"

Thus spoke the enchanter, and no more; his mouth closed up, and he stood fixed and motionless. And Urad, finding her spirits somewhat recovered, hastened out of the hut, and perceived that it was morning.

She had now no more peppercorns to depend upon; wherefore she cried to Houadir to succour her; but the genius was deaf to her entreaties.

"Poor miserable wretch!" said Urad to herself, "what will become of thee, inclosed in a forest through which thou knowest no path? But," continued she, "why should I not examine the enchanter, who perhaps is yet immovable in the cottage? I saw him fold them in the plaits of his garments, and they may yet become mine."

So saying, she returned to the hut, where entering, the very sight of the dumb enchanter affrighted her so much, that it was a long time before she could venture near him. At length she put out her hand, and pulled forth her beloved peppercorns, the enchanter still standing motionless.

Away flew Urad like lightning from the hut, and ran till she had again reached the road from which she had been decoyed.

She continued her journeying for seven days, feeding on the fruits of the forest, and sleeping in the densest thickets.

The eighth day, as she was endeavouring to pass a ford where a small rivulet had been swelled by the rains, she perceived a large body of horsemen riding through the woods, and doubted not that it was the remainder of the gang of robbers whom she had before met with.

Urad was now in some measure reconciled to danger; and therefore, without much fear, dropped a peppercorn, and expected relief.

The peppercorn had been dropped some time, the horsemen advanced, and no one appeared to her succour.

"Alas!" said Urad, "why has Houadir deceived me? Neither her advice, nor her magical peppercorns, can save me from these cruel robbers. O genius, genius! why hast thou forsaken me in my severest trials!"

By this time the robbers were come up, and were highly rejoiced to find such a beautiful prize.

Their captain leaped from his horse to seize her, and the trembling Urad gave a loud shriek, which was answered from the woods by the roaring of a hundred lions.

"O Allah," said the chief, "the lions are upon us!"

"That may be," said he who was dismounted; "but were the whole world set against me, I would secure my prize." So saying, he took Urad in his arms to place her on his horse.

The roaring of the lions continued, and many of them came howling out of the woods: the robbers fled in dismay, all but the ruffian who had seized on the fair Urad, who was striving in vain to fix her on his horse. A lion furiously made at him, and tore him limb from limb, while Urad expected the same fate from several others who came roaring around.

"But," said she, "better is death than infamy, and the paw of the hungry lion, than slavery to a robber."

The noble beast, having devoured his prey, came fawning at the feet of Urad, who was surprised at his behaviour and gentleness; but much more was her astonishment increased when she heard him speak.

"O virgin (for none other can experience the assistance of our race, or stand unhurt before us), I am the King and Sovereign of these mighty forests, and am sent by the genius Houadir to thy protection. But why did the distrustful Urad despair, or why did she accuse Providence of deserting her? should not the relieved wait with patience on the hand that supports him, and not cry out with impatience, and charge its benefactor with neglect?"

"True, O royal lion," answered the fair Urad; "but fear is irresistible, and the children of men are but weakness and ingratitude. But blessed be Allah, who, though justly provoked at my discontent, yet sent to my assistance the guardian of the fair. Yet how cometh it to pass, O royal protector, that you, who are so bold and so fierce in your nature, should yet behave with such tenderness and kindness to a helpless virgin, whom you might with pleasure to yourself in a moment devour?"

"The truly great and noble spirit," answered the lion, "takes a pride in protecting innocence, neither can he wish to oppress it. Hence learn, fair virgin, that of all mankind he only is noble, generous, and truly virtuous, who is ready to defend helpless womanhood. What, then, must you think of those mean wretches who cajole you under the appearance of affection, and yet tell you that it was only to try you? He that is suspicious is mean: he that is mean is unworthy of the chaste affections of the virtuous maid. Wherefore, O Urad, shun him, however honoured by mankind, or covered by the specious characters of virtue, whoever attempts the honour of your chastity, for he cannot be just: to deceive you he must himself swear falsely, and therefore cannot be good; or if he tell the truth, he must be weak and ungenerous, and unworthy of you."

In such conversation they passed along the forest, till, after a few days, they were alarmed at the noise of the hunters and the music of the chase.

"Alas!" said the beautiful Urad, "what is this that I hear?"

"It is," answered the royal beast, "the noise of the hunters; and thou shalt escape, but me will they in sport destroy. The lion you call cruel, who kills to devour. What, then, is he who wantons in the death of those who advantage him not? But man is lord of all: let him look to it how he governs!"

"Nay, but," answered Urad, "leave me, gentle protector, and provide for your safety; nor fear but Houadir will prevent the storms that hover over from breaking upon me."

"No," answered the royal beast, "she has commanded me to follow you till I see her presence; and where can I better sacrifice my life than in the service of chastity and virtue?"

The hunters were now in sight, but advanced not towards the lion; they turned their coursers as ide, and only one of superior mien, with several attendants, rode towards Urad.

The lion erecting his mane, his eyes glowing with vivid lightnings, drew up the wide sinews of his broad back, and with wrathful front leaped towards him who seemed to have the command.

The horseman, perceiving his intention, poised his spear in his right hand, and spurred his courser to meet him.

Ere the royal beast had reached the horseman, the rider threw his spear, which, entering between the fore-paws of the lion, nailed him to the ground. The enraged animal tore his paw from the ground; but the spear still remained in his foot, and the anguish of the wound made him shake the whole forest with his lordly roarings.

The stranger then rode up to the fair Urad, whom viewing, he cried out, "By Allah! thou art worthy of the seraglio of the Vizier Mussapulta: take her, my eunuchs, behind you, and bear her through the forest of Bagdad, to the home of my ancestors."

The eunuchs obeyed, and bore her away, though Urad dropped her corn upon the ground; but still she trusted in the help of Houadir.

The Vizier Mussapulta then ordered that one of his slaves should stay behind, and destroy and bury the lion; which he commanded to be done with the utmost caution, as Almurah had made a decree that if any subjects should wound, maim, or destroy any lion in his forests, the same should be put to death.

The eunuchs bore away Urad to the seraglio, taking her through by-ways to the palace of the Vizier, lest her shrieks should be heard. Mussapulta followed at a distance, and the slave was left with the tortured and faithful lion.

In a few hours they reached the palace, and Urad, being conducted to the seraglio, was ordered to be dressed, as the Vizier intended visiting her.

Urad was thunderstruck at the news, and now began to fear Houadir had forgotten her, and resolved, as soon as the eunuchs had left her, to drop a second peppercorn. But poor Urad had forgotten to take her bag from her old garments, which the women who dressed her had carried away. She dissolved in fresh tears at this piece of carelessness.

"Well," said she, "surely Houadir will neglect me, if I so easily neglect myself."

She waited that night with fear and trembling; but no Vizier appeared.

This eased her greatly, and the next day, when the eunuchs came, they informed her that Mussapulta had that evening been sent by the Sultan to quell an insurrection, and that they did not expect him home under twenty days.

During this time no pains were spared with Urad to teach her the accomplishments of the country, all which, in spite of her unwillingness to learn in such a detestable place, she nevertheless acquired with the utmost ease and facility.

The insurrection being quelled, the Vizier returned, and, not unmindful of his fair captive, ordered that she might be prepared for his reception in the evening.

Accordingly Urad was sumptuously adorned with jewels and brocades, and looked more beautiful than the fairest Circassian; and the dignity of her virtue added such a grace to her charms, that even her keepers, the eunuchs, dared not look upon her. In the evening the chief eunuch led her into the presence of Mussapulta. She shrank from him with horror.

"What!" said he, "cannot a fortnight's pleasure in this palace efface the remembrance of your sorrows? But be gay and cheerful, for know that the Vizier Mussapulta esteems you beyond any of his wives."

"The esteem of a robber, the esteem of a lawless ranger," answered Urad, "charms not the ears of virtue."

"What," said Mussapulta, sternly, "dost thou refuse my proffered love? Then shalt thou die! Slay this proud maiden in my sight. Cut off her head at once."

The eunuch hesitated.

"Why," said the proud Vizier, "do you delay to obey me?"

As he said this an eunuch came running in haste, crying, "The Sultan, the Sultan Almurah, approaches!"

All was instant confusion. Mussapulta turned pale and trembled. He ordered the eunuch to release the fair Urad, and at that moment the faithful lion entered with the Sultan Almurah.

The lion instantly seized on the Vizier Mussapulta, and tore him limb from limb. Yet the generous animal would not defile himself with the carcass, but with great wrath tossed the bloody remains among the females of the seraglio.

Almurah commanded Urad to advance, and at the sight of her,

"O royal beast," said he to the lion, "I wonder not that thou wert unable to describe the beauties of this lovely maid, since they are almost too dazzling to behold. O virtuous maid," continued Almurah, "whose excellencies I have heard from this faithful animal, if thou canst deign to accept of the heart of Almurah, thy Sultan will be the happiest of mankind; but I swear, by my unalterable will, that no power on earth shall force or distress you."

"Oh," sighed Urad, "royal Sultan, you honour your poor slave too much; yet happy should I be were Houadir here!"

As she spoke, the genius Houadir entered the room: the face of the sage instructress still remained, but a glowing splendour surrounded her, and her walk was majestic and commanding. Almurah bowed to the ground, Urad made obeisance, and the rest fell prostrate before her.

"My advice," said Houadir, "is necessary now, O Urad, nor ought young virgins to enter into such engagements without counsel and the approbation of those above them, how splendid and lucrative soever the union may appear. I, who know the heart of Almurah, the servant of Mahomet, know him to be virtuous: some excesses he has been guilty of, but they were chiefly owing to his villanous Vizier, Mussapulta." (Here the lion gave a dreadful roar.) "Against your command, Almurah, did he wound this animal, which I endowed with speech for the service of Urad, to teach her that strength and nobleness of soul would always support the innocent.

"Mussapulta having wounded him, commanded his slave to put the royal beast to death; but I gave the slave bowels of mercy, and he carried him home to his cottage till the wound was healed, when the lion, faithful to his trust, came towards you as you were hunting, and being endowed with speech, declared the iniquity of Mussapulta—but he is no more.

"Now, Urad, if thy mind incline to Almurah, receive his vows, but give not thine hand where thy heart is estranged, for no splendour can compensate the want of affection."

"If Almurah, my gracious lord," answered Urad, "will swear in three things to do my desire, his handmaid will be happy to serve him."

"I swear," answered the fond Almurah. "Hadst thou three thousand desires, Almurah would satisfy them or die."

"What strange things," said Houadir, "has Urad to ask of the Sultan Almurah?"

"Whatever they are, gracious genius," said Almurah, "Urad, the lovely Urad, may command me."

"Then," said Urad, "first I require that the poor inhabitants of the forest be restored to their native lands, whence thou hast driven them."

"By the great Allah, and Mahomet the Prophet of the just," answered Almurah, "the deed was proposed and executed by the villain Mussapulta! Yes, my lovely Urad shall be obeyed. But now, Urad," continued the Sultan, "ere you proceed in your requests, let me make one sacrifice to chastity and justice, by vowing, in the presence of the good genius Houadir, to dismiss my seraglio, and take thee only for my wife."

"So noble a sacrifice," answered Urad, "demands my utmost returns; wherefore, beneficent Sultan, I release thee from any further compliance with my requests."

"Lovely Urad," said Almurah, "permit me, then, to dive into your thoughts:—yes, by your kind glances on that noble beast, I perceive you meditated to ask some bounty for your deliverer. He shall, fair virgin, be honoured as Urad's guardian, and the friend of Almurah; he shall live in my royal palace, with slaves to attend him; and, that his rest may not be inglorious or his life useless, once every year shall those who have injured the innocent be delivered up to his honest rage."

The lovely Urad fell at the feet of her Sultan, and blessed him for his favours; and the sage Houadir approved of Urad's request and the promises of Almurah. The lion came and licked the feet of his benefactors; and the genius Houadir, at parting, poured her blessings on the royal pair.

## The End

# Discovering the Middle East

1. Discuss everything you learned about Middle Eastern culture by careful examination of these characters. Remember, we read literature to learn about the place, the people, and the time in which they lived. What struck a chord in you the most about the people from this region?

2. How does literature advance our knowledge about the people who read it?

3. Compare any other these stories to either Indian literature or Western literature. How are the characters' motivations alike? How are they different? How do the styles in which these stories are told differ in pacing, rhythm, style, and theme?

4. Looking at the many symbolic images in these stories, which one stood out to you most?

# Mwindo

*An Oral Tale*

FROM THE DEMOCRATIC REPUBLIC OF THE CONGO

# *Episode I*

## THE BIRTH OF THE SACRED WARRIOR

A long time ago in the state of Ihimbi, there lived a king named Shemwindo who ruled the village of Tubondo. Shemwindo married seven women, after which he summoned together a council of all his people. There, in the midst of this assembly of juniors and seniors, advisers, counselors, and nobles, Shemwindo decreed, "You my wives must all give birth to girls. Any among you who shall bear a boy, I will kill that child." Then the assembly was dismissed, and Shemwindo hurriedly visited the house of each of his seven wives, planting his seed into each one as they lay together. After several weeks it became known to all that Shemwindo's wives got pregnant from the king's first visit to them.

Now Shemwindo was famed throughout the country, and the birth of his children was eagerly awaited by the villagers of Tubondo. After many months had passed, six of Shemwindo's seven wives gave birth to female children all on the same day. But Nyamwindo, the seventh wife and preferred one, remained inexplicably pregnant and worried what her long gestation might portend.

Then suddenly, strange things began to happen: cut firewood magically appeared at her doorstep; a water jar seemed to fill itself; and raw vegetables turned up on her table. In each case, Nyamwindo felt it was the child still in her womb who was performing these miraculous deeds, but she had no idea how. Meanwhile, the inhabitants of Tubondo began to disdain Nyamsvindo for failing to deliver her child. But the child dwelling in the womb of the preferred one meditated to itself: I do not wish to come out the birth canal of my mother, for then others may not understand that I am no ordinary man.

When the pains of childbirth began, old midwives, wives of the counselors, arrived at Nyamwindo's house. But the child dwelling in her womb climbed up into her belly, then farther up toward her shoulder, descending down her arm where it was born through the preferred one's middle finger.

Seeing him wailing on the ground, the old midwives were astonished. "What kind of child is this?" they asked. Others answered in a somber tone, "It's a male child." Then some of the old midwives said that they should announce to the village that a male child was born. Many thought this unwise because Shemwindo would surely kill the baby.

Shemwindo, sitting together with his counselors, heard of the preferred one's delivery and demanded to know, "What child is born there?" But the old midwives, sitting in the house with the child, kept silent. They gave him the name Mwindo, because he was the first male child who followed only female children in order of birth.

Mwindo was born laughing, speaking, and walking, holding a conga-scepter in his right hand and an ax in his left. He was born wearing a little bag of the spirit of Kahindo, the goddess of good fortune, slung across the left side of his back, and in that little bag there was a long rope.

In the house where the child was born, there was a little cricket perched on the wall. When the cricket heard that the midwives were unwilling to give Shemwindo an answer, it went to Shemwindo and said, "A male child was born to the preferred one today; his name is Mwindo; that is why no one has answered you."

Shemwindo was enraged upon hearing this news. He sharpened his spear on a whetstone and immediately left for the birth hut. But the moment he prepared to throw the spear into the hut, the child shouted from within, "Each time you throw a spear may it end up at the bottom of the house pole; may it never reach me, these old midwives, or my mother."

Shemwindo threw the spear into the house six times, and each time it fell short of its mark. Failing to kill Mwindo, Shemwindo became exhausted and told his counselors they should dig a grave and throw Mwindo into it. The counselors dug the grave, then went to fetch the child. But after being placed in the grave, Mwindo howled, saying, "O my father, this is the death that you will die, but first you will suffer many sorrows." Shernwindo heard the sound of the little castaway and scolded his people, telling them to cover the grave immediately. Fallen plantain stems were fetched and placed over Mwindo; on top of these stems mounds of soil were heaped. Yet as evening fell, a light as bright as the sun shone from Mwindo's grave. Those still sitting outdoors rushed to tell Shemwindo's counselors what they beheld. The counselors returned, but the great heat, like a fire burning from where Mwindo lay, forced them to stand back. Throughout the night they took turns keeping a vigil over the child's grave. During the first watch, when the rest of Tubondo was already asleep, Mwindo got out of his grave and crept silently into the house of his mother.

Shemwindo, who was awakened by the sound of a child wailing in the house of the preferred one, crept to her hut and questioned his wife:

"Where does this child come from? Did you have another one in your womb?"

"No," she replied, "this child is Mwindo."

Shemwindo left at once to wake up his counselors. "Tomorrow," he ordered, "you will cut a piece from the trunk of a tree; you will carve from it the body of a drum; you will then put the skin of an antelope in the river to soften for the drumhead. You will place this miracle child, Mwindo, in the drum and seal it tightly."

When dawn came, the counselors went to the forest to cut a piece of wood for the shell of the drum. They hollowed the wood, and when they had finished, they went to fetch Mwindo once more. They stuck him into the body of the drum and glued the antelope hide on top.

Shemwindo then summoned two expert divers to throw this drum into the pool where nothing moves, as the entire village looked on. The swimmers entered the pool, and in the middle they released the drum, which quickly sank into the watery depths.

Mwindo moaned inside the drum, stuck his ear to the drumhead, listened attentively, and said resolutely to himself, "I would not be Mwindo if I simply floated. My father, and the others, they will hear the sound of my voice again." And with those words, the drum arose unassisted from the sandy river bottom and floated to the surface of the water, remaining fixed at one point in the middle of the pool where nothing moves.

When a group of maidens came to draw water from the river, they saw Mwindo's drum turning round and round in the middle of the pool, and they heard him singing of his father's perfidy. The frightened women scurried up the riverbank and ran back to the village. When news of the sighting reached

Shemwindo, he too was in disbelief; he again assembled all his people, who headed for the river armed with spears, arrows, and fire torches. Mwindo waited until the residents of Tubondo had gathered along the river's edge, then he threw sweet words of song into his mouth:

> *I am saying farewell to Shemwindo–*
> *Oh, you ungrateful people, do you think I shall die?*
> *The counselors abandoned Shemwindo.*
> *He who appears to die but actually will be safe,*
> *He is going to encounter Iyangura.*

## *Episode II*

### RESCUE BY THE MOTHER

Mwindo's drum headed upstream, for he was not sure where Iyangura lived and thought to begin his journey at the river's source. From Kahungu the Hawk, Mwindo learned that she inhabited an unfathomable realm of the river even deeper than he had ventured so far. Thus began Mwindo's voyage down into the river's depths to meet his aunt Iyangura. He sang to all who might impede his quest:

> *Get out of my way!*
> *You are impotent against Mwindo,*
> *Mwindo is the little-one-just-born-he-walked.*
> *I am going to meet Iyangura.*
> *He who will go up against me, it is he who will die on the way.*

Now Mukiti, master of the unfathomable realm and husband of Iyangura, had placed his younger sister Musoka as a guardian at the portal of his domain. When she saw Mwindo, she dispatched an envoy to Mukiti who, by return messenger, ordered her to keep Mwindo far away, for Mwindo was a threat to him. Musoka tried to block Mwindo's progress, but to no avail; he dove with his drum even farther into the watery depths, burying himself deep within the bottom sand. There he dug a tunnel around Musoka and surfaced farther downstream.

When Mukiti heard Mwindo calling for his aunt and challenging him in song, he began to stir, asking who had just mentioned his wife. He shook heaven and earth.

"I, Mwindo, I spoke of your wife," Mwindo defiantly answered. "We shall meet in battle today," he continued, "for I, Mwindo, am being denied access to my aunt!"

When Mukiti finally saw Mwindo he exclaimed, "You are not the one I expected to see! You are a child inside a drum! Who are you?"

Mwindo referred to himself as the little-one-just-born-he-walked, nephew of Iyangura, who was on his way to meet his aunt.

"Do not even dare to dream that you, of all people, are capable of besting me, Mukiti, lord of the unfathomable realm; you will not pass beyond my guard."

These harsh words were overheard by some of Iyangura's maidens who had come to Mukiti's pool to fetch water. At this mention of their mistress's name, they grew frightened and ran to Iyangura, saying, "There is a little man inside a drum insisting that Mukiti should release him, that he is Mwindo, going to encounter Iyangura, his paternal aunt."

"That is my child," she exclaimed, "let me go to him."* Iyangura made her way to the water hole. She slashed the drumhead, removing the hide, and there beheld the multiple rays of the rising sun and the moon—the radiant beauty of the child Mwindo. Mwindo got out of the drum, still holding his conga-scepter, his ax, and the little bag with rope in it.

# Episode III

## BATTLING THE FORCES OF THE UNFATHOMABLE REALM

When Kahungu the Hawk observed Mwindo meeting with his aunt, he flew to Kasiyembe, whom Mukiti had given the task of keeping watch over his wife.

"Kasiyembe," Kahungu cried, "it is not merely a little man who converses with Iyangura; he is a man of many great feats. Perhaps you have more trouble than you think."

"Go tell this Mwindo he should not even try to venture past the area I guard," proclaimed the brazen Kasiyembe. "Otherwise 1 will tear out his spinal column. I am already setting traps, pits, pointed sticks, and razors in the ground, so he will be unable to step anywhere."

Now, Katee the Hedgehog overheard this talk between Kahungu and Kasiyembe and immediately sought out Mwindo. "Mwindo," said Katee, "Kahungu and Kasiyembe are holding secret council against you; they are even preparing pit traps against you, with pointed sticks and razors. But I am Katee, a hedgehog," he continued. "I am going to dig a tunnel for you, a road that begins right here and comes out inside the house of your aunt."

Mwindo then told his aunt Iyangura to return to her home where he would join her shortly. "And tell your bodyguard, Kasiyembe, to be careful," he warned.

When Katee's tunnel was complete, Mwindo followed it until he came out in Iyangura's house, to the astonishment of Kasiyembe. Meanwhile Mwindo was also receiving unseen help at the hands of Master Spider who had been watching Kasiyembe build the pits.

"As far as I am concerned," Master Spider said to himself, "Mwindo will not perish." So the spider began building bridges over the top of the pits he knew Mwindo would have to cross.

When Iyangura saw that her nephew Mwindo had arrived, she said to him, "My son, don't cat food yet; come, first let us dance to the rhythm of the drum."

Mwindo stepped outside with Iyangura and told her that if he danced without food he might faint.

"What shall we do then?" pleaded Iyangura. "Kasiyembe is demanding that you dance." Mwindo understood he was dancing into a trap laid by Kasiyembe, but still he agreed. And dance he did: round and round the middle of the pits, with his body bent over them; with glee, he danced everywhere that traps had been set for him, and he remained uninjured, thanks to Master Spider. And all the while Mwindo waved his conga-scepter and taunted Kasiyembe's impotence against him.

Instead Nkuba sent down seven bolts of lightning that missed Mwindo intentionally each time. Now angered by Kasiyemhe's intransigence, Mwindo cast an eye in his direction, and suddenly the guard's hair flared up in flames.

People went to fetch water in jars to extinguish the fire, but when they arrived, the jars were empty; the water had magically evaporated.

"Kasiyembe is about to die," they intoned. "Let us go to his master, Mukiti, for help." But they were too late. Mwindo, in his anger, had also dried up the pool where Mukiti lived.

When Iyangura saw that Mwindo had killed both Mukiti and Kasiyembe she begged of her nephew, "Widen your heart, my child. Did you come here to attack us? Set your heart down; untie your anger; undo my husband and his guardian Kasiyembe; heal them without harboring further resentment."

Mwindo was moved by his aunt's compassionate request; he opened his heart, waking first Kasiyembe by waving his conga-scepter above him. Suddenly, Kasiyembe returned to life, water returned to the jars, the river was full again, and Mukiti awoke from death. Everyone who witnessed Mwindo's feat was astonished. "Lo! Mwindo, he too is a great nian," they said. Even Kasiyembe gave Mwindo a salute: "Hail! Hail, Mwindo!"

After Mwindo had accomplished this great deed, he announced to his aunt that tomorrow he would be going to Tubondo alone to fight with his father.

"Don't go alone," she implored her nephew. "The lonely path is never nice."

But Mwindo refused to listen, and when she realized that her appeals had fallen on deaf ears, she said only, "I do not wish you, my young man, to go fight with your father, but if you persist on going, then I shall go with you to witness this terrible event."

## Episode IV

### THE FATHER QUEST

Mwindo, his aunt, and her servants set off on a war march to Tubondo. Along the way they enlisted recruits. The fighting began shortly after they arrived on the outskirts of the city. Mwindo's forces were badly beaten, so he called on Nkuba to help, and the lightning hurler unleashed seven bolts against Tubondo, turning to dust the village and all who lived there. But after entering the devastated city, Mwindo soon learned that Shemwindo, his father, had fled before the holocaust, escaping to the underworld realm of Muisa, "the place where no one ever gathers around the fire."

Again his aunt Iyangura tried to dissuade him from pursuing his father, but Mwindo paid her no heed. He told her to remain in Tubondo, holding one end of his birth rope. If the rope became still, then she could assume he was dead.

Suddenly, Sparrow appeared to Mwindo with these words: "Come here for me to show you the path that your father took upon entering the underground realm of Muisa at the base of the root of the kikoka fern." When Mwindo arrived at the kikoka fern, he pulled the plant out of the ground and entered the underworld realm.

Mwindo was met by Kahindo, the daughter of Muisa and guardian of the entrance to the underworld, whose repulsive body was covered from head to foot with yaws. She cautioned him against going farther: "No one ever gets through Muisa's village," she warned. "Do you think you with all your pride will succeed?"

But Mwindo persisted, and Kahindo then supplied him with the oaths and knowledge needed to procure his safe passage: "When you arrive in the village meeting place, you will see a very tall, very big man, curled up in the ashes near the hearth," she informed Mwindo. "That is Muisa, and if he greets you, 'Blessing be with you, my father,' you too will answer, 'Yes, my father.' Then he will offer you a stool, but you must refuse it.

"Next," Kahindo continued, "he will offer you some banana beer to drink; you must refuse that too. Finally, Muisa will invite you to have some gruel to eat; that, Mwindo, you must also refuse."

Mwindo's heart reached out to the disfigured Kahindo, and he realized he could not leave without washing her scabs. He cleansed and soothed the lesions, then healed her entirely of her yaws before taking leave.

Mwindo headed on to Muisa's village. On seeing him, Muisa greeted Mwindo, "Blessing be with you, my father." Mwindo answered, "Yes, my father." Muisa then offered Mwindo a stool on which to sit, some banana beer to drink, and some gruel to eat, all of which Mwindo refused. Seeing Mwindo escape these ordeals, Muisa suggested that he might like to go back and rest at his daughter's house for a while.

So he went back to Kahindo's, who in the meantime had made herself like the "anus of a snail": dressing up, then rubbing herself with red powder and castor oil. Mwindo was taken aback by her radiant beauty. "Come in, Mwindo," Kahindo exclaimed, "please, come in."

"Oh, my sister," he replied, "I would harm myself if I stayed outside."

Kahindo went to prepare some food, but Muisa, who had observed her tender behavior toward Mwindo, quickly intervened. Before giving him his father, Muisa told Mwindo he would have to face a series of challenges to prove his worth.

"Tomorrow you will start cultivating a new banana grove for me," Muisa ordered. "You must first cut leaves, then plant the banana trees, then fell the trees; then cut the newly grown weeds, then prune the banana trees, then prop them up, then bring ripe bananas. After you have performed all these tasks," Muisa concluded, "I shall give you your father."

In the morning Mwindo left to accomplish the tasks. He laid out his tools on the ground; then all by themselves the tools went to work: first, they cut the grasses; then the tools having cut the grasses, the banana trees planted themselves; the banana trees having planted themselves, Mwindo sent a bunch of axes to fell the trees; when the axes finished their work, he sent niany weeding tools that went across the banana grove cutting the newly grown weeds. After his weeding tools had finished, his other tools now cut supporting staffs; the staffs themselves propped up the banana trees. The staffs having finished sustaining the trees, the banana stems were ripe. In one day, Mwindo cleared, planted, and cultivated an entire field of bananas.

While Mwindo was harvesting his crop, an astonished informant told Muisa of these miraculous events. Muisa then determined to send his karemba belt against Mwindo, for he never intended to hand over Mwindo's father. "You, my karemba, you are going to fight Mwindo," he said. "When you see him, you will bend him, then smash him against the ground."

Karemba, having heard the instructions of its master, went to the banana grove. When it saw Mwindo, the belt fell upon him, making him scream. Muisa's belt crushed him; it planted his mouth against the ground and froth came out. Mwindo could neither breathe nor could he control his bladder and bowels. Then, seeing its master with no way out, Mwindo's conga awoke to its duty; it wagged itself above his head, and he succeeded in taking a short breath, then a sneeze; and finally he opened his eyes and gazed about.

All the while, Mwindo's birth rope was quiet, and his aunt in the upperworld began crying, "Mwindo is dead! His rope has become still. He must escape this terrible fate," she implored the divinities, "he is my child."

Mwindo remembered his aunt and communicated to her through the power of his thoughts: "My aunt there in Tubondo, my rope did not move because Muisa had trapped me; he wrapped me up like a bunch of bananas in his karemba; but don't worry now, I am saved; my conga has rescued me."

Mwindo then sent his conga-scepter to attack Muisa. "You, my conga," he commanded, "when you arrive at Muisa's, you will smash him with force; you must plant his mouth to the ground; his tongue must penetrate the earth; do not release him until I return."

Whirling through the air, the conga went on its way, and arriving at Muisa's, it did smash him; it planted his mouth to the ground; his tongue dug into the earth; his bladder and bowels left him; and his breath was cut off.

Mwindo remained in the banana grove, preparing a load of green and ripe bananas. When he returned to the village, he cast his eyes at Muisa and saw foam oozing out of his mouth and nostrils. "Now give me my father," he said to Kahindo, who met him as he moved toward Muisa, "so I may go home with him."

"Begin first by healing my father," she pleaded, "so I may find out where your father is and give him to you."
> Mwindo sang while awakening Muisa:
> He who went to sleep wakes up.
> Muisa, you are powerless against Mwindo,
> because Mwindo is the little-one-just-born-he-walked.

Mwindo went on singing like that while beating Muisa incessantly on the head with his conga in order to wake him up. When Muisa was revived, he pointed to a tree some distance from where he stood and said, "Mwindo, if you want to get your father, go tomorrow and extract honey for me from that tree."

That evening Kahindo cooked for Mwindo, and after eating, she put her leg across him and they slept. When daylight came, Mwindo, equipped with his ax and with fire, went into the forest to extract the honey. He arrived at the base of the tree and climbed up high to where the honey was. But Muisa did not mean for Mwindo to succeed at this task either. Once again he sent his karemba belt after Mwindo; it smashed Mwindo on the tree; it planted his mouth into the trunk of the tree; he could not breathe; his bladder and bowels left him.

Once again Mwindo's aunt felt his birth rope grow still, and she feared the end had come. But Mwindo's conga, lying on the ground at the base of the tree, realized that its master was dying. It climbed up the tree to where he was and began to beat and beat Mwindo about his head, Mwindo sneezed, lifted his eyes slightly, and a bit of breath came out.

When Nkuba, the lightning hurler, heard the cry of his friend Mwindo, he unleashed a lightning bolt that split the tree into pieces. Mwindo got down from the tree without a single wound. He then went back with a basket of honey and set it down before Muisa, demanding to be given his father. Muisa, pretending to comply with Mwindo's demand, sent a boy to fetch Shemwindo from his hiding place. But the boy arrived and found Shemwindo was no longer there.

Suddenly, Kahungu the Hawk, who had previously abetted Muisa, swooped down from the sky squawking, "Muisa lies; he has warned your father to flee, saying that you were too tough an opponent."

Now Mwindo was furious. "Give me my father immediately, you scoundrel! Make him come out from where you have hidden him so that I may return to the upperworld with him. You said that when I cultivated a field for you, when I extracted honey for you, you would then give me my father. You lied! I want him right now; don't let your saliva dry up before giving him to me."

Muisa did not bring his father out, and Mwindo gave up on polite words. He beat Muisa on the top of his head with his conga; Muisa lost control of his bladder and bowels; he fainted and froth came out of his nose, his eyes, and his mouth; he tossed his feet up into the air; he stiffened like a dead snake.

"Stay like that, you dog," Mwindo yelled. "I will heal you when I have finally caught my father."

Meanwhile Shemwindo had sought refuge with the god Sheburungu, and Mwindo followed him there, wrapped in his hatred.

"Oh, Mwindo," Sheburungu shouted, "let us play wiki together first.

Mwindo accepted Sheburungu's challenge to play; if he won, he could then retrieve his father. Through superior play, Sheburungu won everything Mwindo had—his money, his possessions, his aunt, even his claim to the village of Tubondo. In desperation Mwindo wagered his conga against the god, and finally his fortune turned; ultimately he won everything the god possessed—people, cattle, goats—and most important, the ability to capture his fugitive father.

"Mwindo, come quickly," sang Kahungu the Hawk, "your father wants to flee again." Mwindo hastily abandoned the wiki game and headed off to intercept his father in a banana grove.

Seeing Shemwindo, Mwindo inquired sarcastically, "O my father, is it you here?"

Shemwindo answered meekly, "Here I am."

After seizing his father, Mwindo returned to Sheburungu's, telling the god he did not want any of the things he had won during the game. Then Mwindo bid farewell to Sheburungu and tugged on the rope to remind his aunt he was still alive. On his return home he went into Muisa's house, where Kahindo came running. "You see my father here, his bones fill a basket; what shall 1 do then? It is befitting that you heal my father; please don't leave him like that; wake him up; he is the chief of all these people."

Mwindo resurrected Muisa once more, striking him with his conga, telling him, "You have offended me in vain; you have tried to equal Mwindo. But only I am Mwindo, the little-one-just-born-he-walked, the little one who does not eat earthly foods; and the day he was born, he did not drink at the breasts of his mother."

Mwindo tugged on the rope again, and this time Iyangura knew that he was on his way home with his father.

# Episode V

## ATONEMENT WITH THE FATHER

Mwindo journeyed back from the underworld, exiting from the kikoka fern with his father and triumphantly arriving in Tubondo. Reunited with his aunt Iyangura, he recounted his adventures for her. Iyangura sought a public apology from her brother, but first she made a special re quest of Mwindo:

"My son, shall we go on living always in this desolate village alone without other people? I, Iyangura, want you first to save all the people who lived here in this village; only when they have been resuscitate shall I ask Shemwindo to confess how he acted toward you and the evil he perpetrated against you. You, my son, are the eternal savior of people."

For three days, Mwindo resurrected those who had fallen in the battle for Tubondo. He beat his conga over the bones of the dead, and miraculously they arose, resuming precisely the activity they had been engaged in at the time of their death.

After the inhabitants of Tubondo had been resurrected, Iyangura asked Shemwindo to call together all the people, and those three radiant stars—Mwindo, Shemwindo, and Iyangura—appeared to the pleasure of the assembled crowd.

Turning to his father Mwindo beckoned: "Now you, my father, it is your turn. Explain to the chiefs the reason why you have had a grudge against me; tell the chiefs so that they may understand."

Sweat rose from Shemwindo's body, shame welled up in his eyes. He uttered his confession in quivering tones, broken by a spitting cough:

"All you chiefs," Shemwindo stammered, "I don't deny the evil that I have done against my son; indeed, I passed a decree that I would kill all male children. I tried many times to kill this child, but each time, instead of harming him, I only made him stronger. I fled to the underworld thinking I would be safe, but my son set out in search of me; he came to take me away from the abyss of evil in which I was involved. I was at that time withered like dried bananas. And it is like that I arrived here in the village of Tubondo. So may the male progeny be saved. My son has let me see the way in which the dark sky becomes daylight and given me the joy of witnessing again the warmth of the people and of all the things here in Tubondo."

After that Iyangura spoke: "You, Shemwindo, together with your counselors and nobles, acted badly. If it were a counselor from whom this plan of torment against Mwindo had emanated, then his throat would be cut here in the council. You discriminated against the children, saying that male children were bad and female children were good. You did not know what was in the womb of your preferred wife, what you were given by Sheburungu, but you saw it to be bad."

Iyangura turned to the counselors and nobles, concluding her remarks: "Shemwindo has committed a heinous deed. If the people of Tubondo had been exterminated, Shemwindo would have been guilty of exterminating them."

Finally, Mwindo stood up and with great compassion said, "I, Mwindo, man of many feats, the little-one-just-born-he-walked, I am not holding a grudge against my father; may my father not be frightened, believing that I am still angry with him; no, 1 am not angry with my father. What my father did against me and what 1 did against my father, all that is already over. Now let us examine what is to come, the evil and the good. If either of us starts quarreling again, it is he who will be in the wrong, and all the elders here will be the witnesses of it. Now, let us live in harmony in our country, let us care for our people well."

Full of shame and repentant, Shemwindo wished to cede his throne to his son. He voluntarily stripped himself of the trappings of kingship, giving them to Mwindo; then he blessed Mwindo and left on a self-imposed exile to a mountain retreat. After his enthronement, Mwindo proclaimed that now he had become famous, and would never act like his father.

## *Episode VI*

### A FINAL JOURNEY AMONG THE GODS

Many days after his ascension to the throne, Mwindo had a terrible craving to eat some wild pig meat, so he sent the Forest People to hunt for a fresh pig. Following the trail of a red-haired pig, they encountered Kirimu the Dragon, master of the deep forest. He appeared to them in horrific form, a huge animal with a black hide, seven heads, seven horns, seven eyes, teeth like a dog, a huge belly, and the tail of an eagle.

Kirimu devoured the Forest People, whereupon it then fell to Mwindo to save Tubondo from the beast's reign of terror. Mwindo fearlessly met the monster in battle; then just as Kirimu was about to swallow him whole, Mwindo unleashed his conga and slew the dragon instead. The people rejoiced at the sight of this plentiful supply of fresh meat and were even more pleased when, once the dragon was cut open, all those whom he had ever swallowed were released unharmed from his belly.

But it so happened that Nkuba, the lightning hurler, had made a blood pact with Kirimu. When he inhaled the odor of his dead friend carried on the wind, tears came to his eyes. "What shall I do with this Mwindo?" Nkuba said to himself.

"If I make him suffer up here among the gods, then perhaps he will learn and I can return him to earth to his village again," he mused. "If Mwindo had known I had exchanged blood with Kirimu, then he would not have killed my friend. If he had known, yet still killed Kirimu, I would kill Mwindo right here and now without ever returning him to his country. But he is safe because he did not know that Dragon was my friend."

Nkuba descended for Mwindo and said, "I have come to take you, my friend; I want to teach you because I am very displeased with you since you dared to kill Dragon, who was my friend. You must know this time that you have done wrong."

Still Mwindo showed no deference or fear toward Nkuba, though all the people of Tubondo were stricken with terror, believing their chief was lost forever.

Mwindo sang taunts of his greatness to Nkuba while the pair climbed slowly up into the air. "I have rescued you many times from many dangers," Nkuba reminded Mwindo. "Still you sing so arrogantly. Do you think that you are now equal to me?"

543

Once in the celestial realm, Mwindo experienced cold weather and icy winds. And there was no house! They lived as nomads, never settling in one spot. Nkuba seized Mwindo; he climbed with him up to Mbura the Rain. When Rain saw Mwindo, he told him, "You, Mwindo, you never accept being criticized; the news about your toughness, your heroism, we surely have heard the news, but here, there is no room for your heroism." Rain fell upon Mwindo seven and seven times more; he had Hail fall upon him, and he soaked him thoroughly. Mwindo thought to himself, "This time I am in trouble in a big way."

Nkuba then lifted Mwindo up again and had him scramble across to Mweri the Moon's domain. When Moon saw Mwindo, he pointed at him: "The news has been given us of your pride, but here in the sky there is no room for your pride." Then Moon burned Mwindo's hair.

Nkuba lifted Mwindo up again; he went with him to the domain of Kentse the Sun. When Sun saw Mwindo, he burned him with his heat. Mwindo lacked all means of defense against Sun; his throat became dry; thirst strangled him; he asked for water. The gods said to him, "No, here there is no water for you; now we advise you to grit your teeth and to put your heart on your knee."

After Sun had made Mwindo sustain these pains, Nkuba lifted Mwindo up and brought him to the domain of Kubikubi the Star. When Star saw him, he too echoed the words of the other gods: "The news comes that you are a great hero, but here there is no room for your heroism." Star ordered the Rain and Sun and Moon to come, and all of the assembled gods—Nkuba, Mbura, Mweri, Kentse, Kubikubi—delivered Mwindo a message in unison:

"We have respect for you, but just that much; otherwise, you would vanish right here. You, Mwindo, you are ordered to go back; never a day should you kill an animal of the forest or of the village or even an insect like a centipede or a water spider. If one day we learn that you have begun killing such animals, you will die and your people will never see you again."

They pulled his ears seven times and seven more, saying, "Understand?" And Mwindo said, "Yes, I understand." They also admonished him: "Nkuba will oversee your behavior and comportment; if you stray from our commands Nkuba will report to us, and that day he will seize you instantly, without even a moment to say farewell to your people."

Finally, after one year of wandering in the abode of the sky, Mwindo was allowed to return home. He assembled all his people and told them of his ordeal: "I, Mwindo, the little-one-just-born-he-walked, performer of many wonderful things, I tell you the news from where I have visited in the heavens. When I arrived in the sky, I met with Rain and Moon and Sun and Star and Lightning. These five gods forbade me to kill the animals of the forest and of the village, saying that the day I would dare to touch a living thing in order to kill it, that day my life-fire would be extinguished; then Nkuba would come to take me without my saying farewell to my people and my hope of return would be lost forever. He also told them, "I have seen in the sky things I cannot divulge."

Mwindo then passed good laws for his people, saying,
> May you grow many foods and many crops.
> May you live in good houses and a beautiful village.
> Don't quarrel with one another.
> Don't pursue another's spouse.

*Don't mock the invalid passing in the village.*
*Accept the chief; fear him; may he also fear you.*
*May you agree with one another, harboring no enmity nor too much hate.*
*May you bring forth tall and short children; in so doing you will bring*
*them forth for the chief.*

Mwindo's fame grew and stretched widely; it spread to other countries from which people came to pay their allegiance to him. And among children, none was thought bad; whether males or females, whether able or disabled, they were not rejected. For Mwindo realized there was nothing bad in what God has given to humankind.

## Uncover the Mysterious Mwindo

1.  What elements are in these stories that were not in the others we've read?

2.  What do we learn about some of the customs of people in Central Africa?

3.  Does this tale, which was originally an oral one, lose anything in the translation in writing?

4.  Mwindo used his magic scepter to save himself. Is there a difference between magic and miracles?

# Nigerian Folk Stories

*By Elphinstone Dayrell*

FROM SOUTHERN NIGERIA

# The Tortoise with a Pretty Daughter

There was once a king who was very powerful. He had great influence over the wild beasts and animals. Now the tortoise was looked upon as the wisest of all beasts and men. This king had a son named Ekpenyon, to whom he gave fifty young girls as wives, but the prince did not like any of them. The king was very angry at this, and made a law that if any man had a daughter who was finer than the prince's wives, and who found favour in his son's eyes, the girl herself and her father and mother should be killed.

Now about this time the tortoise and his wife had a daughter who was very beautiful. The mother thought it was not safe to keep such a fine child, as the prince might fall in love with her, so she told her husband that her daughter ought to be killed and thrown away into the bush. The tortoise, however, was unwilling, and hid her until she was three years old. One day, when both the tortoise and his wife were away on their farm, the king's son happened to be hunting near their house, and saw a bird perched on the top of the fence round the house. The bird was watching the little girl, and was so entranced with her beauty that he did not notice the prince coming. The prince shot the bird with his bow and arrow, and it dropped inside the fence, so the prince sent his servant to gather it. While the servant was looking for the bird he came across the little girl, and was so struck with her form, that he immediately returned to his master and told him what he had seen. The prince then broke down the fence and found the child, and fell in love with her at once. He stayed and talked with her for a long time, until at last she agreed to become his wife. He then went home, but concealed from his father the fact that he had fallen in love with the beautiful daughter of the tortoise.

But the next morning he sent for the treasurer, and got sixty pieces of cloth  and three hundred rods , and sent them to the tortoise. Then in the early afternoon he went down to the tortoise's house, and told him that he wished to marry his daughter. The tortoise saw at once that what he had dreaded had come to pass, and that his life was in danger, so he told the prince that if the king knew, he would kill not only himself (the tortoise), but also his wife and daughter. The prince replied that he would be killed himself before he allowed the tortoise and his wife and daughter to be killed. Eventually, after much argument, the tortoise consented, and agreed to hand his daughter to the prince as his wife when she arrived at the proper age. Then the prince went home and told his mother what he had done. She was in great distress at the thought that she would lose her son, of whom she was very proud, as she knew that when the king heard of his son's disobedience he would kill him. However, the queen, although she knew how angry her husband would be, wanted her son to marry the girl he had fallen in love with, so she went to the tortoise and gave him some money, clothes, yams, and palm-oil as further dowry on her son's behalf in order that the tortoise should not give his daughter to another man. For the next five years the prince was constantly with the tortoise's daughter, whose name was Adet, and when she was about to be put in the fatting house , the prince told his father that he was going to take Adet as his wife. On hearing this the king was very angry, and sent word all round his kingdom that all people should come on a certain day to the marketplace to hear the palaver. When the appointed day arrived the market-place was quite full of people, and the stones belonging to the king and queen were placed in the middle of the market-place.

When the king and queen arrived all the people stood up and greeted them, and they then sat down on their stones. The king then told his attendants to bring the girl Adet before him. When she arrived the king was quite astonished at her beauty. He then told the people that he had sent for them to tell them that he was angry with his son for disobeying him and taking Adet as his wife without his knowledge, but that now he had seen her himself he had to acknowledge that she was very beautiful, and that his son had made a good choice. He would therefore forgive his son.

When the people saw the girl they agreed that she was very fine and quite worthy of being the prince's wife, and begged the king to cancel the law he had made altogether, and the king agreed and as the law had been made under the "Egbo" law, he sent for eight Egbos , and told them that the order was cancelled throughout his kingdom, and that for the future no one would be killed who had a daughter more beautiful than the prince's wives, and gave the Egbos palm wine and money to remove the law, and sent them away. Then he declared that the tortoise's daughter, Adet, should marry his son, and he made them marry the same day. A great feast was then given which lasted for fifty days, and the king killed five cows and gave all the people plenty of foo-foo  and palm-oil chop, and placed a large number of pots of palm wine in the streets for the people to drink as they liked. The women brought a big play to the king's compound, and there was singing and dancing kept up day and night during the whole time. The prince and his companions also played in the market square. When the feast was over the king gave half of his kingdom to the tortoise to rule over, and three hundred slaves to work on his farm. The prince also gave his father-in-law two hundred women and one hundred girls to work for him, so the tortoise became one of the richest men in the kingdom. The prince and his wife lived together for a good many years until the king died, when the prince ruled in his place. And all this shows that the tortoise is the wisest of all men and animals.

**MORAL.**--Always have pretty daughters, as no matter how poor they may be, there is always the chance that the king's son may fall in love with them, and they may thus become members of the royal house and obtain much wealth.

## How a Hunter obtained Money from his Friends

Many years ago there was a Calabar hunter called Effiong, who lived in the bush, killed plenty of animals, and made much money. Every one in the country knew him, and one of his best friends was a man called Okun, who lived near him. But Effiong was very extravagant, and spent much money in eating and drinking with every one, until at last he became quite poor, so he had to go out hunting again; but now his good luck seemed to have deserted him, for although he worked hard, and hunted day and night, he could not succeed in killing anything. One day, as he was very hungry, he went to his friend Okun and borrowed two hundred rods from him, and told him to come to his house on a certain day to get his money, and he told him to bring his gun, loaded, with him.

Now, some time before this Effiong had made friends with a leopard and a bush cat, whom he had met in the forest whilst on one of his hunting expeditions; and he had also made friends with a goat and a cock at a farm where he had stayed for the night. But though Effiong had borrowed the money from Okun, he could not think how he was to repay it on the day he had promised. At last, however, he thought of a plan, and on the next day he went to his friend the leopard, and asked him to lend him two hundred rods, promising to return the amount to him on the same day as he had promised to pay Okun; and he also told the leopard, that if he were absent when he came for his money, he could kill anything he saw in the house and eat it. The leopard was then to wait until the hunter arrived, when he would pay him the money; and to this the leopard agreed. The hunter then went to his friend the goat, and borrowed two hundred rods from him in the same way. Effiong also went to his friends the bush cat and the cock, and borrowed two hundred rods from each of them on the same conditions, and told each one of them that if he were absent when they arrived, they could kill and eat anything they found about the place.

When the appointed day arrived the hunter spread some corn on the ground, and then went away and left the house deserted. Very early in the morning, soon after he had begun to crow, the cock remembered what the hunter had told him, and walked over to the hunter's house, but found no one there. On looking round, however, he saw some corn on the, ground, and, being hungry, he commenced to eat. About this time the bush cat also arrived, and not finding the hunter at home, he, too, looked about, and very soon he espied the cock, who was busy picking up the grains of corn. So the bush cat went up very softly behind and pounced on the cock and killed him at once, and began to eat him. By this time the goat had come for his money; but not finding his friend, he walked about until he came upon the bush cat, who was so intent upon his meal off the cock, that he did not notice the goat approaching; and the goat, being in rather a bad temper at not getting his money, at once charged at the bush cat and knocked him over, butting him with his horns. This the bush cat did not like at all, so, as he was not big enough to fight the goat, he picked up the remains of the cock and ran off with it to the bush, and so lost his money, as he did not await the arrival of the hunter. The goat was thus left master of the situation and started bleating, and this noise attracted the attention of the leopard, who was on his way to receive payment from the hunter. As he got nearer the smell of goat became very strong, and being hungry, for he had not eaten anything for some time, he approached the goat very carefully. Not seeing any one about he stalked the goat and got nearer and nearer, until he was within springing distance. The goat, in the meantime, was grazing quietly, quite unsuspicious of any danger, as he was in his friend the hunter's compound. Now and then he would say Ba!! But most of the time he was busy eating the young grass, and picking up the leaves which had fallen from a tree of which he was very fond. Suddenly the leopard sprang at the goat, and with one crunch at the neck brought him down. The goat was dead almost at once, and the leopard started on his meal.

It was now about eight o'clock in the morning, and Okun, the hunter's friend, having had his early morning meal, went out with his gun to receive payment of the two hundred rods he had lent to the hunter. When he got close to the house he heard a crunching sound, and, being a hunter himself, he approached very cautiously, and looking over the fence saw the leopard only a few yards off busily engaged eating the goat. He took careful aim at the leopard and fired, whereupon the leopard rolled over dead. The death of the leopard meant that four of the hunter's creditors were now disposed of, as the bush cat had killed the cock, the goat had driven the bush cat away (who thus forfeited his claim), and in his turn the goat had been killed by the leopard, who had just been slain by Okun. This meant a saving of eight hundred rods to Effiong; but he was not content with this, and directly he heard the report of the gun he ran out from where he had been hiding all the time, and found the leopard lying dead with Okun standing over it. Then in very strong language Effiong began to upbraid his friend, and asked him why he had killed his old friend the leopard, that nothing would satisfy him but that he should report the whole matter to the king, who would no doubt deal with him as he thought fit. When Effiong said this Okun was frightened, and begged him not to say anything more about the matter, as the king would be angry; but the hunter was obdurate, and refused to listen to him; and at last Okun said, "If you will allow the whole thing to drop and will say no more about it, I will make you a present of the two hundred rods you borrowed from me." This was just what Effiong wanted, but still he did not give in at once; eventually, however, he agreed, and told Okun he might go, and that he would bury the body of his friend the leopard.

Directly Okun had gone, instead of burying the body Effiong dragged it inside the house and skinned it very carefully. The skin he put out to dry in the sun, and covered it with wood ash, and the body he ate. When the skin was well cured the hunter took it to a distant market, where he sold it for much money. And now, whenever a bush cat sees a cock he always kills it, and does so by right, as he takes the cock in part payment of the two hundred rods which the hunter never paid him.

**MORAL.**--Never lend money to people, because if they cannot pay they will try to kill you or get rid of you in some way, either by poison or by setting bad Ju Ju's for you.

## The Woman with Two Skins

Eyamba I. of Calabar was a very powerful king. He fought and conquered all the surrounding countries, killing all the old men and women, but the able-bodied men and girls he caught and brought back as slaves, and they worked on the farms until they died.

This king had two hundred wives, but none of them had borne a son to him. His subjects, seeing that he was becoming an old man, begged him to marry one of the spider's daughters, as they always had plenty of children. But when the king saw the spider's daughter he did not like her, as she was ugly, and the people said it was because her mother had had so many children at the same time. However, in order to please his people he married the ugly girl, and placed her among his other wives, but they all complained because she was so ugly, and said she could not live with them. The king, therefore, built her a separate house for herself, where she was given food and drink the same as the other wives. Every one jeered at her on account of her ugliness; but she was not really ugly, but beautiful, as she was born with two skins, and at her birth her mother was made to promise that she should never remove the ugly skin until a certain time arrived save only during the night, and that she must put it on again before dawn. Now the king's head wife knew this, and was very fearful lest the king should find it out and fall in love with the spider's daughter; so she went to a Ju Ju man and offered him two hundred rods to make a potion that would make the king forget altogether that the spider's daughter was his wife. This the Ju Ju man finally consented to do, after much haggling over the price, for three hundred and fifty rods; and he made up some "medicine," which the head wife mixed with the king's food. For some months this had the effect of making the king forget the spider's daughter, and he used to pass quite close to her without recognising her in any way. When four months had elapsed and the king had not once sent for Adiaha (for that was the name of the spider's daughter), she began to get tired, and went back to her parents. Her father, the spider, then took her to another Ju Ju man, who, by making spells and casting lots, very soon discovered that it was the king's head wife who had made the Ju Ju and had enchanted the king so that he would not look at Adiaha. He therefore told the spider that Adiaha should give the king some medicine which he would prepare, which would make the king remember her. He prepared the medicine, for which the spider had to pay a large sum of money; and that very day Adiaha made a small dish of food, into which she had placed the medicine, and presented it to the king. Directly he had eaten the dish his eyes were opened and he recognised his wife, and told her to come to him that very evening. So in the afternoon, being very joyful, she went down to the river and washed, and when she returned she put on her best cloth and went to the king's palace.

Directly it was dark and all the lights were out she pulled off her ugly skin, and the king saw how beautiful she was, and was very pleased with her; but when the cock crowed Adiaha pulled on her ugly skin again, and went back to her own house.

This she did for four nights running, always taking the ugly skin off in the dark, and leaving before daylight in the morning. In course of time, to the great surprise of all the people, and particularly of the king's two hundred wives, she gave birth to a son; but what surprised them most of all was that only one son was born, whereas her mother had always had a great many children at a time, generally about fifty.

The king's head wife became more jealous than ever when Adiaha had a son; so she went again to the Ju Ju man, and by giving him a large present induced him to give her some medicine which would make the king sick and forget his son. And the medicine would then make the king go to the Ju Ju man, who would tell him that it was his son who had made him sick, as he wanted to reign instead of his father. The Ju Ju man would also tell the king that if he wanted to recover he must throw his son away into the water.

And the king, when he had taken the medicine., went to the Ju Ju man, who told him everything as had been arranged with the head wife. But at first the king did not want to destroy his son. Then his chief subjects begged him to throw his son away, and said that perhaps in a year's time he might get another son. So the king at last agreed, and threw his son into the river, at which the mother grieved and cried bitterly.

Then the head wife went again to the Ju Ju man and got more medicine, which made the king forget Adiaha for three years, during which time she was in mourning for her son. She then returned to her father, and he got some more medicine from his Ju Ju man, which Adiaha gave to the king. And the king knew her and called her to him again, and she lived with him as before. Now the Ju Ju who had helped Adiaha's father, the spider, was a Water Ju Ju, and he was ready when the king threw his son into the water, and saved his life and took him home and kept him alive. And the boy grew up very strong.

After a time Adiaha gave birth to a daughter, and her the jealous wife also persuaded the king to throw away. It took a longer time to persuade him, but at last he agreed, and threw his daughter into the water too, and forgot Adiaha again. But the Water Ju Ju was ready again, and when he had saved the little girl, he thought the time had arrived to punish the action of the- jealous wife; so he went about amongst the head young men and persuaded them to hold a wrestling match in the market-place every week.

This was done, and the Water Ju Ju told the king's son, who had become very strong, and was very like to his father in appearance, that he should go and wrestle, and that no one would be able to stand up before him. It was then arranged that there should be a grand wrestling match, to which all the strongest men in the country were invited, and the king promised to attend with his head wife.

On the day of the match the Water Ju Ju told the king's son that he need not be in the least afraid, and that his Ju Ju was so powerful, that even the strongest and best wrestlers in the country would not be able to stand up against him for even a few minutes. All the people of the country came to see the great contest, to the winner of which the king had promised to present prizes of cloth and money, and all the strongest men came. When they saw the king's son, whom nobody knew, they laughed and said, "Who is this small boy? He can have no chance against us." But when they came to wrestle, they very soon found that they were no match for him. The boy was very strong indeed, beautifully made and good to look upon, and all the people were surprised to see how like he was to the king.

After wrestling for the greater part of the day the king's son was declared the winner, having thrown every one who had stood up against him; in fact, some of his opponents had been badly hurt, and had their arms or ribs broken owing to the tremendous strength of the boy. After the match was over the king presented him with cloth and money, and invited him to dine with him in the evening. The boy gladly accepted his father's invitation; and after he had had a good wash in the river, put on his cloth and went up to the palace, where he found the bead chiefs of the country and some of the king's most favoured wives. They then sat down to their meal, and the king had his own son, whom he did not know, sitting next to him. On the other side of the boy sat the jealous wife, who had been the cause of all the trouble. All through the dinner this woman did her best to make friends with the boy, with whom she had fallen violently in love on account of his beautiful appearance, his strength, and his being the best wrestler in the country. The woman thought to herself, It I will have this boy as my husband, as my husband is now an old man and will surely soon die." The boy, however, who was as wise as he was strong, was quite aware of everything the jealous woman had done, and although he pretended to be very flattered at the advances of the king's head wife, he did not respond very readily, and went home as soon as he could.

When he returned to the Water Ju Ju's house he told him everything that had happened, and the Water Ju Ju said—

"As you are now in high favour with the king, you must go to him to-morrow and beg a favour from him. The favour you will ask is that all the country shall be called together, and that a certain case shall be tried, and that when the case is finished, the man or woman who is found to be in the wrong shall be killed by the Egbos before all the people."

So the following morning the boy went to the king, who readily granted his request, and at once sent all round the country appointing a day for all the people to come in and hear the case tried. Then the boy went back to the Water Ju Ju, who told him to go to his mother and tell her who he was, and that when the day of the trial arrived, she was to take off her ugly skin and appear in all her beauty, for the time had come when she need no longer wear it. This the son did.

When the day of trial arrived, Adiaha sat in a corner of the square, and nobody recognised the beautiful stranger as the spider's daughter. Her son then sat down next to her, and brought his sister with him. Immediately his mother saw her she said-

"This must be my daughter, whom I have long mourned as dead," and embraced her most affectionately.

The king and his head wife then arrived and sat on their stones in the middle of the square, all the people saluting them with the usual greetings. The king then addressed the people, and said that he had called them together to hear a strong palaver at the request of the young man who had been the victor of the wrestling, and who had promised that if the case went against him he would offer up his life to the Egbo. The king also said that if, on the other hand, the case was decided in the boy's favour, then the other party would be killed, even though it were himself or one of his wives; whoever it was would have to take his or her place on the killing-stone and have their heads cut off by the Egbos. To this all the people agreed, and said they would like to hear what the young man had to say. The young man then walked round the square, and bowed to the king and the people, and asked the question, "Am I not worthy to be the son of any chief in the country?" And all the people answered "Yes!"

The boy then brought his sister out into the middle, leading her by the hand. She was a beautiful girl and well made. When every one had looked at her he said, "Is not my sister worthy to be any chief's daughter?" And the people replied that she was worthy of being any one's daughter, even the king's. Then he called his mother Adiaha, and she came out, looking very beautiful with her best cloth and beads on, and all the people cheered, as they had never seen a finer woman. The boy then asked them, "Is this woman worthy of being the king's wife?" And a shout went up from every one present that she would be a proper wife for the king, and looked as if she would be the mother of plenty of fine healthy sons.

Then the boy pointed out the jealous woman who was sitting next to the king, and told the people his story, how that his mother, who had two skins, was the spider's daughter; how she had married the king, and how the head wife was jealous and had made a bad Ju Ju for the king, which made him forget his wife; how she had persuaded the king to throw himself and his sister into the river, which, as they all knew, had been done, but the Water Ju Ju had saved both of them, and had brought them up.

Then the boy said--"I leave the king and all of you people to judge my case. If I have done wrong, let me be killed on the stone by the Egbos; if, on the other hand, the woman has done evil, then let the Egbos deal with her as you may decide."

When the king knew that the wrestler was his son he was very glad, and told the Egbos to take the jealous woman away, and punish her in accordance with their laws. The Egbos decided that the woman was a witch; so they took her into the forest and tied her up to a stake, and gave her two hundred lashes with a whip made from hippopotamus hide, and then burnt her alive, so that she should not make any more trouble, and her ashes were thrown into the river. The king then embraced his wife and daughter, and told all the people that she, Adiaha, was his proper wife, and would be the queen for the future.

When the palaver was over, Adiaha was. dressed in fine clothes and beads, and carried back in state to the palace by the king's servants.

That night the king gave a big feast to all his subjects, and told them how glad he was to get back his beautiful wife whom he had never known properly before, also his son who was stronger than all men, and his fine daughter. The feast continued for a hundred and sixty-six days; and the king made a law that if any woman was found out getting medicine against her husband, she should be killed at once. Then the king built three new compounds, and placed many slaves in them, both men and women. One compound he gave to his wife, another to his son, and the third he gave to his daughter. They all lived together quite happily for some years until the king died, when his son came to the throne and ruled in his stead.

## The King's Magic Drum

Efriam Duke was an ancient king of Calabar. He was a peaceful man, and did not like war. He had a wonderful drum, the property of which, when it was beaten, was always to provide plenty of good food and drink. So whenever any country declared war against him, he used to call all his enemies together and beat his drum; then to the surprise of every one, instead of fighting the people found tables spread with all sorts of dishes, fish, foo-foo, palm-oil chop, soup, cooked yams and ocros, and plenty of palm wine for everybody. In this way he kept all the country quiet and sent his enemies away with full stomachs, and in a happy and contented frame of mind. There was only one drawback to possessing the drum, and that was, if the owner of the drum walked over any stick on the road or stept over a fallen tree, all the food would immediately go bad, and three hundred Egbo men would appear with sticks and whips and beat the owner of the drum and all the invited guests very severely.

Efriam Duke was a rich man. He had many farms and hundreds of slaves, a large store of kernels on the beach, and many puncheons of palm-oil. He also had fifty wives and many children. The wives were all fine women and healthy; they were also good mothers, and all of them had plenty of children, which was good for the king's house.

Every few months the king used to issue invitations to all his subjects to come to a big feast, even the wild animals were invited; the elephants, hippopotami, leopards, bush cows, and antelopes used to come, for in those days there was no trouble, as they were friendly with man, and when they were at the feast they did not kill one another. All the people and the animals as well were envious of the king's drum and wanted to possess it, but the king would not part with it.

One morning lkwor Edem, one of the king's wives, took her little daughter down to the spring to wash her, as she was covered with yaws, which are bad sores all over the body. The tortoise happened to be up a palm tree, just over the spring, cutting nuts for his midday meal; and while he was cutting, one of the nuts fell to the ground, just in front of the child. The little girl, seeing the good food, cried for it, and the mother, not knowing any better, picked up the palm nut and gave it to her daughter. Directly the tortoise saw this he climbed down the tree, and asked the woman where his palm nut was. She replied that she had given it to her child to eat.

Then the tortoise, who very much wanted the king's drum, thought he would make plenty palaver over this and force the king to give him the drum, so he said to the mother of the child—

"I am a poor man, and I climbed the tree to get food for myself and my family. Then you took my palm nut and gave it to your child. I shall tell the whole matter to the king, and see what he has to say when he hears that one of his wives has stolen my food," for this, as every one knows, is a very serious crime according to native custom.

Ikwor Edem then said to the tortoise—

"I saw your palm nut lying on the ground, and thinking it had fallen from the tree, I gave it to my little girl to eat, but I did not steal it. My husband the king is a rich man, and if you have any complaint to make against me or my child, I will take you before him."

So when she had finished washing her daughter at the spring she took the tortoise to her husband, and told him what had taken place. The king then asked the tortoise what he would accept as compensation for the loss of his palm nut, and offered him money, cloth, kernels or palm-oil, all of which things the tortoise refused one after the other.

The king then said to the tortoise, "What will you take? You may have anything you like."

And the tortoise immediately pointed to the king's drum, and said that it was the only thing he wanted.

In order to get rid of the tortoise the king said, "Very well, take the drum," but he never told the tortoise about the bad things that would happen to him if he stept over a fallen tree, or walked over a stick on the road.

The tortoise was very glad at this, and carried the drum home in triumph to his wife, and said, "I am now a rich man, and shall do no more work. Whenever I want food, all I have to do is to beat this drum, and food will immediately be brought to me, and plenty to drink."

His wife and children were very pleased when they heard this, and asked the tortoise to get food at once, as they were all hungry. This the tortoise was only too pleased to do, as he wished to show off his newly acquired wealth, and was also rather hungry himself, so he beat the drum in the same way as he had seen the king do when he wanted something to eat, and immediately plenty of food appeared, so they all sat down and made a great f east. The tortoise did this for three days, and everything went well; all his children got fat, and had as much as they could possibly eat. He was therefore very proud of his drum, and in order to display his riches he sent invitations to the king and all the people and animals to come to a feast. When the people received their invitations they laughed, as they knew the tortoise was very poor, so very few attended the feast; but the king, knowing about the drum, came, and when the tortoise beat the drum, the food was brought as usual in great profusion, and all the people sat down and enjoyed their meal very much. They were much astonished that the poor tortoise should be able to entertain so many people, and told all their friends what fine dishes had been placed before them, and that they had never had a better dinner. The people who had not gone were very sorry when they heard this, as a good feast, at somebody else's expense, is not provided every day. After the feast all the people looked upon the tortoise as one of the richest men in the kingdom, and he was very much respected in consequence. No one, except the king, could understand how the poor tortoise could suddenly entertain so lavishly, but they all made up their minds that if the tortoise ever gave another feast, they would not refuse again.

When the tortoise had been in possession of the drum for a few weeks he became lazy and did no work, but went about the country boasting of his riches, and took to drinking too much. One day after he had been drinking a lot of palm wine at a distant farm, he started home carrying his drum; but having had too much to drink, he did not notice a stick in the path. He walked over the stick, and of course the Ju Ju was broken at once. But he did not know this, as nothing happened at the time, and eventually he arrived at his house very tired, and still not very well from having drunk too much. He threw the drum into a corner and went to sleep. When he woke up in the morning the tortoise began to feel hungry, and as his wife and children were calling out for food, he beat the drum; but instead of food being brought, the house was filled with Egbo men, who beat the tortoise, his wife and children, badly. At this the tortoise was very angry, and said to himself-

"I asked everyone to a feast, but only a few came, and they had plenty to eat and drink. Now, when I want food for myself and my family, the Egbos come and beat me. Well, I will let the other people share the same fate, as I do not see why I and my family should be beaten when I have given a feast to all people."

He therefore at once sent out invitations to all the men and animals to come to a big dinner the next day at three o'clock in the afternoon.

When the time arrived many people came, as they did not wish to lose the chance of a free meal a second time. Even the sick men, the lame, and the blind got their friends to lead them to the feast. When they had all arrived, with the exception of the king and his wives, who sent excuses, the tortoise beat his drum as usual, and then quickly hid himself under a bench, where he could not be seen. His wife and children he had sent away before the feast, as he knew what would surely happen. Directly he had beaten the drum three hundred Egbo men appeared with whips, and started flogging all the guests, who could not escape, as the doors had been fastened. The beating went on for two hours, and the people were so badly punished, that many of them had to be carried home on the backs of their friends. The leopard was the only one who escaped, as directly he saw the Egbo men arrive he knew that things were likely to be unpleasant, so he gave a big spring and jumped right out of the compound.

When the tortoise was satisfied with the beating the people had received he crept to the door and opened it. The people then ran away, and when the tortoise gave a certain tap on the drum all the Egbo men vanished. The people who had been beaten were so angry, and made so much palaver with the tortoise, that he made up his mind to return the drum to the king the next day. So in the morning the tortoise went to the king and brought the drum with him. He told the king that he was not satisfied with the drum, and wished to exchange it for something else; he did not mind so much what the king gave him so long as he got full value for the drum, and he was quite willing to accept a certain number of slaves, or a few farms, or their equivalent in cloth or rods.

The king, however, refused to do this; but as he was rather sorry for the tortoise, he said he would present him with a magic foo-foo tree, which would provide the tortoise and his family with food, provided he kept a certain condition. This the tortoise gladly consented to do. Now this foo-foo tree only bore fruit once a year, but every day it dropped foo-foo and soup on the ground. And the condition was, that the owner should gather sufficient food for the day, once, and not return again for more. The tortoise, when he had thanked the king for his generosity, went home to his wife and told her to bring her calabashes to the tree. She did so, and they gathered plenty of foo-foo and soup quite sufficient for the whole family for that day, and went back to their house very happy.

That night they all feasted and enjoyed themselves. But one of the sons, who was very greedy, thought to himself—

"I wonder where my father gets all this good food from? I must ask him."

So in the morning he said to his father—

"Tell me where do you get all this foo-foo and soup from?"

But his father refused to tell him, as his wife, who was a cunning woman, said-

"If we let our children know the secret of the foo-foo tree, some day when they are hungry, after we have got our daily supply, one of them may go to the tree and gather more, which will break the Ju Ju."

But the envious son, being determined to get plenty of food for himself, decided to track his father to the place where he obtained the food. This was rather difficult to do, as the tortoise always went out alone, and took the greatest care to prevent any one following him. The boy, however, soon thought of a plan, and got a calabash with a long neck and a hole in the end. He filled the calabash with wood ashes, which he obtained from the fire, and then got a bag which his father always carried on his back when he went out to get food. In the bottom of the bag the boy then made a small hole, and inserted the calabash with the neck downwards, so that when his father walked to the foo-foo tree he would leave a small trail of wood ashes behind him. Then when his father, having slung his bag over his back as usual, set out to get the daily supply of food, his greedy son followed the trail of the wood ashes, taking great care to hide himself and not to let his father perceive that he was being followed. At last the tortoise arrived at the tree, and placed his calabashes on the ground and collected the food for the day, the boy watching him from a distance. When his father had finished and went home the boy also returned, and having had a good meal, said nothing to his parents, but went to bed. The next morning he got some of his brothers, and after his father had finished getting the daily supply, they went to the tree and collected much foo-foo and soup, and so broke the Ju Ju.

At daylight the tortoise went to the tree as usual, but he could not find it, as during the night the whole bush had grown up, and the foo-foo tree was hidden from sight. There was nothing to be seen but a dense mass of prickly tie-tie palm. Then the tortoise at once knew that some one had broken the Ju Ju, and had gathered foo-foo from the tree twice in the same day; so he returned very sadly to his house, and told his wife. He then called all his family together and told them what had happened, and asked them who had done this evil thing. They all denied having had anything to do with the tree, so the tortoise in despair brought all his family to the place where the foo-foo tree had been, but which was now all prickly tie-tie palm, and said-

"My dear wife and children, I have done all that I can for you, but you have broken my Ju Ju; you must therefore for the future live on the tie-tie palm."

So they made their home underneath the prickly tree, and from that day you will always find tortoises living under the prickly tie-tie palm, as they have nowhere else to go to for food.

# Ituen and the King's Wife

Ituen was a young man of Calabar. He was the only child of his parents, and they were extremely fond of him, as he was of fine proportions and very good to look upon. They were poor people, and when Ituen grew up and became a man, he had very little money indeed, in fact he had so little food, that every day it was his custom to go to the market carrying an empty bag, into which he used to put anything eatable he could find after the market was over.

At this time Offiong was king. He was an old man, but he had plenty of wives. One of these women, named Attem, was quite young and very good-looking. She did not like her old husband, but wished for a young and handsome husband. She therefore told her servant to go round the town and the market to try and find such a man and to bring him at night by the side door to her house, and she herself would let him in, and would take care that her husband did not discover him.

That day the servant went all round the town, but failed to find any young man good-looking enough. She was just returning to report her ill-success when, on passing through the market-place, she saw Ituen picking up the remains of corn and other things which had been left on the ground. She was immediately struck with his fine appearance and strength, and saw that he was just the man to make a proper lover for her mistress, so she went up to him, and said that the queen had sent for him, as she was so taken with his good looks. At first Ituen was frightened and refused to go, as he knew that if the king discovered him he would be killed. However, after much persuasion he consented, and agreed to go to the queen's side door when it was dark.

When the night came he went with great fear and trembling, and knocked very softly at the queen's door. The door was opened at once by the queen herself, who was dressed in all her best clothes, and had many necklaces, beads, and anklets on. Directly she saw Ituen she fell in love with him at once, and praised his good looks and his shapely limbs. She then told her servant to bring water and clothes, and after he had had a good wash and put on a clean cloth, he rejoined the queen. She hid him in her house all the night.

In the morning when he wished to go she would not let him, but, although it was very dangerous, she hid him in the house, and secretly conveyed food and clothes to him. Ituen stayed there for two weeks, and then he said that it was time for him to go and see his mother; but the queen persuaded him to stay another week, much against his will.

When the time came for him to depart the queen got together fifty carriers with presents for Ituen's mother, who, she knew, was a poor woman. Ten slaves carried three hundred rods; the other forty carried yams, pepper, salt, tobacco, and cloth. When all the presents arrived Ituen's mother was very pleased and embraced her son, and noticed with pleasure that he was looking well, and was dressed in much finer clothes than usual; but when she heard that he had attracted the queen's attention she was frightened, as she knew the penalty imposed on any one who attracted the attention of one of the king's wives.

Ituen stayed for a. month in his parents' house and worked on the farm; but the queen could not be without her lover any longer, so she sent for him to go to her at once. Ituen went again, and, as before, arrived at night, when the queen was delighted to see him again.

In the middle of the night some of the king's servants, who had been told the story by the slaves who had carried the presents to Ituen's mother, came into the queen's room and surprised her there with Ituen. They hastened to the king, and told him what they had seen. Ituen was then made a prisoner, and the king sent out to all his people to attend at the palaver house to hear the case tried. He also ordered eight Egbos to attend armed with matchets. When the case was tried Ituen was found guilty, and the king told the eight Egbo men to take him into the bush and deal with him according to native custom. The Egbos then took Ituen into the bush and tied him up to a tree; then with a sharp knife they cut off his lower jaw, and carried it to the king.

When the queen heard the fate of her lover she was very sad, and cried for three days. This made the king angry, so he told the Egbos to deal with his wife and her servant according to their law. They took the queen and the servant into the bush, where Ituen was still tied up to the tree dying and in great pain. Then, as the queen had nothing to say in her defence, they tied her and the girl up to different trees, and cut the queen's lower jaw off in the same way as they had her lover's. The Egbos then put out both the eyes of the servant, and left all three to die of starvation. The king then made an Egbo law that for the future no one belonging to Ituen's family was to go into the market on market day, and that no one was to pick up the rubbish in the market. The king made an exception to the law in favour of the vulture and the dog, who were not considered very fine people, and would not be likely to run off with one of the king's wives, and that is why you still find vultures and dogs doing scavenger in the market-places even at the present time.

## Of the Pretty Stranger who Killed the King

Mbotu was a very famous king of Old Town, Calabar. He was frequently at war, and was always successful, as he was a most skilful leader. All the prisoners he took were made slaves. He therefore became very rich, but, on the other hand, he had many enemies. The people of Itu in particular were very angry with him and wanted to kill him, but they were not strong enough to beat Mbotu in a pitched battle, so they had to resort to 'craft. The Itu people had an old woman who was a witch and could turn herself into whatever she pleased, and when she offered to kill Mbotu, the people were very glad, and promised her plenty of money and cloth if she succeeded in ridding them of their worst enemy. The witch then turned herself into a young and pretty girl, and having armed herself with a very sharp knife, which she concealed in her bosom, she went to Old Town, Calabar, to seek the king.

It happened that when she arrived there was a big play being held in the town, and all the people from the surrounding country had come in to dance and feast. Oyaikan, the witch, went to the play, and walked about so that every one could see her. Directly she appeared the people all marvelled at her beauty, and said that she was as beautiful as the setting sun when all the sky was red. Word was quickly brought to King Mbotu, who, it was well known, was fond of pretty girls, and he sent for her at once, all the people agreeing that she was quite worthy of being the king's wife. When she appeared before him he fancied her so much, that he told her he would marry her that very day. Oyaikan was very pleased at this, as she had never expected to get her opportunity so quickly. She therefore prepared a dainty meal for the king, into which she placed a strong medicine to make the king sleep, and then went down to the river to wash.

*560*

When she had finished it was getting dark, so she went to the king's compound, carrying her dish on her head, and was at once shown in to the king, who embraced her affectionately. She then offered him the food, which she said, quite truly, she had prepared with her own hands. The king ate the whole dish, and immediately began to feel very sleepy, as the medicine was strong and took effect quickly.

They retired to the king's chamber, and the king went to sleep at once. About midnight, when all the town was quiet, Oyaikan drew her knife from her bosom and cut the king's head off. She put the head in a bag and went out very softly, shutting and barring the door behind her. Then she walked through the town without any one observing her, and went straight to Itu, where she placed King Mbotu's head before her own king.

When the people heard that the witch had been successful and that their enemy was dead, there was great rejoicing, and the king of Itu at once made up his mind to attack Old Town, Calabar. He therefore got his fighting men together and took them in canoes by the creeks to Old Town, taking care that no one carried word to Calabar that he was coming.

The morning following the murder of Mbotu his people were rather surprised that he did not appear at his usual time, so his head wife knocked at his door. Not receiving any answer she called the household together, and they broke open the door. When they entered the room they found the king lying dead on his bed covered in blood, but his head was missing. At this a great shout went up, and the whole town mourned. Although they missed the pretty stranger, they never connected her in their minds with the death of their king, and were quite unsuspicious of any danger, and were unprepared for fighting. In the middle of the mourning, while they were all dancing, crying, and drinking palm wine, the king of Itu with all his soldiers attacked Old Town, taking them quite by surprise, and as their leader was dead, the Calabar people were very soon defeated, and many killed and taken prisoners.

**MORAL.**--Never marry a stranger, no matter how pretty she may be.

## Why the Bat flies by Night

A bush rat called Oyot was a great friend of Emiong, the bat; they always fed together, but the bat was jealous of the bush rat. When the bat cooked the food it was always very good, and the bush rat said, "How is it that when you make the soup it is so tasty?"

The bat replied, "I always boil myself in the water, and my flesh is so sweet, that the soup is good."

He then told the bush rat that he would show him how it was done; so he got a pot of warm water, which he told the bush rat was boiling water, and jumped into it, and very shortly afterwards came out again. When the soup was brought it was as strong and good as usual, as the bat had prepared it beforehand.

The bush rat then went home and told his wife that he was going to make good soup like the bat's. He therefore told her to boil some water, which she did. Then, when his wife was not looking, he jumped into the pot, and was very soon dead.

When his wife looked into the pot and saw the dead body of her husband boiling she was very angry, and reported the matter to the king, who gave orders that the bat should be made a prisoner. Every one turned out to

561

catch the bat, but as he expected trouble he flew away into the bush and hid himself. All day long the people tried to catch him, so he had to change his habits, and only came out to feed when it was dark, and that is why you never see a bat in the daytime.

# The Disobedient Daughter who Married a Skull

Effiong Edem was a native of Cobham Town. He had a very fine daughter, whose name was Afiong. All the young men in the country wanted to marry her on account of her beauty; but she refused all offers of marriage in spite of repeated entreaties from her parents, as she was very vain, and said she would only marry the best-looking man in the country, who would have to be young and strong, and capable of loving her properly. Most of the men her parents wanted her to marry, although they were rich, were old men and ugly, so the girl continued to disobey her parents, at which they were very much grieved. The skull who lived in the spirit land heard of the beauty of this Calabar virgin, and thought he would like to possess her; so he went about amongst his friends and borrowed different parts of the body from them, all of the best. From one he got a good head, another lent him a body, a third gave him strong arms, and a fourth lent him a fine pair of legs. At last he was complete, and was a very perfect specimen of manhood.

He then left the spirit land and went to Cobham market, where he saw Afiong, and admired her very much.

About this time Afiong heard that a very fine man had been seen in the market, who was better-looking than any of the natives. She therefore went to the market at once, and directly she saw the Skull in his borrowed beauty, she fell in love with him, and invited him to her house. The Skull was delighted, and went home with her, and on his arrival was introduced by the girl to her parents, and immediately asked their consent to marry their daughter. At first they refused, as they did not wish her to marry a stranger, but at last they agreed.

He lived with Afiong for two days in her parents' house, and then said he wished to take his wife back to his country, which was far off. To this the girl readily agreed, as he was such a fine man, but her parents tried to persuade her not to go. However, being very headstrong, she made up her mind to go, and they started off together. After they had been gone a few days the father consulted his Ju Ju man, who by casting lots very soon discovered that his daughter's husband belonged to the spirit land, and that she would surely be killed. They therefore all mourned her as dead.

After walking for several days, Afiong and the Skull crossed the border between the spirit land and the human country. Directly they set foot in the spirit land, first of all one man came to the Skull and demanded his legs, then another his head, and the next his body, and so on, until in a few minutes the skull was left by itself in all its natural ugliness. At this the girl was very frightened, and wanted to return home, but the skull would not allow this, and ordered her to go with him. When they arrived at the skull's house they found his mother, who was a very old woman quite incapable of doing any work, who could only creep about. Afiong tried her best to help her, and cooked her food, and brought water and firewood for the old woman. The old creature was very grateful for these attentions, and soon became quite fond of Afiong.

One day the old woman told Afiong that she was very sorry for her, but all the people in the spirit land were cannibals, and when they heard there was a human being in their country, they would come down and kill her and eat her. The skull's mother then hid Afiong, and as she had looked after her so well, she promised she would send her back to her country as soon as possible, providing that she promised for the future to obey her parents. This Afiong readily consented to do. Then the old woman sent for the spider, who was a very clever hairdresser, and made him dress Afiong's hair in the latest fashion. She also presented her with anklets and other things on account of her kindness. She then made a Ju Ju and called the winds to come and convey Afiong to her home. At first a violent tornado came, with thunder, lightning and rain, but the skull's mother sent him away as unsuitable. The next wind to come was a gentle breeze, so she told the breeze to carry Afiong to her mother's house, and said good-bye to her. Very soon afterwards the breeze deposited Afiong outside her home, and left her there.

When the parents saw their daughter they were very glad, as they had for some months given her up as lost. The father spread soft animals' skins on the ground from where his daughter was standing all the way to the house, so that her feet should not be soiled. Afiong then walked to the house and her father called all the young girls who belonged to Afiong's company to come and dance, and the feasting and dancing was kept up for eight days and nights. When the rejoicing was over, the father reported what had happened to the head chief of the town. The chief then passed a law that parents should never allow their daughters to marry strangers who came from a far country. Then the father told his daughter to marry a friend of his, and she willingly consented, and lived with him for many years, and had many children.

## The King who Married the Cock's Daughter

King Effiom of Duke Town, Calabar, was very fond of pretty maidens, and whenever he heard of a girl who was unusually good-looking, he always sent for her, and if she took his fancy, he made her one of his wives. This he could afford to do, as he was a rich man, and could pay any dowry which the parents asked, most of his money having been made by buying and selling slaves.

Effiom had two hundred and fifty wives, but he was never content, and wanted to have all the finest women in the land. Some of the king's friends, who were always on the look-out for pretty girls, told Effiom that the Cock's daughter was a lovely virgin, and far superior to any of the king's wives. Directly the king heard this he sent for the Cock, and said he intended to have his daughter as one of his wives. The Cock, being a poor man, could not resist the order of the king, so he brought his daughter, who was very good-looking and pleased the king immensely. When the king had paid the Cock a dowry of six puncheons of palm-oil, the Cock told Effiom that if he married his daughter he must not forget that she had the natural instincts of a hen, and that he should not blame Adia unen (his daughter) if she picked up corn whenever she saw it. The king replied that he did not mind what she ate so long as he possessed her.

The king then took Adia unen as his wife, and liked her so much, that he neglected all his other wives, and lived entirely with Adia unen, as she suited him exactly and pleased him more than any of his other wives. She also amused the king, and played with him and enticed him in so many different ways that he could not live without her, and always had her with him to the exclusion of his former favourites, whom he would not even speak to or notice in any way when he met them This so enraged the neglected wives that they met together, and although they all hated one another, they agreed so far that they hated the Cock's daughter more than any one, as now that she had come to the king none of them ever had a chance with him. Formerly the king, although he always had his favourites, used to favour different girls with his attentions when they pleased him particularly. That was very different in their opinion to being excluded from his presence and all his affections being concentrated on one girl, who received all his love and embraces. In consequence of this they were very angry, and determined if possible to disgrace Adia unen. After much discussion, one of the wives, who was the last favourite, and whom the arrival of the Cock's daughter had displaced, said: "This girl, whom we all hate, is, after all, only a Cock's daughter, and we can easily disgrace her in the king's eyes, as I heard her father tell the king that she could not resist corn, no matter how it was thrown about."

Very shortly after the king's wives had determined to try and disgrace Adia unen, all the people of the country came to pay homage to the king. This was done three times a year, the people bringing yams, fowls, goats, and new corn as presents, and the king entertained them with a feast of foo-foo, palm-oil chop, and tombo . A big dance was also held, which was usually kept up for several days and nights. Early in the morning the king's head wife told her servant to wash one head of corn, and when all the people were present she was to bring it in a calabash and throw it on the ground and then walk away. The corn was to be thrown in front of Aida unen, so that all the people and chiefs could see.

About ten o'clock, when all the chiefs and people had assembled, and the king had taken his seat on his big wooden chair, the servant girl came and threw the corn on the ground as she had been ordered. Directly she had done this Adia unen started towards the corn, picked it up, and began to eat. At this all the people laughed, and the king was very angry and ashamed. The king's wives and many people said that they thought the king's finest wife would have learnt better manners than to pick up corn which had been thrown away as refuse. Others said: "What can you expect from a Cock's daughter? She should not be blamed for obeying her natural instincts." But the king was so vexed, that he told one of his servants to pack up Adia unen's things and take them to her father's house. And this was done, and Aida unen returned to her parents.

That night the king's third wife, who was a friend of Adia unen's, talked the whole matter over with the king, and explained to him that it was entirely owing to the jealousy of his head wife that Adia unen had been disgraced. She also told him that the whole thing had been arranged beforehand in order that the king should get rid of Adia unen, of whom all the other wives were jealous. When the king heard this he was very angry, and made up his mind to send the jealous woman back to her parents empty-handed, without her clothes and presents. When she arrived at her father's house the parents refused to take her in, as she had been given as a wife to the king, and whenever the parents wanted anything, they could always get it at the palace. It was therefore a great loss to them. She was thus turned into the streets, and walked about very miserable, and after a time died, very poor and starving.

The king grieved so much at having been compelled to send his favourite wife Adia unen away, that he died the following year. And when the people saw that their king had died of a broken heart, they passed a law that for the future no one should marry any bird or animal.

## The Woman, the Ape, and the Child

Okun Archibong was one of King Archibong's slaves, and lived on a farm near Calabar. He was a hunter, and used to kill bush buck and other kinds of antelopes and many monkeys. The skins he used to dry in the sun , and when they were properly cured, he used to sell them in the market; the monkey skins were used for making drums, and the antelope skins were used for sitting mats. The flesh, after it had been well smoked over a wood fire, he also sold, but he did not make much money.

Okun Archibong married a slave woman of Duke's house named Nkoyo. He paid a small dowry to the Dukes, took his wife home to his farm, and in the dry season time she had a son. About four months after the birth of the child Nkoyo took him to the farm while her husband was absent hunting. She placed the little boy under a shady tree and went about her work, which was clearing the ground for the yams which would be planted about two months before the rains. Every day while the mother was working a big ape used to come from the forest and play with the little boy; he used to hold him in his arms and carry him up a tree, and when Nkoyo had finished her work, he used to bring the baby back to her. There was a hunter named Edem Effiong who had for a long time been in love with Nkoyo, and had made advances to her, but she would have nothing to do with him, as she was very fond of her husband. When she had her little child Effiong Edem was very jealous, and meeting her one day on the farm without her baby, he said: "Where is your baby?" And she replied that a big ape had taken it up a tree and was looking after it for her. When Effiong Edem saw that the ape was a big one, he made up his mind to tell Nkoyo's husband. The very next day he told Okun Archibong that he had seen his wife in the forest with a big ape. At first Okun would not believe this, but the hunter told him to come with him and he could see it with his own eyes. Okun Archibong therefore made up his mind to kill the ape. The next day he went with the other hunter to the farm and saw the ape up a tree playing with his son, so he took very careful aim and shot the ape, but it was not quite killed. It was so angry, and its strength was so great, that it tore the child limb from limb and threw it to the ground.

This so enraged Okun Archibong that seeing his wife standing near he shot her also. He then ran home and told King Archibong what had taken place. This king was very brave and fond of fighting, so as he knew that King Duke would be certain to make war upon him, he immediately called in all his fighting men. When he was quite prepared he sent a messenger to tell King Duke what had happened. Duke was very angry, and sent the messenger back to King Archibong to say that he must send the hunter to him, so that he could kill him in any way he pleased. This Archibong refused to do, and said he would rather fight. Duke then got his men together, and both sides met and fought in the market square. Thirty men were killed of Duke's men, and twenty were killed on Archibong's side; there were also many wounded. On the whole King Archibong had the best of the fighting, and drove King Duke back. When the fighting was at its hottest the other chiefs sent out all the Egbo men with drums and stopped the fight, and the next day the palaver was tried in Egbo house. King Archibong was found guilty, and was ordered to pay six thousand rods to King Duke. He refused to pay this amount to Duke , and said he would rather go on fighting, but he did not mind paying the six thousand rods to the town, as the Egbos had decided the case. They were about to commence fighting again when the whole country rose up and said they would not have any more fighting, as Archibong said to Duke that the woman's death was not really the fault of his slave Okun Archibong, but of Effiong Edem, who made the false report. When Duke heard this he agreed to leave the whole matter to the chiefs to decide, and Effiong Edem was called to take his place on the stone. He was tried and found guilty, and two Egbos came out armed with cutting whips and gave him two hundred lashes on his bare back, and then cut off his head and sent it to Duke, who placed it before his Ju Ju. From that time to the present all apes and monkeys have been frightened of human beings; and even of little children. The Egbos also passed a law that a chief should not allow one of his men slaves to marry a woman slave of another house, as it would probably lead to fighting.

## The Fish and the Leopard's Wife;

Many years ago, when King Eyo was ruler of Calabar, the fish used to live on the land; he was a great friend of the leopard, and frequently used to go to his house in the bush, where the leopard entertained him. Now the leopard had a very fine wife, with whom the fish fell in love. And after a time, whenever the leopard was absent in the bush, the fish used to go to his house and make love to the leopard's wife, until at last an old woman who lived near informed the leopard what happened whenever he went away. At first the leopard would not believe that the fish, who had been his friend for so long, would play such a low trick, but one night he came back unexpectedly, and found the fish and his wife together; at this the leopard was very angry, and was going to kill the fish, but he thought as the fish had been his friend for so long, he would not deal with him himself, but would report his behaviour to King Eyo. This he did, and the king held a big palaver, at which the leopard stated his case quite shortly, but when the fish was put upon his defence he had nothing to say, so the king addressing his subjects said, "This is a very bad case, as the fish has been the leopard's friend, and has been trusted by him, but the fish has taken advantage of his friend's absence, and has betrayed him." The king, therefore, made an order that for the future the fish should live in the water, and that if he ever came on the land he should die; he also said that all men and animals should kill and eat the fish whenever they could catch him, as a punishment for his behaviour with his friend's wife.

## Why the Bat is Ashamed to be seen in the Daytime

There was once an old mother sheep who had seven lambs, and one day the bat, who was about to make a visit to his father-in-law who lived a long day's march away, went to the old sheep and asked her to lend him one of her young lambs to carry his load for him. At first the mother sheep refused, but as the young lamb was anxious to travel and see something of the world, and begged to be allowed to go, at last she reluctantly consented. So in the morning at daylight the bat and the lamb set off together, the lamb carrying the bat's drinking-horn. When they reached half-way, the bat told the lamb to leave the horn underneath a bamboo tree. Directly he arrived at the house, he sent the lamb back to get the horn. When the lamb had gone the bat's father-in-law brought him food, and the bat ate it all, leaving nothing for the lamb. When the lamb returned, the bat said to him, "Hullo! you have arrived at last I see, but you are too late for food; it is all finished." He then sent the lamb back to the tree with the horn, and when the lamb returned again it was late, and he went supperless to bed.

The next day, just before it was time for food, the bat sent the lamb off again for the drinking-horn, and when the food arrived the bat, who was very greedy, ate it all up a second time. This mean behaviour on the part of the bat went on for four days, until at last the lamb became quite thin and weak. The bat decided to return home the next day, and it was all the lamb could do to carry his load. When he got home to his mother the lamb complained bitterly of the treatment he had received from the bat, and was baa-ing all night, complaining of pains in his inside. The old mother sheep, who was very fond of her children, determined to be revenged on the bat for the cruel way he had starved her lamb; she therefore decided to consult the tortoise, who, although very poor, was considered by all people to be the wisest of all animals. When the old sheep had told the whole story to the tortoise, he considered for some time, and then told the sheep that she might leave the matter entirely to him, and he would take ample revenge on the bat for his cruel treatment of her son.

Very soon after this the bat thought he would again go and see his father-in-law, so he went to the mother sheep again and asked her for one of her sons to carry his load as before. The tortoise, who happened to be present, told the bat that he was going in that direction, and would cheerfully carry his load for him. They set out on their journey the following day, and when they arrived at the half-way halting-place the bat pursued the same tactics that he had on the previous occasion. He told the tortoise to hide his drinking-horn under the same tree as the lamb had hidden it before; this the tortoise did, but when the bat was not looking he picked up the drinking-horn again and hid it in his bag. When they arrived at the house the tortoise hung the horn up out of sight in the back yard, and then sat down in the house. just before it was time for food the bat sent the tortoise to get the drinking-horn, and the tortoise went outside into the yard, and waited until he heard that the beating of the boiled yams into foo-foo had finished; he then went into the house and gave the drinking-horn to the bat, who was so surprised and angry, that when the food was passed he refused to eat any of it, so the tortoise ate it all; this went on for four days, until at last the bat became as thin as the poor little lamb had been on the previous occasion. At last the bat could stand the pains of his inside no longer, and secretly told his mother-in-law to bring him food when the tortoise was not looking. He said, "I am now going to sleep for a little, but you can wake me up when the food is ready." The tortoise, who had been listening all the time, being hidden in a corner out of sight, waited until the bat was fast asleep, and then carried him very gently into the next room and placed him on his own bed; he then very softly and quietly took off the bat's cloth and covered him self in it, and lay down where the bat had been; very soon the bat's mother-in-law brought the food and placed it next to where the bat was supposed to be sleeping, and having pulled his cloth to wake him, went away. The tortoise then got up and ate all the food; when he had finished he carried the bat back again, and took some of the palm-oil and foo-foo and placed it inside the bat's lips while he was asleep; then the tortoise went to sleep himself. In the morning when he woke up the bat was more hungry than ever, and in a very bad temper, so he sought out his mother-in-law and started scolding her, and asked her why she had not brought his food as he had told her to do. She replied she had brought his food, and that he had eaten it; but this the bat denied, and accused the tortoise of having eaten the food. The woman then said she would call the people in and they should decide the matter; but the tortoise slipped out first and told the people that the best way to find out who had eaten the food was to make both the bat and himself rinse their mouths out with clean water into a basin. This they decided to do, so the tortoise got his tooth-stick which he always used, and having cleaned his teeth properly, washed his mouth out, and returned to the house.

When all the people had arrived the woman told them how the bat had abused her, and as he still maintained stoutly that he had had no food for five days, the people said that both he and the tortoise should wash their mouths out with clean water into two clean calabashes; this was done, and at once it could clearly be seen that the bat had been eating, as there were distinct traces of the palm-oil and foo-foo which the tortoise had put inside his lips floating on the water. When the people saw this they decided against the bat, and he was so ashamed that he ran away then and there, and has ever since always hidden himself in the bush during the daytime, so that no one could see him, and only comes out at night to get his food.

The next day the tortoise returned to the mother sheep and told her what he had done, and that the bat was for ever disgraced. The old sheep praised him very much, and told all her friends, in consequence of which the reputation of the tortoise for wisdom was greatly increased throughout the whole country.

## Why the Worms live Underneath the Ground

When Eyo III. was ruling over all men and animals, he had a very big palaver house to which he used to invite his subjects at intervals to feast. After the feast had been held and plenty of tombo had been drunk, it was the custom of the people to make speeches. One day after the feast the head driver ant got up and said he and his people were stronger than any one, and that no one, not even the elephant, could stand before him, which was quite true. He was particularly offensive in his allusions to the worms (whom he disliked very much), and said they were poor wriggling things.

The worms were very angry and complained, so the king said that the best way to decide the question who was the stronger was for both sides to meet on the road and fight the matter out between themselves to a finish. He appointed the third day from the feast for the contest, and all the people turned out to witness the battle.

The driver ants left their nest in the early morning in thousands and millions, and, as is their custom, marched in a line about one inch broad densely packed, so that it was like a dark-brown band moving over the country. In front of the advancing column they had out their scouts, advance guard, and flankers, and the main body followed in their millions close behind.

When they came to the battlefield the moving band spread out, and as the thousands upon thousands of ants rolled up, the whole piece of ground was a moving mass of ants and bunches of struggling worms. The fight was over in a very few minutes, as the worms were bitten in pieces by the sharp pincer-like mouths of the driver ants. The few worms who survived squirmed away and buried themselves out of sight.

King Eyo decided that the driver ants were easy winners, and ever since the worms have always been afraid and have lived underground; and if they happen to come to the surface after the rain they hide themselves under the ground whenever anything approaches, as they fear all people.

# The Elephant and the Tortoise

When Ambo was king of Calabar, the elephant was not only a very big animal, but he had eyes in proportion to his immense bulk. In those days men and animals were friends, and all mixed together quite freely. At regular intervals King Ambo used to give a feast, and the elephant used to eat more than any one, although the hippopotamus used to do his best; however, not being as big as the elephant, although he was very fat, he was left a long way behind.

As the elephant ate so much at these feasts, the tortoise, who was small but very cunning, made up his mind to put a stop to the elephant eating more than a fair share of the food provided. He therefore placed some dry kernels and shrimps, of which the elephant was very fond, in his bag, and went to the elephant's house to make an afternoon call.

When the tortoise arrived the elephant told him to sit down, so he made himself comfortable, and, having shut one eye, took one palm kernel and a shrimp out of his bag, and commenced to eat them with much relish.

When the elephant saw the tortoise eating, he said, as he was always hungry himself, "You seem to have some good food there; what are you eating?"

The tortoise replied that the food was "sweet too much," but was rather painful to him, as he was eating one of his own eyeballs; and he lifted up his head, showing one eye closed.

The elephant then said, "If the food is so good, take out one of my eyes and give me the same food."

The tortoise, who was waiting for this, knowing how greedy the elephant was, had brought a sharp knife with him for that very purpose, and said to the elephant, "I cannot reach your eye, as you are so big."

The elephant then took the tortoise up in his trunk and lifted him up. As soon as he came near the elephant's eye, with one quick scoop of the sharp knife he had the elephant's right eye out. The elephant trumpeted with pain; but the tortoise gave him some of the dried kernels and shrimps, and they so pleased the elephant's palate that he soon forgot the pain.

Very soon the elephant said, That food is so sweet, I must have some more but the tortoise told him that before he could have any the other eye must come out. To this the elephant agreed; so the tortoise quickly got his knife to work, and very soon the elephant's left eye was on the ground, thus leaving the elephant quite blind. The tortoise then slid down the elephant's trunk on to the ground and hid himself. The elephant then began to make a great noise, and started pulling trees down and doing much damage, calling out for the tortoise but of course he never answered, and the elephant could not find him.

The next morning, when the elephant heard the people passing, he asked them what the time was, and the bush buck, who was nearest, shouted out, "The sun is now up, and I am going to market to get some yams and fresh leaves for my food."

Then the elephant perceived that the tortoise had deceived him, and began to ask all the passers-by to lend him a pair of eyes, as he could not see, but every one refused, as they wanted their eyes themselves. At last the worm grovelled past, and seeing the big elephant, greeted him in his humble way.

He was much surprised when the king of the forest returned his salutation, and very much flattered also.

The elephant said, " Look here, worm, I have mislaid my eyes. Will you lend me yours for a few days? I will return them next market-day."

The worm was so flattered at being noticed by the elephant that he gladly consented, and took his eyes out-which, as every one knows, were very small-and gave them to the elephant. When the elephant had put the worm's eyes into his own large eye-sockets, the flesh immediately closed round them so tightly that when the market-day arrived it was impossible for the elephant to get them out again to return to the worm; and although the worm repeatedly made applications to the elephant to return his eyes, the elephant always pretended not to hear, and sometimes used to say in a very loud voice, " If there are any worms about, they had better get out of my way, as they are so small I cannot see them, and if I tread on them they will be squashed into a nasty mess."

Ever since then the worms have been blind, and for the same reason elephants have such small eyes, quite out of proportion to the size of their huge bodies.

## Why a Hawk kills Chickens

In the olden days there was a very fine young hen who lived with her parents in the bush.

One day a hawk was hovering round, about eleven o'clock in the morning, as was his custom, making large circles in the air and scarcely moving his wings. His keen eyes were wide open, taking in everything (for nothing moving ever escapes the eyes of a hawk, no matter how small it may be or how high up in the air the hawk may be circling). This hawk saw the pretty hen picking up some corn near her father's house. He therefore closed his wings slightly, and in a second of time was close to the ground; then spreading his wings out to check his flight, he alighted close to the hen and perched himself on the fence, as a hawk does not like to walk on the ground if he can help it.

He then greeted the young hen with his most enticing whistle, and offered to marry her. She agreed, so the hawk spoke to the parents, and paid the agreed amount of dowry, which consisted mostly of corn, and the next day took the young hen off to his home.

Shortly after this a young cock who lived near the hen's former home found out where she was living, and having been in love with her for some months-in fact, ever since his spurs had grown-determined to try and make her return to her own country. He therefore went at dawn, and, having flapped his wings once or twice, crowed in his best voice to the young hen. When she heard the sweet voice of the cock she could not resist his invitation, so she went out to him, and they walked off together to her parent's house, the young cock strutting in front crowing at intervals.

The hawk, who was hovering high up in the sky, quite out of sight of any ordinary eye, saw what had happened, and was very angry. He made up his mind at once that he would obtain justice from the king, and flew off to Calabar, where he told the whole story, and asked for immediate redress. So the king sent for the parents of the hen, and told them they must repay to the hawk the amount of dowry they had received from him on the marriage of their daughter, according to the native custom; but the hen's parents said that they were so poor that they could not possibly afford to pay. So the king told the hawk that he could kill and eat any of the cock's children whenever and wherever he found them as payment of his dowry, and, if the cock made any complaint, the king would not listen to him.

From that time until now, whenever, a hawk sees a chicken he swoops down and carries it off in part-payment of his dowry.

## Why the Sun and the Moon live in the Sky

Many years ago the sun and water were great friends, and both lived on the earth together. The sun very often used to visit the water, but the water never returned his visits. At last the sun asked the water why it was that he never came to' see him in his house, the water replied that the sun's house was not big enough, and that if he came with his people he would drive the sun out.

He then said, "If you wish me to visit you, you must build a very large compound; but I warn you that it will have to be a tremendous place, as my people are very numerous, and take up a lot of room."

The sun promised to build a very big compound, and soon afterwards he returned home to his wife, the moon, who greeted him with a broad smile when he opened the door. The sun told the moon what he had promised the water, and the next day commenced building a huge compound in which to entertain his friend.

When it was completed, he asked the water to come and visit him the next day.

When the water arrived, he called out to the sun, and asked him whether it would be safe for- him to enter, and the sun answered, "Yes, come in, my friend."

The water then began to flow in, accompanied by the fish and all the water animals.

Very soon the water was knee-deep, so he asked the sun if it was still safe, and the sun again said, "Yes," so more water came in.

When the water was level with the top of a man's head, the water said to the sun, "Do you want more of my people to come?" and the sun and moon both answered, "Yes, not knowing any better, so the water flowed on, until the sun and moon had to perch themselves on the top of the roof.

Again the water addressed the sun, but receiving the same answer, and more of his people rushing in, the water very soon overflowed the top of the roof, and the sun and moon were forced to go up into the sky, where they have remained ever since.

## Why the Flies Bother the Cows

When Adiaha Umo was Queen of Calabar, being very rich and hospitable, she used to give big feasts to all the domestic animals, but never invited the wild beasts, as she was afraid of them.

At one feast she gave there were three large tables, and she told the cow to sit at the head of the table, as she was the biggest animal present, and share out the food. The cow was quite ready to do this, and the first course was passed, which the cow shared out amongst the people, but forgot the fly, because he was so small.

When the fly saw this, he called out to the cow to give him his share, but the cow said: "Be quiet, my friend, you must have patience."

When the second course arrived, the fly again called out to the cow, but the cow merely pointed to her eye, and told the fly to look there, and he would get food later.

At last all the dishes were finished, and the fly, having been given no food by the cow, went supperless to bed.

The next day the fly complained to the queen, who decided that , as the cow had presided at the feast, and had not given the fly his share, but had pointed to her eye, for the future the fly could always get his food from the cow's eyes wherever she went; and even at the present time, wherever the cows are, the flies can always be seen feeding off their eyes in accordance with the queen's orders.

## Why the Cat kills Rats

Ansa was King of Calabar for fifty years. He had a very faithful cat as a housekeeper, and a rat was his house-boy. The king was an obstinate, headstrong man, but was very fond of the cat, who had been in his store for many years.

The rat, who was very poor, fell in love with one of the king's servant girls, but was unable to give her any presents, as he had no money.

At last he thought of the king's store, so in the night-time, being quite small, he had little difficulty, having made a hole in the roof, in getting into the store. He then stole corn and native pears, and presented them to his sweetheart.

At the end of the month, when the cat had to render her account of the things in the store to the king, it was found that a lot of corn and native pears were missing. The king was very angry at this, and asked the cat for an explanation. But the cat-could not account for the loss, until one of her friends told her that the rat had been stealing the corn and giving it to the girl.

When the cat told the king, he called the girl before him and had her flogged. The rat he handed over to the cat to deal with, and dismissed them both from his service. The cat was so angry at this that she killed and ate the rat, and ever since that time whenever a cat sees a rat she kills and eats it.

## The Story of the Lightning and the Thunder

In the olden days the thunder and lightning lived on the earth amongst all the other people, but the king made them live at the far end of the town, as far as possible from other people's houses.

The thunder was an old mother sheep, and the lightning was her son, a ram. Whenever the ram got angry he used to go about and burn houses and knock down trees; he even did damage on the farms, and sometimes killed people. Whenever the lightning did these things, his mother used to call out to him in a very loud voice to stop and not to do any more damage; but the lightning did not care in the least for what his mother said, and when he was in a bad temper used to do a very large amount of damage. At last the people could not stand it any longer, and complained to the king.

So the king made a special order that the sheep (Thunder) and her son, the ram (Lightning), should leave the town and live in the far bush. This did not do much good, as when the ram got angry he still burnt the forest, and the flames sometimes spread to the farms and consumed them.

So the people complained again, and the king banished both the lightning and the thunder from the earth and made them live in the sky, where they could not cause so much destruction. Ever since, when the lightning is angry, he commits damage as before, but you can hear his mother, the thunder, rebuking him and telling him to stop. Sometimes, however, when the mother has gone away some distance from her naughty son, you can still see that he is angry and is doing damage, but his mother's voice cannot be heard.

## Why the Cow and the Elephant are bad Friends

The bush cow and the elephant were always bad friends, and as they could not settle their disputes between themselves, they agreed to let the head chief decide.

The cause of their unfriendliness was that the elephant was always boasting about his strength to all his friends, which made the bush cow ashamed of himself, as he was always a good fighter and feared no man or animal. When the matter was referred to the head chief, he decided that the best way to settle the dispute was for the elephant and bush cow to meet and fight one another in a large open space. He decided that the fight should take place in the market-place on the next market-day, when all the country people could witness the battle.

When the market-day arrived, the bush cow went out in the early morning and took up his position some distance from the town on the main road to the market, and started bellowing and tearing up the ground. As the people passed he asked them whether they had seen anything of the "Big, Big one," which was the name of the elephant.

A bush buck, who happened to be passing, replied, I am only a small antelope, and am on my way to the market. How should I know anything of the 'Big, Big one?'" The bush cow then allowed him to pass.

After a little time the bush cow heard the elephant trumpeting, and could hear him as he came nearer breaking down trees and trampling down the small bush.

When the elephant came near the bush cow, they both charged one another, and a tremendous fight commenced, in which a lot of damage was done to the surrounding farms, and many of the people were frightened to go to the market, and returned to their houses.

At last the monkey, who had been watching the fight from a distance whilst he was jumping from branch to branch high up in the trees, thought he would report what he had seen to the head chief. Although he forgot several times what it was he wanted to do, which is a little way monkeys have, he eventually reached the chief's house, and jumped upon the roof, where he caught and ate a spider. He then climbed to the ground again, and commenced playing with a small stick. But he very soon got tired of this, and then, picking up a stone, he rubbed it backwards and forwards on the ground in an aimless sort of way, whilst looking in the opposite direction. This did not last long, and very soon he was busily engaged in a minute personal inspection.

His attention was then attracted by a large praying mantis, which had

573

fluttered into the house, making much clatter with its wings. When it settled, it immediately assumed its usual prayerful attitude.

The monkey, after a careful stalk, seized the mantis, and having deliberately pulled the legs off one after the other, he ate the body, and sat down with his head on one side, looking very wise, but in reality thinking of nothing.

Just then the chief caught sight of him while he was scratching himself, and shouted out in a loud voice, "Ha, monkey, is that you? What do you want here?"

At the chief's voice the monkey gave a jump, and started chattering like anything. After a time he replied very nervously: "Oh yes, of course! Yes, I came to see you." Then he said to himself, "I wonder what on earth it was I came to tell the chief?" but it was no use, everything had gone out of his head.

Then the chief told the monkey he might take one of the ripe plantains hanging up in the verandah. The monkey did not want telling twice, as he was very fond of plantains. He soon tore off the skin, and holding the plantain in both hands, took bite after bite from the end of it, looking at it carefully after each bite.

Then the chief remarked that the elephant and the bush cow ought to have arrived by that time, as they were going to have a great fight. Directly the monkey heard this he remembered what it was he wanted to tell the chief; so, having swallowed the piece of plantain he had placed in the side of his cheek, he said: "Ah I that reminds me," and then, after much chattering and making all sorts of funny grimaces, finally made the chief understand that the elephant and bush cow, instead of fighting where they had been told, were having it out in the bush on the main road leading to the market, and had thus stopped most of the people coming in.

When the chief heard this he was much incensed, and called for his bow and poisoned arrows, and went to the scene of the combat. He then shot both the elephant and the bush cow, and throwing his bow and arrows away, ran and hid himself in the bush. About six hours afterwards both the elephant and bush cow died in great pain.

Ever since, when wild animals want to fight between themselves, they always fight in the big bush and not on the public roads; but as the fight was never definitely decided between the elephant and the bush cow, whenever they meet one another in the forest, even to the present time, they always fight.

## The Cock who caused a Fight between two Towns

Ekpo and Etim were half-brothers, that is to say they had the same mother, but different fathers. Their mother first of all had married a chief of Duke Town, when Ekpo was born; but after a time she got tired of him and went to Old Town, where she married Ejuqua and gave birth to Etim.

Both of the boys grew up and became very rich. Ekpo had a cock, of which he was very fond, and every day when Ekpo sat down to meals the cock used to fly on to the table and feed also. Ama Ukwa, a native of Old Town, who was rather poor, was jealous of the two brothers, and made up his mind if possible to bring about a quarrel between them, although he pretended to be friends with both.

One day Ekpo, the elder brother, gave a big dinner, to which Etim and many other people were invited. Ama Ukwa was also present. A very good dinner was laid for the guests, and plenty of palm wine was provided. When they had commenced to feed, the pet cock flew on to the table and began to feed off Etim's plate. Etim then told one of his servants to seize the cock and tie him up in the house until after the feast. So the servant carried the cock to Etim's house and tied him up for safety.

After much eating and drinking, Etim returned home late at night with his friend Ama Ukwa, and just before they went to bed, Ama Ukwa saw Ekpo's cock tied up. So early in the morning he went to Ekpo's house, who received him gladly.

About eight o'clock, when it was time for Ekpo to have his early morning meal, he noticed that his pet cock was missing. When he remarked upon its absence, Ama Ukwa told him that his brother had seized the cock the previous evening during the dinner, and was going to kill it, just to see what Ekpo would do. When Ekpo heard this, he was very vexed, and sent Ama Ukwa back to his brother to ask him to return the cock immediately. Instead of delivering the message as he had been instructed, Ama Ukwa told Etim that his elder brother was so angry with him for taking away his friend, the cock, that he would fight him, and had sent Ama Ukwa on purpose to declare war between the two towns.

Etim then told Ama Ukwa to return to Ekpo, and say he would be prepared for anything his brother could do. Ama Ukwa then advised Ekpo to call all his people in from their farms, as Etim would attack him, and on his return he advised Etim to do the same. He then arranged a day for the fight to take place between -the two brothers and their people. Etim then marched his men to the other side of the creek, and waited for his brother; so Ama Ukwa went to Ekpo and told him that Etim had got all his people together and was waiting to fight. Ekpo then led his men against his brother, and there was a big battle, many men being killed on both sides. The fighting went on all day, until at last, towards evening, the other chiefs of Calabar met and determined to stop it; so they called the Egbo men together and sent them out with their drums, and eventually the fight stopped.

Three days later a big palaver was held, when each of the brothers was told to state his case. When they had done so, it was found that Ama Ukwa had caused the quarrel, and the chiefs ordered that he should be killed. His father, who was a rich man, offered to give the Egbos five thousand rods, five cows, and seven slaves to redeem his son, but they decided to refuse his offer.

The next day, after being severely flogged, he was left for twenty-four hours tied up to a tree, and the following day his head was cut off.

Ekpo was then ordered to kill his pet cock, so that it should not cause any further trouble between himself and his brother, and a law was passed that for the future no one should keep a pet cock or any other tame animal.

## The Affair of the Hippopotamus and the Tortoise

Many years ago the hippopotamus, whose name was Isantim, was one of the biggest kings on the land; he was second only to the elephant. The hippo had seven large fat wives, of whom he was very fond. Now and then he used to give a big feast to the people, but a curious thing was that, although every one knew the hippo, no one, except his seven wives, knew his name.

At one of the feasts, just as the people were about to sit down, the hippo said, "You have come to feed at my table, but none of you know my name. If you cannot tell my name, you shall all of you go away without your dinner."

As they could not guess his name, they had to go away and leave all the good food and tombo behind them. But before they left, the tortoise stood up and asked the hippopotamus what he would do if he told him his name at the next feast? So the hippo replied that he would be so ashamed of himself, that he and his whole family would leave the land, and for the future would dwell in the water.

Now it was the custom for the hippo and his seven wives to go down every morning and evening to the river to wash and have a drink. Of this custom the tortoise was aware. The hippo used to walk first, and the seven wives followed. One day when they had gone down to the river to bathe, the tortoise made a small hole in the middle of the path, and then waited. When the hippo and his wives returned, two of the wives were some distance behind, so the tortoise came out from where he had been hiding, and half buried himself in the hole he had dug, leaving the greater part of his shell exposed. When the two hippo wives came along, the first one knocked her foot against the tortoise's shell, and immediately called out to her husband, "Oh! Isantim, my husband, I have hurt my foot." At this the tortoise was very glad, and went joyfully home, as he had found out the hippo's name.

When the next feast was given by the hippo, he made the same condition about his name; so the tortoise got up and said, "You promise you will not kill me if I tell you your name?" and the hippo promised. The tortoise then shouted as loud as he was able, "Your name is Isantim," at which a cheer went up from all the people, and then they sat down to their dinner.

When the feast was over, the hippo, with his seven wives, in accordance with his promise, went down to the river, and they have always lived in the water from that day till now; and although they come on shore to feed at night, you never find a hippo on the land in the daytime.

## Why Dead People are Buried

In the beginning of the world when the Creator had made men and women and the animals, they all lived together in the creation land. The Creator was a big chief, past all men, and being very kindhearted, was very sorry whenever anyone died. So one day he sent for the dog, who was his head messenger, and told him to go out into the world and give his word to all people that for the future whenever anyone died the body was to be placed in the compound, and wood ashes were to be thrown over it; that the dead body was to be left on the ground, and in twenty-four hours it would become alive again.

When the dog had travelled for half a day he began to get tired; so as he was near an old woman's house he looked in, and seeing a bone with some meat on it he made a meal off it, and then went to sleep, entirely forgetting the message which had been given him to deliver.

After a time, when the dog did not return, the Creator called for a sheep, and sent him out with the same message. But the sheep was a very foolish one, and being hungry, began eating the sweet grasses by the wayside. After a time, however, he remembered that he had a message to deliver, but forgot what it was exactly; so as he went about among the people he told them that the message the Creator had given him to tell the people, was that whenever any one died they should be buried underneath the ground.

A little time afterwards the dog remembered his message, so he ran into the town and told the people that they were to place wood ashes on the dead bodies and leave them in the compound, and that they would come to life again after twenty-four hours. But the people would not believe him, and said, "We have already received the word from the Creator by the sheep, that all dead bodies should be buried." In consequence of this the dead bodies are now always buried, and the dog is much disliked and not trusted as a messenger, as if he had not found the bone in the old woman's house and forgotten his message, the dead people might still be alive.

## Of the Fat Woman who Melted Away

There was once a very fat woman who was made of oil. She was very beautiful, and many young men applied to the parents for permission to marry their daughter, and offered dowry, but the mother always refused, as she said it was impossible for her daughter to work on a farm, as she would melt in the sun. At last a stranger came from a far-distant country and fell in love with the fat woman, and he promised if her mother would hand her to him that he would keep her in the shade. At last the mother agreed, and he took his wife away.

When he arrived at his house, his other wife immediately became very jealous, because when there was work to be done, firewood to be collected, or water to be carried, the fat woman stayed at home and never helped, as she was frightened of the heat.

One day when the husband was absent, the jealous wife abused the fat woman so much that she finally agreed to go and work on the farm, although her little sister, whom she had brought from home with her, implored her not to go, reminding her that their mother had always told them ever since they were born that she would melt away if she went into the sun. All the way to the farm the fat woman managed to keep in the shade, and when they arrived at the farm the sun was very hot, so the fat woman remained in the shade of a big tree. When the jealous wife saw this she again began abusing her, and asked her why she did not do her share of the work. At last she could stand the nagging no longer, and although her little sister tried very hard to prevent her, the fat woman went out into the sun to work, and immediately began to melt away. There was very soon nothing left of her but one big toe, which had been covered by a leaf. This her little sister observed, and with tears in her eyes she picked up the toe, which was all that remained of the fat woman, and having covered it carefully with leaves, placed it in the bottom of her basket. When she arrived at the house the little sister placed the toe in an earthen pot, filled it with water, and covered the top up with clay.

When the husband returned, he said, "Where is my fat wife?" and the little sister, crying bitterly, told him that the jealous woman had made her go out into the sun, and that she had melted away. She then showed him the pot with the remains of her sister, and told him that her sister would come to life again in three months' time quite complete, but he must send away the jealous wife, so that there should be no more trouble; if he refused to do this, the little girl said she would take the pot back to their mother, and when her sister became complete again they would remain at home.

The husband then took the jealous wife back to her parents, who sold her as a slave and paid the dowry back to the husband, so that he could get another wife. When he received the money, the husband took it home and kept it until the three months had elapsed, when the little sister opened the pot and the fat woman emerged, quite as fat and beautiful as she had been before. The husband was so delighted that he gave a feast to all his friends and neighbours, and told them the whole story of the bad behaviour of his jealous wife.

Ever since that time, whenever a wife behaves very badly the husband returns her to the parents, who sell the woman as a slave, and out of the proceeds of the sale reimburse the husband the amount of dowry which he paid when he married the girl.

## Concerning the Leopard, the Squirrel, and the Tortoise

Many years ago there was a great famine throughout the land, and all the people were starving. The yam crop had failed entirely, the plantains did not bear any fruit, the ground-nuts were all shrivelled up, and the corn never came to a head; even the palm-oil nuts did not ripen, and the peppers and ocros also gave out.

The leopard, however, who lived entirely on "beef," did not care for any of these things; and although some of the animals who lived on corn and the growing crops began to get rather skinny, he did not mind very much. In order to save himself trouble, as everybody was complaining of the famine, he called a meeting of all the animals and told them that, as they all knew, he was very powerful and must have food, that the famine did not affect him, as he only lived on flesh, and as there were plenty of animals about he did not intend to starve. He then told all the animals present at the meeting that if they did not wish to be killed themselves they must bring their grand mothers to him for food, and when they were finished he would feed off their mothers. The animals might bring their grandmothers in succession, and he would take them in turn; so that, as there were many different animals, it would probably be some time before their mothers were eaten, by which time it was possible that the famine would be over. But in any case, he warned them that he was determined to have sufficient food for himself, and that if the grandmothers or mothers were not forthcoming he would turn upon the young people themselves and kill and eat them.

This, of course, the young generation, who had attended the meeting, did not appreciate, and in order to save their own skins, agreed to supply the leopard with his daily meal.

The first to appear with his aged grandmother was the squirrel. The grandmother was a poor decrepit old thing, with a mangy tail, and the leopard swallowed her at one gulp, and then looked round for more. In an angry voice he growled out: "This is not the proper food for me; I must have more at once."

Then a bush cat pushed his old grandmother in front of the leopard, but he snarled at her and said, "Take the nasty old thing away; I want some sweet food."

It was then the turn of a bush buck, and after a great deal of hesitation a wretchedly poor and thin old doe tottered and fell in front of the leopard, who immediately despatched her, and although the meal was very unsatisfactory, declared that his appetite was appeased for that day.

The next day a few more animals brought their old grandmothers, until at last it became the tortoise's turn; but being very cunning, he produced witnesses to prove that his grandmother was dead, so the leopard excused him.

After a few days all the animals' grandmothers were exhausted, and it became the turn of the mothers to supply food for the ravenous leopard. Now although most of the young animals did not mind getting rid of their grandmothers, whom they had scarcely even known, many of them had very strong objections to providing their mothers, of whom they were very fond, as food for the leopard. Amongst the strongest objectors were the squirrel and the tortoise. The tortoise, who had thought the whole thing out, was aware that, as every one knew that his mother was alive (she being rather an amiable old person and friendly with all-comers), the same excuse would not avail him a second time. He therefore told his mother to climb up a palm tree, and that he would provide her with food until the famine was over. He instructed her to let down a basket every day, and said that he would place food in it for her. The tortoise made the basket for his mother, and attached it to a long string of tie-tie. The string was so strong that she could haul her son up whenever he wished to visit her.

All went well for some days, as the tortoise used to go at daylight to the bottom of the tree where his mother lived and place her food in the basket; then the old lady would pull the basket up and have her food, and the tortoise would depart on his daily round in his usual leisurely manner.

In the meantime the leopard had to have his daily food, and the squirrel's turn came first after the grandmothers had been finished, so he was forced to produce his mother for the leopard to eat, as he was a poor, weak thing and not possessed of any cunning. The squirrel was, however, very fond of his mother, and when she had been eaten he remembered that the tortoise had not produced his grandmother for the leopard's food. He therefore determined to set a watch on the movements of the tortoise.

The very next morning, while he was gathering nuts, he saw the tortoise walking very slowly through the bush, and being high up in the trees and able to travel very fast, had no difficulty in keeping the tortoise in sight without being noticed. When the tortoise arrived at the foot of the tree where his mother lived, he placed the food in the basket which his mother had let down already by the tie-tie, and having got into the basket and given a pull at the string to signify that everything was right, was hauled up, and after a time was let down again in the basket. The squirrel was watching all the time, and directly the tortoise had gone, jumped from branch to branch of the trees, and very soon arrived at the place where the leopard was snoozing.

When he woke up, the squirrel said:

"You have eaten my grandmother and my mother, but the tortoise has not provided any food for you. It is now his turn, and he has hidden his mother away in a tree."

At this the leopard was very angry, and told the squirrel to lead him at once to the tree where the tortoise's mother lived. But the squirrel said:

"The tortoise only goes at daylight, when his mother lets down a basket; so if you go in the morning early, she will pull you up, and you can then kill her."

To this the leopard agreed, and the next morning the squirrel came at cockcrow and led the leopard to the tree where the tortoise's mother was hidden. The old lady had already let down the basket for her daily supply of food, and the leopard got into it and gave the line a pull; but except a few small jerks nothing happened, as the old mother tortoise was not strong enough to pull a heavy leopard off the ground. When the leopard saw that he was not going to be pulled up, being an expert climber, he scrambled up the tree, and when he got to the top he found the poor old tortoise, whose shell was so tough that he thought she was not worth eating, so he threw her down on to the ground in a violent temper, and then came down himself and went home.

Shortly after this the tortoise arrived at the tree, and finding the basket on the ground gave his usual tug at it, but there was no answer. He then looked about, and after a little time came upon the broken shell of his poor old mother, who by this time was quite dead. The tortoise knew at once that the leopard had killed his mother, and made up his mind that for the future he would live alone and have nothing to do with the other animals.

## Why the Moon Waxes and Wanes

There was once an old woman who was very poor, and lived in a small mud hut thatched with mats made from the leaves of the tombo palm in the bush. She was often very hungry, as there was no one to look after her.

In the olden days the moon used often to come down to the earth, although she lived most of the time in the sky. The moon was a fat woman with a skin of hide, and she was full of fat meat. She was quite round, and in the night used to give plenty of light. The moon was sorry for the poor starving old woman, so she came to her and said, "You may cut some of my meat away for your food." This the old woman did every evening, and the moon got smaller and smaller until you could scarcely see her at all. Of course this made her give very little light, and all the people began to grumble in consequence, and to ask why it was that the moon was getting so thin.

At last the people went to the old woman's house where there happened to be a little girl sleeping. She had been there for some little time, and had seen the moon come down every evening, and the old woman go out with her knife and carve her daily supply of meat out of the moon. As she was very frightened, she told the people all about it, so they determined to set a watch on the movements of the old woman.

That very night the moon came down as usual, and the old woman went out with her knife and basket to get her food; but before she could carve any meat all the people rushed out shouting, and the moon was so frightened that she went back again into the sky, and never came down again to the earth. The old woman was left to starve in the bush.

Ever since that time the moon has hidden herself most of the day, as she was so frightened, and she still gets very thin once a month, but later on she gets fat again, and when she is quite fat she gives plenty of light all the night; but this does not last very long, and she begins to get thinner and thinner, in the same way as she did when the old woman was carving her meat from her.

## The Story of the Leopard, the Tortoise, and the Bush Rat

At the time of the great famine all the animals were very thin and weak from want of food; but there was one exception, and that was the tortoise and all his family, who were quite fat, and did not seem to suffer at all. Even the leopard was very thin, in spite of the arrangement he had made with the animals to bring him their old grandmothers and mothers for food.

In the early days of the famine (as you will remember) the leopard had killed the mother of the tortoise, in consequence of which the tortoise was very angry with the leopard, and determined if possible to be revenged upon him. The tortoise, who was very clever, had discovered a shallow lake full of fish in the middle of the forest, and every morning he used to go to the lake and, without much trouble, bring back enough food for himself and his family. One day the leopard met the tortoise and noticed how fat he was. As he was very thin himself he decided to watch the tortoise, so the next morning he hid himself in the long grass near the tortoise's house and waited very patiently, until at last the tortoise came along quite slowly, carrying a basket which appeared to be very heavy. Then the leopard sprang out, and said to the tortoise:

"What have you got in that basket?

The tortoise, as he did not want to lose his breakfast, replied that he was carrying firewood back to his home. Unfortunately for the tortoise the leopard had a very acute sense of smell, and knew at once that there was fish in the basket, so he said:

"I know there is fish in there, and I am going to eat it."

The tortoise, not being in a position to refuse, as he was such a poor creature, said:

"Very well. Let us sit down under this shady tree, and if you will make a fire I will go to my house and get pepper, oil, and salt, and then we will feed together."

To this the leopard agreed, and began to search about for dry wood, and started the fire. In the meantime the tortoise waddled off to his house, and very soon returned with the pepper, salt, and oil; he also brought a long piece of cane tie-tie, which is very strong. This he put on the ground, and began boiling the fish. Then he said to the leopard:

"While we are waiting for the fish to cook, let us play at tying one another up to a tree. You may tie me up first, and when I say 'Tighten,' you must loose the rope, and when I say 'Loosen,' you must tighten the rope."

The leopard, who was very hungry, thought that this game would make the time pass more quickly until the fish was cooked, so he said he would play. The tortoise then stood with his back to the tree and said, "Loosen the rope," and the leopard, in accordance with the rules of the game, began to tie up the tortoise. Very soon the tortoise shouted out, "Tighten!" and the leopard at once unfastened the tie-tie, and the tortoise was free. The tortoise then said, "Now, leopard, it is your turn; " so the leopard stood up against the tree and called out to the tortoise to loosen the rope, and the tortoise at once very quickly passed the rope several times round the leopard and got him fast to the tree. Then the leopard said, "Tighten the rope;" but instead of playing the game in accordance with the rules he bad laid down, the tortoise ran faster and faster with the rope round the leopard, taking great care, however, to keep out of reach of the leopard's claws, and very soon had the leopard so securely fastened that it was quite impossible for him to free himself.

All this time the leopard was calling out to the tortoise to let him go, as he was tired of the game; but the tortoise only laughed, and sat down at the fireside and commenced his meal. When he had finished he packed up the remainder of the fish for his family, and prepared to go, but before he started he said to the leopard:

"You killed my mother and now you want to take my fish. It is not likely that I am going to the lake to get fish for you, so I shall leave you here to starve."

He then threw the remains of the pepper and salt into the leopard's eyes and quietly went on his way, leaving the leopard roaring with pain.

All that day and throughout the night the leopard was calling out for some one to release him, and vowing all sorts of vengeance on the tortoise; but no one came, as the people and animals of the forest do not like to hear the leopard's voice.

In the morning, when the animals began to go about to get their food, the leopard called out to everyone he saw to come and untie him, but they all refused, as they knew that if they did so the leopard would most likely kill them at once and eat them. At last a bush rat came near and saw the leopard tied up to the tree and asked him what was the matter, so the leopard told him that he had been playing a game of "tight" and "loose" with the tortoise, and that he had tied him up and left him there to starve. The leopard then implored the bush rat to cut the ropes with his sharp teeth. The bush rat was very sorry for the leopard; but at the same time he knew that, if he let the leopard go, he would most likely be killed and eaten, so he hesitated, and said that he did not quite see his way to cutting the ropes. But this bush rat, being rather kind-hearted, and having had some experience of traps himself, could sympathise with the leopard in his uncomfortable position. He therefore thought for a time, and then hit upon a plan. He first started to dig a hole under the tree, quite regardless of the leopard's cries. When he had finished the hole he came out and cut one of the ropes, and immediately ran into his hole, and waited there to see what would happen; but although the leopard struggled frantically, he could not get loose, as the tortoise had tied him up so fast. After a time, when he saw that there was no danger, the bush rat crept out again and very carefully bit through another rope, and then retired to his hole as before. Again nothing happened, and he began to feel more confidence, so he bit several strands through one after the other until at last the leopard was free. The leopard, who was ravenous with hunger, instead of being grateful to the bush rat, directly he was free, made a dash at the bush rat with his big paw, but just missed him, as the bush rat had dived for his hole; but he was not quite quick enough to escape altogether, and the leopard's sharp claws scored his back and left marks which he carried to his grave.

Ever since then the bush rats have had white spots on their skins, which represent the marks of the leopard's claws.

## The King and the Ju Ju Tree

Udo Ubok Udom was a famous king who lived at Itam, which is an inland town, and does not possess a river. The king and his wife therefore used to wash at the spring just behind their house.

King Udo had a daughter, of whom he was very fond, and looked after her most carefully, and she grew up into a beautiful woman.

For some time the king had been absent from his house, and had not been to the spring for two years. When he went to his old place to wash, he found that the Idem Ju Ju tree had grown up all round the place, and it was impossible for him to use the spring as he had done formerly. He therefore called fifty of his young men to bring their machetes and cut down the tree. They started cutting the tree, but it had no effect, as, directly they made a cut in the tree, it closed up again; so, after working all day, they found they had made no impression on it.

When they returned at night, they told the king that they had been unable to destroy the tree. He was very angry when he heard this, and went to the spring the following morning, taking his own machete with him.

When the Ju Ju tree saw that the king had come himself and was starting to try to cut his branches, he caused a small splinter of wood to go into the king's eye. This gave the king great pain, so he threw down his machete and went back to his house. The pain, however, got worse, and he could not eat or sleep for three days.

He therefore sent for his witch men, and told them to cast lots to find out why he was in such pain. When they had cast lots, they decided that the reason was that the Ju Ju tree was angry with the king because he wanted to wash at the spring, and had tried to destroy the tree.

They then told the king that he must take seven baskets of flies, a white goat, a white chicken, and a piece of white cloth, and make a sacrifice of them in order to satisfy the Ju Ju.

The king did this, and the witch men tried their lotions on the king's eye, but it got worse and worse.

He then dismissed these witches and got another lot. When they arrived they told the king that, although they could do nothing themselves to relieve his pain, they knew one man who lived in the spirit land who could cure him; so the king told them to send for him at once, and he arrived the next day,

Then the spirit man said, "Before I do anything to your eye, what will you give me? " So King Udo, said, ""will give you half my town with the people in it, also seven cows and some money." But the spirit man refused to accept the king's offer. As the king was in such pain, he said, "Name your own price, and I will pay you." So the spirit man said the only thing he was willing to accept as payment was the king's daughter. At this the king cried very much, and told the man to go away, as he would rather die than let him have his daughter.

That night the pain was worse than ever, and some of his subjects pleaded with the king to send for the spirit man again and give him his daughter, and told him that when he got well he could no doubt have another daughter but that if he died now he would lose everything.

The king then sent for the spirit man again, who came very quickly, and in great grief, the king handed his daughter to the spirit.

The spirit man then went out into the bush, and collected some leaves, which he soaked in water and beat up. The juice he poured into the king's eye, and told him that when he washed his face in the morning he would be able to see what was troubling him in the eye.

The king tried to persuade him to stay the night, but the spirit man refused, and departed that same night for the spirit land, taking the king's daughter with him.

Before it was light the king rose up and washed his face, and found that the small splinter from the Ju Ju tree, which had been troubling him so much, dropped out of his eye, the pain disappeared, and he was quite well again.

When he came to his proper senses he realised that he had sacrificed his daughter for one of his eyes, so he made an order that there should be general mourning throughout his kingdom for three years.

For the first two years of the mourning the king's daughter was put in the fatting house by the spirit man, and was given food; but a skull, who was in the house, told her not to eat, as they were fatting her up, not for marriage, but so that they could eat her. She therefore gave all the food which was brought to her to the skull, and lived on chalk herself.

Towards the end of the third year the spirit man brought some of his friends to see the king's daughter, and told them he would kill her the next day, and they would have a good feast off her.

When she woke up in the morning the spirit man brought her food as usual; but the skull, who wanted to preserve her life, and who had heard what the spirit man had said, called her into the room and told her what was going to happen later in the day. She handed the food to the skull, and he said, "When the spirit man goes to the wood with his friends to prepare for the feast, you must run back to your father."

He then gave her some medicine which would make her strong for the journey, and also gave her directions as to the road, telling her that there were two roads but that when she came to the parting of the ways she was to drop some of the medicine on the ground and the two roads would become one.

He then told her to leave by the back door, and go through the wood until she came to the end of the town; she would then find the road. If she met people on the road she was to pass them in silence, as if she saluted them they would know that she was a stranger in the spirit land, and might kill her. She was also not to turn round if any one called to her, but was to go straight on till she reached her father's house.

Having thanked the skull for his kind advice, the king's daughter started off, and when she reached the end of the town and found the road, she ran for three hours, and at last arrived at the branch roads. There she dropped the medicine, as she had been instructed, and the two roads immediately became one; so she went straight on and never saluted any one or turned back, although several people called to her.

About this time the spirit man had returned from the wood, and went to the house, only to find the king's daughter was absent. He asked the skull where she was, and he replied that she had gone out by the back door, but he did not know where she had gone to. Being a spirit, however, he very soon guessed that she had gone home; so he followed as quickly as possible, shouting out all the time.

When the girl heard his voice she ran as fast as she could, and at last arrived at her father's house, and told him to take at once a cow, a pig, a sheep, a goat, a dog, a chicken, and seven eggs, and cut them into seven parts as a sacrifice, and leave them on the road, so that when the spirit man saw these things he would stop and not enter the town. This the king did immediately, and made the sacrifice as his daughter had told him.

When the spirit man saw the sacrifice on the road, he sat down and at once began to eat.

When he had satisfied his appetite, he packed up the remainder and returned to the spirit land, not troubling any more about the king's daughter.

When the king saw that the danger was over, he beat his drum, and declared- that for the future, when people died and went to the spirit land, they should not come to earth again as spirits to cure sick people.

## How the Tortoise overcame the Elephant and the Hippo

The elephant and the hippopotamus always used to feed together, and were good friends.

One day when they were both dining together, the tortoise appeared and said that although they were both big and strong, neither of them could pull him out of the water with a strong piece of tie-tie, and he offered the elephant ten thousand rods if he could draw him out of the river the next day. The elephant, seeing that the tortoise was very small, said, "If I cannot draw you out of the water, I will give you twenty thousand rods." So on the following morning the tortoise got some very strong tie-tie and made it fast to his leg, and went down to the river. When he got there, as he knew the place well, he made the tie-tie fast round a big rock, and left the other end on the shore for the elephant to pull by, then went down to the bottom of the river and hid himself. The elephant then came down and started pulling, and after a time he smashed the rope.

Directly this happened, the tortoise undid the rope from the rock and came to the land, showing all people that the rope was still fast to his leg, but that the elephant had failed to pull him out. The elephant was thus forced to admit that the tortoise was the winner, and paid to him the twenty thousand rods, as agreed. The tortoise then took the rods home to his wife, and they lived together very happily.

After three months had passed, the tortoise, seeing that the money was greatly reduced, thought he would make some more by the same trick, so he went to the hippopotamus and made the same bet with him. The hippopotamus said, "I will make the bet, but I shall take the water and you shall take the land; I will then pull you into the water."

To this the tortoise agreed, so they went down to the river as before, and having got some strong tie-tie, the tortoise made it fast to the hippopotamus' hind leg, and told him to go into the water. Directly the hippo had turned his back and disappeared, the tortoise took the rope twice round a strong palm-tree which was growing near, and then hid himself at the foot of the tree.

When the hippo was tired of pulling, he came up puffing and blowing water into the air from his nostrils. Directly the tortoise saw him coming up, he unwound the rope, and walked down towards the hippopotamus, showing him the tie-tie round his leg. The hippo had to acknowledge that the tortoise was too strong for him, and reluctantly handed over the twenty thousand rods.

The elephant and the hippo then agreed that they would take the tortoise as their friend, as he was so very strong; but he was not really so strong as they thought, and had won because he was so cunning.

He then told them that he would like to live with both of them, but that, as he could not be in two places at the same time, he said that he would leave his son to live with the elephant on the land, and that he himself would live with the hippopotamus in the water.

This explains why there are both tortoises on the land and tortoises who live in the water. The water tortoise is always much the bigger of the two, as there is plenty of fish for him to eat in the river, whereas the land tortoise is often very short of food.

## Of the Pretty Girl and the Seven Jealous Women

There was once a very beautiful girl called Akim. She was a native of Ibibio, and the name was given to her on account of her good looks, as she was born in the spring-time. She was an only daughter, and her parents were extremely fond of her. The people of the town, and more particularly the young girls, were so jealous of Akim's good looks and beautiful form-for she was perfectly made, very strong, and her carriage, bearing, and manners were most graceful-that her parents would not allow her to join the young girls' society in the town, as is customary for all young people to do, both boys and girls belonging to a company according to their age; a company consisting, as a rule, of all the boys or girls born in the same year.

Akim's parents were rather poor, but she was a good daughter, and gave them no trouble, so they had a happy home. One day as Akim was on her way to draw water from the spring she met the company of seven girls, to which in an ordinary way she would have belonged, if her parents had not for bidden her. These girls told her that they were going to hold a play in the town in three days' time, and asked her to join them. She said she was very sorry, but that her parents were poor, and only had herself to work for them, she therefore had no time to spare for dancing and plays. She then left them and went home.

In the evening the seven girls met together, and as they were very envious of Akim, they discussed how they should be revenged upon her for refusing to join their company, and they talked for a long time as to how they could get Akim into danger or punish her in some way.

At last one of the girls suggested that they should all go to Akim's house every day and help her with her work, so that when they had made friends with her they would be able to entice her away and take their revenge upon her for being more beautiful than themselves. Although they went every day and helped Akim and her parents with their work, the parents knew that they were jealous of their daughter, and repeatedly warned her not on any account to go with them, as they were not to be trusted.

At- the end of the year there was going to be a big play, called the new yam play, to which Akim's parents had been invited. The play was going to be held at a town about two hours' march from where they lived. Akim was very anxious to go and take part in the dance, but her parents gave her plenty of work to do before they started, thinking that this would surely prevent her going, as she was a very obedient daughter, and always did her work properly.

On the morning of the play the jealous seven came to Akim and asked her to go with them, but she pointed to all the water-pots she had to fill, and showed them where her parents had told her to polish the walls with a stone and make the floor good; and after that was finished she had to pull up all the weeds round the house and clean up all round. She therefore said it was impossible for her to leave the house until all the work was finished. When the girls heard this they took up the water-pots, went to the spring, and quickly returned with them full; they placed them in a row, and then they got stones, and very soon had the walls polished and the floor made good; after that they did the weeding outside and the cleaning up, and when everything was completed they said to Akim, "Now then, come along; you have no excuse to remain behind, as all the work is done."

Akim really wanted to go to the play; so as all the work was done which her parents had told her to do, she finally consented to go. About half-way to the town, where the new yam play was being held, there was a small river, about five feet deep, which had to be crossed by wading, as there was no bridge. In this river there was a powerful Ju Ju, whose law was that whenever any one crossed the river and returned the same way on the return journey, whoever it was, had to give some food to the Ju Ju. If they did not make the proper sacrifice the Ju Ju dragged them down and took them to his home, and kept them there to work for him. The seven jealous girls knew all about this Ju Ju, having often crossed the river before, as they walked about all over the country, and had plenty of friends in the different towns. Akim, however, who was a good girl, and never went anywhere, knew nothing about this Ju Ju, which her companions had found out.

When the work was finished they all started off together, and crossed the river without any trouble. When they had gone a small distance on the other side they saw a small bird, perched on a high tree, who admired Akim very much, and sang in praise of her beauty, much to the annoyance of the seven girls; but they walked on without saying anything, and eventually arrived at, the town where the play was being held. Akim had not taken the trouble to change her clothes, but when she arrived at the town, although her companions had on all their best beads and their finest clothes, the young men and people admired Akim far more than the other girls, and she was declared to be the finest and most beautiful woman at the dance. They gave her plenty of palm wine, foo-foo, and everything she wanted, so that the seven girls became more angry and jealous than be fore. The people danced and sang all that night, but Akim managed to keep out of the sight of her parents until the following morning, when they asked her how it was that she had disobeyed them and neglected her work; so Akim told them that the work had all been done by her friends, and they had enticed her to come to the play with them Her mother then told her to return home at once, and that she was not to remain in the town any longer.

When Akim told her friends this they said, "Very well, we are just going to have some small meal, and then we will return with you." They all then sat down together and had their food, but each of the seven jealous girls hid a small quantity of foo-foo and fish in her clothes for the Water Ju Ju. However Akim, who knew nothing about this, as her parents had forgotten to tell her about the Ju Ju, never thinking for one moment that their daughter would cross the river, did not take any food as a sacrifice to the Ju Ju with her.

When they arrived at the river Akim saw the girls making their small sacrifices, and begged them to give her a small share so that she could do the same, but they refused, and all walked across the river safely. Then when it was Akim's turn to cross, when she arrived in the middle of the river, the Water Ju Ju caught hold of her and dragged her underneath the water, so that she immediately disappeared from sight. The seven girls had been watching for this, and when they saw that she had gone they went on their way, very pleased at the success of their scheme, and said to one another, "Now Akim is gone for ever, and we shall hear no more about her being better-looking than we are."

As there was no one to be seen at the time when Akim disappeared they naturally thought that their cruel action had escaped detection, so they went home rejoicing; but they never noticed the little bird high up in the tree who had sung of Akim's beauty when they were on their way to the play. The little bird was very sorry for Akim, and made up his mind that, when the proper time came, he would tell her parents what he had seen, so that perhaps they would be able to save her. The bird had heard Akim asking for a small portion of the food to make a sacrifice with, and had heard all the girls refusing to give her any.

The following morning, when Akim's parents returned home, they were much surprised to find that the door was fastened, and that there was no sign of their daughter anywhere about the place, so they inquired of their neighbours, but no one was able to give them any information about her. They then went to the seven girls, and asked them what had become of Akim. They replied that they did not know what had become of her, but that she had reached their town safely with them, and then said she was going home. The father then went to his Ju Ju man, who, by casting lots, discovered what had happened, and told him that on her way back from the play Akim had crossed the river without making the customary sacrifice to the Water Ju Ju, and that, as the Ju Ju was angry, he had seized Akim and taken her to his home. He therefore told Akim's father to take one goat, one basketful of eggs, and one piece of white cloth to the river in the morning, and to offer them as a sacrifice to the Water Ju Ju; then Akim would be thrown out of the water seven times, but that if her father failed to catch her on the seventh time, she would disappear forever.

Akim's father then returned home, and, when he arrived there, the little bird who had seen Akim taken by the Water Ju Ju, told him everything that had happened, confirming the Ju Ju's words. He also said that it was entirely the fault of the seven girls, who had refused to give Akim any food to make the sacrifice with.

Early the following morning the parents went to the river, and made the sacrifice as advised by the Ju Ju. Immediately they had done so, the Water Ju Ju threw Akim up from the middle of the river.

Her father caught her at once, and returned home very thankfully.

He never told anyone, however, that he had recovered his daughter, but made up his mind to punish the seven jealous girls, so he dug a deep pit in the middle of his house, and placed dried palm leaves and sharp stakes in the bottom of the pit. He then covered the top of the pit with new mats, and sent out word for all people to come and hold a play to rejoice with him, as he had recovered his daughter from the spirit land. Many people came, and danced and sang all the day and night, but the seven jealous girls did not appear, as they were frightened. However, as they were told that everything had gone well on the previous day, and that there had been no trouble, they went to the house the following morning and mixed with the dancers; but they were ashamed to look Akim in the face, who was sitting down in the middle of the dancing ring.

When Akim's father saw the seven girls he pretended to welcome them as his daughter's friends, and presented each of them with a brass rod, which he placed round their necks. He also gave them tombo to drink.

He then picked them out, and told them to go and sit on mats on the other side of the pit he had prepared for them. When they walked over the mats which hid the pit they all fell in, and Akim's father immediately got some red-hot ashes from the fire and threw them in on top of the screaming girls, who were in great pain. At once the dried palm leaves caught fire, killing all the girls at once.

When the people heard the cries and saw the smoke, they all ran back to the town.

The next day the parents of the dead girls went to the head chief, and complained that Akim's father had killed their daughters, so the chief called him before him, and asked him for an explanation.

Akim's father went at once to the chief, taking the Ju Ju man, whom everybody relied upon, and the small bird, as his witnesses.

When the chief had heard the whole case, he told Akim's father that he should only have killed one girl to avenge his daughter, and not seven. So he told the father to bring Akim before him.

When she arrived, the head chief, seeing how beautiful she was, said that her father was justified in killing all the seven girls on her behalf, so he dismissed the case, and told the parents of the dead girls to go away and mourn for their daughters, who had been wicked and jealous women, and had been properly punished for their cruel behaviour to Akim.

**MORAL**.--Never kill a man or a woman because you are envious of their beauty, as if you do, you will surely be punished.

## How the Cannibals drove the People to the Cross River

Very many years ago, before the oldest man alive at the present time can remember, the towns of Ikom, Okuni, Abijon, Insofan, Obokum, and all the other Injor towns were situated round and near the Insofan Mountain, and the head chief of the whole country was called Agbor. Abragba and Enfitop also lived there, and were also under King Agbor. The Insofan Mountain is about two days' march inland from the Cross River, and as none of the people there could swim, and knew nothing about canoes, they never went anywhere outside their own country, and were afraid to go down to the big river. The whole country was taken up with yam farms, and was divided amongst the various towns, each town having its own bush. At the end of each year, when it was time to dig the yams, there was a big play held, which was called the New Yam feast. At this festival there was always a big human sacrifice, fifty slaves being killed in one day. These slaves were tied up to trees in a row, and many drums were beaten; then a strong man, armed with a sharp matchet, went from one slave to another and cut their heads off. This was done to cool the new yams, so that they would not hurt the stomachs of the people. Until this sacrifice was made no one in the country would eat a new yam, as they knew, if they did so, they would suffer great pain in their insides.

When the feast was held, all the towns brought one hundred yams each as a present to King Agbor. When the slaves were all killed fires were lit, and the dead bodies were placed over the fires to burn the hair off. A number of plantain leaves were then gathered and placed on the ground, and the bodies, having been cut into pieces, were placed on the plantain leaves.

When the yams were skinned, they were put into large pots, with water, oil, pepper, and salt. The cut-up bodies were then put in on top, and the pots covered up with other clay pots and left to boil for an hour.

589

The king, having called all the people together, then declared the New Yam feast had commenced, and singing and dancing were kept up for three days and nights, during which time much palm wine was consumed, and all the bodies and yams, which had been provided for them, were eaten by the people.

The heads were given to the king for his share, and, when he had finished eating them, the skulls were placed before the Ju Ju with some new yams, so that there should be a good crop the following season.

But although these natives ate the dead bodies of the slaves at the New Yam feast, they did not eat human flesh during the rest of the year.

This went on for many years, until at last the Okuni people noticed that the graves of the people who had been buried were frequently dug open and the bodies removed. This caused great wonder, and, as they did not like the idea of their dead relations being taken away, they made a complaint to King Agbor. He at once caused a watch to be set on all newly dug graves, and that very night they caught seven men, who were very greedy, and used to come whenever a body was buried, dig it up, and carry it into the bush, where they made a fire, and cooked and ate it.

When they were caught, the people made them show where they lived, and where they cooked the bodies.

After walking for some hours in the forest, they came to a place where large heaps of human bones and skulls were found.

The seven men were then securely fastened up and brought before King Agbor, who held a large palaver of all the towns, and the whole situation was discussed.

Agbor said that this bad custom would necessitate all the towns separating, as they could not allow their dead relations to be dug up and eaten by these greedy people, and he could see no other way to prevent it. Agbor then gave one of the men to each of the seven towns, and told some of them to go on the far side of the big river and make their towns there. The others were to go farther down the river on the same side as Insofan Mountain, and when they found suitable places, they were each to kill their man as a sacrifice and then build their town.

All the towns then departed, and when they had found good sites, they built their towns there.

When they had all gone, after a time Agbor began to feel very lonely, so he left the site of his old town and also went to the Cross River to live, so that he could see his friends.

After that the New Yam feast was held in each town, and the people still continued to kill and eat a few slaves at the feast, but the bodies of their relations and friends were kept for a long time above ground until they had become rotten, so that the greedy people should not dig them up and eat them.

This is why, even at the present time, the people do not like to bury their dead relations until they have become putrid.

## The Lucky Fisherman

In the olden days there were no hooks or casting nets, so that when the natives wanted to catch fish they made baskets and set traps at the river side.

One man named Akon Obo, who was very poor, began to make baskets and traps out of bamboo palm, and then when the river went down he used to take his traps to a pool and set them baited with palm-nuts. In the night the big fish used to smell the palm-nuts and go into the trap, when at once the door would fall down, and in the morning Akon Obo would go and take the fish out. He was very successful in his fishing, and used to sell the fish in the market for plenty of money. When he could afford to pay the dowry he married a woman named Eyong, a native of Okuni, and had three children by her, but he still continued his fishing. The eldest son was called Odey, the second Yambi, and the third Atuk. These three boys, when they grew up, helped their father with his fishing, and he gradually became wealthy and bought plenty of slaves. At last he joined the Egbo society, and became one of the chiefs of the town. Even after he became a chief, he and his sons still continued to fish.

One day, when he was crossing the river in a small dug-out canoe, a tornado came on very suddenly and the canoe capsized, drowning the chief, When his sons heard of the death of their father, they wanted to go and drown themselves also, but they were persuaded not to by the people. After searching for two days, they found the dead body some distance down the river, and brought it back to the town. They then called their company together to play, dance, and sing for twelve days, in accordance with their native custom, and much palm wine was drunk.

When the play was finished, they took their father's body to a hollowed-out cavern, and placed two live slaves with it, one holding a native lamp of palm-oil, and the other holding a matchet. They were both tied up, so that they could not escape, and were left there to keep watch over the dead chief, until they died of starvation.

When the cave was covered in, the sons called the chiefs together, and they played Egbo for seven days, which used up a lot of their late father's money. When the play was over, the chiefs were surprised at the amount of money which the sons had been able to spend on the funeral of their father, as they knew how poor he had been as a young man. They therefore called him the lucky fisherman.

## The Orphan Boy and the Magic Stone

A chief of Inde named Inkita had a son named Ayong Kita, whose mother had died at his birth.

The old chief was a hunter, and used to take his son out with him when he went into the bush. He used to do most of his hunting in the long grass which grows over nearly all the Inde country, and used to kill plenty of bush buck in the dry season.

In those days the people had no guns, so the chief had to shoot everything he got with his bow and arrows, which required a lot of skill.

When his little son was old enough, he gave him a small bow and some small arrows, and taught him how to shoot. The little boy was very quick at learning, and by continually practising at lizards and small birds, soon became expert in the use of his little bow, and could hit them almost every time he shot at them.

When the boy was ten years old his father died, and as he thus became the head of his father's house, and was in authority over all the slaves, they became very discontented, and made plans to kill him, so he ran away into the bush.

Having nothing to eat, he lived for several days on the nuts which fell from the palm trees. He was too young to kill any large animals, and only had his small bow and arrows, with which he killed a few squirrels, bush rats, and small birds, and so managed to live.

Now once at night, when he was sleeping in the hollow of a tree, he had a dream in which his father appeared, and told him where there was plenty of treasure buried in the earth, but, being a small boy, he was frightened, and did not go to the place.

One day, sometime after the dream, having walked far and being very thirsty, he went to a lake, and was just going to drink, when he heard a hissing sound, and heard a voice tell him not to drink. Not seeing any one, he was afraid, and ran away without drinking.

Early next morning, when he was out with his bow trying to shoot some small animal, he met an old woman with quite long hair. She was so ugly that he thought she must be a witch, so he tried to run, but she told him not to fear, as she wanted to help him and assist him to rule over his late father's house. She also told him that it was she who had called out to him at the lake not to drink, as there was a bad Ju Ju in the water which would have killed him. The old woman then took Ayong to a stream some little distance from the lake, and bending down, took out a small shining stone from the water, which she gave to him, at the same time telling him to go to the place which his father had advised him to visit in his dream. She then said, "When you get there you must dig, and you will find plenty of money; you must then go and buy two strong slaves, and when you have got them, you must take them into the forest, away from the town, and get them to build you a house with several rooms in it. You must then place the stone in one of the rooms, and whenever you want anything, all you have to do is to go into the room and tell the stone what you want, and your wishes will be at once gratified."

Ayong did as the old woman told him, and after much difficulty and danger bought the two slaves and built a house in the forest, taking great care of the precious stone, which he placed in an inside room. Then for some time, whenever he wanted anything, he used to go into the room and ask for a sufficient number of rods to buy what he wanted, and they were always brought at once.

This went on for many years, and Ayong grew up to be a man, and became very rich, and bought many slaves, having made friends with the Aro men, who in those days used to do a big traffic in slaves. After ten years had passed Ayong had quite a large town and many slaves, but one night the old woman appeared to him in a dream and told him that she thought that he was sufficiently wealthy, and that it was time for him to return the magic stone to the small stream from whence it came. But Ayong, although he was rich, wanted to rule his father's house and be a head chief for all the Inde country, so he sent for all the Ju Ju men in the country and two witch men, and marched with all his slaves to his father's town. Before he started he held a big palaver, and told them to point out any slave who had a bad heart, and who might kill him when he came to rule the country. Then the Ju Ju men consulted together, and pointed out fifty of the slaves who, they said, were witches, and would try to kill Ayong. He at once had them made prisoners, and tried them by the ordeal of Esere bean  to see whether they were witches or not. As none of them could vomit the beans they all died, and were declared to be witches. He then had them buried at once. When the remainder of his slaves saw what had happened, they all came to him and begged his pardon, and promised to serve him faithfully. Although the fifty men were buried they could not rest, and troubled Ayong very much, and after a time he became very sick himself, so he sent again for the Ju Ju men, who told him that it was the witch men who, although they were dead and buried, had power to come out at night and used to suck Ayong's blood, which was the cause of his sickness. They then said, "We are only three Ju Ju men; you must get seven more of us, making the magic number of ten." When they came they dug up the bodies of the fifty witches, and found they were quite fresh. Then Ayong had big fires made, and burned them one after the other, and gave the Ju Ju men a big present. He soon after became quite well again, and took possession of his father's property, and ruled over all the country.

Ever since then, whenever any one is accused of being a witch, they are tried by the ordeal of the poisonous Esere bean, and if they can vomit they do not die, and are declared innocent, but if they cannot do so, they die in great pain.

## The Slave Girl who tried to Kill her Mistress

A man called Akpan, who was a native of Oku, a town in the Ibibio country, admired a girl called Emme very much, who lived at Ibibio, and wished to marry her, as she was the finest girl in her company. It was the custom in those days for the parents to demand such a large amount for their daughters as dowry, that if after they were married they failed to get on with their husbands, as they could not redeem themselves, they were sold as slaves. Akpan paid a very large sum as dowry for Emme, and she was put in the fatting-house until the proper time arrived for her to marry.

Akpan told the parents that when their daughter was ready they must send her over to him. This they promised to do. Emme's father was a rich man, and after seven years had elapsed, and it became time for her to go to her husband, he saw a very fine girl, who had also just come out of the fatting-house, and whom the parents wished to sell as a slave. Emme's father therefore bought her, and gave her to his daughter as her handmaiden.

The next day Emme's little sister, being very anxious to go with her, obtained the consent of her mother, and they started off together, the slave girl carrying a large bundle containing clothes and presents from Emme's father. Akpan's house was a long day's march from where they lived. When they arrived just outside the town they came to a spring, where the people used to get their drinking water from, but no one was allowed to bathe there. Emme, however, knew nothing about this. They took off their clothes to wash close to the spring, and where there was a deep hole which led to the Water Ju Ju's house. The slave girl knew of this Ju Ju, and thought if she could get her mistress to bathe, she would be taken by the Ju Ju, and she would then be able to take her place and marry Akpan. So they went down to bathe, and when they were close to the water the slave girl pushed her mistress in, and she at once disappeared. The little girl then began to cry, but the slave girl said, "If you cry any more I will kill you at once, and throw your body into the hole after your sister." And she told the child that she must never mention what had happened to any one, and particularly not to Akpan, as she was going to represent her sister and marry him, and that if she ever told anyone what she had seen, she would be killed at once. She then made the little girl carry her load to Akpan's house.

When they arrived, Akpan was very much disappointed at the slave girl's appearance, as she was not nearly as pretty and fine as he had expected her to be; but as he had not seen Emme for seven years, he had no suspicion that the girl was not really Emme, for whom he had paid such a large dowry. He then called all his company together to play and feast, and when they arrived they were much astonished, and said, "Is this the fine woman for whom you paid so much dowry, and whom you told us so much about?" And Akpan could not answer them.

The slave girl was then for some time very cruel to Emme's little sister, and wanted her to die, so that her position would be more secure with her husband. She beat the little girl every day, and always made her carry the largest water-pot to the spring; she also made the child place her finger in the fire to use as firewood. When the time came for food, the slave girl went to the fire and got a burning piece of wood and burned the child all over the body with it. When Akpan asked her why she treated the child so badly, she replied that she was a slave that her father had bought for her. When the little girl took the heavy water-pot to the river to fill it there was no one to lift it up for her, so that she could not get it on to her head; she therefore had to remain a long time at the spring, and at last began calling for her sister Emme to come and help her.

When Emme heard her little sister crying for her, she begged the Water Ju Ju to allow her to go and help her, so he told her she might go, but that she must return to him again immediately. When the little girl saw her sister she did not want to leave her, and asked to be allowed to go into the hole with her. She then told Emme how very badly she had been treated by the slave girl, and her elder sister told her to have patience and wait, that a day of vengeance would arrive sooner or later. The little girl went back to Akpan's house with a glad heart as she had seen her sister, but when she got to the house, the slave girl said, "Why have you been so long getting the water?" and then took another stick from the fire and burnt the little girl again very badly, and starved her for the rest of the day.

This went on for some time, until, one day, when the child went to the river for water, after all the people had gone, she cried out for her sister as usual, but she did not come for a long time, as there was a hunter from Akpan's town hidden near watching the hole, and the Water Ju Ju told Emme that she must not go; but, as the little girl went on crying bitterly, Emme at last persuaded the Ju Ju to let her go, promising to return quickly. When she emerged from the water, she looked very beautiful with the rays of the setting sun shining on her glistening body. She helped her little sister with her water-pot, and then disappeared into the hole again.

The hunter was amazed at what he had seen, and when he returned, he told Akpan what a beautiful woman had come out of the water and had helped the little girl with her water-pot. He also told Akpan that he was convinced that the girl he had seen at the spring was his proper wife, Emme, and that the Water Ju Ju must have taken her.

Akpan then made up his mind to go out and watch and see what happened, so, in the early morning the hunter came for him, and they both went down to the river, and hid in the forest near the water-hole.

When Akpan saw Emme come out of the water, he recognised her at once, and went home and considered how he should get her out of the power of the Water Ju Ju. He was advised by some of his friends to go to an old woman, who frequently made sacrifices to the Water Ju Ju, and consult her as to what was the best thing to do.

When he went to her, she told him to bring her one white slave, one white goat, one piece of white cloth, one white chicken, and a basket of eggs. Then, when the great Ju Ju day arrived, she would take them to the Water Ju Ju, and make a sacrifice of them on his behalf. The day after the sacrifice was made, the Water Ju Ju would return the girl to her, and she would bring her to Akpan.

Akpan then bought the slave, and took all the other things to the old woman, and, when the day of the sacrifice arrived, he went with his friend the hunter and witnessed the old woman make the sacrifice. The slave was bound up and led to the hole, then the old woman called to the Water Ju Ju and cut the slave's throat with a sharp knife and pushed him into the hole. She then did the same to the goat and chicken, and also threw the eggs and cloth in on top of them.

After this had been done, they all returned to their homes. The next morning at dawn the old woman went to the hole, and found Emme standing at the side of the spring, so she told her that she was her friend, and was going to take her to her husband. She then took Emme back to her own home, and hid her in her room, and sent word to Akpan to come to her house, and to take great care that the slave woman knew nothing about the matter.

So Akpan left the house secretly by the back door, and arrived at the old woman's house without meeting anybody.

When Emme saw Akpan, she asked for her little sister, so he sent his friend, the hunter, for her to the spring, and he met her carrying her water-pot to get the morning supply of water for the house, and brought her to the old woman's house with him.

When Emme had embraced her sister, she told her to return to the house and do something to annoy the slave woman, and then she was to run as fast as she could back to the old woman's house, where, no doubt, the slave girl would follow her, and would meet them all inside the house, and see Emme, who she believed she had killed.

The little girl did as she was told, and, directly she got into the house, she called out to the slave woman: "Do you know that you are a wicked woman, and have treated me very badly? I know you are only my sister's slave, and you will be properly punished." She then ran as hard as she could to the old woman's house. Directly the slave woman heard what the little girl said, she was quite mad with rage, and seized a burning stick from the fire, and ran after the child; but the little one got to the house first, and ran inside, the slave woman following close upon her heels with the burning stick in her hand.

Then Emme came out and confronted the slave woman, and she at once recognised her mistress, whom she thought she had killed, so she stood quite still.

Then they all went back to Akpan's house, and when they arrived there, Akpan asked the slave woman what she meant by pretending that she was Emme, and why she had tried to kill her. But, seeing she was found out, the slave woman had nothing to say.

Many people were then called to a play to celebrate the recovery of

595

Akpan's wife, and when they had all come, he told them what the slave woman had done.

After this, Emme treated the slave girl in the same way as she had treated her little sister. She made her put her fingers in the fire, and burnt her with sticks. She also made her beat foo-foo with her head in a hollowed-out tree, and after a time she was tied up to a tree and starved to death.

Ever since that time, when a man marries a girl, he is always present when she comes out of the fatting-house and takes her home himself, so that such evil things as happened to Emme and her sister may not occur again.

## The King and the 'Nsiat Bird

When 'Ndarake was King of Idu, being young and rich, he was very fond of fine girls, and had plenty of slaves. The 'Nsiat bird was then living at Idu, and had a very pretty daughter, whom 'Ndarake wished to marry. When he spoke to the father about the matter, he replied that of course he had no objection personally, as it would be a great honour for his daughter to marry the king, but, unfortunately, when any of his family had children, they always gave birth to twins, which, as the king knew, was not allowed in the country; the native custom being to kill both the children and throw them into the bush, the mother being driven away and allowed to starve. The king, however, being greatly struck with Adit, the bird's daughter, insisted on marrying her, so the 'Nsiat bird had to agree. A large amount of dowry was paid by the king, and a big play and feast was held. One strong slave was told to carry Adit 'Nsiat during the whole play, and she sat on his shoulders with her legs around his neck; this was done to show what a rich and powerful man the king was.

After the marriage, in due course Adit gave birth to twins, as her mother had done before her. The king immediately became very fond of the two babies, but according to the native custom, which was too strong for anyone to resist, he had to give them up to be killed, When the 'Nsiat bird heard this, he went to the king and reminded him that he had warned the king before he married what would happen if he married Adit, and rather than that the twins should be killed, he and the whole of his family would leave the earth and dwell in the air, taking the twins with them. As the king was so fond of Adit and the two children, and did not want them to be killed, he gladly consented, and the 'Nsiat bird took the whole of his family, as well as Adit and her two children, away, and left the earth to live and make their home in the trees; but as they had formerly lived in the town with all the people, they did not like to go into the forest, so they made their nests in the trees which grew in the town, and that is why you always see the 'Nsiat birds living and making their nests only in places where human beings are. The black birds are the cocks, and the golden-coloured ones are the hens. It was the beautiful colour of Adit which first attracted the attention of 'Ndarake and caused him to marry her.

## Concerning the Fate of Essido and his Evil Companions

Chief Oborri lived at a town called Adiagor, which is on the right bank of the Calabar River. He was a wealthy chief, and belonged to the Egbo Society. He had many large canoes, and plenty of slaves to paddle them. These canoes he used to fill up with new yams-each canoe being under one head slave and containing eight paddles; the canoes were capable of holding three puncheons of palm-oil, and cost eight hundred rods each. When they were full, about ten of them used to start off together and paddle to Rio del Rey. They went through creeks all the way, which run through mangrove swamps, with palm-oil trees here and there. Sometimes in the tornado season it was very dangerous crossing the creeks, as the canoes were so heavily laden, having only a few inches above the water, that quite a small wave would fill the canoe and cause it to sink to the bottom. Although most of the boys could swim, it often happened that some of them were lost, as there are many large alligators in these waters. After four days' hard paddling they would arrive at Rio del Rey where they had very little difficulty in exchanging their new yams for bags of dried shrimps and sticks with smoked fish on them .

Chief Oborri had two sons, named Eyo I. and Essido. Their mother having died when they were babies, the children were brought up by their father. As they grew up, they developed entirely different characters. The eldest was very hard-working and led a solitary life; but the younger son was fond of gaiety and was very lazy, in fact, he spent most of his time in the neighbouring towns playing and dancing. When the two boys arrived at the respective ages of eighteen and twenty their father died, and they were left to look after themselves. According to native custom, the elder son, Eyo I., was entitled to the whole of his father's estate; but being very fond of his younger brother, he gave him a large number of rods and some land with a house. Immediately Essido became possessed of the money he became wilder than ever, gave big feasts to his companions, and always had his house full of women, upon whom he spent large sums. Although the amount his brother had given him on his father's death was very large, in the course of a few years

Essido had spent it all. He then sold his house and effects, and spent the proceeds on feasting.

While he had been living this gay and unprofitable life, Eyo I. had been working harder than ever at his father's old trade, and had made many trips to Rio del Rey himself. Almost every week he had canoes laden with yams going down river and returning after about twelve days with shrimps and fish, which Eyo I. himself disposed of in the neighbouring markets, and he very rapidly became a rich man. At intervals he remonstrated with Essido on his extravagance, but his warnings had no effect; if anything, his brother became worse. At last the time arrived when all his money was spent, so Essido went to his brother and asked him to lend him two thousand rods, but Eyo refused, and told Essido that he would not help him in any way to continue his present life of debauchery, but that if he liked to work on the farm and trade, he would give him a fair share of the profits. This Essido indignantly refused, and went back to the town and consulted some of the very few friends he had left as to what was the best thing to do.

The men he spoke to were thoroughly bad men, and had been living upon Essido for a long time. They suggested to him that he should go round the town and borrow money from the people he had entertained, and then they would run away to Akpabryos town, which was about four days' march from Calabar. This Essido did, and managed to borrow a lot of money, although many people re fused to lend him anything. Then at night he set off with his evil companions, who carried his money, as they had not been able to borrow any themselves, being so well known. When they arrived at Akpabryos town they found many beautiful women and graceful dancers. They then started the same life again, until after a few weeks most of the money had gone. They then met and consulted together how to get more money, and advised Essido to return to his rich brother, pretending that he was going to work and give up his old life; he should then get poison from a man they knew of, and place it in his brother's food, so that he would die, and then Essido would become possessed of all his brother's wealth, and they would be able to live in the same way as they had formerly. Essido, who had sunk very low, agreed to this plan, and they left Akpabryos town the next morning. After marching for two days, they arrived at a small hut in the bush where a man who was an expert poisoner lived, called Okponesip. He was the head Ju Ju man of the country, and when they had bribed him with eight hundred rods he swore them to secrecy, and gave Essido a small parcel containing a deadly poison which he said would kill his brother in three months. All he had to do was to place the poison in his brother's food.

When Essido returned to his brother's house he pretended to be very sorry for his former mode of living, and said that for the future he was going to work. Eyo I. was very glad when he heard this, and at once asked his brother in, and gave him new clothes and plenty to eat.

In the evening, when supper was being prepared, Essido went into the kitchen, pretending he wanted to get a light from the fire for his pipe. The cook being absent and no one about, he put the poison in the soup, and then returned to the living-room. He then asked for some tombo, which was brought, and when he had finished it, he said he did not want any supper, and went to sleep. His brother, Eyo I., had supper by himself and consumed all the soup. In a week's time he began to feel very ill, and as the days passed he became worse, so he sent for his Ju Ju man.

When Essido saw him coming, he quietly left the house; but the Ju Ju man, by casting lots, very soon discovered that it was Essido who had given poison to his brother. When he told Eyo I. this, he would not believe it, and sent him away. However, when Essido returned, his elder brother told him what the Ju Ju man had said, but that he did not believe him for one moment, and had sent him away. Essido was much relieved when he heard this, but as he was anxious that no suspicion of the crime should be attached to him, he went to the Household Ju Ju , and having first sworn that he had never administered poison to his brother, he drank out of the pot.

Three months after he had taken the poison Eyo I. died, much to the grief of every one who knew him, as he was much respected, not only on account of his great wealth, but because he was also an upright and honest man, who never did harm to any one.

Essido kept his brother's funeral according to the usual custom, and there was much playing and dancing, which was kept up for a long time. Then Essido paid off his old creditors in order to make himself popular, and kept open house, entertaining most lavishly, and spending his money in many foolish ways. All the bad women about collected at his house, and his old evil companions went on as they had done before.

Things got so bad that none of the respectable people would have anything to do with him, and at last the chiefs of the country, seeing the way Essido was squandering his late brother's estate, assembled together, and eventually came to the conclusion that he was a witch man, and had poisoned his brother in order to acquire his position. The chiefs, who were all friends of the late Eyo, and who were very sorry at the death, as they knew that if he had lived he would have become a great and powerful chief, made up their minds to give Essido the Ekpawor Ju Ju, which is a very strong medicine, and gets into men's heads, so that when they have drunk it they are compelled to speak the truth, and if they have done wrong they die very shortly. Essido was then told to dress himself and attend the meeting at the palaver house, and when he arrived the chiefs charged him with having killed his brother by witchcraft. Essido denied having done so, but the chiefs told him that if he were innocent he must prove it by drinking the bowl of Ekpawor medicine which was placed before him. As he could not refuse to drink, he drank the bowl off in great fear and trembling, and very soon the Ju Ju having got hold of him, he confessed that he had poisoned his brother, but that his friends had advised him to do so. About two hours after drinking the Ekpawor, Essido died in great pain.

The friends were then brought to the meeting and tied up to posts, and questioned as to the part they had taken in the death of Eyo. As they were too frightened to answer, the chiefs told them that they knew from Essido that they had induced him to poison his brother. They were then taken to the place where Eyo was buried, the grave having been dug open, and their heads were cut off and fell into the grave, and their bodies were thrown in after them as a sacrifice for the wrong they had done. The grave was then filled up again.

Ever since that time, whenever any one is suspected of being a witch, he is tried by the Ekpawor Ju Ju.

## Concerning the Hawk and the Owl

In the olden days when Effiong was king of Calabar, it was customary at that time for rulers to give big feasts, to which all the subjects and all the birds of the air and animals of the forest, also the fish and other things that lived in the water, were invited. All the people, birds, animals, and fish, were under the king, and had to obey him. His favourite messenger was the hawk, as he could travel so quickly.

The hawk served the king faithfully for several years, and when he wanted to retire, he asked what the king proposed to do for him, as very soon he would be too old to work any more. So the king told the hawk to bring any living creature, bird or animal, to him, and he would allow the hawk for the future to live on that particular species without any trouble. The hawk then flew over a lot of country, and went from forest to forest, until at last he found a young owl which had tumbled out of its nest. This the hawk brought to the king, who told him that for the future he might eat owls. The hawk then carried the owlet away, and told his friends what the king had said.

One of the wisest of them said, "Tell me when you seized the young owlet, what did the parents say?" And the hawk replied that the father and mother owls kept quite quiet, and never said anything. The hawk's friend then advised him to return the owlet to his parents, as he could never tell what the owls would do to him in the nighttime, and as they had made no noise, they were no doubt plotting in their minds some deep and cruel revenge.

The next day the hawk carried the owlet back to his parents and left him near the nest. He then flew about, trying to find some other bird which would do as his food; but as all the birds had heard that the hawk had seized the owlet, they hid themselves, and would not come out when the hawk was near. He therefore could not catch any birds.

As he was flying home he saw a lot of fowls near a house, basking in the sun and scratching in the dust. There were also several small chickens running

599

about and chasing insects, or picking up anything they could find to eat, with the old hen following them and clucking and calling to them from time to time. When the hawk saw the chickens, he made up his mind that he would take one, so he swooped down and caught the smallest in his strong claws. Immediately he had seized the chicken the cocks began to make a great noise, and the hen ran after him and tried to make him drop her child, calling loudly, with her feathers fluffed out and making dashes at him. But he carried it off, and all the fowls and chickens at once ran screaming into the houses, some taking shelter under bushes and others trying to hide themselves in the long grass. He then carried the chicken to the king, telling him that he had returned the owlet to his parents, as he did not want him for food; so the king told the hawk that for the future he could always feed on chickens.

The hawk then took the chicken home, and his friend who dropped in to see him, asked him what the parents of the chicken had done when they saw their child taken away; so the hawk said-

"They all made a lot of noise, and the old hen chased me, but although there was a great disturbance amongst the fowls,
nothing happened."

His friend then said as the fowls had made much palaver, he was quite safe to kill and eat the chickens, as the people who made plenty of noise in the day-time would go to sleep at night and not disturb him, or do him any injury; the only people to be afraid of were those who when they were injured, kept quite silent; you might be certain then that they were plotting mischief, and would do harm in the night-time.

## The Story of the Drummer and the Alligators

There was once a woman named Aftiong Any who lived at 'Nsidung, a small town to the south of Calabar. She was married to a chief of Hensham Town called Etim Ekeng. They had lived together for several years, but had no children. The chief was very anxious to have a child during his lifetime, and made sacrifices to his Ju Ju, but they had no effect. So he went to a witch man, who told him that the reason he had no children was that he was too rich. The chief then asked the witch man how he should spend his money in order to get a child, and he was told to make friends with everybody, and give big feasts, so that he should get rid of some of his money and become poorer.

The chief then went home and told his wife. The next day his wife called all her company together and gave them a big dinner, which cost a lot of money; much food was consumed, and large quantities of tombo were drunk. Then the chief entertained his company, which cost a lot more money. He also wasted a lot of money in the Egbo house. When half of his property was wasted, his wife told him that she had conceived. The chief, being very glad, called a big play for the next day.

In those days all the rich chiefs of the country belonged to the Alligator Company, and used to meet in the water. The reason they belonged to the company was, first of all, to protect their canoes when they went trading, and secondly, to destroy the canoes and property of the people who did not belong to their company, and to take their money and kill their slaves.

Chief Etim Ekeng was a kind man, and would not join this society, although he was repeatedly urged to do so. After a time a son was born to the chief, and he called him Edet Etim. The chief then called the Egbo society together, and all the doors of the houses in the town were shut, the markets were stopped, and the women were not allowed to go outside their houses while the Egbo was playing. This was kept up for several days, and cost the chief a lot of money. Then he made up his mind that he would divide his property, and give his son half when he became old enough. Unfortunately after three months the chief died, leaving his sorrowing wife to look after their little child.

The wife then went into mourning for seven years for her husband, and after that time she became entitled to all his property, as the late chief had no brothers. She looked after the little boy very carefully until he grew up, when he became a very fine, healthy young man, and was much admired by all the pretty girls of the town; but his mother warned him strongly not to go with them, because they would make him become a bad man. Whenever the girls had a play they used to invite Edet Etim, and at last he went to the play, and they made him beat the drum for them to dance to. After much practice he became the best drummer 'in the town, and whenever the girls had a play they always called him to drum for them. Plenty of the young girls left their husbands, and went to Edet and asked him to marry them. This made all the young men of the town very jealous, and when they met together at night they considered what would be the best way to kill him. At last they decided that when Edet went to bathe they would induce the alligators to take him. So one night, when he was washing, one alligator seized him by the foot, and others came and seized him round the waist. He fought very hard, but at last they dragged him into the deep water, and took him to their home.

When his mother heard this, she determined to do her best to recover her son, so she kept quite quiet until the morning.

When the young men saw that Edet's mother remained quiet, and did not cry, they thought of the story of the hawk and the owl, and determined to keep Edet alive for a few months.

At cockcrow the mother raised a cry, and went to the grave of her dead husband in order to consult his spirit as to what she had better do to recover her lost son. After a time she went down to the beach with small young green branches in her hands, with which she beat the water, and called upon all the Ju Jus of the Calabar River to help her to recover her son. She then went home and got a load of rods, and took them to a Ju Ju man in the farm. His name was Ininen Okon; he was so called because he was very artful, and had plenty of strong Ju Jus.

When the young boys heard that Edet's mother had gone to Ininen Okon, they all trembled with fear, and wanted to return Edet, but they could not do so, as it was against the rules of their society. The Ju Ju man having discovered that Edet was still alive, and was being detained in the alligators' house, told the mother to be patient. After three days Ininen himself joined another alligators' society, and went to inspect the young alligators' house. He found a young man whom he knew, left on guard when all the alligators had gone to feed at the ebb of the tide, and came back and told the mother to wait, as he would make a Ju Ju which would cause them all to depart in seven days, and leave no one in the house. He made his Ju Ju, and the young alligators said that, as no one had come for Edet, they would all go at the ebb tide to feed, and leave no one in charge of the house. When they returned they found Edet still there, and everything as they had left it, as Ininen had not gone that day.

Three days afterwards they all went away again, and this time went a long way off, and did not return quickly. When Ininen saw that the tide was going down he changed himself into an alligator, and swam to the young alligators' home, where he found Edet chained to a post. He then found an axe and cut the post, releasing the boy. But Edet, having been in the water so long, was deaf and dumb. He then found several loin cloths which had been left behind by the young alligators, so he gathered them together and took them away to show to the king, and Ininen left the place, taking Edet with him.

He then called the mother to see her son, but when she came the boy could only look at her, and could not speak. The mother embraced her boy, but be took no notice, as he did not seem capable of understanding anything, but sat down quietly. Then the Ju Ju man told Edet's mother that he would cure her son in a few days, so be made several Ju Jus, and gave her son medicine, and after a time the boy recovered his speech and became sensible again.

Then Edet's mother put on a mourning cloth, and pretended that her son was dead, and did not tell the people he had come back to her. When the young alligators returned, they found that Edet was gone, and that someone had taken their loin cloths. They were therefore much afraid, and made inquiries if Edet had been seen, but they could hear nothing about him, as he was hidden in a farm, and the mother continued to wear her mourning cloth in order to deceive them.

Nothing happened for six months, and they had quite forgotten all about the matter. Affiong, the mother, then went to the chiefs of the town, and asked them to hold a large meeting of all the people, both young and old, at the palaver house, so that her late husband's property might be divided up in accordance with the native custom, as her son had been killed by the alligators.

The next day the chiefs called all the people together, but the mother in the early morning took her son to a small room at the back of the palaver house, and left him there with the seven loin cloths which the Ju Ju man had taken from the alligators' home. When the chiefs and all the people were seated, Affiong stood up and addressed them, saying-

"Chiefs and young men of my town, eight years ago my husband was a fine young man. He married me, and we lived together for many years without having any children. At last I had a son, but my husband died a few months afterwards. I brought my boy up carefully, but as he was a good drummer and dancer the young men were jealous, and had him caught by the alligators. Is there any one present who can tell me what my son would have become if he had lived?" She then asked them what they thought of the alligator society, which had killed so many young men.

The chiefs, who had lost a lot of slaves, told her that if she could produce evidence against any members of the society they would destroy it at once. She then called upon Ininen to appear with her son Edet. He came out from the room leading Edet by the hand, and placed the bundle of loin cloths before the chiefs.

The young men were very much surprised when they saw Edet, and wanted to leave the palaver house; but when they stood up to go the chiefs told them to sit down at once, or they would receive three hundred lashes. They then sat down, and the Ju Ju man explained how he had gone to the alligators' home, and had brought Edet back to his mother. He also said that he had found the seven loin cloths in the house, but he did not wish to say anything about them, as the owners of some of the cloths were sons of the chiefs.

The chiefs, who were anxious to stop the bad society, told him, however, to speak at once and tell them everything. Then he undid the bundle and took the cloths out one by one, at the same time calling upon the owners to come and take them. When they came to take their cloths, they were told to remain where they were; and they were then told to name their company. The seven young men then gave the names of all the members of their society, thirty-two in all. These men were all placed in a line, and the chiefs then passed sentence, which was that they should all be killed the next morning on the beach. So they were then all tied together to posts, and seven men were placed as a. guard over them. They made fires and beat drums all the night.

Early in the morning, at about 4 A.M., the big wooden drum was placed on the roof of the palaver house, and beaten to celebrate the death of the evildoers, which was the custom in those days.

The boys were then unfastened from the posts, and had their hands tied behind their backs, and were marched down to the beach. When they arrived there, the head chief stood up and addressed the people. "This is a small town of which I am chief, and I am determined to stop this bad custom, as so many men have been killed." He then told a man who had a sharp matchet to cut off one man's head. He then told another man who had a sharp knife to skin another young man alive. A third man who had a heavy stick was ordered to beat another to death, and so the chief went on and killed all the thirty-two young men in the most horrible ways he could think of. Some of them were tied to posts in the river, and left there until the tide came up and drowned them. Others were flogged to death.

After they had all been killed, for many years no one was killed by alligators, but some little time afterwards on the road between the beach and the town the land fell in, making a very large and deep hole, which was said to be the home of the alligators, and the people have ever since tried to fill it up, but have never yet been able to do so.

## The 'Nsasak Bird and the Odudu Bird

A long time ago, in the days of King Adam of Calabar, the king wanted to know if there was any animal or bird which was capable of enduring hunger for a long period. When he found one the king said he would make him a chief of his tribe.

The 'Nsasak bird is very small, having a shining breast of green and red; he also has blue and yellow feathers and red round the neck, and his chief food consists of ripe palm nuts. The Odudu bird, on the other hand, is much larger, about the size of a magpie, with plenty of feathers, but a very thin body; he has a long tail, and his colouring is black and brown with a cream-coloured breast. He lives chiefly on grasshoppers, and is also very fond of crickets, which make a noise at night.

Both the 'Nsasak bird and the Odudu were great friends, and used to live together. They both made up their minds that they would go before the king and try to be made chiefs, but the Odudu bird was quite confident that he would win, as he was so much bigger than the 'Nsasak bird. He therefore offered to starve for seven days.

The king then told them both to build houses which he would inspect, and then he would have them fastened up, and the one who could remain the longest without eating would be made the chief.

They both then built their houses, but the 'Nsasak bird, who was very cunning, thought that he could not possibly live for seven days without eating anything. He therefore made a tiny hole in the wall (being very small himself), which he covered up so that the king would not notice it on his inspection. The king then came and looked carefully over both houses, but failed to detect the little hole in the 'Nsasak bird's house, as it had been hidden so carefully. He therefore declared that both houses were safe, and then ordered the two birds to go inside their respective houses, and the doors were carefully fastened on the outside.

Every morning at dawn the 'Nsasak bird used to escape through the small opening he had left high up in the wall, and fly away a long distance and enjoy himself all day, taking care, however, that none of the people on the farms should see him. Then when the sun went down he would fly back to his little house and creep through the hole in the wall, closing it carefully after him. When he was safely inside he would call out to his friend the Odudu and ask him if he felt hungry, and told him that he must bear it well if he wanted to win, as he, the 'Nsasak bird, was very fit, and could go on for a long time.

For several days this went on, the voice of the Odudu bird growing weaker and weaker every night, until at last he could no longer reply. Then the little bird knew that his friend must be dead. He was very sorry, but could not report the matter, as he was supposed to be confined inside his house.

When the seven days had expired the king came and had both the doors of the houses opened. The 'Nsasak bird at once flew out, and, perching on a branch of a tree which grew near, sang most merrily; but the Odudu bird was found to be quite dead, and there was very little left of him, as the ants had eaten most of his body, leaving only the feathers and bones on the floor.

The king therefore at once appointed the 'Nsasak bird to be the head chief of all the small birds, and in the Ibibio country even to the present time the small boys who have bows and arrows are presented with a prize, which sometimes takes the shape of a female goat, if they manage to shoot a 'Nsasak bird, as the 'Nsasak bird is the king of the small birds, and most difficult to shoot on account of his wiliness and his small size.

The Election of the King Bird (the black and-white Fishing Eagle)

Old town, Calabar, once had a king called Essiya, who, like most of the Calabar kings in the olden days, was rich and powerful; but although he was so wealthy, he did not possess many slaves. He therefore used to call upon the animals and birds to help his people with their work. In order to get the work done quickly and well, he determined to appoint head chiefs of all the different species. The elephant he appointed king of the beasts of the forest, and the hippopotamus king of the water animals, until at last it came to the turn of the birds to have their king elected.

Essiya thought for some time which would be the best way to make a good choice, but could not make up his mind, as there were so many different birds who all considered they had claims. There was the hawk with his swift flight, and of hawks there were several species. There were the herons to be considered, and the big spur-winged geese, the hornbill or toucan tribe, and the game birds, such as guinea-fowl, the partridge, and the bustards. Then again, of course, there were all the big crane tribe, who walked about the sandbanks in the dry season, but who disappeared when the river rose, and the big black-and-white fishing eagles. When the king thought of the plover tribe, the sea-birds, including the pelicans, the doves, and the numerous shy birds who live in the forest, all of whom sent in claims, he got so confused, that he decided to have a trial by ordeal of combat, and sent word round the whole country for all the birds to meet the next day and fight it out between themselves, and that the winner should be known as the king bird ever afterwards.

The following morning many thousands of birds came, and there was much screeching and flapping of wings. The hawk tribe soon drove all the small birds away, and harassed the big waders so much, that they very shortly disappeared, followed by the geese, who made much noise, and winged away in a straight line, as if they were playing "Follow my leader." The big forest birds who liked to lead a secluded life very soon got tired of all the noise and bustle, and after a few croaks and other weird noises went home. The game birds had no chance and hid in the bush, so that very soon the only birds left were the hawks and the big black-and-white fishing eagle, who was perched on a tree calmly watching everything. The scavenger hawks were too gorged and lazy to take much interest in the proceedings, and were quietly ignored by the fighting tribe, who were very busy circling and swooping on one another, with much whistling going on. Higher and higher they went, until they disappeared out of sight. Then a few would return to earth, some of them badly torn and with many feathers missing. At last the fishing eagle said—

"When you have quite finished with this foolishness please tell me, and if any of you fancy yourselves at all, come to me, and I will settle your chances of being elected head chief once and for all;" but when they saw his terrible beak and cruel claws, knowing his great strength and ferocity, they stopped fighting between themselves, and acknowledged the fishing eagle to be their master.

Essiya then declared that Ituen, which was the name of the fishing eagle, was the head chief of all the birds, and should thenceforward be known as the king bird .

From that time to the present day, whenever the young men of the country go to fight they always wear three of the long black-and-white feathers of the king bird in their hair, one on each side and one in the middle, as they are believed to impart much courage and skill to the wearer; and if a young man is not possessed of any of these feathers when he goes out to fight, he is looked upon as a very small boy indeed.

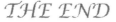

*THE END*

# Relating to Folktales from Nigeria

1. Religion plays a large role in many of the tales we read. Compare and contrast the beliefs of the Africans and those of the Greeks and Indians.

2. Looking at the characters in these folktales, what characteristics do they all seem to have in common? What do these commonalities say about the culture?

3. Conversely, how are the characters different? What specific actions lead you to believe that this culture's heroes are different from everyone else's?

4. What can you deduce about gender differences from these tales? Are the women stronger or weaker, or non-existent compared to Western literature?

# APUS ePress Colophon

For end matter, APUS ePress draws on a convention from the birth of writing on clay tablets to the days of the handwritten codex. Our colophon, the final stroke, identifies the source of the manuscript-but also a bit more. APUS ePress volumes are designed for Web output. Print is a secondary option. As befits a Web conceit, the colophon thus goes a step further to point the reader beyond the covers.

APUS ePress publications are designed to avoid such printed book trappings as indexes and bibliographies. Instead, the index function is subsumed by the ability for electronic searching across the full text. At the low level, this assumes the simple employ word/string matching with wildcards. At a higher plane and especially if employing our Online Library's copy, you may be able to use a relevance engine and even search across multiple volumes. Rather than a bibliography, we also typically proffer a related campus guide with its range of librarian-vetted Web resources. In this case: LITR 201, World Literature through the Renaissance-http://apus.campusguides.com/LITR201.

Frederick J. Stielow, Ph.D., M.L.S.
Chief Editor, APUS ePress
111 W. Congress Street
Charles Town, WV 25414

CPSIA information can be obtained at www.ICGtesting.com
Printed in the USA
BVOW020924200911

271685BV00002B/5/P